China and
the Question of Taiwan

edited by
Hungdah Chiu

The Praeger Special Studies program—
utilizing the most modern and efficient book
production techniques and a selective
worldwide distribution network—makes
available to the academic, government, and
business communities significant, timely
research in U.S. and international economic, social, and political development.

China and
the Question of Taiwan
Documents and Analysis

PRAEGER SPECIAL STUDIES IN INTERNATIONAL POLITICS AND GOVERNMENT

Praeger Publishers   New York   Washington   London

PRAEGER PUBLISHERS
111 Fourth Avenue, New York, N.Y. 10003, U.S.A.
5, Cromwell Place, London S.W.7, England

Published in the United States of America in 1973
by Praeger Publishers, Inc.

Library of Congress Catalog Card Number: 72-89644

Printed in the United States of America

CONTENTS

	Page
LISTS OF TABLES AND FIGURES	xv
INTRODUCTION by Shao-chuan Leng	xvi
MAP SHOWING TAIWAN AND THE MAINLAND	xx

PART I: BACKGROUND AND ANALYSIS

Chapter

1 HISTORY OF TAIWAN
  Ting-yee Kuo ... 3

  Introduction ... 3
  Early History ... 3
  The Dutch Occupation ... 6
  Chinese Recovery of Taiwan ... 8
  Ch'ing Policy Toward Taiwan ... 13
  Taiwan in the Late Ch'ing Dynasty ... 15
  The Japanese Occupation ... 17
  Japanese Administration of Taiwan ... 19
  Resistance of the Chinese in Taiwan and in
    Mainland China ... 21
  Restoration to China ... 23
  Concluding Observations ... 24
  Notes ... 24

2 THE ECONOMIC DEVELOPMENT OF TAIWAN
  Ramon H. Myers ... 28

  Introduction ... 28
  The Traditional Economy ... 29
  The Economy in Transition: Japanese Colonial
    Management ... 33
  Transformation of the Taiwan Economy ... 42
  Conclusion ... 58
  Notes ... 64

v

Chapter		Page

3   POLITICAL DEVELOPMENT IN THE REPUBLIC
     OF CHINA ON TAIWAN
     Yung Wei   74

    Introduction   74
    Reasons for the Lack of Interest in Studying the
      ROC on Taiwan   75
    The Republic of China After 1949: A Brief
      Historical Survey   76
    Political Development of the ROC on Taiwan   83
      Political Ideology   84
      Political Structure   86
      Political Integration   90
      Political Participation   96
    Conclusions   102
    Notes   104

4   CHINA, THE UNITED STATES, AND THE QUESTION
     OF TAIWAN
     Hungdah Chiu   112

    Introduction   112
    The Origin of the Taiwan Question   112
    The Question of Taiwan at the United Nations,
      1950-51   117
    The Question of Taiwan and the Japanese Peace
      Settlement   122
    The International Legal Status of Taiwan   127
    The Question of Taiwan in Sino-American
      Relations   142
    Concluding Observations   171
    Notes   176

PART II: DOCUMENTS AND MATERIALS

5   OFFICIAL DOCUMENTS CONCERNING THE
     QUESTION OF TAIWAN, 1662-1950   195

    Document 1: Koxinga-Dutch Treaty, February 1,
      1662   195
    Document 2: Treaty of Shimonoseki, April 17,
      1895   197

Document 3: Telegram from Governor of
Taiwan, T'ang Ching-sung, to the Chün wu-ch'u,
April 28, 1895   198
Document 4: Telegram from Governor of Taiwan,
T'ang, to the Chief Officers of All the Provinces,
May 25, 1895   199
Document 5: Statement of T'ang Ching-sung,
President of the Republic of Taiwan, May
[25?], 1895   199
Document 6: Declaration of the People of Taiwan,
May 25, 1895   200
Document 7: Telegram Governor of Taiwan, T'ang
Ching-sung, to the Tsung-shu, May 27, 1895   203
Document 8: President Chiang Kai-shek's Speech
to the Provisional National Convention of the
Kuomintang, April 1, 1938   203
Document 9: China's Declaration of War on Japan,
December 9, 1941   204
Document 10: Declaration by the United Nations,
January 1, 1942   204
Document 11: The Cairo Conference: The Chinese
Record of the November 26, 1943, Meeting   205
Document 12: The Cairo Declaration, November
26, 1943   207
Document 13: U.S. President Roosevelt's Address,
December 24, 1943   208
Document 14: Potsdam Proclamation, July 26, 1945   208
Document 15: Japanese Instrument of Surrender,
September 2, 1945   209
Document 16: Proclamation of the National Govern-
ment of the Republic of China, September 4, 1945   210
Document 17: Japanese Instrument of Surrender on
Taiwan, October 25, 1945   211
Document 18: Taiwan Administrator Chen I's State-
ment at the Japanese Surrender Ceremony, Taipei,
October 25, 1945   212
Document 19: Decree on the Resumption of Chinese
Nationality for the Taiwanese People, January 12,
1946   213
Document 20: Measures Concerning the Nationality
of Overseas Taiwanese, June 22, 1946   213
Document 21: Statement of President Hsieh Hsueh-
hung of the Taiwan Democratic Self-Government
League, September 3, 1949   215

Document 22: "American Scheme of Aggression
Against Taiwan in the Past Four Years"   216
Document 23: U.S. Department of State's Policy
Memorandum on Formosa, December 23, 1949   217
Document 24: President Truman's Statement on
U.S. Policy Respecting the Status of Formosa
(Taiwan), January 5, 1950   220
Document 25: Secretary of State Acheson's Remarks
Elaborating the Policy Respecting the Status of
Formosa (Taiwan), January 5, 1950   221
Document 26: Review of U.S. Policy in Relation to
China   222
Notes   225

6   OFFICIAL DOCUMENTS CONCERNING THE QUESTION
OF TAIWAN, 1950-58   228

Document 27: President Truman's Statement on the
Mission of the U.S. Seventh Fleet in the Formosa
Area, June 27, 1950   228
Document 28: ROC's Suspension of Military Opera-
tions Against the China Mainland, June 27-28,
1950   228
Document 29: PRC Chairman Mao Tse-tung's Address
at the Eighth Meeting of the Central People's
Government, June 28, 1950   230
Document 30: PRC Foreign Minister Chou En-lai's
Statement Refuting Truman's Statement of June
27, 1950, June 28, 1950   230
Document 31: PRC Foreign Minister Chou En-lai's
Cable to the President of the Security Council and
the Secretary-General of the United Nations,
August 24, 1950   231
Document 32: PRC Delegate Wu Hsiu-chuan's State-
ment at the United Nations Security Council,
November 28, 1950   232
Document 33: Record of the Conversation Between
Ambassador Koo and Dulles Concerning the
Japanese Peace Treaty, October 20, 1950   236
Document 34: Record of the Conversation Between
Ambassador Koo and Dulles Concerning the
Japanese Peace Treaty, December 19, 1950   237

Document 35: Memorandum Containing General
Observations of the Chinese Government on the
U.S. Tentative Proposals Regarding the Peace
Treaty with Japan, January 22, 1951   238
Document 36: Record of the Conversation Between
Ambassador Koo and Dulles Concerning the
Japanese Peace Treaty, April 24, 1951   239
Document 37: Record of the Conversation Between
Ambassador Koo and Dulles Concerning the
Japanese Peace Treaty, May 29, 1951   240
Document 38: ROC President Chiang Kai-shek's
Statement on the Peace Treaty with Japan, June
18, 1951   243
Document 39: PRC Foreign Minister Chou En-lai's
Statement on the U.S. Proposal of the Japanese
Peace Treaty, August 15, 1951   244
Document 40: Treaty of Peace Between the Republic
of China and Japan, April 28, 1952   245
Document 41: PRC Premier Chou En-lai's Report on
the Work of the Government to the First Session of
the First National People's Congress, September
23, 1954   249
Document 42: Mutual Defense Treaty Between the
United States and the Republic of China, December
2, 1954   250
Document 43: PRC Foreign Minister Chou En-lai's
Statement on U.S.-Chiang Kai-shek "Mutual
Security Treaty," December 8, 1954   253
Document 44: U.S. Congressional Authorization for
the President to Employ the Armed Forces of the
United States to Protect Formosa, the Pescadores,
and Related Positions and Territories of That Area   257
Document 45: ROC President Chiang Kai-shek's
Review of the International Situation, February 8,
1955   258
Document 46: ROC President Chiang Kai-shek's
Replies to Questions Asked in a Press Conference,
February 14, 1955   260
Document 47: U.S. Secretary of State Dulles' State-
ment on Negotiations with Communist China for a
Cease-fire in the Formosa Area, July 26, 1955   261
Document 48: PRC Foreign Ministry Statement on
Sino-American Talks at Geneva, January 18, 1956   263

Document 49: ROC President Chiang Kai-shek's
Replies to Questions Submitted by William
Randolph Hearst, Jr., March 15, 1956   268
Document 50: PRC Premier Chou En-lai's Speech
to the Third Session of the First National People's
Congress, June 28, 1956   268
Document 51: Liu Shao-chi's Political Report of the
Central Committee of the Chinese Communist
Party to the Eighth National Congress of the Party,
September 15, 1956   273
Document 52: PRC Premier Chou En-lai's Report to
the Chinese People's Consultative Conference,
March 5, 1957   274
Document 53: ROC President Chiang Kai-shek's
Replies to Questions Submitted by Sven Steenberg,
October 4, 1957   275
Document 54: PRC Premier Chou En-lai's Report to
the Fifth Session of the First National People's
Congress, February 10, 1958   276
Document 55: The U.S. Position on the Question of
Recognition of the Chinese Communist Regime   277
Document 56: U.S. Secretary of State Dulles' State-
ment, September 4, 1958   279
Document 57: PRC's Declaration on the Territorial
Sea, September 4, 1958   281
Document 58: PRC Premier Chou En-lai's State-
ment, September 6, 1958   282
Document 59: ROC President Chiang Kai-shek's
Replies to Questions Submitted by the New York
Journal-American, September 15, 1958   283
Document 60: ROC President Chaing Kai-shek's
Replies to Questions Submitted by Chinese and
Foreign Press, Broadcasters, and Cameramen,
September 29, 1958   284
Document 61: ROC-U.S. Joint Communiqué, October
23, 1958   286
Document 62: PRC Defense Minister P'eng Teh-huai's
Second Message to Compatriots in Taiwan, October
25, 1958   288
Document 63: "On the Chiang Kai-shek-Dulles
Talks," People's Daily, October 30, 1958   290
Document 64: Ely Maurer, "Legal Problems Regarding
Formosa and the Offshore Islands"   293
Notes   294

7   OFFICIAL DOCUMENTS CONCERNING THE
     QUESTION OF TAIWAN, 1959-72   297

        Document 65: U.S. President Eisenhower's Reply
        to a Question at a News Conference, October 22,
        1959   297
        Document 66: Excerpt from a 1959 Mao Interview   297
        Document 67: ROC President Chiang Kai-shek's
        Address at the Opening of the Third Session of
        the First National Assembly, February 20, 1960   298
        Document 68: ROC President Chiang Kai-shek's
        Answers to Questions Submitted by the Honolulu
        Advertiser, July 9, 1960   300
        Document 69: PRC Premier Chou En-lai's Replies
        to Questions Submitted by Felix Greene, September
        5, 1960   301
        Document 70: "100 Meetings of Sino-U.S. Talks,"
        People's Daily, September 8, 1960   302
        Document 71: U.S. Secretary of State Rusk's Reply
        to a Question Asked by a Representative of the
        British Broadcasting Corporation, March 3, 1961   304
        Document 72: ROC President Chiang Kai-shek's
        Answers to Questions Submitted by Marvin
        Liebman, June 11, 1961   304
        Document 73: PRC Vice-Premier Ch'en Yi's Tele-
        vision Interview with Russel Spurr and Alexandre
        Des Fontaines, June 29, 1961   306
        Document 74: "There Is Only One China, Not Two,"
        People's Daily, July 14, 1961   306
        Document 75: ROC-U.S. Joint Communiqué, August
        2, 1961   310
        Document 76: "A Brief Account of the U.S. Two
        Chinas Plot," People's Daily, August 7, 1961   312
        Document 77: NCNA Correspondent, "Chiang
        Kai-shek Gang Prepares for Military Adventure,"
        June 23, 1962   317
        Document 78: PRC Spokesman's Comment on the
        U.S.S.R. Government's Statement of August 21,
        1963, September 1, 1963   318
        Document 79: PRC Premier Chou En-lai's Press
        Conference in Dacca, February 25, 1964   319
        Document 80: ROC Foreign Ministry Spokesman's
        Reply to a Question Asked by a Reporter, March
        3, 1964   320

Document 81: ROC President Chiang Kai-shek's
Answers to Questions Submitted by Armando
Rivas Torres, March 26, 1964   321
Document 82: China's Sovereignty over Taiwan
Brooks No Intervention," People's Daily, May
12, 1964   322
Document 83: Hsu Meng-shan, "Resolutely Oppose
the 'One China and One Taiwan' Scheme," People's
Daily, May 24, 1964   324
Document 84: ROC President Chiang Kai-shek's New
Year Message, January 1, 1965   327
Document 85: "The Chinese People Are Determined
to Liberate Taiwan," People's Daily, June 27, 1965   328
Document 86: Vice-Premier and Foreign Minister
Ch'en Yi's Press Conference, Peking, September
29, 1965   329
Document 87: "The Five-Star Red Flag Must Be
Planted on Taiwan Province," People's Daily, June
27, 1966   330
Document 88: PRC Foreign Ministry's Note to the
Soviet Embassy in China, March 21, 1968   331
Document 89: ROC Ambassador to the United States
Chow Shu-kai's Letter on the "Status of Taiwan"   332
Document 90: PRC Foreign Ministry's Statement on
Sino-American Negotiations, November 26, 1968   333
Document 91: Communiqué on Talks Between Chinese
and Japanese Representatives of Memorandum
Trade Offices, April 4, 1969   334
Document 92: "U.S.-Japanese Reactionaries Step up
'Taiwan Independence Movement' Plot," People's
Daily, February 24, 1970   335
Document 93: ROC President Chiang Kai-shek's
Interview, May 23, 1970   338
Document 94: ROC Foreign Minister Wei Tao-ming's
Statement on the Representation of China in the
United Nations   339
Document 95: U.S. Department of State's Statement
on the Status of Taiwan, April 28, 1971   340
Document 96: ROC Foreign Ministry Statement,
April 30, 1971   341
Document 97: Commentator, "Fresh Evidence of the
U.S. Government's Hostility Toward the Chinese
People," People's Daily, May 4, 1971   342

Document 98: ROC President Chiang Kai-shek's
Statement on the Withdrawal of the ROC from
the United Nations, October 26, 1971   344
Document 99: Nixon-Chou Communiqué, February
28, 1972   346
Document 100: ROC Foreign Ministry's Statement
on Nixon-Chou Communiqué, February 28, 1972   346
Notes   348

8   UNOFFICIAL MATERIALS RELATING TO THE
     QUESTION OF TAIWAN, 1925-69   350

Item 1: The First Manifesto of the Taiwan Com-
rades Association of Amoy, April 18, 1925   350
Item 2: "Editorial: China Must Recover Taiwan"   351
Item 3: Letter from the Taiwan Revolution
Alliance Association to the National Government
Requesting Establishment of a Taiwan Provincial
Government, 1943   354
Item 4: Shao Chin-fu, "The Absurd Theory of 'Two
Chinas' and Principles of International Law"   354
Item 5: The Conlon Report, November 1, 1959   369
Item 6: Lin Yutang and Chin-tung Liang, "An
Analysis of the Conlon Report: Its Fallacies and
Contradictions as Viewed by Asians," 1960   372
Item 7: " 'One China, One Taiwan' Plot Denounced"   376
Item 8: "Editorial: No Need for Concealment, No
Room for Appeasement—on the Government's
Attitude Toward the So-called 'Taiwan Indepen-
dence' Conspiracy"   377
Item 9: Statement of President Liao Wen-yi on the
Dissolution of the Provisional Government of the
Republic of Taiwan, May 14, 1965   378
Item 10: Statement of Liao Wen-yi, May 17, 1965   379
Item 11: Statement of Cheng Wen-fu, President of
the Taiwan Democratic-Political Party, May 20,
1965   380
Item 12: Wang Shao-p'ing, "Can Taiwan Become
Independent"?   381
Item 13: Chao Kuang-yu, "Mr. Ts'ai Pei-ho Talks
About His Trip Around the World"   382
Item 14: Ssu-ma Lu, "Forward to 'A Taiwanese
Speaks about the Future of Taiwan' "   383

Item 15: Wu Yu-lin, "A Taiwanese Speaks About
the Future of Taiwan"   384
Item 16: Ch'en Shao-shun, "On the Problem of
Taiwan Independence—a Comment on 'A Taiwanese
Speaks About the Future of Taiwan' "   386
Item 17: Sun Ch'ih-p'ing, "While Wu Yu-lin's
Opinion May Speak for Some People, Its Reasons
Are Not Convincing"   388
Item 18: Nixon-Chou Joint Communiqué and the
Future of Taiwan.   389
Notes   390

SELECTED BIBLIOGRAPHY   392

ABOUT THE EDITOR AND THE CONTRIBUTORS   396

LISTS OF TABLES AND FIGURES

Table   Page

2.1   Basic Indicators of the Taiwan Economy, 1946-68   44

2.2   Total Value of Exports and Percentage of Exports
       of Four Leading Agricultural Commodities,
       Selected Years, 1910-65   56

2.3   Total Value of Imports and Percentage of Food and
       Fiber Imports, 1910-65   56

2.4   Annual Average Growth Rate of Agricultural Output
       in Taiwan, 1910-60   59

2.5   Annual Population Growth Rates, 1911-41   60

2.6   Ten-Year Average Changes in Area, Yield, and Pro-
       duction of Taiwan's Four Main Crops, 1901-65   61

Figure

2.1   Shares of Major Sectors in National Product
       Corresponding to Growth in Per Capita Income,
       1951-68   47

3.1   Organization Chart of the Government of the Republic
       of China   87

INTRODUCTION
Shao-chuan Leng

Taiwan (Formosa) continues to be the most difficult problem
for the U.S. China policy despite the recent course of events moving
toward improved relations between Washington and Peking. The United
States is by treaty committed to defend the Republic of China (ROC)
on Taiwan against attack, but the People's Republic of China (PRC)
remains adamant about the "liberation" of the island as a Chinese
province. To find a way out of this dilemma, there have been conferences and books specially designed to examine policy options for the
United States.[1]

With all types of arguments that have been advanced, the Taiwan
question is essentially a political one. Between 1661 and 1895 the
island was administered as a part of China. In 1895 it was ceded to
Japan by the Treaty of Shimonoseki. In both the Cairo Declaration of
November, 1943 and the Potsdam Proclamation of July, 1945, the
Allied Powers pledged the return of Taiwan to China. In October, 1945,
the ROC accepted the surrender of the Japanese forces in Taiwan and
thereafter ruled the island as a province. Before the Korean conflict
no one challenged the Chinese control of Taiwan. In fact, Secretary
of State Dean Acheson had this to say on January 5, 1950:

> The Chinese have administered Formosa for 4 years.
> Neither the United States nor any other ally ever ques-
> tioned that authority and that occupation. When Formosa
> was made a province of China nobody raised any lawyers'
> doubts about that. That was regarded as in accordance
> with the commitments.
>   Now in the opinion of some the situation is changed.
> They believe that forces now in control of the mainland of
> China . . . are not friendly to us and therefore they want
> to say, "Well, we have to wait for a treaty." We did not
> wait for a treaty on Korea. We did not wait for a treaty
> on the Kuriles. We did not wait for a treaty on the islands
> over which we have trusteeship.[2]

However, the outbreak of the Korean War in June, 1950, drastically changed the American position regarding Taiwan. In a statement
made on June 27, President Truman declared that he had ordered the
Seventh Fleet to "prevent any attack on Formosa" and had also requested the Nationalist government on Taiwan to "cease all air and
sea operations against the mainland." "The determination of the

future status of Formosa," he stated, "must await the restoration of security in the Pacific, a peace settlement with Japan, or consideration by the United Nations."[3]

Thus was born the "Formosa question." Since then the status of Taiwan has remained "legally undetermined" in the eyes of the United States, although both the Chinese Communists and the Chinese Nationalists have insisted that Taiwan is an integral part of China. The U.S. policy toward the Taiwan issue is further complicated by the fact that while Washington has given the ROC government on Taiwan various measures of support, there are also people in and outside the American government who have shown considerable sympathy for an exile-led Taiwanese independent movement based primarily in Japan and the United States.

Much has been published on Taiwan under the KMT (Kuomintang) rule. There are a number of detached studies on specific political or economic issues of the island.[4] Many of the other writings, nevertheless, tend to be colored by pro- or anti-KMT bias. By and large, liberal writers usually have such a distaste for the KMT regime that they proceed to espouse the cause of "Formosa nationalism."[5] Some authors, for instance, take pains to emphasize the differences between the mainlanders and the Taiwanese and strongly support the movement for "Formosan independence" against the "oppressive and alien" rule of the Chinese Nationalists.[6] Others use legal arguments to underline the "unsettled" status of Taiwan and advocate military intervention by the United States to help establish an independent Formosan state in the name of national self-determination.[7]

Granting the existence of discontent among the Taiwanese, these writers nonetheless appear to have used the term "nationalism" too loosely. It is well-known that provincialism has existed in many parts of China and that prejudice of one region against another is not uncommon on the mainland. During the Sino-Japanese War the great influx of population from other parts of China into Szechwan resulted in tensions and frictions between the native Szechwanese and the "Hsia-chiang jen" (people from the lower part of the Yangtze). However, this, along with the Szechwanese warlords' "independent kingdom" orientation, failed to generate any separatist movement.* Admittedly, Taiwan is unique in that it had an interlude of 50 years under the Japanese occupation. Still, the Taiwanese are ethnically and culturally more closely tied to the mainlanders than the Tibetans are to the Chinese. No one has disputed that Tibet belongs to China.

---

*The author is himself a Szechwanese and personally knew some top warloads in Szechwan.

Furthermore, governments can come and go. The nature of the Nationalist regime alone is not a sufficient justification for Taiwan's independence. One must seek the answer to the question of Taiwan's relations with mainland China in studying all pertinent historical, cultural, political, and legal factors.

It is to these issues that the present volume addresses itself. In editing this comprehensive work, Dr. Hungdah Chiu of the Harvard Law School has combined numerous original documents with analytical chapters contributed by specialists. In Chapter 1 Ting-yee Kuo traces the history of Taiwan from the beginning of its recorded history to 1945, when Chinese rule was restored to the island. The Japanese occupation during 1895-1945, according to the author, failed to alter the close ties between the people of Taiwan and those of mainland China in terms of cultural affinity and ethnic origins. In Chapter 2 Ramon Myers examines the economic development of Taiwan. With supporting statistics he shows how the island has been transformed from a traditional agrarian economy to a modern industrial society over the past half-century. In his words the seedbed by which the roots of modernization were nourished was established between 1895 and 1945, but it was not until the early 1960's that these roots became sufficiently strong and deeply imbedded to yield fruit.

Political development in the ROC on Taiwan is treated in Chapter 3 by Yung Wei. In an effort to present a balanced picture of this rather controversial subject, the author examines in detail the nature of the political system on Taiwan, its inherent limitations and resultant problems, and the achievements it has made under trying conditions. In Chapter 4 Hungdah Chiu discusses the Taiwan question with special reference to the Chinese attitude toward it. From a legal perspective he carefully analyzes the origins of the Taiwan question, the international status of the island, and the Taiwan issue in Sino-American relations. After examining divergent arguments on the legal status of Taiwan, he concludes that China has a legitimate claim to the island on the basis of historical records and the principles of international law, particularly those of occupation and prescription.

The second part of the book contains an impressive collection of primary source material on Taiwan. The materials selected cover the period from 1661 to 1970 and are divided into official and unofficial documents. The former include excerpts from agreements, communications, policy statements, and editorials of official newspapers. The latter present views expressed by individuals and semiofficial or unofficial groups in China. Together they constitute an invaluable source of information on Taiwan that will enable readers to draw their own conclusions or to carry on further research in the field.

NOTES

1. For instance, The League of Women Voters Education Fund and the National Committee on United States-China Relations held a conference in Washington, D.C., on March 5 and 6, 1971, to discuss U.S. policy toward Taiwan. A book has resulted from this conference: Jerome A. Cohen, Edward Friedman, Harold C. Hinton, and Allen S. Whiting, Taiwan and American Policy (New York: Praeger, 1971). Other books on the same issue include A. Doak Barnett, A New U.S. Policy Toward China (Washington, D.C.: The Brookings Institution, 1971); William M. Bueler, U.S. China Policy and the Problem of Taiwan (Boulder, Colo.: Colorado Associated University Press, 1971); Richard Moorsteen and Morton Abramowitz, Remaking China Policy (Cambridge, Mass.: Harvard University Press, 1971).

2. American Foreign Policy, 1950-1955, Public Documents, II (Washington, D.C.: U.S. Government Printing Office, 1957), 2449-51.

3. Ibid., p. 2468.

4. See, for example, Sheldon Appleton, "Taiwanese and Mainlanders on Taiwan: A Survey of Student Attitudes," The China Quarterly, No. 44 (October-December 1970), pp. 38-65; J. Bruce Jacobs, "Leadership and Political Trends in Taiwan," ibid., No. 45 (January-March 1971), pp. 129-54; Ramon H. Myers, "Taiwan," in R. T. Shand, ed., Agricultural Development in Asia (Berkeley and Los Angeles; University of California Press, 1969) pp. 25-52 (Canberra: Australian National University Press, 1969).

5. For instance, Maurice Meisner, "The Development of Formosan Nationalism," in Mark Mancall, ed., Formosa Today (New York: Praeger, 1964), pp. 147-62.

6. See George H. Kerr, Formosa Betrayed (Boston: Houghton Mifflin, 1965); and Douglas Mendel, The Politics of Formosan Nationalism (Berkeley: University of California Press, 1970).

7. See Lung-chu Chen and Harold D. Lasswell, Formosa, China and the United Nations (New York: St. Martin's Press, 1967). An opposite view is expressed in Frank Morello, International Legal Status of Formosa (The Hague: Martinus Nijhoff, 1966).

MAP SHOWING TAIWAN AND THE MAINLAND

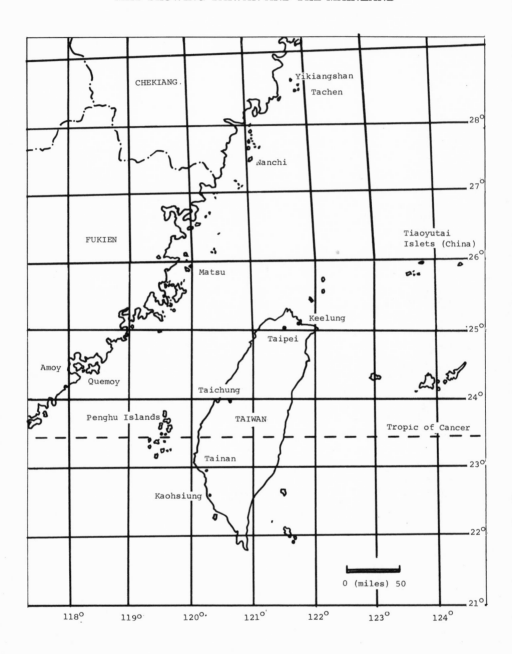

I

BACKGROUND
AND
ANALYSIS

INTRODUCTION

The island of Taiwan, which Westerners called Formosa, is roughly parallel to the mainland of southeast China and is separated from the Chinese coast by the Taiwan Straits, which are 90 to 120 miles in breadth. Lying between 21°45'25" and 25°37'53" north latitude and 119°18'3" and 122°6'25" east longitude, the island straddles the Tropic of Cancer. Shaped like a tobacco leaf, Taiwan is about 250 miles long and about 80 miles across. The area of the island, with all the adjacent islands such as the Penghu (Pescadores) Islands and the Tiaoyutai Islets, is about 14,000 square miles.

The history of Taiwan is intimately linked with the history of China. The development of Taiwan has resulted almost entirely from the painstaking efforts of migrants from southern Fukien and eastern Kwangtung. The geographic proximity of Taiwan and southern Fukien and Kwangtung was a principal reason for the mass migration. However, the Hakkas and the people of southern Fukien came primarily from central China. First they migrated to the coastal regions and then, gradually, to Penghu and Taiwan. The reasons for the migration were varied. Some were forced to move for political reasons; others, by economic pressures. Others migrated for personal and unknown reasons. But migration does not mean, and never has meant, a breaking of ties with China. Most of the migrants merely intended to stay in Taiwan for a short period and to return to their motherland.

EARLY HISTORY

Recent geological studies indicate that in prehistoric times Taiwan was probably part of mainland China but, because of geological changes,

was severed from the mainland and became an island.[1] The discovery
of prehistorical material in eastern Taiwan tends to suggest cultural
ties between this island and Chinese mainland. In any case, it is
probable that the ancient culture and civilization that emerged in
central China along the valleys of the Yellow River spread to the
island of Taiwan.[2]

The earliest book of history in China, Shang Shu, has a chapter
known as "Yu Kung" that is believed by historians to be a geographic
survey of China made approximately 4,000 years ago. The "Yu Kung"
describes China in terms of nine parts, one of which was the Yang
Chou area, covering the southeast coast. According to Taiwan Fu-chih
(The Taiwan gazeteer), Taiwan once belonged to the Yang Chou area.
The description is not entirely clear; but since the "Yu Kung" chapter
of the Shang Shu reports tributes from the people on "eastern islands," it is not impossible that the Taiwan Fu-chih is correct.[3]

Even assuming that the Fu-chih is accurate in describing the
relationship between Taiwan and China, it can be taken as merely a
prehistorical relationship. There is no historical record to verify
that the Chinese people had arrived on the island when Shang Shu was
written. Despite various interpretations made in later years—one of
them being that one Hsu Fu was sent by the first emperor of the
Ch'in dynasty (221-06 B.C.) on expeditions in the eastern sea and that
Hsu reached an island called I-chou, which was subsequently identified
as Taiwan—there has been no positive historical evidence to prove
them.[4]

A new era began when Sun Ch'üan, emperor of Wu of the Three
Kingdoms (A.D. 222-80), sent troops to conquer offshore islands; the
military victories included capture of a few thousand natives on the
island of I-chou, believed to be Taiwan.[5] While its sovereignty was
not established over Taiwan, China's military influence was extended
to the island.

A more definite historical record can be found in the Sui Shu
(History of the Sui dynasty [A.D. 589-618]). It notes that Emperor
Yang Ti sent Chu Kuan to investigate a report of a mysterious land
seen in the eastern sea. Crossing the eastern sea, Chu Kuan reached
a land called Liu Chiu, the inhabitants of which were peaceful in their
approach. However, because of language difficulties, no conversation
with them was possible.[6]

Four years later General Ch'en Ling was ordered to fit out a
second expedition and explore the new land. Ch'en took an interpreter
with him, but this time they met a far more hostile tribe. When Ch'en
demanded tribute as recognition of the sovereignty of Emperor Yang
Ti, he met not only with a flat refusal but also with a challenge to arms.
In the ensuing conflict Ch'en defeated the tribesmen and killed their
leader, Kaishi Harato. When the Chinese troops ventured further

inland, they were confronted with another military challenge. They
finally won a second victory and killed another tribe leader, Damori
(or Ramori). As nothing was to be gained by remaining longer, Ch'en
returned to China.[7]

The T'ang relationship with Taiwan (Liu Chiu) was not clear,
though the people of T'ang should have known about the island. The
Chu-fang-chih (A description of the barbarous people) of the southern
Sung dynasty (A.D. 1127-1280) consisted of descriptions of Penghu
(Pescadores) and statements that Chinese had migrated to the offshore
island to avoid warfare on the mainland.[8]

The first emperor of the Yüan dynasty (A.D. 1280-1368), Shih-
tsu, was more active in his policy of cultivating the lands in the
eastern and southeastern seas than his predecessors in the Sui and
T'ang dynasties. For example, in 1292 he sent Admiral Yang Tsiang
to establish a base on the eastern sea from which to attack Taiwan.
Yang sailed to an island that he told the emperor was Liu Chiu
(Taiwan). Yang's discovery, however, was disputed by his staff
members and the question was never settled.[9] During the period of
Emperor Shun-ti (A.D. 1340-68), the Yüan government formally
established an administrative post (Hsün-chien Szu) at Penghu, under
the jurisdiction of Chuanchow Fu of Fukien province.[10]

At the beginning of the Ming dynasty (A.D. 1368-1644), Liu Chiu
(Taiwan) was differentiated from Okinawa, the latter being identified
as Ryukyu. Thereafter Taiwan was called Little Liu-chiu (Shao Liu-
chiu). The distinction between Taiwan and Okinawa was accomplished
by the establishment of a tributary relationship between China and
Okinawa in the early Ming dynasty.

Why the island of Little Liu-chiu was subsequently called Taiwan,
however, is not clear. For quite a time the term Taiwan referred to
the port of Anping. During the Dutch occupation of the island, the
place that is now Tainan was called Tayovan, Tayan, Tayoun, Tyovan,
or Taivan. As time passed, this name for a local place was used to
identify the whole island.

In the early Ming period Mongols in the north still constituted
the major threat to the government. Therefore, national defense on
the northern frontier was emphasized and, because the preceding
Yüan dynasty was frustrated in its expedition to Japan, the first Ming
emperor, T'ai-tzu, adopted a rather passive policy toward the eastern
sea. Moreover, during the period between 1369 and 1387, Japanese
pirates in the eastern sea repeatedly invaded the offshore islands,
including the Penghu and the coastal areas of China. As a result, in
1388 the government adopted the policy of moving the inhabitants of
these areas inland, prohibiting migration to the offshore islands, and
abolishing the Chinese administration at Penghu.[11] For a short period
the mass movement to Taiwan was suspended.

The successors of T'ai-tzu were more active in their policies toward the eastern sea. In the reign of Emperor Ch'en-tzu, Cheng Ho led seven expeditions to the southern sea and voyaged as far as the Somali coast of East Africa and Ormuz on the Persian Gulf. It has been said that he used troops to conquer Taiwan. Another account is that in 1430-1433 a typhoon drove his junks off their course as far east as southern Taiwan, where Cheng Ho ordered the crew to take on water from the land.[12] Despite all this, there is no positive historical evidence that Cheng Ho personally visited Taiwan. In view of the large size of the fleet that he led and the number of expeditions he made, it is likely that parts of his crew may have landed on Taiwan.

During the 16th century Japan attempted to invade Taiwan as part of her plan to conquer the Ryukyu Islands. In 1593 the Japanese sent an ultimatum to Taiwan, demanding that the latter pay tribute to Japan. This request was ignored; in 1601 and 1615 Japan sent troops to Taiwan. Both attempts were unsuccessful. The Japanese designs on Taiwan aroused the Ming court, which established guards on Penghu.

Since the Sung dynasty many Chinese have moved from the mainland to Taiwan. Among them were adventurers who used the island as a base for piracy. The best-known figure in the late Ming era was Cheng Chih-lung. Born in Fukien in 1602, Cheng spent some time in Macao and Manila and gained a working knowledge of Portuguese and Spanish. Eventually he made his way to Japan, where he married a woman of the Tagawa family, samurai of humble origin, known as Ashgaru.

Cheng worked with a leader of a pirate band, Yen Ssu-chi, from whom he subsequently acquired a fleet of pirate ships. By 1626 Cheng commanded 1,000 junks and had become the most powerful pirate leader in the eastern sea. While Cheng terrorized the Ming officials and troops along the eastern coast, he had much popular support because of his benevolent attitude toward ordinary people. More significant is the fact that Cheng encouraged mass migration to his base on Taiwan. His pirate fleet never interfered with Chinese ships trading between China and Taiwan; the Dutch, Portuguese, and Spanish were his prey.

In 1645 the Manchus defeated the Ming troops and took over the provisional capital, Nanking. The Ming court moved to Foochow, where Emperor Lung Wu was enthroned. Cheng Chih-lung was appointed to a high rank in the Ming government. Later he left Taiwan, and his influence in the area decreased rapidly. The next year Cheng surrendered to the Manchus, and Taiwan was left to Dutch occupation.

THE DUTCH OCCUPATION[13]

For decades the Dutch had wanted to enter the China trade, which was monopolized by the Portuguese. In 1595 Cornelius Houtman had

opened up trade with Java; this led to the formation of the Dutch East
India Company in 1602 and the subsequent annexation of the East
Indies. After these successes the company decided to challenge the
Spaniards, who had established a trading base by taking over the
Philippines in 1571, and the Portuguese, who from their base at Macao
had controlled the China trade since 1557. In 1604 a Dutch officer,
Wijbland van Waerwijek, occupied the Pescadores. Chinese tactics
were to evade a direct military conflict but to isolate the Pescadores.
As the result of this economic isolation, the Dutch retreated four
months after the occupation. Between 1607 and 1622 the Dutch made
several requests to China for permission to establish a trading post,
but they were always refused. In 1622 Kornelis Rayerszoon and his
fleet approached Macao but were defeated by the Portuguese. They
then sailed northward to the Taiwan Straits and, for the second time,
occupied the Pescadores. This time they began the construction of
a naval base.

In July, 1622, Rayerszoon arrived in Taiwan and was satisfied
with the condition of the island. In 1622 and 1624 the Chinese launched
attacks against the Dutch in the Pescadores, but these were largely
fruitless. In 1624 a compromise was reached, and the Chinese
permitted the Dutch to establish a trading post on Taiwan. On August
30, 1624, Commander Sonk arrived in Taiwan, and within a month
all Dutch remaining in the Pescadores were moved to Taiwan.

The aim of the Dutch was to make Taiwan a colony. Casteel
Zeelandia, the fort erected at Anping, at the entrance to the harbor
that serves the present city of Tainan, was a military warning to the
people. Other military forts were built for the purpose of maintaining
Dutch control over the island.

The Dutch rule was oppressive, and the island was ruthlessly
exploited. Chinese families, seeking to eke out a precarious livelihood
in remote places, were reduced to beggary. Heavy taxes were imposed,
and all profit went into the pockets of the Dutch merchants. A spirit
of rebellion gradually spread, and eventually revolts broke out against
the Dutch rulers. The revolt led by Kuo Huei-i and the many other
rebellions that followed were met with massacres of the Chinese.
After these revolts the Dutch built a series of forts on the central,
western, and northern coasts of Taiwan. By the end of 1650, 25
military centers had been established throughout the island. The
Chinese population, comprising some 50 clans, was brought under
rigid control through several administrative centers. Colonization
was reaching its peak, and the Dutch were determined that the Kuo
Huei-i rebellion not be repeated.

The Dutch occupation of Taiwan jeopardized the trade of the
Japanese and Spanish in the eastern sea.[14] The Spaniards, fearing
that from their base in southern Taiwan the Dutch would interfere

with their trading ships bound for China or Japan, decided to establish their own base in northern Taiwan. In 1626 they built their fort, Santísima Trinidad, at the entrance to Keelung harbor. In 1629 a second settlement was established on the northwestern coast at the mouth of the Tamsui River and a fort erected.

The Spanish purpose was, of course, to safeguard their trade; they had no colonizing plans. Understandably the Dutch viewed the advent of the Spaniards as a direct threat to their colonization program. Thus, in 1640 the Dutch determined to expel the Spaniards from Taiwan. The Spaniards, outnumbered by the well-equipped Dutch troops, were soon defeated and in August, 1642 were forced from Taiwan.

Japan had also been uneasy about the Dutch occupation of Taiwan. This was due not only to the menace to the Japanese ships passing through the Taiwan Straits but also to the fact that Japanese merchants on Taiwan had been exploited by the Dutch just as the Chinese inhabitants had been. Matters came to a head with the Yahei incident in 1628. Yamade Yahei, a merchant-pirate living at Nagasaki, had clashed with the Dutch some years earlier; he had suffered from Dutch interference in the Pescadores on his way to China. Deciding on revenge, he mustered 470 men and, with the assistance of Daimyo and the Shogun, sailed to Taiwan. There he captured Governor Nuyts and forced an agreement from the Dutch. Yet the ensuing discussion between the Japanese and the Dutch was fruitless, and many of the Japanese settlers decided to return to Japan. In later years the Japanese authorities prohibited the Japanese from going to Taiwan, and for a period the commercial and migratory relations between Japan and Taiwan were virtually severed.

On the island the Dutch attempted to win over the aborigines, one of the ways being through religion. The first missionaries to be recruited for work in Taiwan were Georgius Candidus and Robertus Junius. They taught the natives the rudiments of Christianity, practiced what medical knowledge they possessed, and introduced an elementary educational system. The effect of these efforts is shown by the fact that, during 1638 and 1639, approximately 2,000 aborigines were baptized. The small school that Robertus Junius established with 50 pupils soon expanded into a chain of schools with more than 500 pupils; they used a romanized form of their own language that the missionaries had devised.

CHINESE RECOVERY OF TAIWAN

One of the national heroes in Chinese history is Cheng Ch'en-kung (Koxinga). He is remembered principally for two undertakings when he was in Taiwan during the late Ming and early Ch'ing periods: the resistance to the Manchus and the recovery of Taiwan.

Cheng Ch'en-kung[15] was born on August 27, 1624, at Hirado, Japan. His mother was of the Tagawa family. At the age of seven he was taken to China and at fifteen was registered as a salaried licentiate.

In 1644, the Manchus were established in Peking and their troops were advancing southward. Emperor Lung Wu was enthroned in 1646 at Foochow. Cheng Chih-lung, possessing a powerful fleet and army, was for a short time uncertain which court, the Ming or the Manchu, he would choose to serve.

His son, Cheng Ch'en-kung, was determined to be a patriot for the Ming. Legend has it that he was so handsome and talented that when Emperor Lung Wu first saw him, he exclaimed, "What a pity that I have no daughter so that you could become my son-in-law!"

Lung Wu's government was firmly supported by Cheng, who was subsequently invested with the imperial surname Chu and was popularly known as Kuo-hsing-yeh (lord of the imperial surname) or Koxinga. During the reign of Lung Wu, Cheng was in command of the Ming armies in southern China. When Foochow fell to the Manchus and his father, Cheng Chih-lung, surrendered to Peking, Cheng made his way to Kulang-yu, a small island off Amoy, to collect the scattered Ming forces, take over his father's fleet, and plan his future operations against the Manchus.

While the Manchu army controlled the greater part of China, the spirit of the Mings was still very much alive; and after Emperor Yung Li took the throne in Yunnan, southwestern China rallied to the Ming side. The fact that Szechwan, Yunnan, and Shensi were under Ming control strengthened Cheng's conviction that the Ming could be restored and continued.

During the period between 1646 and 1660, Cheng Ch'en-kung stationed his troops in Amoy and Quemoy and fought the Manchus along the southeastern coast of China. In a very short time the size of his army expanded to roughly 200,000 and he had about 3,000 warships. The troops were well trained, equipped, and disciplined; and they had popular support wherever they operated.

Cheng's plan was threefold. First, he undertook to strengthen and enlarge his military bases on the southeastern coast. Second, he planned to advance into southwestern China and establish a tie with the Ming court, then in Yunnan. Third, he wanted to recover Nanking, which was to be used as a base for future operations in central and northern China. His ultimate goal was to recover Peking and expel the Manchus from China. Moving in 1654 to realize his second plan, Cheng led his army toward Canton but turned back halfway because his base, Amoy, was being attacked by the Manchus.

Three years later Cheng attempted to realize his third plan by sending troops to fight along the eastern coast. In 1659 he led his entire force in a drive toward Nanking. On August 3, Cheng's troops reached the vicinity of Nanking, but they were defeated at the last moment by the Manchus. Heavy casualties forced him to retreat immediately to Amoy. But he was not thoroughly defeated, for in 1660, when the Manchu troops challenged him at Amoy, Cheng won a decisive victory after a bloody battle. However, recognizing the difficulties in his initial plan, Cheng was now contemplating a long-range plan to restore the Ming dynasty. To realize this plan he first had to find a permanent political as well as military base, and it is no surprise that he thought of Taiwan as the place to which he should retire his forces and rebuild them for a future assault on the Manchus.

Despite objections from his staff, Cheng Ch'en-kung finally decided to use military force to expel the Dutch from Taiwan. In 1661 a fleet of warships carrying thousands of handpicked troops sailed from Amoy for the Pescadores, leaving Cheng Ching, son of Cheng Ch'en-kung, to hold Amoy with the rest of the forces. After weathering violent storms, the fleet arrived off the coast of Tainan at the end of April. Because of the bad weather Cheng's arrival was unexpected. The defense was surprised, and Cheng's tactics of entering a river mouth at a point north of Tainan, which usually was not suitable for ships sailing at low tides, was successful. While the Dutch were misled into thinking that activity was confined to the sea battle that was going on, the junks landed Chinese troops in a constant stream. In a few days a strong Chinese force had landed and moved to the rear of the Dutch line of defense.

On June 21, 1661, Batavia learned the bad news and immediately sent a fleet under the command of Jacob Caeuw to Taiwan. It arrived off the island on August 12. During September and October there were battles between the Chinese and the Dutch. Both sides suffered casualties, but Cheng's control over Taiwan seemed firm and Dutch chances to defeat him seemed remote. In December the Dutch on Taiwan held talks with Cheng and, under an agreement containing 18 articles, the Dutch were allowed to take with them from Taiwan everything they possessed but arms and munitions (Doc. 1).

On assuming control, Cheng Ch'en-kung dedicated himself to the twofold task of making Taiwan a prosperous island and, using it as a base, launching an expedition for the recovery of the Chinese mainland from the Manchus.

By introducing Chinese laws, customs, and forms of government, Cheng Ch'en-kung restored the Ming way of life in Taiwan. Under his administration land was distributed without payment to families prepared to settle on it. For a period the families were exempted from taxation. All males were required to undergo a period of military

training, and the army also was put to work on the land. Special areas
adjacent to the military posts were set aside for the troops to cultivate.

Soon after Cheng Ch'en-kung's occupation of Taiwan, the Manchus
issued an edict directing all coastal villages to be evacuated and the
inhabitants moved inland not less than 30 li (10 miles).[16] Peking
feared that the villagers would cooperate with Cheng's men when they
landed, for an invasion was regarded as imminent. This policy, however, antagonized many Chinese in the area, for it deprived most of
them their farms and their living. As a result, thousands of peasants
in Fukien and Kwangtung migrated to the island to find a new life.
And so did the literati. Hundreds of scholars from southern China
made their homes on Taiwan during 1662-64; many of them set up
their own schools for the promotion of Chinese culture.

Cheng's agriculture programs were realistic and devoted to
realizing the potential of the island. Today's rice paddies and sugar
and fruit plantations originated with his programs. Having set the
foundation for agricultural development, he turned his attention to
foreign trade. He encouraged trade with Japan, the Philippines,
Indochina, Siam, and the East Indies. Soon Tainan became an important port in the western Pacific.

Huang Tsung-hsi (Huang Li-chou), a great scholar in Chinese
history, summarized Cheng Ch'en-kung's achievements in Taiwan in
the following words:

> He pronounced laws, and established prisons for crimi-
> nals. He set up schools and conducted a population
> survey. He ordered a social security program to
> protect the young and to assist the old. He emphasized
> transportation, and stressed production. He listened
> to scholars. As a result, the talented Chinese people
> gathered in Taiwan, and the local people were pros-
> perous. The Cheng government had thus established
> a base upon which it could expect security.[17]

Before assuming the control of Taiwan, Cheng Ch'en-kung had
long had a plan to develop trade with the Philippines. Probably his
desire was for more than trading; he may have had an ambition to
take military control of the islands. After the first plank of his
platform, the building up of Taiwan, was achieved, Cheng set his
mind to the second, the utilization of Taiwan as a base from which
to expel the Manchus from China. To this end he looked to the
Philippines as a vital stage in the execution of his grand designs.
His first move was to send a representative, Victorio Riccio, to
Manila. While the envoy was in Manila, the Spaniards noted that

the local Chinese showed elation over the visit—perhaps denoting
the likelihood that a Chinese uprising could be stirred up by Cheng's
efforts. The Spaniards therefore lost no time in taking preventive
action. The Spanish army was dispatched into and around Manila
and slaughtered 10,000 Chinese.

Receiving the report of the Spanish suppression of the Chinese,
Cheng was infuriated and decided to take retaliatory measures. However, he was soon struck by illness and died suddenly on June 23,
1662.

Upon Cheng's death the Manchus offered terms of agreement to
his son, Cheng Ching, at Amoy. Cheng Ching declined. But in the
government bitter polarization appeared as disputes developed over
Cheng Ching's right of succession. Officials in Taiwan attempted to
raise his uncle to the throne. Angered by the plot, Cheng Ching used
force to gain what he considered his rightful position. Triumphing in
a military conflict, he finally took the throne and announced that he
would dedicate himself to carrying on the work his father had begun.

Following Cheng Ch'en-kung's plan, in 1674 Cheng Ching entered
into an alliance with Keng Ching-chung, who then controlled Fukien
and had rebelled against the Manchu dynasty. Cheng landed at Amoy
but, suspecting Keng of treachery, he decided to go it alone. He had
some success in his military expeditions; but after four years of
sporadic fighting he was driven from his base at Amoy and forced to
retreat to Taiwan. There, with the aid of Ch'eng Yung-hua, Cheng
Ching developed a good domestic program. He died in 1681, at the
age of 39.

With the death of Cheng Ching, the fortunes of the Taiwan government began to decline. Within two years palace intrigue, leading to
internal dissension, hastened its end. The home front cracked, thus
providing an opportunity for which those outside Taiwan had long
waited.

This opportunity to overthrow Taiwan was seized by Shih Lang,
a general for Peking. While the palace quarrel in Taiwan was at its
peak, he prepared his fleet and troops on the mainland. In July,
1683, he sailed from Fukien for the Pescadores, where he soon
destroyed the entire fleet of the Cheng government. Meanwhile, there
was great unrest in Taiwan, as was evidenced by civilian uprisings
and military disobedience. When Shih's troops landed on Taiwan,
Cheng K'e-shuang, successor to Cheng Ching, offered surrender.
The 22-year Chinese rule over Taiwan under the Chengs was thus
destroyed by the Manchus.

There have been disputes over the extent of the Cheng government's achievements on Taiwan, but it is undeniable that there were
achievements. Economically the Cheng period was an age of reconstruction. Its basis, the land policy, was its greatest accomplishment.

It allowed each peasant to own the land he tilled. This involved the division of estates held by privileged families who had acquired the land in earlier times. The result was that production increased startlingly and contentment rapidly spread over the island. During the Cheng period Taiwan was peaceful and prosperous.

On the cultural side the arts flourished. Schools, academies, and libraries were established. Education was gradually promoted all over the island.

Perhaps most significant is the political achievement of the Cheng government. The Cheng period saw the birth of a real national purpose in Taiwan. Previously the population had been a loose gathering of families. Nationalism was aroused by the Chengs' pledge to restore China from the Manchus and to unite Taiwan with mainland China.

CH'ING POLICY TOWARD TAIWAN[18]

Taiwan was reintegrated into China in 1683 and was placed under the control of the Fukien provincial government. But Peking's attention was given to imminent national problems, and the policy toward Taiwan was at best passive. China was occupied with other pressing problems, both from within and from without. There was great unrest in the southern provinces.

Under these circumstances Peking could give no thought to the island across the sea. The Fukien government appointed officials, but attention was drawn more to the Pescadores than to Taiwan. By and large, the inefficient and corrupt Ch'ing administration in Taiwan resulted in numerous uprisings on the island. Some secret societies organized by the Han Chinese there took advantage of the Ch'ing government's ignorance of Taiwan and organized a number of revolts under the motto "Destroy the Ch'ing, restore the Ming."

One of the Ch'ing measures was to prohibit migration from the mainland and to prevent the families of those already on Taiwan from joining them. This policy virtually prevented most of the Chinese from southern China from staying on Taiwan permanently. Despite this prohibition, however, migration continued, mainly for two reasons: the law was not rigorously enforced, and certain local officials on Taiwan actually encouraged migration for cultivation of the island. Emperor Yung Chen (1723-35) finally abrogated the prohibition and allowed their families to go with the migrants. In 1732 an order was issued to encourage Chinese families to settle on Taiwan. However, in 1736 Emperor Chien Lung again issued a prohibition against migration.[19] The law continued to exist throughout the 19th century. But because of nonenforcement, migration was never substantially interrupted.

In 1858 the Treaty of Tientsin brought Taiwan within the orbit of the ambitious schemes of the West; Keelung and Tamsui became ports of call for Western ships.[20] Europeans and Americans set up consulates and trading posts on Taiwan. The treaty brought more foreign merchants to make profits throughout the island. But the ambitions of certain Western nations may have been more than trading.

As early as 1833 British merchants in China urged the British government to occupy Taiwan as a "convenient and desirable acquisition." During the Opium War, some British vessels were wrecked on the Taiwan coast and most of the crews killed. When the war was over, the British plenipotentiary to China demanded the punishment of officials in Taiwan, with the warning that the British might occupy the island if China failed to discipline her officials there.[21] However, the British ambition toward Taiwan was never realized.

The Americans also had ideas about Taiwan. In 1854 Commodore Perry urged his government to occupy the island.[22] Townsend Harris, American commissioner to Japan, suggested that America purchase Taiwan from China.[23] Gideon Nye, an American merchant in China, even presented the American commissioner to China, Peter Parker (1854-56), with a plan for the "colonization" of Taiwan.[24] Parker enthusiastically supported the idea and made a formal suggestion to the U.S. government.[25] However, all these plans were left unrealized because America then had many internal problems that occupied her attention.

Taiwan itself was in turmoil. In 1853 Hung Hsui-ch'uan had established Nanking as the capital of his T'ai-p'ing T'ien-kuo. The people on Taiwan were greatly encouraged. In June, 1853, an uprising, led by the San Ho Hui (Triad Society) took place on Taiwan; and for a time the rebels were so strong that the uprising "shocked the whole island of Taiwan." However, the rebellion was suppressed by the Ch'ing troops. In 1862-64, however, Tai Chao-chuen led a second revolt and declared himself the East King of the T'ai-p'ing T'ien-kuo.

To the Chinese literati the revolt under the banner of T'ai-p'ing was not a good cause; the most objectionable feature was the novel religion and values proclaimed by its leaders. The Taiwan literati thus defended themselves against the revolt that failed in 1864.

The real challenge came from Japan. The first step taken by the Japanese government was to review Japan's relations with Liu Chiu. For many years both China and Japan had received allegiance from the king of Okinawa; but Japan was not content with the status quo, for she intended to bring this group of islands into her territory. In 1871 a vessel from Liu Chiu was driven ashore during a storm off the coast of southern Taiwan, and 54 of the 66 survivors were killed

by tribesmen. Since Liu Chiu had always been a tributary state of
China, the incident had nothing to do with Japan. The Chinese government ordered the authorities on Taiwan to investigate the matter and
compensated the 12 survivors and repatriated them to Liu Chiu.[26]
Japan, however, decided to use this incident as a pretext to invade
Taiwan. At the same time the American consul to Taiwan and Amoy,
Charles Uriliam LeGendre strongly urged the Japanese government
to take military action against Taiwan. He himself supplied important
local information to Japan to aid in the action.[27] In 1874 a punitive
expedition, led by Saigo Judo, was sent to Taiwan.

China protested the expedition, charging that it was a violation
of international law. Meanwhile, Peking sent Shen Pao-chen to Taiwan
to cope with the situation. After an inspection of the island, Shen
made four suggestions to the court at Peking. It should bring international pressure upon Japan; equip the troops on Taiwan with modern
weapons; appoint capable officials; and develop close communications
system between Taiwan and the mainland.[28] Peking approved all of
the suggestions, and more than 10,000 troops were immediately sent
to Taiwan for its defense.

Reactions of the Western powers were not favorable to Japan.
Britain expressed suspicion that Japan was seeking an excuse to
involve China in a war. Americans and Europeans with interests in
China stated that Japan planned to occupy Taiwan as a steppingstone
for imperialist movement into the western Pacific.[29] The British
minister, Thomas Wade, and the American minister, B. P. Avery,
intervened in the matter to seek a peaceful settlement of the Sino-
Japanese dispute. These international reactions were such that Japan
had to stay her hand for the time being.[30]

An agreement was finally reached between Japan and China, in
which China recognized that Japan's expedition was for the purpose
of protecting her subjects—a provision that implicitly recognized
Japan's sovereignty over Liu Chiu.[31]

TAIWAN IN THE LATE CH'ING DYNASTY

During the conflict between China and Japan, Shen Pao-chen
urged that Peking take Taiwan seriously. He suggested that the system
of administration on Taiwan be overhauled, and particularly that
education facilities be extended to include the mountain tribes. Natural resources, especially gold and coal, were to be exploited. Moreover, fortresses should be constructed along the coast for defense.
Peking then directed the Fukien authorities to set up new administrative units on Taiwan.

Following Shen, the governor of Fukien, Ting Jih-ch'ang, contributed to the development of Taiwan. He made inspections on Taiwan and put forward plans for the training of naval and land forces, the exploitation of coal, the construction of highways, the setting up of cables for communication, and the promotion of education. Ting resigned in 1877 and died in 1882.

During the 1850's France had been acquiring territory in Southeast Asia. In 1863 it had annexed three provinces of Annam (Vietnam). Then François Garnier, and others, suggested that the time had come to tap the rich mineral sources of the Chinese province of Yunnan. When war broke out between China and France in 1884-85, France decided to acquire a naval base on Taiwan from which to attack China.

When the invasion of Taiwan was imminent, Liu Ming-ch'uan was sent there with instructions to take over its defense.[32] On August 4, 1884, he drove back the French at Keelung. The next year he held Taipei in the face of a massive assault by French troops. The French were successful merely in taking the Pescadores. Their attempts to take Taiwan and Liu's vigorous defense aroused Peking, which for the first time began to realize the importance of the island in terms of China's national defense. On October 12, 1885, Peking announced that Taiwan had become a province of China and that Liu was appointed governor of Taiwan.[33]

Assuming the new position, Liu moved the capital from Tainan to Taipei. There, in 1887, he constructed the first electric power station on Taiwan.

Next he planned the strengthening of Taiwan's defensive forces. By 1887 there were Western batteries at a number of strategic ports. Also, supplies of heavy modern armament were bought from European countries. Efforts were made to build the Pescadores into a modern naval base.

Third, Liu turned to the communication system. He extended the telegraph line that had been set up by Ting Jih-ch'ang throughout the island, and a school for the training of telegraph operators was established in Taipei. Taiwan and the Pescadores were linked by a cable.

Liu had urged Peking to construct a railway system on the mainland, but his suggestions were not accepted by the court at Peking. With Taiwan under his control, he began to carry out his plan. In 1889 the first railway track was built from Taipei to Keelung. Liu also constructed many roads.

As his attention turned to industry, Liu ordered the exploitation of camphor and emphasized tea production. He also drew up plans for the building of ships and the construction of ports.

Finally, Liu extended education to all inhabitants on Taiwan, including the mountain tribesmen. This education emphasized Chinese philosophy and also stressed Western scientific knowledge and technology. Taiwan was rapidly becoming the most modern and progressive province of China.

THE JAPANESE OCCUPATION

In 1891 Liu was succeeded by Shao Yu-ling, a weak man who cared more for the easy life than for maintaining the defense of Taiwan. He was succeeded by T'ang Ching-sung. In 1894 Taiwan underwent a great change. In that year, when the Tong Hake, a secret society in Korea, attempted to take over control of that country, China sent forces to Korea, over which it had suzerainty, in answer to an appeal from the Korean ruler. Japan did likewise, with the result that Chinese and Japanese armies were face to face. This conflict finally led to an open war. China was defeated; and by the 1895 Treaty of Shimonoseki, Korea was declared independent and China lost Taiwan to Japan (Doc. 2).

The cession of Taiwan to Japan was vigorously opposed by the people of Taiwan. They made it clear that under no circumstances would the island accept Japanese rule (Doc. 3).

The whole country also strongly opposed the cession of Taiwan. On May 1, 1895, K'ang Yu-wei, the famous reform movement leader, led more than 1,200 chü-jen (recommended men, persons qualified for taking the imperial examination at Peking) from various provinces to plead that the government reject the treaty. Governors of various provinces also appealed to the government not to cede Taiwan.

Various attempts were made to save Taiwan. A group of Chinese officials offered to raise China's indemnity to Japan as the price for keeping the island out of Japanese hands. A number of Westerners also volunteered their financial assistance. Peking even tried to invite Britain to take over Taiwan on China's behalf. Suggestions were also made to invite a French take-over of the island.

Faced with strong opposition at home, Peking directed Li Hung-chang to reopen discussion with Japan over the cession clause. But the Japanese representatives were adamant in insisting that Taiwan and the Pescadores must be handed over. Having no alternative, Peking finally ratified the treaty.

When the news reached Taiwan, the island was in an uproar. On May 25, 1895, T'ang Ching-sung proclaimed Taiwan an independent republic (Docs. 4, 5). He pleaded with the court at Peking for forgiveness, pledged that Taiwan would remain loyal to China, and claimed that independence was intended only to be temporary and solely for

the purpose of defending the island against a Japanese take-over
(Doc. 7). The declaration of independence had not only popular
support on Taiwan (Doc. 6) but also moral support from China.

The new Taiwan government consisted of three branches: military, interior affairs, and foreign affairs. An executive council was
immediately constituted and commissioned to draw up the policy of
the republic and devise means by which it could be carried out. A
state lottery was set up to provide funds for the conduct of the war,
and a postal system was introduced. The government also assured
the people that after the Japanese were driven out of Taiwan, a
program of railway construction, the opening of mines, and trade
would be carried out.

On May 28, 1895, the Japanese forces appeared on the sea outside
Keelung. The troops of the new republic launched a defensive attack,
but it was an uneven battle. On June 3 the Japanese occupied Keelung.
On June 8 they reached and took Taipei, the capital of the republic.
On June 14 the first Japanese governor of Taiwan arrived in Taipei.

Liu Yung-fu, well-known for his army of "Black Flags," was
still in southern Taiwan; and he pledged to fight the Japanese to the
last. For three months there were a number of bloody battles. On
August 16 the Japanese troops took Feng-Shang. Three days later
Tainan was occupied. That was the end of the Taiwan republic.[34]

The Japanese take-over of Taiwan had proved more difficult
than they had imagined. The Hakkas fought bravely, and even the
Taiyal tribesmen played a role of distinction in one battle in northern
Taiwan. In southern Taiwan the Bunums from the mountains wiped
out a Japanese force converging on the city of Tainan. In fact, the
entire population of the island—Hoklos and Hakkas, and the tribesmen
of the mountains, men and women alike—united in a single effort to
drive back the Japanese invader. The short-lived Taiwan republic
had been created to preserve Chinese culture and maintain Chinese
rule, rather than to establish a state independent of China (Docs. 6,
7). The battles against the Japanese had indeed been fought with a
national spirit.

The cession of Taiwan to Japan fully exposed the incompetence
of the Ch'ing government, and many reform-minded Chinese were
now disillusioned with the imperial court and turned to radical means
of change. This was a significant episode in modern Chinese history,
as one Western commentator wrote:

> [I]t is clear that the prolonged defense of Taiwan and the
> establishment of the republic and its vestiges were
> manifestations of a rising nationalist spirit among the
> Chinese. The backers of the republic evinced a marked
> degree of patriotism in their utterances. Furthermore,

their resistance effort, conducted in the name of the people and on behalf of China, certainly was indicative of an outgrowth of modern nationalism.[35]

JAPANESE ADMINISTRATION OF TAIWAN[36]

From the beginning Japanese occupation of Taiwan was designed to be the first step in a campaign of imperialist expansion. Thus, Japanese migration to Taiwan was not encouraged. Most Japanese on Taiwan were in the armed forces, government service, or industrial enterprises.

Economic development of the island was emphasized. The Chinese population was regimented in most ruthlessly. The objective of the industries was to exploit the island, and the population's labor was the only thing that permitted survival.

The domestic policy was discriminatory. The Japanese imposed heavy taxation on the native people. Land was easily confiscated and individual rights were virtually nonexistent. The people of Taiwan were a conquered people and could not claim any political rights.

In 1898, three years after Japan extended her power to Taiwan, a police force was established to take the place of the troops who had been used to suppress the local resistance. Between 1898 and 1903 the police force was used largely to suppress Taiwanese revolts. When, in 1903, most of the organized underground resistance groups had reportedly been eliminated, the police force, which by then had become very strong, was utilized for ordinary crime prevention and administrative measures. The organization and functions of this Japanese police force on Taiwan were basically different from those in Japan—in addition to preserving the peace, the police on Taiwan were used to support and enforce every administrative measure.

One of the important pieces of legislation was an administrative decree for the suppression of "undesirable elements" promulgated in November, 1900 (The Taiwan Peace Preservation Rules, Administrative Decree No. 21).[37] Under this decree the police had exclusive power to arrest and confine, without a trial, the following persons:

1. One who has no legitimate employment and wanders about on the streets;
2. One whose behavior has been rude, or who slanders or gossips about another's daily behavior;
3. One who threatens another, regardless of his reason for doing so, or who interferes with another's business, or another's personal freedom;
4. One who fabricates rumors through words or written materials;

5. One who instigates another to commit one of the
above acts.

Under the ambiguous and broad terms of this decree, any individual could easily be put in confinement for an indefinite period by
the police, without being accorded any opportunity to defend himself.

By Administrative Decree No. 2, promulgated in March, 1896,[38]
the police were authorized to arrest and confine all Taiwanese who,
in the official view, had a propensity to endanger society. Individuals
were to be confined on an outer island near Taiwan after being arrested. No trial was necessary.

The most rigorous enactment seems to have been the Decree
for Punishment of Bandits, promulgated on November 5, 1898 (Administrative Decree No. 24).[39] It consisted of seven articles, all
but article 5 imposing the death penalty on the offender. Moreover,
the law was enforced retroactively and analogously. The trial for an
act against this law was not held in a regular court, but in a special
tribunal. No appeal was allowed. It bears emphasis that all these
administrative decrees, having the function of law, were not applicable
to the Japanese inhabitants in Taiwan but applied exclusively to the
Taiwanese.

To illustrate the harshness of these decrees, in one case the
Japanese government, applying these provisions, arrested 1,957 persons and the special tribunal that had put the defendants on a summary
trial announced the death sentence for 866 of the accused.[40]

All education was designed to further the imperialist purposes
of Japan. All instruction in elementary schools was in Japanese, and
the doors to a general advanced education were closed to the native
people. Two different school systems coexisted in Taiwan throughout
the Japanese occupation. A superior system, consisting of a broader
range of curricula and better facilities, was designed for the Japanese
in Taiwan. All Taiwanese, on the other hand, were allowed to go only
to schools where the curricula were specially arranged for the students and facilities were generally inadequate. For example, the public schools for Japanese students were financed by the government,
but those for Taiwanese were supported by local funds. Taiwanese
students, moreover, were required to attend school for a shorter
period of time than their Japanese counterparts. The curriculum in
the schools for local students was oriented toward technology, but the
courses in the schools for Japanese students encompassed a much
broader range, including both theory and practice.

Furthermore, very few Taiwanese were permitted to enter the
only university on Taiwan and their fields were confined to medicine,
agriculture, and other practical sciences. Very few were allowed to
study political science, law, or history.

As a result of this discriminatory education, few Taiwanese possessed knowledge comparable with that of an ordinary Japanese college student.[41] After the restoration of Taiwan to China, the Chinese government gave preferential treatment to local Taiwanese youngsters in school examinations for 10 years so that they could compete equally with the Chinese mainlanders who came to Taiwan after 1949.

Despite the efforts to colonize Taiwan, however, the island was never pacified from the day the Japanese occupied it in 1895 until they left in 1945. Records indicate that a great number of people were arrested, persecuted, and massacred for attempts to overthrow the Japanese. During the entire period of occupation there were 19 major uprisings, each brutally suppressed.[42]

RESISTANCE OF THE CHINESE IN TAIWAN AND IN MAINLAND CHINA

During the Japanese occupation, restrictions against traveling to China were imposed upon the Chinese on Taiwan. As a result, in the early years only a limited number of them had a chance to tour China. By 1922, however, a great many young Taiwanese had been deprived of the opportunity to pursue college education in Taiwan; and most of them began to think of returning to the mainland regardless of the Japanese prohibitions. Some of them went to China via Japan, a route that required no special Japanese official permit. Others went surreptitiously by ship. In the 1920's the number of people from Taiwan who went to China rapidly increased.

Early in 1922 the Chinese from Taiwan who were staying at Peking organized a society for the promotion of a nationalistic movement for Taiwan. Honorary members of this society were such prominent Chinese scholars as Ts'ai Yuan-p'ai, Liang Ch'i-ch'ao, Li Shih-tseng, and Hu Shih.[43] In the same year the society issued a declaration calling upon the people on Taiwan to organize themselves against the Japanese.[44] Similar societies were set up in Shanghai and other major cities by the Chinese from Taiwan.

In 1924 a number of protest meetings were convened in Shanghai to bring the attention of the country and the world to the inhuman Japanese administration on Taiwan. On May 9, 1924, for example, they declared that the people on Taiwan had awakened and were willing to unite themselves with the people on the mainland against the "common enemy"—Japan.[45] Taking the opportunity provided by the anti-Japan sentiments among the Chinese after the May 30 Incident and, subsequently, the 1931 Mukden Incident,* the Chinese from Taiwan issued various declarations designed to promote the nationalistic movement on Taiwan and unite it with the general nationalism in China.

During the same period the Chinese from Taiwan at Amoy and Foochow also organized and convened meetings against the Japanese occupation of Taiwan.[46] These activities were carried out despite the close surveillance of the Japanese consulate at Amoy. On January 30, 1925, for example, the oppressive rule of the Japanese government in Taiwan was publicly denounced.[47] This announcement was followed by many other statements of the same nature. In 1926 a number of these people returned to Taiwan and attempted to organize a revolt but were arrested and convicted by the Japanese.[48]

In Kwangtung the Chinese from Taiwan published a periodical in order to arouse a nationalistic feeling among the people of Taiwan. Tai Chi-t'ao, president of Chung-shan University, showed himself in great sympathy with them.[49] In 1932 the Taiwan Democratic Party was organized to fulfill the objective of recovering Taiwan.[50] The leaders of this party traveled extensively in the coastal provinces of China to promulgate their views and to instigate an organized movement against the Japanese on Taiwan. The Japanese consulates in China arrested some of these people and extradited them to Taiwan for trial and punishment. But most of the leaders of the movement remained in China and thus were able to escape Japanese persecution.

After Japan started all-out aggression against China in 1937, the Japanese tried to draft Taiwanese to fight on the mainland. Many Chinese on Taiwan participated in antiwar movements and refused to be drafted into the Japanese imperialist army. On October 8 and 10, 1938, antiwar riots broke out at Liu-chia and Kaohsiung. The Japanese ruthlessly suppressed the riots by slaughtering some 200 individuals and arresting 500 Taiwanese.[51] On October 10, 1939, the national day of the Republic of China, 300 Taiwanese draftees refused to go to mainland China to fight against the Chinese. Many Japanese officers

---

*The May 30 Incident occurred in Shanghai in 1925, when the foreign-controlled police in the International Settlement opened fire upon Chinese demonstrators, killing more than 10 persons. The incident created a fervor of patriotism among Chinese and aroused a strong anti-British and anti-Japanese sentiment. The Mukden Incident occurred on September 18, 1931, when Japanese troops suddenly occupied the city of Mukden by force. The Japanese soon expanded their occupation to all of Manchuria. The Mukden Incident brought the anti-Japanese feeling of the Chinese to a peak.

and soldiers were killed as a result of the mutiny, though more
Taiwanese were then and later slaughtered.[52]

In 1938 the Chinese from Taiwan residing in China organized
the Taiwanese Volunteers to fight on the Chinese side.[53] On March
29, 1940, all Taiwanese resistance groups organized themselves in
a united front under the Great Alliance for Taiwanese Revolution at
Chungking, the provisional capital of the Republic of China. In 1941
the alliance was renamed the Taiwan Revolution Alliance Association.
In 1943, anticipating the ultimate victory over Japan, the association
formally asked the Chinese government that a Taiwan provincial
government be established for the future recovery of Taiwan (Item
3).[54]

Between 1937 and 1945 some 50,000 Taiwanese went to China
to join in the "war of resistance." Their activities on the mainland
consisted of three aspects: to organize an army of the Chinese from
Taiwan intended to liberate the island from the Japanese militarists;
to form a provincial government for Taiwan; and to work on plans
for revolt on Taiwan to overthrow the Japanese authorities.[55] These
Taiwanese patriots contributed a great deal, both psychologically and
physically, to the morale of the Chinese government during the war.

RESTORATION TO CHINA

Soon after Japan started all-out aggression against China in
1937, President Chiang Kai-shek announced at the Provisional National
Convention of the Kuomintang on April 1, 1938, the determination of
China to recover Taiwan after the war (Doc. 8). On December 9,
1941, the Chinese government formally declared war against Japan
and abrogated all treaties between China and Japan, including the
1895 Treaty of Shimonoseki (Doc. 9). At the same time Foreign
Minister T. V. Soong explicitly stated in a press conference that
"after the war, China is determined to recover Penghu, Taiwan and
the four northeastern provinces [Manchuria]."[56]

In November, 1943, President Chiang Kai-shek met at Cairo
with President Franklin D. Roosevelt of the United States and Prime
Minister Winston Churchill of Great Britain. On December 1, 1943,
they released a communiqué signed on November 26 pledging, among
other things, the return of Taiwan and Penghu to China (Doc. 12).
The Potsdam Proclamation of July 26, 1945, declared that "the terms
of the Cairo Declaration shall be carried out" (Doc. 14). This was
accepted by Japan in its instrument of surrender executed on September
2, 1945, (Doc. 15). On October 25, 1945, Taiwan was formally restored
to the Republic of China (Docs. 17 and 18) and has since been administered as one of the provinces of the Republic of China.

CONCLUDING OBSERVATIONS

The fate of Taiwan has historically been intertwined with that of China. A turning point in modern Chinese history was the 1895 Sino-Japanese War, as it was in the history of Taiwan. From 1895 to 1945 Japan ruthlessly expanded its imperialist plans over mainland China. However, sooner or later China had to curb this expansion. As a result, the Chinese "war of resistance" that began in 1937, viewed with hindsight, was inevitable. For half a century Japan inflicted immeasurable evils on China, but Taiwan suffered the most. Chinese nationalism has been aimed at preserving an integrated China and uniting the Chinese people. Taiwan certainly has been a part of this nationalism. In other words, the Taiwan question is a part of the China problem.

The war of resistance against Japan was fought to save not only China but also Taiwan. There has been an unbreakable tie between the people of Taiwan and those of mainland China, both in terms of cultural affinity and in terms of ethnic origins. There is no doubt, therefore, that the island should be returned to China.

The history of Taiwan cannot be adequately understood without reference to the history of China. War or peace on the mainland has invariably affected the fate of the island. This has been even more the case in modern history. The reason is apparent—Taiwan, as part of China, undergoes whatever changes the nation as a whole undergoes.

NOTES

1. See Chiao-min Hsieh, Taiwan—ilha Formosa, a Geography in Perspective (Washington, D.C.: Butterworths, 1964), pp. 7-8.

2. Ibid., pp. 125-27.

3. Kuo Ting-yee, T'ai-wan shih-shih kai-shu (General history of Taiwan) (3d. printing; Taipei: Cheng chung shu chu, 1964), pp. 1-2.

4. Ibid., p. 2. See also Lien Heng, T'ai-wan t'ung-shih (A comprehensive history of Taiwan), edited from 1921 Taiwan ed., I (Taipei: Chung hua ts'ung shu wei yuan hui, 1954), pp. 1-2.

5. Kuo Ting-yee, T'ai-wan shih-shih kai-shu, pp. 3-4.

6. See Lien Heng, T'ai-wan t'ung-shih, pp. 2-4.

7. Kuo Ting-yee, T'ai-wan shih-shih kai-shu, pp. 4-5.

8. See Chau Ju-kua, Chu-fan-chi (A description of barbarous peoples), translated from Chinese and annotated by Friedrich Hirth and W. W. Rockhill (St. Petersburg: Printing Office of the Imperial Academy of Sciences, 1911; repr. Taipei: Literature House, 1965), pp. 162-66.

9. Lien Heng, T'ai-wan t'ung-shih, p. 6.

10. Ibid., p. 7.

11. Ibid.

12. Ibid.

13. For a study of the history of this period, see William Campbell, Formosa Under the Dutch (London: Kegan Paul, Trench, Trubner & Co., 1903); and James W. Davidson, The Island of Formosa (n.p., 1903; repr. Taipei: Wen hsing shu chu, 1964), pp. 9-48. For a Chinese record of the Dutch occupation of Taiwan, see Lien Heng, T'ai-wan t'ung-shih, pp. 9-16; Kuo Ting-yee, T'ai-wan shih-shih kai-shu, pp. 18-33; and Huang Shun-ch'ing and Lin Hsiung-hsiang, eds., T'ai-wan sheng t'ung-chih kao (Draft history of Taiwan province), IX, Ke-min chih-Ch'ü ho pien (History of revolution—driving out of the Dutch) (Taipei: T'ai-wan sheng wen-hsien wei yüen hui, 1954).

14. For a survey of the Spanish occupation of Taiwan, see Kuo Ting-yee, T'ai-wan shih-shih kai-shu, pp. 28-29, Huang Shun-ch'ing and Lin Hsiung-hsiang, Ke-min chih-Ch'ü ho pien, pp. 21-24, 41-56; and W. G. Goddard, Formosa, a Study in Chinese History (London: Macmillan, 1966), pp. 53-54.

15. For a biography of Cheng Ch'en-kung, see Goddard, Formosa, pp. 70-86; and Donald R. Keene, trans., The Battle of Coxinga (London: Taylor's Foreign Press, 1951).

16. For details, see Hsieh Kuo-chen, "Removal of Coastal Population in the Early Tsing [Ch'ing] Period," T. H. Chen, trans., Chinese Social and Political Science Review (Peking), XV (1930-31), 559-96.

17. Cited in Kuo Ting-yee, T'ai-wan shih-shih kai-shu, p. 60.

18. For Ch'ing's administration in Taiwan, see Lien Heng, T'ai-wan t'ung-shih, pp. 43-65.

19. See Kuo Ting-yee, T'ai-wan shih-shih kai-shu, pp. 100-01.

20. Article XI of Sino-British Treaty, Tientsin, June 26, 1858, provided that "it is agreed that British subjects may frequent the Cities and Ports of . . . Taiwan [Formosa] . . . ." China, Maritime Customs, Treaties, Conventions, Etc., Between China and Foreign States, I (2d ed.; Shanghai: Inspectorate General of Customs, 1917), p. 408. For details of the opening of Taiwan to foreigners, see Sophia Su-fei Yen, Taiwan in China's Foreign Relations 1836-1874 (Hamden, Conn.: The Shoe String Press, 1965), pp. 74-95.

21. See Davidson, The Island of Formosa, pp. 104-09; and Sophia Su-fei Yen, Taiwan in China's Foreign Relations, pp. 36-39.

22. See Davidson, The Island of Formosa, pp. 112-14; Sophia Su-fei Yen, Taiwan in China's Foreign Relations, pp. 53-56; and Huang Chia-mo, Mei-kuo yu T'ai-wan, 1784-1895 (The United States and Taiwan, 1784-1895) (Taipei: Chung yang yen-chiu yen, 1966), pp. 135-42.

23. See Sophia Su-fei Yen, Taiwan in China's Foreign Relations, p. 55; Huang Chia-mo, Mei-kuo yu T'ai-wan 1784-1895, pp. 127-34.

24. See Sophia Su-fei Yen, Taiwan in China's Foreign Relations, pp. 59-60; Huang Chia-mo, Mei-kuo yu T'ai-wan 1784-1895, pp. 145-46; and Davidson, The Island of Formosa, p. 172.

25. Davidson, The Island of Formosa, pp. 171-72; Huang Chia-mo, Mei-kuo yu T'ai-wan 1784-1895, pp. 143-54; and Sophia Su-fei Yen, Taiwan in China's Foreign Relations, pp. 56-63.

26. Kuo Ting-yee, T'ai-wan shih-shih kai-shu, pp. 157-58; Lien Heng, T'ai-wan t'ung shih, pp. 316-17; and Sophia Su-fei Yen, Taiwan in China's Foreign Relations, p. 157.

27. For details see Huang Chia-mo, Mei-kuo yu T'ai-wan 1784-1895, pp. 259-74.

28. Ch'ing-tai ch'ou-pan i-wu shih-mo (History of the management of barbarian affairs of the Ch'ing dynasty), book III, "T'ung-ch'ih ch'ao," chüan 95 (Peiping: Palace Museum, 1930), pp. 3-5; see also T. F. Tsiang, "Sino-Japanese Diplomatic Relations, 1870-1874," Chinese Social and Political Science Review (Peking), XVII (1933-34), 22.

29. Kuo Ting-yee, T'ai-wan shih-shih kai-shu, pp. 159-63; Sophia Su-fei Yen, Taiwan in China's Foreign Relations, pp. 212-20.

30. Kuo Ting-yee, T'ai-wan shih-shih kai-shu, p. 163; Sophia Su-fei Yen, Taiwan in China's Foreign Relations, pp. 272-73.

31. Sino-Japanese Agreement, Peking, October 31, 1874. China, Maritime Customs . . ., II, pp. 1313-15.

32. For a study of Liu's career on Taiwan, see William M. Spiedel, "Liu Ming-ch'uan in Taiwan, 1884-91," Ph. D. Dissertation, Yale University, 1967.

33. Lien Heng, T'ai-wan t'ung-shih, pp. 77-78.

34. For a study of the history of the Taiwan republic, see Harry J. Lamley, "The 1895 Taiwan Republic: A Significant Episode in Modern Chinese History," Journal of Asian Studies, XXVII, 4 (August 1968), 739-62; Lien Heng, T'ai-wan t'ung-shih, pp. 66-76; and Davidson, The Island of Formosa, pp. 275-89.

35. Lamley, "The 1895 Taiwan Republic," p. 761.

36. For a study of Japanese rule on Taiwan, see Huang Ching-chia, Jih-chü shih-ch'i chih T'ai-wan chih-min-ti fa-chih yü chih-min t'ung-chih (Taiwan colonial legal system and colonial rule under the Japanese occupation) Published by the author. (Taipei, 1960).

37. Ibid., pp. 178-79.

38. Ibid., p. 179.

39. Ibid., p. 120. Between 1907 and 1915 at least 903 Taiwanese were sentenced to death under this decree. See ibid., p. 130.

40. Ibid., p. 147.

41. In 1944, of 357 students in Taiwan University (the only university on Taiwan) only 85 were Taiwanese. Among the 85 Taiwanese students, 80 were majoring in medicine. The university employed 692 staff and faculty members, only 142 of whom were Taiwanese, all except one being of lower rank. See Lin Hsiung-hsiang and Li Teng-yü, eds., T'ai-wan sheng t'ung-chih kao (draft history of Taiwan), V, Chiao-yü chih-chiao-yü shih-she pien (History of education—educational facilities) (Taipei: T'ai-wan sheng wen hsien wei yüan hui, 1955), pp. 141-42.

42. For details, see Lin Hsiung-hsiang and Huang wang-cheng, eds., T'ai-wan sheng t'ung-chih kao (draft history of Taiwan), IX, Ke-min chih-k'ang-jih pien (History of revolution—resistance against Japan) (Taipei: T'ai-wan sheng wen hsien wei yüan hui, 1954), 1-125.

43. Ibid., p. 215.

44. For the text of the declaration, see ibid., pp. 217-19.

45. Ibid., p. 221.

46. Ibid., p. 228.

47. Ibid., p. 229.

48. Ibid., p. 239.

49. Ibid., p. 241.

50. Ibid., p. 251.

51. Shen Pao, Shanghai, October 14, 1938, cited in Li Chich-fu, T'ai-wan en-min Ke-min tou-cheng chien-shih (The revolutionary struggle of the Taiwanese people), Canton: Hua-nan ien-min ch'u pan she, 1955, p. 153

52. Associated Press dispatch, October 31, 1939, cited in T'ai-wan jen-min tou-cheng chien-shih, p. 159.

53. See Feng Hao, T'ai-wan min-tsu yuen-tung hsiao-shih (A concise history of the nationalist movement in Taiwan) (Taipei: Cheng chung shu chü, 1951), pp. 40-42.

54. Ibid.

55. Ibid.

56. Huang Shun-ch'ing, Lin Hsiung-hsiang, and Kuo Hai-ming, eds., T'ai-wan sheng t'ung-chih kao (Draft history of Taiwan province), X, Kuang-fu chih (History of restoration) (Taipei: T'ai-wan sheng wen-hsien wei-yuan hui, 1952), p. 2.

2

THE ECONOMIC DEVELOPMENT OF TAIWAN
Ramon H. Myers

INTRODUCTION

Ironically, the only Asian countries that have achieved a high degree of industrialization have been islands poor in farmland and mineral resources. Industrial development has enabled Japan, Taiwan, Singapore, and Hong Kong to narrow the wealth gap between themselves and the advanced countries of the West. In 1895 Taiwan was exceedingly backward, yet it found the appropriate substitutes for the scarcities that normally inhibit economic growth. In effect, Taiwan managed to create for itself "substitutes for those factors which in more advanced countries had substantially facilitated economic development."[1]

Before 1895 Taiwan was a frontier area managed by the Manchu government. The transport system was appallingly inefficient. Only the coastal regions were farmed by the Chinese, while the vast mountainous hinterland remained in the hands of aborigine tribes. Probably a third of the Chinese inhabitants smoked opium at one time or another. There was a high death rate, caused by malaria and other tropical diseases.[2] Between 1895 and 1945 Japanese occupation resulted in the improvement of agriculture and the establishment of a basic infrastructure that eventually contributed to industrialization. After 1945 the Nationalist Chinese government took up where the Japanese left off and, with the assistance of U.S. economic aid, built upon pre-existing foundations. A quarter of a century later modern industries emerged, only four out of ten families worked in agriculture (compared with seven out of ten in 1938), and urban industry contributed more to gross national output than did agriculture. The labor force was rapidly becoming as skilled and professionalized as that of Japan and other advanced countries.

To dramatize this sharp break with tradition, we must examine the characteristics of the 19th-century Chinese economy and the changes that occurred afterward under Japan's enlightened colonial administration. The seed bed in which the roots of modernization were nourished was established between 1895 and 1945, but it was not until the early 1960's that these roots became sufficiently strong and deeply embedded to yield fruit. The results were industrialization and urbanization, two congruent processes moving Taiwan from a traditional agrarian economy to a modern industrial society.

THE TRADITIONAL ECONOMY

The traditional Chinese economic structure consisted of walled cities producing and exchanging products with scattered villages in the countryside. The typical walled city contained central marketplaces handicraft enterprises, and countless shops that received products from overseas and the countryside. One group of merchants supplied food and fibers to handicraft establishments for processing while another distributed perishable items of grain, vegetables, and meat to city households. The urban labor force participated in policing and defense, engaged in small-scale industry, trades, and services, and worked for government officials. Taiwan-fu, or contemporary Tainan, provides an excellent illustration of the model Chinese city in Taiwan.

By the 1850s' it contained around 70,000 people protected by a seven-meter-high wall extending nine kilometers around the city.[3] The main roads, intersecting at right angles, were lined with merchants' homes and shops; most of the residential homes were constructed of bamboo or earth, covered with straw. The most impressive edifices were the Taotai's headquarters (or yamen), the home of the military general, a large examination hall where prospective candidates gathered, and two temples. Gardens and parks dotted the city, giving it a calm absent in the adjacent countryside, where villages frequently did battle and aborigines clashed with Chinese settlers.[4]

Poor communication and transport barely enabled the urban centers to exchange goods with the countryside and to control its inhabitants. The few roads going forth from Taiwan-fu soon ended in footpaths impossible to traverse during poor weather. Not a paved road existed in the province, and travelers desiring to reach the north found it more convenient, cheaper, and quicker to go by sea. An official of the Imperial Maritime Customs Service complained that "in South Formosa there are no roads in the European sense of the word,—the foot paths and dry water-courses which do duty as roads have no claim to be so entitled, for they are in no way kept in repair, nor have they been macadamised, raised or drained in any way."[5] C. Imbault-Huart reported it normally required 10 days to travel from Tainan to Tamsui, a time regarded as excellent, as excursions into the central highlands could prolong such a trip by as much as four days.[6]

The type of village pattern, based chiefly upon settlement and mode of farming, distinguished the south from the north. Southern villages tended to be rather large, with concentrations of households bearing the same family surname;[7] farming required a fairly developed irrigation system for units of such large size and compactness. In contrast, northern villages were small, with farms more dispersed and belonging to different families; as rainfall was more dependable and abundant, irrigation systems were less developed.

Local officials exercised little direct control over villages, preferring to delegate taxation, security, and census-taking to individuals called ti-pao, who performed these tasks on a hereditary basis.[8] For all practical purposes villages settled their disputes and provided for their defense. In return for minimal government interference in their lives, villagers neither received nor expected support and protection in the event of natural disasters. Their contact with the central authority was infrequent in comparison with the relationship of governments in modern societies to their localities.

The agrarian system stemmed from land tenure customs borrowed from Fukien and modified to suit local conditions.[9] Migrants from the mainland cleared the land belonging to wealthy families who had earlier staked claim to vast tracts of land as a reward for services rendered to the government. These families, called ta-tau-hu, usually refrained from investing in their tenants, merely collected a rent in kind, and rarely saw their tenants except to agree upon the terms of the next period's rent.[10] Many tenants, called hsiao-tsu-hu, managed to accumulate enough wealth to clear land of their own, which they in turn leased to other migrants at rents higher than they paid to the ta-tsu.[11] The administration tolerated this system because the landed wealthy helped the poor to gain a footing in agriculture without the government's assuming any burden or obligation to colonize the island. But as farmers were not eager to pay taxes to an administration that spent nothing to assist them, they refused to report newly cultivated land. As a result, by 1890 roughly four-fifths of the existing farmland was not taxed.[12]

The island's soil and climate were especially well suited for rice, sweet potatoes, sugarcane, indigo, tea, ramie, beans, vegetables, and fruits. Chinese records extolled the favorable conditions that produced higher yields than on the mainland.

> Though the coast line is sandy, the land is flat and fertile
> and exceptionally suited for planting crops. The landscape
> is verdant with bushes and trees; rice husks are as large
> as beans. The fall harvest is usually twice as large as
> the mainland. Moreover, sugar is grown. Because all
> kinds of plants can be cultivated and harvested, the in-
> ferior crops grown on the mainland find no market in
> Taiwan.[13]

The mildly acidic, rich, humus soil provided two rice harvests yearly
at yields higher than those of the mainland.[14] The early-ripening
rice seed, which had revolutionized rice production during the Ming
period, had also found its way to Taiwan.[15]

The island's wealth and prosperity attracted wave after wave
of migrants from Fukien and Kwangtung to ignore Ch'ing imperial
edicts forbidding emigration, and the population increased by leaps
and bounds. In the 1680's the Chinese population probably numbered
around 16,000, but by 1738 it had increased to an alleged 73,000—
undoubtedly a gross underestimate of true numbers. In 1812 the
population was believed to have jumped to slightly over 2 million,
and by the century's end it stood at roughly 3 million. The magistrate
of Taiwan-fu commented in 1753 that "there were tens of thousands
of poor people here from the mainland. The parents and children
collect their meagre property and come to Taiwan to raise their
families. As the law prevents them from migrating freely, small
pirate fleets operate in small groups, using fishing vessels to cross
at night and unload their passengers."[16] In 1716 farmers had pene-
trated as far as present-day Taichung. "Thus the greater part of
the entire Formosan plain was turned into cultivated land, but all this
work was done solely by the people without any aid or protection
from the government, which was slow and hesitating in respect of
all enterprises."[17]

A wide chasm separated the common merchant and farmer
from the large, wealthy urban families whose property generated
annual incomes as high as $10,000 to $100,000 Chinese dollars,
compared with middle-class incomes of $500 to $10,000 per year.[18]
Skilled and unskilled laborers usually earned less than $500 per
year, so that middle-class families earned roughly 18 times more
than the average laborer and his family. As landless peasants,
tenant farmers, and urban craftsmen constituted the majority of
households, the income gap between the masses and the enormously
wealthy was incredibly large.

A distinctive feature of trade was the expansion of sugar and
rice exports. In the first quarter of the 18th century Taiwan was
already shipping large quantities of rice to Chekiang and Fukien,

often depleting stocks, so that rice prices rose considerably. Some officials complained that rice shipments to the mainland should be restricted, but mainland officials countered that "the people of the coastal provinces need to buy rice, and the people of Taiwan must sell their rice."[19] Free trade was allowed to continue. Sugar was produced by small mills around Tainan and Kaohsiung; and in the 1730's some 3,000 small boats annually sailed the Taiwan Straits, carrying sugar to the mainland.[20] During the 18th century sugar export increased rapidly, becoming one of the island's leading cash crop exports by the nineteenth century. Tea exports also rose rapidly after the 1860's, a development owing entirely to an Englishman, John Dodd, who advanced loans to merchants to buy tea from farmers around Tamsui in 1866.[21] He built kilns to fire the leaf, and soon more than half a dozen foreign firms followed suit: between 1866 and 1890 tea exports rose from a mere 13,000 silver dollars to 4.5 million dollars.[22] The industry grew so rapidly that land and labor were diverted from rice production to growing teas, and rice frequently had to be imported from the mainland. Specialization and trade undoubtedly would have developed even more had not each local market possessed its own weights and measures, the unit of currency fluctuated greatly, and transport remained in a poor state.

Passive local administration could not prevent colonization and modest economic advance. Population growth, export expansion, and extension of cultivated land continued unabated while foreign investment to specialize production of export and cash-crop processing promoted a greater division of labor and slow urban development. The island's abundant, fertile land and numerous, advantageous sites for harbor development and commerce encouraged one foreign visitor traveling about the island in the 1870's to remark that "everything there was in its infancy" and merely waiting to be produced.[23]

Fearful of possible foreign invasion and takeover of Taiwan, in the early 1870's the Ch'ing government decided upon a number of ambitious projects to bolster the island's defenses. These projects required continued financial support, sustained market demand, stable business conditions, and much managerial expertise. They were confined to urban centers and designed to increase trade, speed up communications, and strengthen the administration's capability to provide defense. In 1870 the official Shen Pao-chen was dispatched to Taiwan. He tried to promote coal mining and export but was unsuccessful because of his limited tenure in office. In 1876 Ting Jih-ch'ang replaced him, continued a similar policy, and installed a telegraph line between Kaohsiung and Tainan. In July, 1884, the Ch'ing court ordered Liu Ming-ch'uan to assume the governship and prepare for a possible French invasion. After the Sino-French crisis was settled, Liu continued in the footsteps of his predecessors.

In 1886 he rebuilt part of Taipei and enlarged it considerably, even providing it with a small postal system and installing electric street lights. In 1887 he founded a Western school in Taipei and began the financing and building of a railway line from Keelung to Taipei, later extending it as far south as Hsinchu. In addition, he tried to repair the large Keelung coal mine network, which had been flooded—on his orders—in the event of a French takeover of the northern part of the island. Although Liu failed in this attempt as well as that of creating a shipping line between Tamsui and the mainland, he did complete the construction of a telegraph cable between Tamsui and Foochow, as well as a telegraph line between Tainan and Taipei in 1888.[24] These projects constituted a solid beginning, but they required great financing to complete. To raise revenue for this, Liu established the Land Tax Bureau in 1888. In June of that year the bureau began surveying all land and issuing new deeds to landowners. However, Liu lacked the manpower and military authority to carry out this far-reaching reform, and the survey was only partially completed; although a new land tax was imposed and collected most land in the south was inadequately surveyed. Liu did succeed in raising nearly 200,000 taels of additional revenue, but this was not enough, and he had to borrow heavily to promote projects in which the waiting time for repayment of investment was exceedingly long.

Other policies, backed by greater authority and supported by long-term financing, were also clearly needed if the island's resources were to be developed to their full potential. New technology had to be introduced; a modern infrastructure based upon systematized weights, measures, and currency had to be established; stable foreign markets had to be found. Taiwan possessed abundant idle land, and its labor was capable of more intensive effort. Land and labor could also be made more productive and more fully employed if the supply of entrepreneurial management and capital increased.

THE ECONOMY IN TRANSITION: JAPANESE COLONIAL MANAGEMENT

Taiwan was legally ceded to Japan by the Ch'ing government in 1895, but controlling the island and developing it was another matter. Japanese troops first encountered fierce resistance, but this soon ceased, to be "replaced by brigandage so extensive that travel in some districts, at certain times, became so dangerous that Japanese officials off the more frequented routes, did not travel unless provided with a guard, and wealthy Chinese scarcely dared to leave the treaty ports."[25] For the next three years various military

governors-general tried in vain to pacify the island, but mounting
costs to support these operations soon threatened to bankrupt the
administration. Some leading officials suggested selling the island
to the French; commerce was at a standstill, and Chinese merchants
fled to the mainland. In the spring of 1898 the government, perhaps
in a last desperate gamble, dispatched another high-ranking officer
and his civilian adviser to restore order and reduce the mounting
fiscal burden on the government.

The arrival of General Kodama Gentarō and Gotō Shimpei
ushered in a new era for Taiwan. Kodama streamlined the administrative structure, eliminating much deadwood, and established the
Civil Affairs Bureau, with Gotō as head, to be the main instrument
of policy making and the organization with maximum power to formulate a colonial policy.[26] Kodama also informed local officials that
police would replace the military and be given wide authority in dealing
with social matters. Upon Gotō's suggestion the police revived the old
village pao-chia system and integrated it with local administration.
By 1902 the police had restored peace and order throughout the
island.[27] At the same time Kodama and Gotō envisaged making
Taiwan self-sufficient in food production, with a large surplus for
export—chiefly to Japan—and developing commerce and industry.[28]
Their strategy called for the administration to promote the growth
of export industries centered on agricultural production. At first
this policy called for establishing a shipping line to link Taiwan with
Japan, constructing harbors at Keelung and Kaohsiung to handle this
traffic, and building a railway to connect Keelung in the north with
Kaohsiung in the south to improve the state of domestic transport.
Markets were to be standardized; a central bank was to be created
to issue new currency, expand credit, and stabilize the value of
money; agricultural production was to be increased by introducing
new technology to farms through establishment of research stations
and farmer associations; public health facilities were to be built to
improve sanitation conditions and eliminate man-killing tropical
diseases. The initiation and completion of these projects would direct
resources into their most productive, highest-income-earning activities, eventually enabling the administration to accumulate a budget
surplus and become independent of financial support from Japan.
This was the grand plan that Kodama and Gotō followed to manage
Japan's first colony acquired since the imperial restoration of 1868.

Implementation of such a plan required that domestic savings
be greatly increased; but the economy was poor, and skilled labor,
management, and capital were scarce. The administration moved
on two fronts to finance these projects: first, it increased the land
tax, introduced new taxes, and established government control over
the production and distribution of special products to increase fiscal

revenue; second, it issued long-term bonds, the bulk of which were purchased by the Japanese treasury. As soon as the administration increased its revenue, it quickly spent to complete a specific project by a fixed date, from which time that project commenced to provide additional revenue for the administration. By selecting high-yielding revenue projects first, the administration was able to increase its financial resources and continue to finance new projects. Kodama and Gotō singled out agriculture for primary improvement and first developed a modern infrastructure of transport, banking, and public health to enable Taiwan's exports of farm products, such as rice and sugar, to increase rapidly. As a result the supply of skilled labor and capital gradually expanded, and these factors later provided the new foundations for further economic progress.

Between 1897 and 1902 the old land tax continued to be collected in the traditional manner; but in 1897 a land survey had commenced that, though extremely expensive to complete, provided the appropriate information to identify land ownership, estimate land value, produce land maps, and count the ta-tsu families.[29] The administration terminated ta-tsu land rights and transferred land ownership to the so-called hsiao-tsu households, who nominally rented land from the ta-tsu, but actually controlled the use of the land. Ta-tsu family rent income in perpetuity was estimated, and bonds were issued by the administration to compensate for their loss of rental income. Tax officials completed a new land tax schedule that dramatically increased revenue in 1904 to 1.9 million yen, compared with the traditional collection of 900,000 yen per year.[30] In 1905 the land tax revenue rose to 2.9 million yen and gradually increased thereafter.

The colonial administration quickly established a number of monopoly bureaus that garnered considerable additional revenue. Between 1896 and 1904 these monopolies earned income to account for 35 percent of total administration revenue; between 1905 and 1913 they operated even more efficiently, and their income-producing share of total budget revenue rose to 47 percent; in 1914-20 this share rose to an all-time high of nearly 52 percent. A final important source of revenue was the sugar tax, introduced in 1902 as an export levy and collected in ports as customs duty. In the first year this tax produced 700,000 yen, but with the growth of the sugar trade it yielded 5.4 million yen—nearly a quarter of total budget revenue—in 1909.[31]

Despite more revenue, the colonial administration operated with an unbalanced budget between 1896 and 1909; deficits were covered at first by subsidies from the Japanese government and later by bond issues. Between 1896 and 1904 subsidies amounting to 30.5 million yen were received; and between 1899 and 1909, the period when new projects were established, bonds valued at 27.2 million yen were issued. Subsidies ended by 1904, as budget revenue increased from

5.3 million yen in 1897 to 13 million in 1900 and finally 16 million in 1906. Revenue climbed to 32.7 million in 1910, the year the debt issue terminated.32 About 55 percent of the debt issue went to finance railroad construction, 36 percent financed the land survey and compensation of ta-tsu landholders, and 7 percent defrayed costs of harbor construction.33 These examples illustrate very successful project development through bond issue or deficit budget financing.

The infrastructure to promote rural development was established in the following manner. In 1899 the Osaka Commercial Shipping Co. received the right to handle all shipping between Taiwan and Japan. In the same year Keelung harbor was dredged and construction of a new harbor, finally completed in 1902, was begun. Kaohsiung harbor was built between 1908 and 1912. In May, 1899, work began on an island railway system that was completed in April, 1908, costing 27.5 million yen for a rail line extending only 247 miles; however, the line crossed very difficult terrain and required many tunnels and bridges of great length. By 1910 an additional 586 miles of small-gauge railway line had been built to help sugar mills ship their product to mills and harbors. An island-wide telegraph and postal system was also built before 1905, Taipei was greatly enlarged with new government buildings and official residences, hospitals were established in the largest cities, and a public health program was introduced. In July, 1906, a sugarcane experimental station was started in the south. Meanwhile, markets were standardized with uniform weights and measures, and a central bank set up in Taipei. By 1907-08 most of the new infrastructure was virtually complete.

The two principal developments in agriculture that expanded the export trade and increased income greatly were the establishment of the sugar industry and the promotion of rice production. On November 5, 1901, Kodama announced that because "sugar was the principal product of the island," its production could be increased from an annual average of 44,000 metric tons to over 6 million tons if the administration adopted a policy of "selecting improved seeds from overseas and disseminating them about the island; by educating the farmers to plant these seeds, using new farm machinery, and upgrading existing sugar production methods, quality improvement would take place and production costs reduced."34 Kodama's proposals originated from an extensive survey report by Dr. Nitobe Inazō, who had found that this industry had great potential for development in southern Taiwan.

In June, 1902, the Provisional Taiwan Sugar Affairs Bureau was created to promote new sugarcane seed research and dissemination. The encouragement given to this sector of agriculture bore quick fruit. Between 1902-03 and 1912-13 the area devoted to cultivation of sugarcane jumped from 16,526 to 67,358 chia, cane production more than doubled, and yield rose gradually.[35] By 1917-18 cultivated cane area had climbed to 150,450 chia, output was about 4 million metric tons, and yield per chia stood at 2,490 kilograms, compared with 1,840 in 1902-03. Output continued to increase: between 1927 and 1933 it averaged around 5 million metric tons per year; and by 1937 it had risen to 8.5 million metric tons, well above the level predicted by Kodama nearly four decades before. In 1939 the industry occupied a dominant position in agriculture: out of 400,000 farms, 120,000 specialized in producing sugarcane; approximately one-fifth of all farmland grew sugarcane; about 16 percent of annual total farm production value came from sugarcane.[36] Even the island's small industrial base depended upon the new sugar mills: of total factory production value, averaging 360 million yen in 1938-39, 60 percent was accounted for by sugar; and 40 percent of export value originated from sugar. (See Table 2.1.)

Although vigorous steps were taken by the administration to stimulate sugarcane production and sugar export, efforts were not relaxed to increase the production of rice, Taiwan's second most important farm crop. Efforts along this line began in 1903, when the Central Agricultural Research Bureau was founded in Taipei with branch experimental stations later set up in five other districts.[37] In 1908 the administration created farmer associations in each district, with landlords and wealthy farmers paying dues, keeping accounts of association activities, and operating gardens where the latest new seeds and methods tested in the district experimental station were adopted on a trial basis. The associations introduced these same seeds and methods to villages through the pao-chia system or by word of mouth.

The administration moved along two lines to improve rice production. It gradually reduced the number of rice varieties in use, so that by 1911 only 485 circulated, compared with 1,300-odd varieties used three years earlier.[38] In 1924 agricultural associations began introducing a new rice variety called p'eng-lai, which had been imported from Honshu in 1912 and was made suitable for Taiwan's climate and soil a decade later. The p'eng-lai was adopted quickly; and by 1938 the average yield per chia for the second rice crop was 13.57 koku for p'eng-lai, compared with 11.37 for native varieties.[39] As a result of better selection and standardization of native varieties and the adoption of a Japanese variety, rice production increased rapidly; in 1923 output was 695,000 metric tons, increasing to 1.0 million metric tons in 1930 and 1.4 million metric tons in 1938. In the mid 1920's only 20 percent of the total rice crop was exported to Japan; but the rapid increase in output produced at costs cheaper than those in Japan and possessing quality and taste similar to Japanese rice resulted in exports' increasing to 50 percent of output by the late

1930's.[40] The new rice seeds required more inputs of water and
fertilizer; and because the administration spent heavily to construct
new irrigation projects and farmer associations purchased more
inorganic fertilizers, family farms were gradually able to purchase
more of these inputs.

The great attention devoted by the administration to improving
agriculture resulted in a rapid increase in farm output between 1900
and 1940, with growth at annual growth rates of 1.6 and 4.4 percent,
respectively, between 1910-20 and 1921-37.[41] The annual rate of
population growth for these same time intervals was considerably
less, being 1.0 and 2.3 percent, respectively. Most of the farm surplus
was exported: the four leading export crops made up nearly 90 percent
of the total in 1910 and declined to 64 percent in 1940 because other
crops, such as fruits and vegetables, assumed greater importance.
(See Table 2.2.) Food imports as a share of the total declined because of increased production; Taiwan became more self-sufficient
in food as its export of crops slowly diversified.

By the mid-1920's Taiwan was a model of economic progress,
stability, and order. A traveler could leave Taipei in the morning
and by late afternoon arrive in Tainan or Kaohsiung. Between Keelung
and Taipei 14 trains ran daily.[42] All large cities were in communication with one another by telephone and telegraph. Public health
facilities were operative throughout the island, and widespread fatalities
due to malaria and influenza had at last been restricted to the south
and east coast; by the late 1930's these areas were finally safe.
Farmers were now linked through an organizational network to a
system producing modern farming technology. Visitors from China
could easily compare Taiwan with southeastern China, for topography
and climate were similar; and none could fail to be favorably impressed with the tremendous advances achieved by the Japanese in
Taiwan. In December, 1915, an agricultural student from Fukien,
Ch'iu Wen-luan, toured Taiwan; upon arriving at the Taichung farm
research station he was amazed to find certain plants native to Kwangtung province being grown in the farm association garden. He was
told that because Japan spent 2 million yen annually to import these
plants from China, it was decided to grow these same plants in Taiwan;
and if the experiment proved successful, precious foreign exchange
could be saved. Ch'iu's reactions were of anguish:

> Japan's success; our misery! Japan no longer spends 2
> million yen, but China loses 2 million yen. If China's
> major industries are not improved, then we will see our
> wealth dissipated day by day. The people will live in
> poverty, and the future will be too unbearable to consider.
> Will this not come about because of examples like these
> Kwangtung plants?[43]

Another student, Hsieh Wu-k'o, visited Kaohsiung to observe timber processing mills. He commented that the Japanese developed all kinds of primary industries in Taiwan, yet in China, where "we see sections of natural forests, there is no study of forestry; a timber industry has still not been created; there are no forests along the seacoast, and the inland hills stretch endlessly denuded of all timber."[44] Undoubtedly Taiwan was moving ahead of mainland China in the development of her primary industries. As yet, however, urban industry grew at a snail's pace.

Between 1905 and 1930 the share of gainfully employed Taiwanese males in mining, manufacturing, commerce, and transportation in the total work force increased from 17.3 to 25.6 percent. This industrial labor force grew from 187,000 to 350,000, an increase of only about 87 percent over a quarter of a century and an annual growth rate of only 2.5 percent, compared with a total population annual growth rate of around 2.0 percent.[45] This slowly expanding urban industrial labor force could not absorb very much labor from agriculture and reduce the absolute number of rural people even after a century had elapsed. On the basis of existing population trends at this time, by the year 2000 population would rise to 10 times its 1905 level, or roughly 20 million, and the agrarian index or share of population still in agriculture would be only 45 percent, compared with 65 percent in 1905.[46]

The gross value of industrial production rose from 165 to 228 million yen between 1921-24 and 1930-32, and the main industries consisted of food processing for export and consumer goods for the home market. The small capital-goods component of industry—metal products, machinery, and equipment—supplied goods to the Taiwan Railway Corporation and provided service and replacement maintenance for other industries. Japanese colonial policy had created "a corporate superstructure placed on an agrarian base," without any firm industrial sinews.[47]

The expansion of the primary sector, and the resulting prosperity for farms, brought about modest improvements of living standards. Without national income data these improvements cannot be specifically documented, but indirect evidence conclusively demonstrates that living standards gradually rose. First of all, more people survived the early years of infancy and lived longer. Public health developments by the mid-1920's had greatly reduced the threat of mortality from major diseases that traditionally had infested the island. By 1935 the crude death rate had fallen from 35 to 21 per thousand for males and females aged 15-49; infant mortality had declined from 192 to 149, and for females aged 15-49 the rate had fallen from 20 to 8 per thousand. "The gains in survival were being spread more evenly over the various portions of the island as time went on."[48] Age expectancy also increased greatly: in 1936-40, 3,347 out of 10,000 males could expect to live until 60 years of age, whereas in 1906 only 1,153 could have expected to survive as long.[49]

Family farm budget survey data for the 1930's show that in 1931-37 tenant farm income rose 30 percent in real value terms.[50] Annual household expenditures measured on a per capita basis also increased. More important, however, was the increase in real expenditures by various family farm classes for clothing and rent. These survey findings indicate that average living standards were improving over the period.

Textiles improved in quality, and consumers increased their clothing purchases. In value terms textile imports rose more than five times between 1918 and 1938.[51] Domestic textile production rose from 1.7 million Taiwan yuan in 1921 to 9.0 million yuan in 1939.[52] When retail prices are deflated by the general retail price index, the rate of consumption of textile products increased more rapidly than the population growth rate. We possess little information on improvement in furniture and dwellings, but more peasants gradually replaced the straw roofs of their homes with tile and rebuilt the mud-baked walls with brick and cement to ensure durability, comfort, and beauty. These modest gains in everyday living standards strongly suggest that the life of the lower-class farmer, coolie laborer, and merchant became more pleasant by the mid-1930's in comparison with the early 1900's.[53]

In the final eight hectic years of Japanese rule, 1937-45, two new economic developments occurred. First, a movement to build heavy industry was initiated; second, war controls were imposed on the economy and resources were mobilized for the military effort. On March 4, 1935, the governor-general convened a conference in Taipei to determine the future course of economic development.[54] The decision taken was to promote heavy industry with all possible speed, and in mid-1935 the program to achieve this commenced. New industrial corporations were established on the basis of the administration's encouraging Japanese capital to invest in Taiwan. For example, the Taiwan Electrical Company, a subsidiary of the powerful Nissan manufacturing enterprise in Japan, built a factory in Keelung to process minerals.[55] By December 10, 1935, production commenced. On July 21, 1935, the Taiwan Electrical Company created the Japanese Aluminum Company as one of its subsidiaries; and on November 29, 1936, it opened its first factory in Kaohsiung. In 1937 the industrialization momentum accelerated as cotton spinning factories, chemical companies, and thermoelectric plants were established.[56]

In 1942 a Japanese economist wrote that "a notable tendency shown in 1938 in the production industries, especially in the manufacturing industry, was the abandonment of the idea of dependence

on Japan proper."[57] As Japanese industry prepared for war, it reduced its export of intermediate and consumer products to Taiwan.
The scarcity of shipping space also limited trade between the two
regions. For these reasons Taiwan was forced to become more self-
sufficient and to establish new industries. By the end of 1941 there
were 8,683 factories, with roughly 85 percent using electrical power,
compared with 6,775 at the end of 1934. The labor force employed
had doubled.[58] Gross production value from factories also had doubled,
with the share of sugar production falling to 25 percent in 1941, compared with 55 percent in 1936.[59] The physical output of fibers and
metal products more than doubled, and the total kilowatts of electrical
energy produced also more than doubled.[60] If a doubling of net value
of industrial output took place during this seven-year period, and
the available data suggest this to be so, then the annual industrial
output growth rate was roughly 10.3 percent, an impressive, although
short-lived, growth performance.

In October, 1941, the Provisional Taiwan Economic Inquiry
Commission met to evaluate the island's readiness for war and what
contribution it could make if war erupted.[61] The majority view held
that the rate of industrialization must be reduced and controls introduced to mobilize Taiwan's resources for the war effort. As Taiwan
did not possess a highly developed industrial base or any ship repair
and service facilities for the Japanese navy, her major role must be to
supply food, textile products, and labor to the Japanese military.
Price, wage, and rent controls were introduced, and the economy
swiftly moved onto a solid wartime footing in early 1942.[62]

The sugar industry was ordered to withdraw its investments
from northern Taiwan and concentrate sugar production in the south.
Land in the north was to be used for food and fiber production because Japan had acquired sugar production facilities in Java and the
Philippines in 1942.[63] To control prices, in 1941 the administration
created commodity purchasing companies for buying goods at fixed
prices, supplying what the government required, and rationing the
remainder to consumers. More Taiwanese labor was recruited for
local project construction, and labor detachments were also sent to
Southeast Asia. Industrial commodity and raw material scarcities
became serious only in 1942 and thereafter. At the same time capital
inputs to agriculture began to decline. The area of cultivated land
in 1945 stood at 657,446 hectares, compared with 816,017 hectares
in 1941, with the greatest decline occurring for paddy land. Crop
consumption also changed radically, because as rice and sugar prices
were rigidly fixed and demand for food increased, more farmers
switched to food crops such as sweet potatoes. Early in 1945 sweet
potatoes had finally replaced rice as the main food crop cultivated
throughout the south.[64]

Between February and May, 1945, the island was attacked by U.S. bombers, which strafed the railway system, bombed factories, and destroyed harbor installations.[65] Manufacturing activity virtually halted; cities encountered enormous difficulty in obtaining food from the countryside; goods scarcely moved from sources of supply to markets; and shipping costs rose astronomically. Much of the industrial and transport base built by the Japanese was destroyed overnight. On October 25, 1945, a new era began: Taiwan was restored to the Republic of China.

TRANSFORMATION OF THE TAIWAN ECONOMY

In late 1945 and early 1946 Chinese troops and civil affairs officials arrived and stationed themselves throughout Taiwan in order to install Nationalist government authority. The resumption of civil war on the mainland prevented the new government from giving domestic matters careful consideration; in fact, Taiwan was called upon to give material support to the motherland for campaigns against the Communist insurgents. As a result of these extra demands imposed upon an economy already seriously weakened by inflation, economic deterioration quickened and reached an all-time low in late 1947 and early 1948. The departure of the Japanese further intensified the process of economic decline: more than 20,000 technicians and managers, some 40,000 officials, and 10,000 professional workers left by late 1946;[66] their removal caused additional dislocation of the transport, commercial, and banking systems. Although Chinese civil authorities had secured most of these positions, they were unfamiliar with their environment and many did not possess the competence of their predecessors. The government attempted to revive the transport system, but numerous difficulties prevented trains from running on schedule and at prewar frequency until 1950.

Prices climbed rapidly after 1945. If sugar and rice prices represent the trend of general commodity prices, hyperinflation was indeed under way. Between 1945 and 1948 the price of 100 kilos of sugar rose from 748 to 84,412 new Taiwan dollars ($NT) and 100 kilos of rice rose from $NT 686 to $NT 35,369.[67] Prices continued their rise despite a currency reform in 1948, and monthly interest rates also rose to fantastic heights. Before the war the Bank of Taiwan lending rate fluctuated between 1.6 and 2.0 percent per month, but in 1947 monthly market rates rose to 17 percent. Trade between town and countryside also declined as farmers concentrated upon growing food crops to meet household needs and neglected cash crops. The area planted in sugar and cotton fell greatly between 1945 and 1949, but that in rice, sweet potatoes, soybeans, peanuts, and wheat

rose.[68] A final factor contributing to near economic collapse was
the outbreak of a widespread rebellion in February and March, 1947.
This exacerbated tensions between mainlanders and Taiwanese and
left deep resentment and enmity between the people and the new
government.

Thus when a new body politic arrived in full force in 1949, it
was confronted by a population deeply suspicious of and hostile toward its intentions. At the same time it was threatened with a massive attack by the Chinese Communists from the mainland. The
economy moved into deep recession. The year 1949 was a bleak
and discouraging one for the new government.

By 1952 the highest prewar farm output levels, except for
cotton and sugar, had been surpassed; the same performance was
achieved in industry, mining, and construction. Between 1953-54
and 1967-68 economic growth was very rapid, and during the mid-
1960's the growth momentum steadily accelerated. Between 1952
and 1967 gross national product rose eight times in current prices
and more than three times in constant 1964 prices, a performance
that compared favorably with recent growth rates achieved by Japan
and South Korea. If we divide this period at 1960, the annual growth
rate of gross national product averaged 7.2 percent between 1953
and 1960 and 10.0 percent between 1960 and 1968.

In spite of a rapid population growth rate of 3.5 percent per
year, per capita income, measured in 1963 prices, rose from $U.S.
26 to $U.S. 56 between 1951 and 1953; by 1960 it reached $U.S. 114,
and in 1970 it soared to $U.S. 292. Since 1953 real per capita in-
come, expressed in 1964 prices, has increased at an annual rate
of 4.4 percent; and if this rate continues for another decade or more,
per capita real income will rise even faster because of a decline
in the population growth rate. Between 1954 and 1964 the annual
population growth rate was 3.42 percent, but by 1969 and 1970 it
had fallen to 2.20 and 2.16 percent, respectively. This decline is
expected to continue because of the rapid adoption of birth control
methods such as the intra-uterine device by the lower classes.[69]

In Table 2.1 we observe that after 1953, when prewar levels
were achieved, agriculture and industry grew rapidly, the growth
rate gaining momentum after 1960. Farm output grew at 3.0 percent
per year between 1953 and 1960 and 5.9 percent between 1960 and
1967 despite a modest rise in total crop area between 1952 and 1967
of only 11.6 percent.[70] Output expanded because yields were greatly
raised by use of new capital and technology. The sustained growth
of farm production during the 1960's stands as particularly impressive. Farming became an industry with increasing returns to
scale: the average farm size declined by nearly 20 percent, from 1.29
to 1.04 hectares, between 1952 and 1967. Between 1952 and 1967 the

TABLE 2.1

Basic Indicators of the Taiwan Economy, 1946-68
(1953=100)

Year	(1) Primary Production Index	(2) Industrial Production Index	(3) Population (thousands)	(4) National Income (million $NT)	(5) National Income Index
1946	39.8	18.2	—	—	—
1947	50.2	23.7	—	—	—
1948	62.5	39.7	—	—	—
1949	74.0	49.4	7,397	—	—
1950	76.5	54.1	7,554	—	—
1951	78.2	63.7	7,869	8,942	50.9
1952	87.6	80.5	8,128	13,047	73.0
1953	100.0	100.0	8,438	19,542	100.0
1954	102.0	107.2	8,749	20,761	106.24
1955	104.5	119.2	9,078	24,684	126.31
1956	111.3	125.3	9,374	28,079	143.69
1957	122.9	142.3	9,690	32,409	165.84
1958	133.0	153.2	10,039	35,921	183.81
1959	136.0	173.2	10,431	41,592	212.83
1960	135.3	197.2	10,792	50,828	260.10
1961	149.6	217.9	11,149	57,012	291.74
1962	151.5	245.7	11,512	61,222	313.28
1963	156.9	270.6	11,884	70,490	360.71
1964	173.0	343.8	12,257	84,686	433.35
1965	188.0	400.6	12,628	91,891	470.22
1966	199.1	455.5	12,993	101,859	521.23
1967	211.0	535.1	13,297	116,233	594.79
1968	—	637.3	—	132,865	679.89

Year	(11) Imports (million $U.S.)	(12) U.S. Aid (million $U.S.)	(13) Percentage of Industrial Origin of Net Domestic Product Primary Production	Industry	Transport and Communication
1949	34.9	8.9	—	—	—
1950	127.7	20.5	—	—	—
1951	143.3	56.6	33.80	24.9	5.1
1952	207.0	89.1	35.2	22.4	4.5
1953	190.6	100.6	39.4	20.8	3.9
1954	204.0	87.9	33.3	24.2	4.2
1955	190.1	89.2	33.4	24.6	4.4
1956	228.2	96.5	32.9	25.4	4.3
1957	252.2	98.7	32.0	26.6	4.6
1958	232.8	82.3	31.7	26.1	4.5
1959	244.4	73.4	30.5	27.3	4.2
1960	252.2	90.9	32.51	24.72	4.08
1961	324.1	108.2	31.31	24.94	4.75
1962	327.5	80.1	29.16	25.60	4.49
1963	336.8	76.1	26.68	27.25	4.20
1964	410.4	39.7	27.71	27.44	4.09
1965	556.4	67.0	26.89	26.63	4.55
1966	603.1	36.3	25.78	27.20	5.15
1967	847.5	30.6	24.34	28.12	5.02
1968	976.0	—	23.23	29.24	5.16

Sources: Col. (1), Industry of Free China, xiii, 3 (March 1960), 44; xxxi, 2 (February 1969), 54—this index includes 73 commodities and is constructed on the basis of weighted aggregates of value; col. (2), xiii, 3 (March 1960), 52; xxxi, 2 (February 1969), 76—this index covers 207 commodities (including sugar) and is based on the method of weighted aggregates of value, cols. (3)-(5), xiii, 3 (March 1960), 38; xxxi, 2 (February 1969), 54.

(6) Per Capita Income ($NT)	(7) Per Capita Income Index	(8) Wholesale Price Index (Taipei)	(9) Monthly Interest Rate (Taipei)	(10) Exports (million $U.S.)
—	—	—	—	—
—	—	—	—	—
—	—	—	—	—
—	—	11.1	17.4	33.9
—	—	45.1	12.0	93.1
1,056	53.4	74.4	10.5	93.1
1,495	75.5	91.9	6.6	119.5
2,215	100.0	100.0	4.3	129.8
2,273	102.62	102.4	4.1	97.8
2,604	117.56	116.8	4.5	133.4
2,858	129.03	131.6	3.9	130.1
3,198	144.38	141.1	3.6	168.5
3,434	155.03	143.1	3.3	164.4
3,849	173.77	158.6	3.9	160.5
4,557	205.73	181.0	3.9	174.2
4,953	223.61	186.9	2.7	218.3
5,158	232.87	192.5	2.7	244.4
5,760	260.05	205.0	2.4	363.5
6,716	303.21	210.1	2.1	469.5
7,078	319.55	200.3	2.4	495.8
7,630	344.47	203.3	2.1	584.2
8,494	383.48	208.4	2.1	675.1
9,487	428.35	212.5	2.4	843.0

(13) Percentage of Industrial Origin of Net Domestic Product			(14) Fixed Capital Formation (million $NT 1964 prices)	(15) Inventory ($NT)
Commerce	Government	Other		
—	—	—	—	—
—	—	—	—	—
13.0	13.0	10.2	—	—
16.8	11.4	9.7	—	—
18.5	9.9	7.5	5,634	1,027
17.3	12.2	8.2	6,038	1,293
15.7	13.1	8.2	5,224	899
16.5	12.3	8.6	6,061	1,240
16.4	11.8	8.6	6,021	1,429
15.8	12.3	9.6	7,308	1,459
16.3	12.2	9.5	8,863	1,533
14.42	11.94	12.33	10,081	2,485
13.95	12.35	12.70	11,443	2,805
14.42	12.46	13.87	11,611	3,287
15.51	12.12	14.24	13,645	2,139
15.79	11.53	13.44	14,451	4,797
16.51	11.51	13.91	18,304	7,147
16.07	11.92	13.88	22,927	5,537
15.67	13.03	13.82	28,644	5,509
15.89	12.91	13.57	34,999	3,879

Sources: Cols. (6)-(7), Industry of Free China, xiii, 3 (March 1960), p. 38; xxxi, 2 (February 1969), 54; cols. (8)-(12), xiii, 3 (March 1960), 39; xxxi, 2 (February 1969), 55; cols. (13)-(14), Directorate-General of Budgets, Accounts and Statistics, Executive Yüan, National Income of China, 1953-1960 (Taipei, January 1964), p. 19; Industry of Free China, xxxi, 2 (February 1969), 58, 60-61.

industrial production index covering mining, manufacturing, electricity, gas, and water increased at an annual rate of 13.4 percent. If the period is divided at 1960, annual growth rates of 10.4 and 16.1 percent, respectively, were achieved. Industry also expanded rapidly, and its growth accelerated spectacularly after 1960.

In Figure 2.1 the nature of economic structural change can be observed. When sector contribution to net domestic production in percentage terms is plotted against per capita income change between 1951 and 1967, net domestic product originating from primary production gradually declines and that of industry rises. In 1966 industry's share began to exceed that of primary production for the first time, at a level of per capita income of around $U.S. 200. The share for transport, communications, and government remained rather constant, while that of services and commerce rose gradually. This pattern repeats the experience of Japan and Western countries.[71] Rapid economic growth since 1950 has been accompanied by a steady improvement in living standards and an upswing in purchase of domestically produced consumer goods. The sale of electric stoves, television sets, transistor radios, electric fans, and refrigerators increased greatly after 1964, the year from which the most rapid distribution of these items can be dated. For some products sales doubled, while for others they more than quadrupled: between 1964 and 1970 electric fans increased from 198,461 to 400,218, electric stoves from 107,450 to 231,366, television sets from 31,055 to 1,254,125, refrigerators from 21,959 to 153,254, and transistor radios from 487,023 to 3,642,567. When expressed on a population ownership basis, there were 110 radio sets per 1,000 persons and 37 television sets per 1,000 persons in 1970. Building construction also increased dramatically after the early 1960's. Between 1954 and 1964 the square meters of brick building construction rose from 327,714 to 476,604, but in 1970 it reached 3,020,822. Rapid growth was also registered for reinforced concrete and wooden buildings. Consumption of electrical power between 1959 and 1970 more than quadrupled, and gas and water consumption also skyrocketed in the same period.

This great building boom and growth in manufacturing productivity occurred in medium-size cities and large metropolitan centers. In 1967 the rural population stood at 44 percent of total population, compared with 52 percent in 1952. In the principal metropolitan centers population stood at 2.8 million in 1965, compared with 1.3 million in 1950. About one-quarter of the island's population now lives in six large cities. A recent study estimated that roughly 529,000 persons, or 62 percent of the metropolitan population, would have to be displaced in order to obtain the same population distribution that prevailed in 1950.[72]

FIGURE 2.1

Shares of Major Sectors in National Product
Corresponding to Growth in Per Capita Income, 1951-68

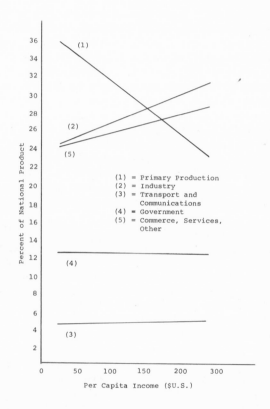

Source: Constructed from data in Industry of Free China, XIII, 1 (March 1960), and Council for International Economic Cooperation and Development, Taiwan Statistical Data Book, 1969 (Taipei 1970).

Associated with urbanization and rising standards are expansion of educational facilities, further reduction in mortality, and improvement in public health facilities. The percentage of population in higher, secondary, and primary education stood at 1.4, 8.18, and 43.5 percent in 1952, but in 1967 these percentages rose to 3.0, 18.1, and 55.8, respectively. Now only one out of five persons is illiterate; and in 1970 only 19.3 percent of the population over 12 years of age could not read, as compared with 24.5 percent in 1966. The crude death rate has fallen below 6.0, and in 1964 a Taiwanese male and female could expect to live 64 and 68 years, respectively.[73] Between 1952 and 1967 registered medical personnel (physicians, dentists and pharmacists, nurses, midwives, and technicians) increased from 11,613 to 25,902, public medical institutions nearly doubled, and the number of persons served by a medical person declined from 700 in 1952 to 513 in 1967, indicating an improvement in the ratio of supply of professionals to total population.[74] Daily caloric consumption in 1970 was 2,665, as compared with nearly 2,500 calories in 1964. Taiwan now exhibits all the attributes of a modernizing society.

How was it possible for an economy so badly dislocated by war, inflation, and unrest to revive so quickly and then move forward into a phase of structural transformation and growth?

Rehabilitating the economy to prewar production levels was achieved as early as 1952-53 because the government took vigorous steps on a number of fronts. First, it rapidly brought inflation under control by tightly controlling the money supply and using American aid (food, etc.) to absorb excess purchasing power. Second, government resources were used to restore the transport system; again U.S. aid played a key role in enabling the railroads to attain full operational efficiency within only a few years. Third, the government introduced land reform between 1949 and 1953 to redistribute land, to enable small farms to acquire additional land, and to assist former landlords to reinvest in urban commerce and industry.

The land reform consisted of three stages. First, tenant rents were reduced from the prewar high of 50 percent of the harvest to 37.50 percent. Second, the government sold public land to farmers on long-term, low-interest loans. Finally, a new land law was enacted requiring all owners to sell their land above a legal minimal holding to the government. A new land bank was created for the purpose of lending to tenant farmers and part owners so they could purchase land formerly held by landlords. These loans were issued at 3 percent annual interest for as long as 15 years. Sellers of land received industrial bonds or cash. With their bonds some landlords were encouraged to invest in urban commerce, banking, and light industry. The new land reform achieved two important goals. First, it created a much larger owner-cultivator farming class than had existed previously. In 1952 only 38 percent of farm households fully owned their land; in 1967 virtually all loans had been repaid and 68 percent of farm households fully owned their land.[75] Second, the reform diverted considerable amounts of landlord liquid assets into capital investment in industry and commerce. The impact of this reform on the rural economy was remarkably neutral in not greatly disrupting social relationships.

With inflation arrested, the prewar infrastructure nearly rebuilt, and agriculture in the process of being reconstructed, the government was immediately confronted with a mounting trade imbalance of serious gravity. The loss of the prewar preferential market of Japan and the scarcity of alternative export markets made it difficult for Taiwan to market her processed food stuffs profitably. Immigration of troops and officials from the mainland and the urgent need to revive the economy had increased the demand for imports. In 1950 imports exceeded exports by $U.S. 29.6 million; this deficit rose to $U.S. 50.2 million in 1951 and $U.S. 87.5 million in 1952. (See Table 2.1.) The government introduced foreign exchange restrictions and import controls to reduce the growing trade imbalance. At the same time it decided upon a course of encouraging the development of capital-intensive industries to produce commodities that would replace imported manufactured goods. The policy of developing import-substitution industries was conceived as logically extending an industrial base already containing a small metallurgical-chemical industrial complex.

The government deliberately reserved profitable openings for private enterprise to manufacture new products like polyvinyl chloride plastics after public enterprises conducted initial basic research. It also allowed certain entrepreneurs access to foreign aid loans, public bank credits, and foreign exchange at more favorable terms than those prevailing in the market. These large manufacturing enterprises also received preferential allocation of electrical power and raw material supplies.[76] Corporate enterprises frequently were given income tax holidays, rebates of customs duties and excise taxes, low-cost export loans, and assistance in developing and acquiring urban plant sites and auxiliary facilities.

U.S. aid during 1951-63 played a critical role in supporting the government's policy of promoting the growth of import-substitution industries.[77] "More than two-thirds of all U.S. capital assistance—aid-generated local currency as well as U.S. dollars—" went to infrastructure and industry.[78] This amounted to a total of $U.S. 299.3 million worth of aid. Between 1952 and 1964 six large hydroelectric and three large thermoelectric plants were completed, thus quadrupling the peak rate of electrical power generated.[79] This aid also helped extend and modernize the transport system: diesel

trains replaced conventional coal-fueled trains; a cross-island highway was constructed; a superhighway linking Taipei with Keelung was
built; the north-south highway was macadamized; harbors at Kaohsiung
and Keelung were enlarged. U.S. aid vitally contributed to the rehabilitation and expansion of the island's telecommunication network.
For industry the bulk of U.S. assistance initiated the constuction
of factories in such areas as fertilizers, cement, aluminum, pulp
and paper, plastics, glass, sugar, chemicals, coal and coke, synthetic
fibers, and pharmaceuticals. Recipient firms needed only to match
these aid funds with their own investment funds.[80]

Between 1950 and 1954 the average annual growth rate of production in manufacturing was 21 percent, but between 1954 and 1960
it fell to 11 percent.[81] This decline was registered in all branches
of manufacturing. At the same time the rate of price change for
manufactures between 1957 and 1958 showed an unusual decline. The
average annual rate of price change between 1952 and 1957 had been
13 percent, but this assumed a negative rate of -2 percent between
1957 and 1958. Industrial surveys undertaken in 1950-60 indicate
that enterprises producing woolen textiles, plywood, paper, rubber
goods, soap, iron rods and bars, insulated wires, sewing machines,
and electric fans were operating at only 40 to 70 percent of capacity.[82]
As industrial plant construction terminated in 1955-56 and production
of consumer goods increased in the subsequent two years, demand
failed to keep pace with supply and excessive inventory accumulation
occurred. Commodities were being offered at prices that consumers
still regarded as unattractive to buy in large quantities. The slackening
of the manufacturing growth rate, the emergence of idle capacity and
inventories, and a leveling off of prices clearly suggested that an
economic recession was pending. A greater buildup of capital-intensive
manufacturing had occurred than the domestic market was able and
willing to accommodate at the existing level of per capita income.

Between 1958 and 1960 several developments combined to
"reorient the economy toward an outward-directed development, resulting in the expansion of exports of manufactures and new agricultural products during the 1960s."[83] In 1958 the government converted
the foreign exchange rate system from a multiple to a single rate.
This enormously simplified business procedures for exporters and
importers and gave their activities a great boost. At the same time
import controls were lifted for some 130 commodities.[84] Export
controls were also lifted for more than 200 commodities, and procedures for exporting were streamlined. The export price floor was
made more flexible, and import duty refund procedures were simplified. Harbor dues were waived for exports. Businessmen seeking
export loans found it much easier to obtain the funds they needed.
They could also obtain materials vitally needed for processing goods

to be exported. This avalanche of foreign trade reforms stimulated industries to reduce their inventories by selling abroad. Exports rose from $U.S. 160.5 million in 1959 to $U.S. 174.2 million in 1960 and then leaped to $U.S. 218.3 million in 1961. Exports continued to climb rapidly thereafter.

In 1958 war threatened on the offshore island of Quemoy: and in the fall of 1959 a typhoon lashed the island, causing severe flooding and a reduction of the harvest. These two events stimulated inflationary pressures once again. Government stockpiling and the sudden scarcity of farm products caused prices to rise. By late 1959 the central bank resorted to stricter lending procedures. Enterprises reacted to this by striving to reduce their unit costs and take advantage of the recent liberalization of trade. Many were able to increase their sales abroad. Their anticipation of further sales expansion prompted new investment outlays. Fixed-capital formation showed a great increase between 1957 and 1960, accelerating at an annual rate of 13.6 percent, as compared with 8.1 percent between 1953 and 1956.[85]

The new export promotion policy launched in 1958-59 marked a decisive change in foreign trade and domestic growth. Exports, in current prices, increased 388 percent between 1959-60 and 1966-67, compared with only 38 percent between 1952-53 and 1959-60. This represented an annual growth rate of 20 and 5 percent, respectively. In 1963 and 1964 Taiwan experienced, for the first time since the prewar period, a favorable balance of trade. The composition of exports altered rapidly after 1958-59. In 1956 manufactured goods other than processed foods made up only 12 percent of export value: this share rose to 29 percent in 1960, 40 percent in 1964, and 76 percent in 1968.[86] The principal industrial exports were textiles, machinery, transport equipment, and chemical products (plywood and cement). On the import side, raw materials as a percentage of total imports, in value terms, rose from 20 percent in 1956 to 28 percent in 1964 and 34 percent in 1968. The share of food imports remained constant over the period; that of capital goods declined from 67 percent in 1956 to 37 percent in 1968. This composition change indicates that the major thrust in export growth has originated from manufactured goods. On the other hand, Taiwan has become increasingly dependent upon raw materials. Like England and Japan before her, she now consumes raw materials to fabricate goods for domestic requirements and export.

In 1964 exports accounted for 40-90 percent of the total output of such manufactures as monosodium glutamate, cotton yarn, cement, and plywood.[87] For manufacturing output as a whole, excluding processed food, beverages, and tobacco, the ratio of output exported to total rose from 11 percent in 1961 to 14 percent in 1964. This suggests that many manufacturing industries finally began selling in the home market and, by doing so, were encouraged to expand output and add new productive capacity. The rise in income generated from export growth, continued good harvests in agriculture, and the spurt in capital formation in preceding years "strengthened domestic demand for more sophisticated consumer goods and also for intermediate and capital goods."[88]

The speed with which manufacturing firms grew is reflected in the relative changes in net product of private and public industries. Between 1952 and 1967 private enterprise's share rose from 42.2 to 74.8 percent, while that of public enterprises fell from 57.8 to 25.2 percent.[89] Private manufacturing firms outpaced the growth of public manufacturing industries, especially after the late 1950's.[90] This burst of speed was also manifested in more registered factories and the growth of the industrial work force (excluding mining and utilities): between 1952 and 1958 the number of registered factories increased from 9,966 to 12,289, but by 1967 reached 29,861; the industrial work force for the same period increased from 272,000 to 477,000, raising industry's share of the total work force from 9 to 12 percent.[91]

The geographic concentration of exports and imports between 1956 and 1965 was fairly high, but the coefficient of commodity concentration of Taiwan's exports has not been high compared with those of Norway, Canada, and Japan.[92] Taiwan depends heavily upon Japan and the United States for buying her foodstuffs and raw materials and a variety of labor-intensive products, such as clothing, plywood, plastic articles, and transistor radios. Capital-intensive goods such as flour, refined petroleum products, chemicals, pulp and paper, rubber goods, textile yarns, cement, metals and fabricated metal goods, and certain machines and electrical supplies are exported mainly to the underdeveloped countries. During the early 1960's exports to the developed countries grew faster than those to less developed countries.[93] The growth of exports to the underdeveloped countries would have been slower had there not been increased demand from South Vietnam. Because Taiwan occupies an intermediate position in trade and produces for two different markets, her industrial structure exhibits some of the characteristics of the dual structure possessed by Japan in the prewar years.

The labor-intensive products exported to Japan and the United States will probably continue to increase, as their demand is highly income-elastic. The growth of the more capital-intensive industries depends in part upon future demand in underdeveloped countries and the growth of domestic demand. To date, the spectacular growth of trade in the 1960's, coupled with the great surge in manufacturing, has created a new production sequence in Taiwan: "import raw materials, create additional selling value by processing, and export finished products."[94] This pattern of growth characterizes an economy with limited resources adjusting to expanding domestic demand. So far Taiwan produces and exports commodities that use relatively less capital per unit and imports items requiring more capital.[95] The new industries have achieved cost reductions through economies of scale and new technology. The industries dependent upon exports have benefited by learning from more advanced competitors and borrowing technology across the board.

Factors of production can be combined and allocated in different ways, but in the final analysis human beings create organizations and make policies that determine how effectively these combinations will lead to the betterment of living standards. The economic development strategy of the Nationalist government has been crucial in engineering Taiwan's successful economic growth since the late 1940's. Inasmuch as the Kuomintang party still dominates in decision making, it is important to understand the basic economic ideology of this party, particularly that of its leadership.

The first statement by a major Kuomintang party leader of an integral economic plan appeared in October, 1921, when Sun Yat-sen published his industrial plan.[96] Sun proposed that foreign loans be obtained to assist China in undertaking a huge industrialization program. The core of the program called for constructing three large port cities on the China coast near the Treaty Ports, building railways from these centers into the interior, developing mining in regions served by these railways, and creating new industries in these centers, such as food processing, textiles, household furnishings, printing, and vehicles.[97] However, Sun never mentioned which concrete steps were required to implement this plan, nor did he estimate project costs and rates of return to justify the very high investment funds he proposed. Japanese aggression and civil war forced the party to shelve the plan.

Upon arriving in Taiwan, the Kuomintang leadership declared that it intended to build Taiwan for the purpose of returning to the mainland.[98] But how was Taiwan to be developed? Chiang Kai-shek had long argued that China must industrialize "by peaceful and gradual stages,"[99] and obviously Taiwan was also to be industrialized. Although a specific blueprint for industrializing Taiwan has never appeared in Kuomintang writings, a broad development strategy can be perceived from comments uttered by the leadership in the early 1950's.

In 1949 the Kuomingtang was extremely sensitive to agrarian matters. Having just lost the mainland because of its failure to control the countryside, the government speedily adopted measures to guarantee that peace and prosperity would prevail in the Taiwanese

countryside. It introduced a land reform to equalize land rights and
restore land to the tiller for nearly two-thirds of farmers owning little
or no land.[100] The party leadership fervently believed such a reform
would strengthen its hold over the countryside and unleash new productive energy. If agriculture could prosper, developing industry
would quickly follow suit; and manufacturing could then favorably
influence the growth of agriculture. President Chiang merely extended the Confucian dictum that agriculture is the mainstay of the
country to argue that agriculture and manufacturing interact to influence one another favorably. "As agriculture supports and nourishes
industry, so too does industry develop agriculture."[101] The leadership now endorsed a balanced growth view of economic development,
in which economic sectors were to be encouraged to develop simultaneously.

The Kuomintang tried to restore as quickly as possible the
large-scale industries established by the Japanese. President
Chiang emphatically asserted that at the same time the government
must encourage new industries, in order to reduce Taiwan's dependency
upon imports of manufactured goods. He proposed that some of the
investment funds to launch these new enterprises be solicited from
overseas Chinese capitalists. In July, 1954, the government passed
a law inviting foreign capital into Taiwan and guaranteeing that a
lion's share of the profits could be withdrawn from the country.
Rather than continue to take the lead in initiating industrial growth,
the government tried to encourage private enterprise to flourish.[102]
It returned public enterprises in cement, paper, agricultural processing, and mining to private entrepreneurs to operate. Although
the price system functioned relatively free of central administrative
control, the government continued to give special attention to certain
economic sectors through subsidies and passing laws to encourage
new business practices in industries it regarded as important to
develop. The government set certain priorities for development in
each of its four four-year economic plans between 1953 and 1968.

For example, the first four-year plan emphasized promoting
new import-substitution industries and encouraging greater capital
investment in agriculture to increase the rate of farm production
growth. The second plan concentrated upon trade liberalization and
building certain infrastructure for the manufacturing sector. The
third plan encouraged the growth of new export industries, while the
fourth continued the objectives of the third plan and urged an increase
in the supply of skilled and professional manpower by expanding secondary and higher educational facilities. The fifth four-year plan,
commencing in 1969, gives special attention to developing electrical
power and transport, increasing the quantity of skilled manpower,
and developing more advanced industries requiring skilled labor and

capital.[103] This plan admitted that "in the past, shortage of capital
and over-protection have combined to retard improvements in productive facilities and technical and managerial capabilities, with
the result that industrial production is still predominated by simple
processing operations."[104] The government now intends to promote
the development of more sophisticated modern industries that require
highly skilled labor, extensive research facilities, and skilled management. Because the government recognizes that foreign trade is indispensable for industrialization, it is more willing to enter into
new bilateral and multilateral economic and technical cooperation
agreements.

    Each four-year plan contains a number of objectives, such as
a limited annual rise in prices, a prescribed annual growth of gross
domestic product, and minimum annual sectoral growth rates in
industry and agriculture. Targets are also set for the amount of
capital funding required, the expected growth of consumer expenditures
and exports, and the anticipated rise in employment. These plans
contain neither provisions for material input procurement nor specific
means by which targets are to be realized. Although few price controls exist, the government has fixed the prices at which farmers
sell rice to the government and purchase fertilizers.[105]

    One ingenious policy to stimulate export development was intro-
duced in 1965. The government designated Kaohsiung for an industrial
zone in which investors and businessmen could establish new export
industries on the model of Hong Kong's free entrepôt economy. A
site of 165 acres was set aside for entrepreneurs to produce optical
equipment, plastics, electrical appliances, chemicals, garments,
furniture, and packaging materials for export. Enterprises were
exempted from paying business and commodity taxes and trade duties,
and foreign investors could recoup all profits the first year and 15
percent of the total capital investment annually two years after the
project was completed. As of August, 1968, a total of 119 factories
had been approved for construction, and 65 were already in operation.

    In April, 1969, the Tenth National Congress of the Kuomintang
convened in Taipei to elect a "new, enlarged Central Committee of
99 members, including many who occupy top managerial and technological posts in and outside the government."[106] The Central
Committee named from its new membership a 22-man committee
that included many university-trained specialists. These are young
men, still in their 40's, and with university degrees. What appears
to be happening is the emergence of a technocratic faction in the
party, very pragmatic and eager to introduce more imaginative,
innovative procedures to accelerate the modernization of the economy.
The principal architect of the successful development of export industries is K. T. Li, formerly minister of economic affairs and now

TABLE 2.2

Total Value of Exports and Percentage of Exports of Four Leading
Agricultural Commodities, Selected Years 1910-65
($1,000)*

| | | Main Agricultural Commodity Exports | | | | | |
| | Total | Sugar | | Rice | | Tea | |
Year	Export Value	Value	Percent	Value	Percent	Value	Percent
1910	59,962	35,163	58,64	6,996	11.66	6,425	10.72
1915	75,623	36,268	47.95	8,307	10.98	8,209	10.85
1920	216,264	142,191	65.75	17,172	7.94	6,693	3.09
1925	263,214	111,552	42.38	72,114	27.40	11,711	4.45
1930	241,441	141,922	58.78	38,697	16.03	8,869	3.67
1935	350,744	151,533	43.20	105,580	30.10	9,365	2.67
1940	566,054	222,554	39.32	87,594	15.47	20,991	3.71
1943	400,903	139,451	34.78	67,181	16.76	31,661	7.80
1950	93,074	74,251	79.77	2,870	3.08	2,693	2.89
1955	133,441	67,920	50.90	32,764	24.55	5,594	4.19
1960	169,866	74,401	43.80	4,320	2.52	6,334	3.74
1961	214,041	61,096	28.54	10,080	4.71	8,890	4.15
1962	238,609	49,588	20.80	7,380	3.08	7,859	3.28
1963	357,524	105,983	29.64	23,354	6.53	8,104	2.27
1964	463,110	135,403	29.24	18,030	3.90	8,426	1.82
1965	487,959	67,956	13.93	42,955	8.80	9,719	1.99

TABLE 2.3

Total Value of Imports and Percentage
of Food and Fibers Imports, 1910-65
($1,000)*

| | | Fiber Imports | | | | | |
| | Total | Total | | Cotton | | Other Fibers | |
Year	Import Value	Value	Percent	Value	Percent	Value	Percent
1910-20	744,865	109,341	14.68	99,610	13.37	9,731	1.31
1920-30	1,620,963	248,664	15.34	217,685	13.43	30,979	1.91
1930-40	2,532,013	400,993	15.82	361,671	14.28	39,322	1.54
1940-44	1,629,566	274,622	16.85	249,568	15.31	25,054	1.54
1950-55	11,252,781	878,967	7.81	810,028	7.20	68,939	0.61
1955-60	1,147,660	130,397	9.35	99,903	8.70	30,434	2.65
1960	252,216	28,982	11.49	21,231	8.42	7,751	3.07
1961	324,050	42,556	13.13	30,391	9.38	12,165	3.75
1962	327,542	53,255	16.26	35,962	10.98	17,293	5.28
1963	336,787	42,847	12.71	26,688	7.92	16,159	4.79
1964	410,401	62,482	15.23	33,680	8.21	28,802	7.02
1965	555,286	71,321	12.85	40,073	7.22	31,248	5.63

| Main Agricultural Commodity Exports | | | | | | Six Leading Export Crops | |
| Bananas | | Pineapples | | Camphor | | | |
Value	Percent	Value	Percent	Value	Percent	Value	Percent
345	0.58	40	0.07	3,958	6.60	52,542	87.62
684	0.85	158	0.21	5,029	6.64	57,813	76.42
1,807	0.84	848	0.39	7,607	3.52	173,663	80.30
9,219	3.50	1,934	0.73	4,514	1.71	204,596	77.73
8,570	3.55	3,593	1.49	2,341	0.97	198,058	82.03
10,243	2.92	8,220	2.34	4,399	1.25	276,721	77.89
28,357	5.01	15,264	2.70	4,719	0.83	359,496	64.51
5,401	1.34	4,872	1.22	2,427	0.61	243,694	60.68
1,254	1.35	117	0.13	1,170	1.26	81,068	87.09
3,991	2.99	5,562	4.17	541	0.41	111,840	83.81
6,851	4.04	8,486	4.99	271	0.16	96,072	56.57
10,670	4.98	12,103	5.66	296	0.14	93,949	53.89
8,041	3.56	10,859	4.54	475	0.19	76,347	32.18
8,655	2.42	11,591	3.24	829	0.23	149,583	41.83
33,344	7.20	13,911	3.00	1,142	0.25	200,688	43.34
55,269	11.33	19,379	3.97	907	0.19	185,559	38.03

*The currency from 1910 to 1943 is the Taiwan dollar; after 1950, the U.S. dollar.

Sources: Computed from Taiwan Civil Affairs Bureau, T'ai-wan sheng wu-shih i-nien lai t' ung-chi t'ai-yao (Taipei, 1946), pp. 946-51; and Bank of Taiwan, Export and Import Exchange Settlements for the Year 1965 (Taipei, 1966).

| | | Food Imports | | | | Total Food and Fibers | |
| Total | | Wheat, Flour, Beans | | Other Food | | | |
Value	Percent	Value	Percent	Value	Percent	Value	Percent
208,756	28.04	59,218	7.95	149,538	20.08	318,097	42.72
485,375	30.07	169,084	10.43	316,291	19.64	734,039	45.41
532,851	20.70	127,984	5.06	395,867	15.64	924,844	36.52
304,308	18.67	88,887	5.54	215,421	13.22	578,930	35.52
1,233,129	10.67	1,233,129	10.97			2,112,096	18.78
154,968	13.50	131,801	11.48	23,167	2.02	285,365	22.85
43,243	17.14	33,981	13.47	9,262	3.67	72,225	28.63
51,336	15.85	33,718	10.41	17,618	5.44	93,892	28.98
41,156	12.57	33,403	10.20	7,753	2.37	94,711	28.83
58,746	17.45	50,072	14.87	8,676	2.58	101,593	30.16
59,771	14.57	42,217	10.29	17,554	4.28	122,253	29.80
65,176	11.74	54,572	9.83	10,604	1.91	136,497	24.59

*1910-44 figures are in Taiwan dollars; 1950-65 figures are in U.S. dollars.

Sources: Taiwan Civil Affairs Bureau, T'ai-wan sheng wu-shih i-nien lai t'ung-chi t'ai-yao (Taipei, 1946), pp. 952-61; Bank of Taiwan, Export and Import Exchange Settlements for the Year 1965 (Taipei; 1966); Taiwan Statistical Abstract, No. 22.

minister of finance. Other key advisers who have played instrumental roles in advising on technical and economic matters are the physicist Wu Ta-yu and the economist T. C. Liu, both of whom teach in universities in the United States but return regularly to Taiwan.[107] The vice-president and premier, C. K. Yen, is also considered a representative of the younger generation of technocrats who have come to the fore.

CONCLUSION

Over the past century Taiwan has experienced dramatic and momentous change. If urban communities of the Ch'ing, Japanese, and contemporary periods are compared, the rapidity of change becomes obvious. In the 1860's the largest city, Tainan, was a typical Chinese walled city with little handicraft industry but many service enterprises. A traveler passing under its gates was impressed by the design and layout of the city, but a visit to a typical urban home immediately revealed how backward living standards were. Homes contained primitive sanitation facilities; poor and simple furnishings barely made these wooden structures livable; residents retired early for lack of artificial lighting. Laborers toiled 12 hours or more a day. Children went uneducated unless their parents were extremely wealthy and could afford a tutor. Disease frequently broke out and took a high toll; and the average life expectancy was less than 50 years.

After the Japanese arrived, the center of urban advance shifted from Tainan to Taipei. The Japanese built large, splendidly ornate administrative buildings connected by broad plazas, gardens, and paved roads. They electrified the city, introduced modern public health measures, constructed wells to install running water, and regulated urban market standards. Many Japanese-style residences were built from the Chinese city quarter, on the gradually silting Tamsui River, to the new National Taiwan University located south near farm fields. Museums and parks circled the center of town. The residential quarters of Taiwanese city dwellers also improved: cement structures replaced wood and bamboo; diet became more varied and dress more modern. Consumer goods from Japan filled the shops. Many families owned bicycles, and shortly before the Pacific War (December 8, 1941) radios appeared throughout the city. As the chief center of attraction on the island, Taipei drew tourists from other parts of the island to visit its museums, walk in its gardens, and shop in its many markets and stores. This calm and peaceful city also contained a well-developed school system to which middle-class Taiwanese families sent their children. Primary

TABLE 2.4

Annual Average Growth Rate of Agricultural Output
in Taiwan, 1910-60

Stage of Development	Period	Average Annual Growth Rate of Agricultural Output (percent)		
		Hsieh and Lee	Myers and Ching	Ho
Initial stage of agricultural development under Japanese rule	1910-20	1.66	.96	1.23
Takeoff stage of agricultural development under Japanese rule	1920-39	4.19	4.48	4.42
Agricultural development during World War II	1939-45	-12.32	-14.72	-15.71
Recovery and rehabilitation under Chinese Nationalist rule	1945-52	12.93	n.a.	13.52
Rapid and sustained growth under Chinese Nationalist Rule	1952-60	3.98	n.a.	4.30
Average annual growth rate of agricultural output, prewar period	1910-39	3.31	3.45	3.35
Average annual growth rate of agricultural output, postwar period	1945-60	8.06	n.a.	8.50
Average annual growth rate of agricultural output, entire period	1910-60	2.67	n.a.	2.65

Sources: S. C. Hsieh and T. H. Lee, Agricultural Development and Its Contributions to Economic Growth in Taiwan—Input-Output and Productivity Analysis of Taiwan Agricultural Development (Taipei: Joint Commission on Rural Reconstruction, 1966), p. 14; Ramon H. Myers and Adrienne Ching, "Agricultural Development in Taiwan Under Japanese Rule," The Journal of Asian Studies, xxiii, 4 (August 1964), 556; Yhi-min Ho, Agricultural Development of Taiwan 1903-1960 (Nashville, Tenn.: Vanderbilt University Press, 1966), pp. 17-18.

TABLE 2.5

Annual Population Growth Rates, 1911-41
(percent)

	1911-27	1927-41	1911-41
Taipei	1.99	2.54	2.25
Hsinchu	1.15	2.00	1.54
Taichung	2.03	2.84	2.42
Tainan	n.a.	2.54	1.20
Kaohsiung	5.19	3.78	4.51
Tai Tung	1.75	5.05	3.45
Hualien	4.96	6.25	5.58
Pescadores	n.a.	n.a.	n.a.
Total	1.60	2.79	2.16

Note: Growth rates were estimated from population data contained in Taiwan Satofuku [Taiwan Governor-General], Taiwan Tokeisha, 1901-1942 [The Statistical Yearbook for Taiwan, 1901-1942], published annually by the Taiwan Governor-General, Taipei.

education was made mandatory for six years. The new university added faculties of law and medicine.

Taipei of the late 1960's bore little resemblance to its prewar cousin. By 1965 its population had soared to over a million people. The city's environs now extended several miles west and south, past the National Taiwan University, to include entirely new districts. Land values in the downtown commercial districts rose more than 3,000 times between 1949 and 1965.[108] Large hotels, business offices, and bank buildings now thrust upward to block out the view of distant hills for local residents. Taipei's international airport, situated west in the Sung-shan district, does a brisk day's business, and its planes fly low to disturb the residential sections north of the city. The traditional pedicab has given way to the blaring taxi. A fleet of buses moves out each morning to convey great throngs of people to their work. Factories are now located on the outer rim of the city, and their chimneys spew forth fumes that frequently darken the sky. Taipei now resembles any great Western city with all its flourishing opportunities and problems. The highest units of government, business, and education are located there; a thriving tourist industry has evolved. The old and new, so neatly juxtaposed in the 1950's, now contest one another. As Taiwan moves into the 1970's,

TABLE 2.6

Ten-Year Average Changes in Area, Yield, and Production of Taiwan's Four Main Crops, 1901-70

Crop	Years	Area (hectares)	Yield (Kilogram/ hectares)	Production (metric tons)	Sugar Prod. (metric tons)
Brown rice	1901-10	432,021	1,324	571,899	
	1911-20	486,365	1,379	670,531	
	1921-30	551,622	1,594	879,516	
	1931-40	654,847	1,926	1,261,187	
	1941-50	646,224	1,657	1,070,780	
	1951-60	776,813	2,227	1,729,782	
	1961-70	779,200	3,162	2,293,000	
Sweet potato	1901-10	90,107	6,837	616,078	
	1911-20	111,950	7,063	790,741	
	1921-30	122,765	9,231	1,133,192	
	1931-40	134,277	11,534	1,548,823	
	1941-50	183,805	9,158	1,683,263	
	1951-60	234,531	10,882	2,547,563	
	1961-70	235,000	13,906	3,270,900	
Peanut	1901-10	17,971	593	10,649	
	1911-20	20,831	599	12,472	
	1921-30	25,347	827	20,964	
	1931-40	30,000	933	27,995	
	1941-50	45,556	695	31,648	
	1951-60	94,396	832	78,493	
	1961-70	106,400	1,259	121,673	
Sugarcane	1902-10	30,823	31,134	959,653	82,236
	1911-20	100,258	28,149	2,822,156	251,498
	1921-30	115,757	43,836	5,074,342	498,353
	1931-40	119,740	68,206	8,166,994	948,344
	1941-50	112,287	51,949	5,833,181	583,756
	1951-60	94,942	68,418	6,495,760	770,387
	1961-70	106,030	83,119	8,048,300	885,039

Source: Data for period 1901-1965 obtained from Chinese-American Joint Commission on Rural Reconstruction, Taiwan Agricultural Statistics 1901-1965 (Joint Commission on Rural Reconstruction: Taipei, 1966). Data for period 1961-70 obtained from Council for International Economic Cooperation and Development, Taiwan Statistical Data Book 1971 (Executive Yüan, Taipei, 1972).

modernity seems to be fast obliterating the traditional quarters of the
city. Such transformation has been initiated by rapid industrialization.

The Japanese and Nationalist governments devoted considerable
attention to developing the basic external economies that nourished
the growth of the agricultural sector. The government made it possible
for family farms of exceedingly small size to become highly productive and capable of bringing a large surplus to market by encouraging exchange, specialization, and the adoption of new technology.
Agriculture was never neglected; and continued investment by the
government to extend and further modernize the rural infrastructure,
as well as introduce new basic inputs, has made possible a growing
surplus. Furthermore, industries producing fertilizers, farm equipment, and machinery have been encouraged to supply farmers. Rapidly
expanding rural demand enabled these enterprises to utilize their
capacity fully and efficiently and reduce average unit costs, thus
passing important gains on to farmers in the form of lower prices
and higher-quality goods.

The growth of the primary sector through export promotion
generated higher incomes and savings, thus making it possible for
private entrepreneurs and government to launch large and medium-
size industrial undertakings. In the crucial period of the early 1950's
U.S. economic aid permitted more of these enterprises to be established than normally would have been possible. As the government
encouraged export dependence to build the domestic industrial structure, a great manufacturing boom took place in the 1960's that seemed
strong enough to continue into the 1970's. Continued government
spending to extend and modernize the infrastructure as well as to
promote agriculture contributed to manufacturing development in
two ways.

First, it increased the skilled manpower force by making primary education mandatory, extending this through secondary school,
and establishing new trade, technical, and engineering schools. These
programs provided industry with a large supply of cheap semiskilled
labor. By paying attention to developing transport, communications,
and electrical power the government also prevented overhead costs
for entrepreneurs from rising too rapidly. By establishing technical
cooperative associations, disseminating trade and technical journals,
and financing commercial and industrial fairs and expositions the
government also assisted businessmen in acquiring new knowledge
for producing and marketing their products.

Second, by improving the farm extension system created by
the Japanese, the Nationalist government established an entirely
new human organizational network in the countryside that now capably
assists farmers in progressively raising their yields. The key
agency, the Joint Commission for Rural Reconstruction, has financed,

coordinated, and stimulated new projects in forestry, fishing, and agriculture. This agency now leads the way in studying the new problems of marketing, commodity quality control, and rural credit that have arisen through recent rural prosperity.

As the government successfully activated its abundant, cheap resources in agriculture, the resulting increase in production and income enabled many entrepreneurs to invest in manufacturing new products. One inducement to invest was the existence of a large, inexpensive, semiskilled labor force. The rate of industrial growth exceeded that of agricultural growth by more than three times because of a much smaller ratio of capital to income for agriculture as compared with manufacturing.[109] Further, the ratio remained relatively constant in agriculture but rose rapidly in manufacturing, and particularly in services, during the early 1960's. Of course beyond this simple ratio it is still necessary to seek the principal factors accounting for growth and their relationship to one another. This task awaits future researchers. Whereas further inflows of capital to agriculture in recent years have accounted for the spectacular rise in farm output despite tilling of a constant land area, entrepreneurs in manufacturing have been able to increase their production and sale by combining even more labor with a small, growing stock of capital. Because entrepreneurs have been particularly successful in operating at nearly full capacity far out on the low segment of their long-run average unit cost curve, their industrial products have sold very competitively overseas and at home have been priced low enough for consumers to buy them in increasing amounts.

When rates of increase of capital formation in Taiwan and the Philippines since 1955 are compared, it is seen that Taiwan obtained a rate of around 3.5 percent, while the Philippines generated a rate near 5.0 percent.[110] Despite the higher growth rate in the Philippines, however, factor productivity increase, and subsequently the growth of income and employment, has not been as high as in Taiwan. What seems to have accounted for the large difference in factor productivity has been the rapid adoption of new technology by Taiwanese enterprises. The major explanation for their superior performance in this regard could very well spring from entrepreneurs' being very export-oriented. These industries are greatly encouraged to adopt the most advanced techniques as soon as they become known, in order to retain and expand their share of world markets. Another reason is that rapid output expansion has enabled enterprises to expand to their optimal scale of operations. Output has continued to expand, rather than becoming kinked at some point because of a failure by firms to increase domestic sales. Output growth has been sustained chiefly by export expansion.

Certainly the rapid export growth of Taiwan has enabled industrial enterprises to produce more efficiently and to adopt the best
technology practices. Of all Asian countries, excluding Japan, only
Taiwan, Hong Kong, and Korea exhibited high export growth rates
between 1956-57 and 1962-63.[111] The key to Taiwan's economic
success story in recent years undeniably lies in the recognition of
Nationalist leadership that export dependence must be encouraged.

NOTES

I want to express my thanks to the Center for Advanced International Studies of the University of Miami for supporting the research to prepare this essay. I also want to acknowledge thanks
to Professor Roy Hensley of the Department of Economics, University
of Miami, for constructive remarks on an early draft of this essay.

1. Alexander Gerschenkron, Economic Backwardness in Historical Perspective (New York: Frederick A. Praeger, 1965), p. 123.
2. The Decennial Reports 1882-91 mention the terrible toll
in human lives that malaria and other diseases took during the 1880's:
"In Formosa the visitation of malarial fever are severe, and thousands
among the Chinese die from this cause every year; there has not,
however, been any such exceptional epidemic of it, except perhaps
among the troops during the French war, as to call for special note.
In August and September 1888 this district was visited by Cholera,
which is said to have then claimed 2,000 victims." See Inspector
General of Customs, Decennial Reports 1882-91, first issue (Shanghai:
Inspector General of Customs, 1893), p. 455.
3. C. Imbault-Huart, L'île Formose: Histoire et description
(Taipei: Ch'eng-wen Publishing Co., 1968), p. 174.
4. The English official Robert Swinhoe reports in the 1850's
visiting Taiwan-fu and later stopping over in a village 25 miles from
present day Kaohsiung where "the rice fields were lying waste on
account of disturbances." See Robert Swinhoe, "Narrative of a Visit
to the Island of Formosa," Journal of the North-China Branch of the
Royal Asiatic Society, No. 2 (May 1859), p. 149.
5. "Inland Communications in China," Journal of the China
Branch of the Royal Asiatic Society, new series, XXVIII (1898), pp.
95-96.
6. Imbault-Huart, L'île Formose, pp. 280-81.
7. Tomita Yoshirō, "Taiwan shuraku no kenkyū" (A study of
Taiwan villages), in Andō Seiji, ed., Taiwan bunka ronsō (Essays on
Taiwanese culture) (Taipei, 1942), pp. 176-78.

8. Tai Teruo, "Taiwan narabi ni Shindai Shina no sonshō oyobi sonshōbyō" (Villages and village temples of Taiwan during the Ch'ing period), in Andó Seiji, ed., Taiwan bunka ronsō, p. 295.

9. Tai Yen-hui, "T'ai-wan ti hsiao-tsu yeh chi k'en-t'ien chih Kuan-hsi," (The relationship between large rent and small rent households in Taiwan), T'ai-wan wen-hsien (Taiwan cultural miscellany), XIV, 2 (June 1963), 164-65.

10. Bank of Taiwan Economic Research Office, T'ai-wan fang-chih hui-k'an ch'uan-shih: Miao-li hsien chih (The revised gazetteer series for Taiwan, volume 10; The local history of Miao-li hsien) (Taipei: Bank of Taiwan, 1959), p. 63. The section on customs mentions that when land was first reclaimed, the tenant paid a fixed rent for five to eight years and bore all farming costs. Later, tenant contracts were set annually and rent paid in kind; the tenant continued to bear all farming costs.

11. The origin of these wealthy families who had acquired land and then leased it to migrants from the mainland is described in Bank of Taiwan Economic Research Office, Ch'ing-tai T'ai-wan ta-tsu tiao-ch'a shu (A survey of the Taiwan large rent households during the Ch'ing period), I (Taipei: Bank of Taiwan, 1963), pp. 14-58.

Chen Ta-yuan, "Taiwan tochi seido to kosaku mondai" (The tenant problem and land system in Taiwan), in Andō Seiji, ed., Taiwan bunka ronsō, p. 117, points out that the hsiao-tsu paid rent to the ta-tsu for field and garden land considerably below what the hsiao-tsu were able to obtain from their tenants. See the following comparison of rent payments.

Land Class	Hsiao-tsu Rent to Ta-tsu (rent per chia in koku of unhulled grain)*	Tenant Rent Paid to Hsiao-tsu in Same Unit of Account
Field		
High	8	32
Medium	6	24
Low	4	16
Garden		
High	6	24
Medium	4	16
Low	2	8

*one koku = 4.9629 bu.

12. Bank of Taiwan Economic Research Office, T'ai-wan t'u-ti chih-tu k'ao ch'a pao-kao shu (a report on the survey of Taiwan's land system) (Taipei: Bank of Taiwan, 1963), p. 22. This study was written by a Chinese official from Fukien who traveled around Taiwan in 1914 to learn how the Japanese colonial administration conducted its land tax survey. He reports that Liu Ming-ch'uan's survey, under-taken in the 1880's, found 361,448 chia of cultivated land instead of the 70,000 chia recorded in the tax records. The rural sector could have yielded a land tax of 970,400 yuan instead of 400,000 yuan. A chia is roughly equivalent to a hectare, or 2.5 acres.

13. Inō Yoshinoru, Taiwan bunkashi (A history of Taiwan civilization), I (Tokyo: Toke Shoin), p. 676; Herbert J. Allen, "Notes of a Journey Through Formosa from Tamsui to Taiwan-fu," Pro-ceedings of the Royal Geographical Society, XXI (1876-77), 265.

14. Ino Yoshinoru, Taiwan bunkashi, pp. 693-94.

15. Chou Hsien-wen, Ch'ing-tai T'ai-wan ching-chi shih (Eco-nomic history of Taiwan in the Ch'ing dynasty) (Taipei: Bank of Taiwan, 1957), p. 26; Bank of Taiwan Economic Research Office, T'ai-wan fang-chih hui-k'an ch'uan-san: Chang-hua hsien-chih (The revised gazetteer series for Taiwan, volume 3: The local history of Chang-hua Hsien) (Taipei: Bank of Taiwan, 1959), p. 137.

16. T'ai-wan fang-chih hui-k'an ch'uan-san: Chang-hua hsien-chih, loc. cit.

17. Santarō Okamatsu, Provisional Report on Investigations of Laws and Customs in the Island of Formosa Compiled by Order of the Governor-General of Formosa (Kobe: Kobe Herald Office, 1900), p. 9.

18. Rinji Taiwan Kyūkan Chōsakai (Temporary commission of the Taiwan government-general for the study of old Chinese customs), Dai-nibu chōsa keizai shiryō hōkoku (Report and materials of the economic investigation by the second section), II (Tokyo, 1905), p. 515.

19. Lien Heng, T'ai-wan t'ung-shih (A general history of Taiwan), IV (Taipei: Bank of Taiwan, 1962), p. 649.

20. Lien Ya-t'ang, T'ai-wan t'ung-shih (a history of Taiwan), III (Taipei: Tsushisha, 1921), p. 728. E. C. Bridgeman, writing in the China Repository, comments as follows: "According to the best accounts we have, there are no less than two millions Chinese in Formosa engaged in the cultivation of sugar and rice, and about 400 vessels continually plying between the island and the Chinese coast. When it is taken into consideration, that a great part of the sugar consumed in the northern provinces of China is produced on this island, and that millions of the people in Fuhkeen depend almost entirely for their support on the rice imported from thence, we may fairly conclude, that great numbers of laborers are always at work to supply these wants. Many parts of the opposite shore in Fuhkeen

are so barren, that without the aid of the oil-cakes from Formosa, used in manuring the sandy hills, even the sweet potato, would not be produced." E. C. Bridgeman, "Remarks on Formosa," China Repository, Vl (January 1838), p. 418.

21. James W. Davidson, The Island of Formosa: Historical View from 1430 to 1900; History, People, Resources, and Commercial Prospects (Taipei: Book World Co., 1961), p. 375. Davidson's account is based upon the report of Dr. W. W. Myers in an 1890 British consular report from Tainan.

22. Chou Hsien-wen, Ch'ing-tai T'ai-wan ching-chi shih, pp. 86-87.

23. Allen, "Notes of a Journey Through Formosa," p. 266.

24. Samuel C. Chu, " Liu Ming-ch'uan and Modernization of Taiwan," The Journal of Asian Studies, XXIII, 1 (November 1963), 37-54; for coal mining see Huan Chia-mo, Chia-wu chan-ch'ien chih T'ai-wan mei-wu (Coal mining in Taiwan prior to the Sino-Japanese War of 1895) (Taiwan: Academia Sinica, 1961), pp. 214-48; Davidson, The Island of Formosa, pp. 243-56.

25. Davidson, The Island of Formosa, p. 364. Davidson's account of the Japanese take-over is excellent.

26. E. Patricia Tsurumi, "Taiwan Under Kodama Gentarō and Gotō Shimpei," in Papers on Japan, IV (Cambridge, Mass.: Harvard University Press, 1967), 104-06; and Chang Han-yu and Ramon H. Myers, "Japanese Colonial Development Policy in Taiwan, 1895-1906: A Case of Bureaucratic Entrepreneurship," The Journal of Asian Studies, XXII, 4 (August 1963), 435-37.

27. Ching-chih Chen, "The Police and Hoko Systems in Taiwan Under Japanese Administration (1895-1945)," in Papers on Japan, IV (Cambridge, Mass.: Harvard University Press, 1967), 157. Ten households were combined into a chia, and ten chia made into a pao. Chia and pao heads were responsible to a policeman.

28. Mochiji Rokusaburō, Taiwan shokumin seisaku (Colonial policy in Taiwan) (Tokyo: Fuzambo, 1913), pp. 174-80.

29. Ramon H. Myers and Adrienne Ching, "Agricultural Development in Taiwan Under Japanese Colonial Rule," The Journal of Asian Studies, XXIII, 4 (August 1964), 561-62.

30. Taiwan sōtokufu zaimukyoku, Taiwan zeisei no enkaku (A history of the Taiwan tax system) (Taipei, 1935), table 5.

31. Rokusaburō, Taiwan shokumin seisaku, p. 121.

32. For discussion of these projects and their costs see the following: Tsurumi, "Taiwan Under Kodama Gentarō and Gotō Shimpei," p. 134 for sanitation; Chang and Myers, "Japanese Colonial Development Policy in Taiwan," pp. 441-42; George W. Barclay, Colonial Development and Population in Taiwan (Princeton: Princeton University Press, 1954), pp. 23-24; Rokusaburō, Taiwan shokumin

seisaku, chs. 8, 9, 10; Chang Han-yu, "Jih-chü shih-tai T'ai-wan ching-chi chih yen-pien," (The transformation of the Taiwan economy during the period of Japanese control), in T'ai-wan ching-chi shih ehrchi (Essays on the Economic history of Taiwan, No. 2) (Taipei: Bank of Taiwan, 1955), pp. 74-78.

33. Chang and Myers, "Japanese Colonial Development Policy in Taiwan," p. 446.

34. Taiwan Sōtokufu Shokusankyoku, Taiwan no tōgyō (The Taiwan sugar industry) (Taipei, 1929), p. 69.

35. Ibid., pp. 10-11; for a good description of the adoption and diffusion of these seeds see Tanaka Kazuji, Taiwan sangyō sōran (A survey of Taiwan industries) (Taipei, 1919), p. 71; Satō Seizō, Kairei yonjunen no Taiwan (Taiwan after forty years of reform) (Taipei, 1935), p. 179; Chang, "Jih-chü shih-tai T'ai-wan ching-chi chih yen-pien," p.80.

36. Taiwan Sōtokufu Shokusankyoku, Taiwan no tōgyō, p. 21.

37. Myers and Ching, "Agricultural Development in Taiwan," p. 563.

38. Tanaka, Taiwan sangyō sōran, p. 37.

39. Myers and Ching, "Agricultural Development in Taiwan," pp. 566-67.

40. Bank of Taiwan Economic Research Office, Jih-chü shih-tai T'ai-wan ching-chi shih t'e-cheng (An economic history of Taiwan under Japanese rule), I (Taipei: Bank of Taiwan, 1958), p. 37.

41. Myers and Ching, "Agricultural Development in Taiwan," p. 556; Yih-min Ho, Agricultural Development of Taiwan 1903-1960 (Nashville, Tenn.: Vanderbilt University Press, 1966), pp. 17-18; S. C. Hsieh and T. H. Lee, Agricultural Development and Its Contributions to Economic Growth in Taiwan—Input-Output and Productivity Analysis of Taiwan Agricultural Development (Taipei: Joint Commission on Rural Reconstruction, 1966), p. 14; Samuel Pao-San Ho, "Agricultural Transformation Under Colonialism: The Case of Taiwan," The Journal of Economic History, XXVIII, 3 (September 1968), 317-18.

42. Harry A. Franck, Glimpses of Japan and Formosa (New York and London: The Century Co., 1924), p. 142.

43. Bank of Taiwan Economic Research Office, T'ai-wan liu-hsing chi (Diaries of travels in Taiwan) (Taipei: Bank of Taiwan, 1965), p. 26.

44. Ibid., p. 105.

45. Barclay, Colonial Development and Population in Taiwan, pp. 60, 71.

46. These estimated projections are based upon the method introduced by Bruce F. Johnston in his "Agriculture and Economic Development: The Relevance of the Japanese Experience," Food

Research Institute Studies, Vl, 3 (1966), 269; see also Bruce F. Johnston and Soren T. Nielsen, "Agricultural and Structural Transformation in a Developing Economy," Economic Development and Cultural Change; XIV, 3 (April 1966), 285. See Table 2.5 for regional population trends between 1911 and 1941.

47. Barclay, Colonial Development and Population in Taiwan, p. 42.

48. Ibid., p. 169.

49. Ibid., p. 172.

50. Han-yu Chang, "A Study of Living Conditions of Farmers in Taiwan, 1931-1950," The Developing Economies, VIII, (March 1969), 42-43, 57-58.

51. Taiwan Civil Affairs Bureau, T'ai-wan sheng wu-shih i-nien lai t'ung-chi t'i-yao (The basic statistics for the past fifty-one years of Taiwan Province) (Taipei: Civil Affairs Bureau; 1946), pp. 564-75 for the growth of fruit and vegetable production between 1905 and 1940. Henceforth this study will be referred to as TTY.

52. Ibid., p. 939.

53. A further bit of supporting evidence is provided by a Chinese scholar who has measured gross value of production for all economic sectors excluding government monopoly products. He found that per capita gross value of output in 1902 stood at 25 yen, compared with 255 yen in 1943—a tenfold rise. As the general price index rose threefold, "generally speaking, the economic livelihood of the Taiwanese was obviously at a higher level than the base level." Kang Shan, "T'ai-wan kung-yeh chih t'e-cheng" (Special characteristics of Taiwan industry), in Bank of Taiwan Economic Research Office, Jih-chü shih-tai T'ai-wan ching-chi chih t'e-cheng, p. 75.

54. T'ai-wan ching-chi nien-piao (Essays on the Taiwan economy), No. 4 (Taipei: Bank of Taiwan, 1956), p. 135.

55. Ibid.

56. Ibid., pp. 139, 142, 145, 149, 158, 166.

57. Taiwan keizai nempō kankōkai, ed., Taiwan keizai nempō (Taiwan economic yearbook), 1943 ed., translated by Military Government Translation Center (New York: Naval School of Military Government and Administration, 1943), p. 71.

58. TTY, p. 763.

59. Ibid., p. 778. This estimate is based upon holding value of 1936 sugar production constant for years up to 1941 as a fixed share of total value of industrial output.

60. Ibid., p. 824; for data on industrial output see pp. 788-813.

61. Taiwan keizai nempō kankōkai, ed., Taiwan keizai nempō (Taiwan economic yearbook), 1942 ed. (Tokyo: Kokushi Nihon Kyokai, 1942), p. 45.

62. Ibid., pp. 63-69.

63. Taiwan keizai nempō, 1943 ed., ch. 1, pp. 29-34.

64. T'ai-wan ching-chi nien-piao, p. 186.

65. Ibid., pp. 186-87.

66. Chien-sheng Shih, "Economic Development in Taiwan After the Second World War," Weltwirtschaftliches Archiv, C, 1 (1968), 116.

67. Kan Ching-jao, "T'ai-wan mi-t'ang pi-chia chih yen-chiu," (A comparative study of rice and sugar prices in Taiwan), in Bank of Taiwan Economic Research Office, T'ai-wan mi-t'ang pi-chia chih yen-chiu (Comparative studies of rice and sugar prices in Taiwan) (Taipei: Bank of Taiwan, 1953), p. 55.

68. Tzu-yu chung-kuo chih kung-yeh (Industry of free China), XIII, 2 (February 1960), 54-57.

69. Ronald Freedman and John Y. Takeshita, Family Planning on Taiwan: An Experiment in Social Change (Princeton: Princeton University Press, 1969), p. 354.

70. Council for International Economic Cooperation and Development, Taiwan Statistical Data Book, 1968, (Taipei, 1968), p. 22.

71. See H. B. Chenery, "Patterns of Industrial Growth," The American Economic Review, L, 4 (September 1960), 636.

72. Paul K. C. Liu, "Population Redistribution and Development in Taiwan, 1951-1965," presented at the Conference on Economic Development sponsored by the China Council on Sino-American Cooperation in the Humanities and Social Sciences and the U.S. Joint Committee on Sino-American Cooperation in the Humanities and Social Sciences, June 19-28, 1967 (Taipei, Taiwan), p. A7.

73. Taiwan Statistical Data Book, 1968, p. 182.

74. Ibid., pp. 167-69.

75. Ibid., p. 23. For an excellent appraisal of land reform see also Chao-chen Chen, "Land Reform and Agricultural Development in Taiwan," presented at Conference on Economic Development of Taiwan, June 19-28, 1967; H. S. Tang and S. C. Hsieh, "Land Reform and Agricultural Development in Taiwan," The Malayan Economic Review, VI, 1 (April 1961), 49-54.

76. Ken C. Y. Lin, "Industrial Development and Changes in the Structure of Foreign Trade," International Monetary Fund Staff Papers, XV, 2 (July 1968), 297.

77. Neil H. Jacoby, U.S. Aid to Taiwan: A Study of Foreign Aid, Self-Help and Development (New York: Frederick A. Praeger, 1966), p. 174. In selecting industrial projects for U. S. aid, the J. G. White Engineering Corporation made engineer and economic analyses of various projects initiated by the U.S. aid mission. The Chinese government strategy was to rehabilitate and modernize the original industrial base of aluminum, fertilizer, petroleum, textiles, and agricultural processing industries. Second, this strategy was designed

to establish new industries such as automotive, electrical appliances, and basic chemicals, which would reduce imports and utilize Taiwan's low-cost labor supply. Finally, the government hoped to establish high-technology industries, such as electronics. See p. 201.

78. Ibid., p. 177.

79. Ibid., p. 190.

80. Ibid., p. 191.

81. Ken C. Y. Lin, "Industrial Development and Changes in the Structure of Foreign Trade," p. 302.

82. Ibid., p. 303.

83. Ibid., p. 304.

84. S. Y. Dao, W. P. Chang, and M. S. Shih, "Industrial Development in Taiwan," a paper prepared for the Conference on Economic Development of Taiwan, June 19-28, 1967, p. 17.

85. Tzu-yu chung-kuo chih kung-yeh (Industry of free China), XXVIII, 2 (February 1969), 58.

86. Ibid., p. 35, for data to calculate export share of total in 1968; Ken C. Y. Lin, "Industrial Development and Changes in the Structure of Foreign Trade," p. 304, for percentage of years 1956-64. See also Tzong-shian Yu, "The Impact of Foreign Trade on Taiwan's Economic Growth," paper prepared for Conference on Economic Development of Taiwan, June 19-28, 1967, p. C9; for the high correlation between growth of imports and gross national product see pp. C17-18.

87. Ken C. Y. Lin, "Industrial Development and Changes in the Structure of Foreign Trade," p. 306.

88. Ibid., p. 307. Ken C. Y. Lin goes on to remark that "notable among the latter [intermediate and capital goods] were increased demands for wood pulp, stemming from growing needs for paperboard for export packing; for petrochemical intermediates, resulting from domestic and export demands for synthetic yarns, resins and plastics, etc.; for steel plates and other fabricated metal products, owing to demand for export containers and increased domestic demand for household durables and transport equipment; and for cement and structural steel for larger buildings, such as tourist hotels and residential construction." See p. 307.

89. Taiwan Statistical Data Book, 1968, p. 53.

90. See Hsing Mo-huan, "An Anatomy of Economic Development in Taiwan, 1951-65," 1968, p. 18. Professor Hsing kindly gave this writer a copy of this draft, which was to be revised before final publication.

91. Taiwan Statistical Data Book, 1968, p. 7.

92. Tsong-shian Yu, "The Impact of Foreign Trade on Taiwan's Economic Growth," pp. C20-21.

93. Ken C. Y. Lin, "Industrial Development and Changes in the Structure of Foreign Trade," pp. 311-13.

94. Ibid., p. 309.

95. To this extent Taiwan had adhered to a criterion for investment recommended by certain Western economists. See H. B. Chenery, "Comparative Advantage and Development Policy," The American Economic Review, LI, 1 (March 1961), 26.

96. Sun Wen, Shih-yeh chi-hua (An industrial plan) (Taipei: Central Literary Supply Co., 1956), Ch. 1.

97. Ibid., pp. 258-85.

98. Yen Chia-kan, Hou Chiu-yuan, and Ch'en Tsung-han, eds., Chiang tsung-t'ung yu Chung-kuo min-sheng chien-she (President Chiang and raising the livelihood of the Chinese people) (Taipei: Yu-t'ai Co. [Hsing-t'ai Printing Co.], 1967), p. 36. In March, 1950, President Chiang declared, "At the moment, I only want to say that our basic task is to build up Taiwan to oppose Communism and resist Soviet Russia."

99. Ibid., p. 18. This source provides an excellent summary of government economic planning in the early 1950's.

100. Ibid., p. 37.

101. Ibid., p. 41.

102. Ibid., p. 40.

103. Council for International Economic Cooperation and Development, Highlights of the Fifth Four-Year Economic Development Plan of the Republic of China (Taipei, 1969), p. 304. In the fall of 1968, the government intended to extend universal public education from six years to nine. The cost of this project would be $90 million and would constitute a new, untold strain on the existing school system. At present 97 percent of school-age children are enrolled in free and compulsory schools. See Frederick Andrews, "The Boom is Even Bigger in Taiwan, " The New York Times, January 19, 1968, p. 54.

104. Ibid., p. 17.

105. For an excellent study of this system and its drawbacks see A. B. Lewis, "The Rice-Fertilizer Barter Price and the Production of Rice in Taiwan, Republic of China (1949-1965)," Journal of Agricultural Economics (Taichung, Taiwan), No. 5 (June 1967), pp. 120-80.

106. "Technocrats Gain Key Role in Taipei," The New York Times, April 13, 1969, p. 9.

107. "Younger Leaders Rising in Taiwan," The New York Times, April 28, 1968, p. 4.

108. Lai Chang, T'ai-pei shih ti-chia wen-t'i yen-chiu (A study of the land price problem in Taipei city) (Taipei: Taiwan Commercial Press, 1967), p. 33.

109. Hsing Mo-huan, "An Anatomy of Economic Development in Taiwan, 1951-65," pp. 38-39.

110. Jeffrey G. Williamson, "Dimensions of Postwar Philippine Economic Progress," The Quarterly Journal of Economics, LXXXIII, 1 (February 1969), 107. Despite rapid industrial development and a high rate of capital formation in the Philippines, employment stagnation has occurred. See Theodore K. Ruprecht, "Output Stimulation and Employment Stagnation-Policy By-products in the Philippines," Economic Development and Cultural Change, XVII, 1 (October 1968), 77-89. The same problem has occurred in numerous Latin American countries that have tried to achieve an import-substitution policy. In general, factor productivity has not risen and technological improvement has been exceedingly low. Nor have employment rates been impressive. See Henry Bruton, "Productivity Growth in Latin America," American Economic Review, LVII, 5 (December 1967), 1099-1116.

111. Seiji Naya, "The Commodity Pattern and Export Performance of Developing Asian Countries to the Developed Areas," Economic Development and Cultural Change, XV (October 1966-July, 1967), p. 430.

3

POLITICAL DEVELOPMENT IN
THE REPUBLIC OF CHINA
ON TAIWAN
Yung Wei

INTRODUCTION

Although it is one of the important political systems in East Asia, the Republic of China on Taiwan has, until very recently, received little attention from political scientists. This is true even among the specialists who have a professed interest in the comparative politics of the Far East. In comparison with the amount of research on Taiwan conducted by economists, sociologists, and anthropologists, that done by political scientists is negligible.

One may point to the presumably "small" size and dimensions of the Republic of China (henceforth the ROC) for this lack of interest, but a quick check of statistical data immediately disproves this explanation. With about 13,950 square miles under effective control,** the ROC is not as small as is generally conceived. The territorial base from which its government operates is slightly smaller than Switzerland but bigger than Belgium. The population of Taiwan, which exceeds 14.8 million, is bigger than those of 70 percent of the nations

---

*The author would like to express his gratitude to Dr. Lung-sheng Tao of Cornell University for his assistance in collecting various materials for this study. It is the author alone, of course, who is solely responsible for all statements.

**Including Taiwan, Penghu (Pescadores), Tiaoyutai Islets, and other scattered islands within the provincial jurisdiction of Taiwan; Kinmen (Quemoy) and Matsu of Fukien Province; and Tungsha (Pratas) and Nansha (Spratly) in the South China Sea.

of the world.[1] With a standing army, navy, and air force 600,000
strong,[2] the ROC can boast that it is the world's sixth biggest military
power. On the basis of these facts, we cannot explain the scarcity of
serious political studies on the ROC either by its "smallness" or by its
lack of significance in the political and military balance among nations
of the world.

It is the purpose of this to review the political development on
Taiwan since 1949 and to evaluate the achievements of the government
of the ROC on that island, along with its limitations and problems.
There are three major parts to this chapter. The first examines some
of the reasons for the lack of interest in studying the political system
of the ROC. The second presents a brief review of the history of the
ROC on Taiwan since 1949. And the third part, which is probably
the most substantive, deals with the various aspects of political development on Taiwan.[3]

The author makes no pretense that this is an exhaustive and con-
clusive study. Rather, it is merely an exploratory study on a dynamic
and ever-changing political system, using the limited hard data that
are presently available. A more complete analysis on the seemingly
simple but actually complex political system of the ROC will have
to wait until more empirical findings on the functioning of that system
have been produced by rigorous political research.

REASONS FOR THE LACK OF INTEREST
IN STUDYING THE ROC ON TAIWAN

There appear to be two underlying reasons for the lack of
interest among political scientists in the Chinese Nationalist political
system on Taiwan. The first can be attributed to the seemingly over-
powering presence of Communist China in international politics,
especially in East and Southeast Asia. The huge size of mainland
China and its overwhelming population, the participation of the Chinese
Communists in the Korean War, their development of nuclear weaponry
and missiles, and their support of "people's wars of national liberation" in underdeveloped areas have rendered any achievements or
impact made by the ROC in international politics insignificant in the
eyes of most Western observers.

A second reason for the lack of serious studies of the ROC seems
to lie in the prejudice of certain political scientists against the Chinese
Nationalists. This is a carryover of the dissillusionment and resultant
resentment caused by the failures of the Chinese Nationalists on the
Chinese mainland before 1949. For many of the "old China hands"
having this kind of prejudice, the ROC is the political regime of a
lost cause and hence does not warrant further investigation. In the

eyes of these China experts, the ROC is a remnant of an ancien régime that sooner or later will either be absorbed by Communist China or become an independent nation. So why should they bother to analyze a political system with such a precarious existence?

A closer examination of the events that have occurred on Taiwan since 1949 and the impact the ROC has made in its relations with other political systems leads us to conclude that neither of these reasons is tenable. As already pointed out, the ROC on Taiwan is not as small or as insignificant as some of the China experts tend to believe. To study the behavior of the Chinese Communists without bringing Taiwan into the frame of analysis would certainly lead to the omission of many important variables affecting the decision-making process of this giant Communist political system in Asia.

With the continuing of the war in Indochina and the increasing nuclear threat of Communist China, the position and future role of the ROC in the international relations of East and Southeast Asia have become more important than ever before. The gradual disengagement of the United States from direct military involvement in these areas in terms of manpower has made the 600,000 men of the ROC's armed forces even more indispensable in the minds of the leaders of non-Communist Asian nations.

Other than the military posture of the ROC, the remarkable economic development on Taiwan is another aspect of the ROC that has attracted the attention and admiration of leaders of many nations, especially of developing nations. The ROC's successful land reform, its agricultural aid to African nations, and its technical assistance to Vietnam, Thailand, and some Latin American countries have further increased its prestige.

THE REPUBLIC OF CHINA AFTER 1949: A BRIEF HISTORICAL SURVEY

In order to appreciate fully the transformation of the ROC from a defeated, threatened political regime on the verge of total collapse toward the end of 1949 into the prosperous, vigorous political system of today, a brief review of events that occurred on Taiwan after 1949 is necessary.

The history of the ROC on Taiwan may be divided into five periods. The first period, which lasted from 1949 to 1953, was one of struggle for survival and of reconstruction. When the Chinese Nationalists moved the seat of government from mainland China to Taiwan in 1949, few political observers had confidence in the continued existence of the ROC as an independent political entity. In the eyes of many Western diplomats stationed in the Far East, it was only a matter of time before the Chinese Communists would take over.[4]

The political situation in and outside of Taiwan at the time seemed to support their observation. The armed forces that had retreated to Taiwan from the mainland were disorganized and badly in need of weapons and supplies. The economy was threatened by inflation caused, among many other elements, by the sudden influx of one million refugees from the mainland. And, worst of all, the Nationalist government was deprived of the official head of state when the acting president, General Li Tsung-jen, suddenly left China for Hong Kong in November and then went to the United States in December, 1949. Probably the only encouraging events of the year were the two decisive defeats that the Chinese Communists suffered at the hands of the Nationalists on two offshore islands near the mainland coast— Kinmen (Quemoy) and Teng-pu. The victories won by the Nationalists on these two islands gave the nearly shattered morale of the Nationalist troops a boost and frustrated the Communist plan to make an early attempt to take Taiwan.

Several events that occurred in 1950 brought drastic changes in the domestic and international environments of Taiwan that helped stabilize the rule of the Nationalists there. First of all, the resumption of the presidency by Chiang Kai-shek early that year again provided the Nationalist government with a rallying point of support and allegiance. Self-government for the province of Taiwan was put into practice. Land reform, starting with the limitation of farm rent to a maximum of 37.5 percent of the annual main crop, was also initiated.

For the Chinese Nationalists the most important development was probably the outbreak of the Korean War on June 25, 1950. The war brought about a quick change in the U.S. attitude toward the future of Taiwan—from one of "wait and see" to one of grave concern. The Seventh Fleet was ordered by President Truman to patrol the Taiwan Straits to prevent a Communist invasion of the island. U.S. military aid and economic assistance also started to pour into Taiwan.

After obtaining a sense of security from the events that occurred in 1950, the government of the ROC wasted no time in improving the social, economic, and political conditions in Taiwan. In 1951 the Taiwan Provincial Assembly was established, with representatives elected by popular vote. The "Land to Tiller" program, the most important step in the land reform, was adopted by the government in 1951 and was implemented in 1953. The essence of this program was for the government of the ROC to purchase the land from the landlords in exchange for land bonds and shares of stock in government enterprises. The land so obtained was then given to the tenant farmers. The entire price of the land was to be paid by the farmers to the government over a period of 10 years. This important step has had a long-lasting effect in improving the livelihood of the farmers. It has also contributed to the increase of political stability on Taiwan and the acceleration of economic development.[5]

1953 was also the year of the execution of the first four-year plan, which marked a policy shift on the part of the government of the ROC from short-term, stopgap measures to long-term developmental efforts.[6] Emphasis was placed on the encouragement of growth in the agricultural sector as well as on the development of electric power, fertilizer, and such light industries as glass, cement, and textiles. This balanced plan for economic development, which was followed by three further four-year plans, has proved to be extremely success-ful in developing the island's limited natural resources.[7]

With the signing of a mutual defense treaty with the United States in 1954, the ROC entered into a new era of its rule on Taiwan—a period of consolidation. This treaty formalized the relations between the ROC and the United States as allies having a mutual obligation to defend each other in the face of aggression, presumably from Communist China. Early in 1955 the U.S. Congress passed a joint resolution that gave further authority to the U.S. president to use American forces to defend Taiwan and the Pescadores.[8]

With the increased assurance that the United States would safe-guard its security, Taiwanese society made significant progress between 1954 and 1958. First of all, because of their improved socio-economic status resulting from the land reform, farmers showed a growing interest in participating in local politics. An increasing number of the former tenant farmers were elected to political offices at the village, county, and even provincial level. Prior to land reform most of the administrative offices in the villages were held by land-lords.[9]

A marked expansion of educational facilities at all levels was inaugurated to meet the demand of increasing numbers of young people of school age. With economic support from the United States, the Ministry of Education of the ROC also made a major effort to attract overseas Chinese students to attend colleges on Taiwan. The result was a diminishing number of Chinese students from Southeast Asia attending colleges and universities in mainland China.

While the ROC was making progress in the social, economic, and educational areas on Taiwan, the Chinese Communists took a drastic turn from the moderate, cautious policies of the early 1950's to more militant postures, both in domestic policies and in international behavior. Along with the establishment of commune systems and back-yard furnaces, in August, 1958, the Communists suddenly decided to undertake a military adventure in the Taiwan Straits by shelling the offshore islands controlled by the Nationalists.[10]

The massive bombardment of the offshore islands—primarily of Quemoy (Kinmen)—was so intense that the Chinese Nationalists were not able to ship supplies to these islands for several weeks after the first day of shelling. For a while it seemed that these islands were in real danger of being seized by the Chinese Communists, but the government of the ROC and the United States responded quickly and resolutely.

The Nationalist garrison forces demonstrated very high morale under heavy bombardment by the Communists. Its navy showed remarkable courage in breaking the blockade imposed by the Communist shelling to bring supplies to the besieged islands. To help deliver the supplies, destroyers of the U.S. Seventh Fleet escorted the Nationalist ships to the limit of three nautical miles from the islands. The Nationalist air force also displayed a dazzling performance by shooting down 28 Communist MIG-17's over the Taiwan Straits within two months.

The determination and effectiveness of the Nationalist armed forces, coupled with the demonstration of the U.S. decision to come to the aid of the ROC in an enlarged war in the Taiwan Straits, finally brought an end to the Quemoy crisis. The lack of full support from the Soviet Union seemed also to be a reason that the Chinese Communists resorted to sporadic bombardment after September 1958.

The Nationalist victory over the Communists in the Quemoy crisis was one of the most important developments since the ROC moved its seat of government from mainland China to Taiwan. It clearly demonstrated that the Chinese Communists could not easily take the offshore islands, to say nothing of Taiwan itself, by force.

With the confidence and self-assurance gained from the Quemoy crisis, the government and people of the ROC entered into a new period in 1959. From 1959 to 1965 the people of Taiwan experienced unprecedented economic growth and social progress. Beginning in 1960 inflation was effectively arrested. Since that year the annual rise of the price level has averaged less than 2 percent.[11] A structural change took place in the Taiwanese economy. The agricultural sector decreased from 37.7 percent of the total national output in 1952 to 32.5 percent in 1960. On the other hand, the industrial output increased from 17.9 percent to 24.7 percent during the same period. A marked increase in the private sector of the economy was also effected by 1960, growing from 42 percent in 1952 to 57 percent in that year.[12]

Adding to the economic and industrial growth of Taiwan was the establishment of the export processing zone in Kaohsiung, a major port in southern Taiwan, which immediately drew large investments from foreign firms and overseas Chinese. The increased income of the Taiwan farmers, who had paid off the entire land loan by 1963,

provided a bigger domestic market for consumer goods. Exports
increased from $U.S.174 million in 1960 to $U.S.490 million in 1964.[13]
The combination of all these factors produced a record annual economic
growth (GNP) of 10.0 percent between 1961 and 1968.[14] The economy
of Taiwan was doing so well in 1964 that the United States decided to
stop the economic aid to Taiwan the next year, a rare occurrence in
the history of American aid to the developing countries after World
War II.

With the cessation of economic aid from the United States in
1965, Taiwan entered into a fourth period of development—one of
prosperity and transformation. Although economic aid from the U.S.
government ended in June, 1965, American dollars continued to flow
into Taiwan in the form of concessional loans and investment from
private firms.[15] The rapid growth of the Taiwanese economy was
evidenced in the mushrooming of factories in the countryside and of
high-rise office buildings, resort hotels, and apartments in the cities.

By the end of 1969, the people of Taiwan had achieved a standard
of living second only to Japan in East and Southeast Asia. Epidemic
diseases were eradicated. Social security was extended to government
employees, laborers, fishermen, and sugarcane farmers. Free and
compulsory education was extended from six to nine years, with an
average attendance ratio of 97.3 percent.[16] Life expectancy showed
significant increase, from 41 years for men and 46 years for women
in 1940 to 65 years for men and 69 years for women in 1967.[17]

In addition to progress in economic development and social
welfare, the government of the ROC also made significant achievements
in consolidating the internal political structure and in broadening its
international support and cooperation. The National Security Council
was established in 1967 to give greater power and flexibility to the
president of the ROC in dealing with problems affecting the security
of Taiwan, mainly threats from the Chinese mainland. In March, 1969,
the Tenth National Congress of Kuomintang (KMT) was held in Taipei,
Taiwan. In contrast with the conflicts and confusion in the Ninth
Party Congress of Communist China, which was held in Peking at about
the same time, the Tenth Party Congress of KMT was far more
orderly; and the leader of KMT had more to report to the delegates
in terms of achievements.

One of the basic criticisms of the Chinese Nationalist government on Taiwan has been its unwillingness—or, to put it more accur-
ately, its inability—to hold national elections to renew the membership in the National Assembly and Legislative Yüan—the two legislative bodies in the Nationalist political structure that resemble the
parliament or congress of Western democracies. After much deliberation and careful planning, the government of the ROC finally decided
to hold a national election in Taiwan in 1969. In a popular election

held in Taipei City and Taiwan Province, 15 new members were elected
to the National Assembly; 2 new members were elected to the Control
Yüan; and 11 new legislators were elected to the Legislative Yüan.
All the newly elected members of these bodies were native Taiwanese.[18]
    In its relations with other nations and with international organi-
zations, the ROC also made important gains in the 1960's. Through its
highly successful agricultural assistance to more than 19 African
states, the ROC was able to increase the votes opposing the seating
of Communist China in the United Nations from 47 in 1965 to 57 in
1966.[19] The confusion created by the Great Proletarian Cultural
Revolution on the Chinese mainland was also a factor in reducing
the support for the Chinese Communists among the U.N. members.
Outside the United Nations the ROC made gains in widening its support among Asian and Pacific nations by initiating and participating
in the nine-nation Asia and Pacific Council (ASPAC), which consists
of (besides the ROC) Japan, the Republic of Korea, Australia, New
Zealand, the Philippines, Thailand, Malaysia, and the Republic of
Vietnam (South Vietnam).[20] Since its establishment in 1966, ASPAC
has been playing an important role in the relations among member
nations, especially in the areas of economic assistance and cooperation.
    With the advent of 1970, the ROC seemed to have entered a new
era of accelerated economic growth coupled with difficulties and
uncertainty in its relations with other nations. During this year the
economy of Taiwan continued to have a very high rate of growth. The
per capita income of the population in the ROC reached an all-time
high of $U.S.292.[21] This increase in per capita income led to marked
increment of per capita consumption of food, clothing, and energy.
It also led to higher per capita ownership of automobiles and television
sets.[22] All these indicators point to a fairly bright future for the
economic development of Taiwan.
    While the economy of the ROC continued to make gains in 1970,
the external relations of the government appeared to be leading toward
problems and difficulties. The recognition of Communist China by
Canada in October, 1970, was a severe blow to the ROC in terms of
its impact on other nations that had, until then, maintained diplomatic
relations with the ROC and rejected Communist China.[23] Following
Canada's recognition of Peking, the one-vote simple majority won
by Communist China for the first time in the U.N. General Assembly
constituted a serious threat to the position of the ROC in that world
body. It was only because of the two-thirds majority vote required
for important issues that Peking was prevented from entering the
United Nations.
    If 1970 was a bad year for the international position of the ROC,
developments in 1971 were even more alarming for the Nationalists.
Among many of the setbacks that the government of the ROC has

suffered since the beginning of 1971, the most serious ones have come,
ironically, from its closest and long-time ally—the United States.
On February 25, President Nixon used, for the first time, the official
title "the People's Republic of China" to refer to the Chinese Communist regime in a major foreign policy report to the U.S. Congress.[24]
In the same report he also indicated that he wished that conflict
between Taipei and Peking could be resolved in a peaceful manner.[25]
Reactions to Nixon's report among government officials, academicians,
and newspaper editors on Taiwan naturally were highly critical.[26]

Two months after Nixon's report to the Congress, the relations
between the United States and Communist China entered a new phase
with the visit of the U.S. table tennis team to Peking in mid-April,
1971.[27] This was followed by the dramatic announcement on July 15
by President Nixon of his acceptance of an invitation from Communist
China to visit Peking by May, 1972.[28] On August 2, U.S. Secretary
of State William Rogers announced in Washington that the United
States would support Communist China's admission into the United
Nations but would vote to keep the ROC in the world organization as
well.

In the 26th session of the U.N. General Assembly, the delegation
of the United States, headed by George Bush, did make some efforts
to retain the seat of the ROC. Yet many delegates of other nations,
especially those from the third world, considered the U.S. position
on the issue self-contradictory and U.S. efforts to save the ROC's
seat merely halfhearted. For on the very day when George Bush,
U.S. ambassador to the U.N., was trying to win votes to support the
"important question" resolution, Henry Kissinger was in Peking, making
arrangements for Nixon's visit to Communist China. Consequently,
by the switch of a few votes, the U.S.-initiated resolution, which calls
the expulsion of the delegation of the ROC an "important question"
requiring a two-thirds majority vote, was defeated in the General
Assembly on the evening of October 25, 1971.[29] Facing almost sure
passing of the Albanian resolution, which called for the seating of
Communist China in the United Nations and the expulsion of the ROC,
the delegation of the ROC, led by Foreign Minister Chow Shu-kai,
walked out of the General Assembly after declaring the withdrawal
of the ROC from U.N. membership.

Four months later, in late February, 1972, President Nixon
visited the Chinese mainland. During the visit Nixon had a series of
extended meetings with Chou En-lai and a one-hour meeting with Mao
Tse-tung in Peking. These conferences were held under the strictest
secrecy, to the frustration and dismay of the U.S. newspaper men
who accompanied the presidential party of Peking. It was generally
assumed, however, that issues such as the war in Indochina, the U.S.
prisoners held by the Communists in mainland China, and the future

relations between the United States, Communist China, and the ROC on Taiwan were discussed.

Judging by the communiqué issued by Nixon and Chou En-lai in Shanghai on February 27, there seemed to be little agreement between the Americans and the Chinese Communists on practically all the issues mentioned in that document. The Chinese Communists simply reiterated their long-held positions. The Americans, however, seem to have made important concessions in at least two areas. First, the U.S. government accepted, in the wording of the communiqué, the five principles of "peaceful coexistence" advocated by Chou En-lai at the Bandung Conference in 1955. Second, the United States also indicated that "it affirms the ultimate objective of the withdrawal of all United States forces and military installations from Taiwan. In the meantime, it will progressively reduce its forces and military installations on Taiwan as the tension in the area diminishes" (Doc. 99).

Although Henry Kissinger and State Department officials later tried to explain that the language in the communiqué does not mean that the United States intends to alter or to discontinue its obligation to defend Taiwan and the Pescadores under the mutual defense treaty signed by the United States and the ROC in 1955, the unilateral declaration by the United States withdrawing its forces from Taiwan has led to suspicion in the minds of government officials and the people of the ROC as to the future moves of the United States on the China question. This section of the communiqué has also generated great concern among the political leaders in Japan, South Korea, and other Southeast Asian nations.

All these new, dramatic, and disturbing developments in the external relations of the ROC constitute probably the most serious challenges to its international posture that the government of the ROC has experienced in recent years. Whether the decision makers in Taipei can successfully overcome these setbacks will determine not only the ROC's standing in the community of nations but also its stability on the island of Taiwan.

POLITICAL DEVELOPMENT OF THE ROC ON TAIWAN

Having given a brief review of the history of the ROC on Taiwan since 1949, we may proceed to examine the various aspects of political development on that island. In examining and evaluating political development on Taiwan, Western observers have tended to look only at the limitations and problems that have faced the government of the ROC. As a result, they are inclined to overlook the achievements

made by the Chinese Nationalists' political system under very trying
domestic and international circumstances. To correct this, a more
balanced discussion on the limitations and problems faced by the
Nationalists, as well as on their political achievements is called for.

Political Ideology

Let us turn first to the ideological foundation of the Chinese
Nationalist political system. The ideological base of the ROC on
Taiwan is San Min Chu I (The three principles of the people). The
essence of this ideology can be found in a series of speeches made by
Dr. Sun Yat-sen, founder of the Chinese Nationalist Party (Kuomintang),
at Canton in 1924.[30] These speeches dealt with three interrelated
principles (Chu i in Chinese), which include the principle of nationalism
(Min Chu Chu I), the principle of democracy (Min Chuan Chu I), and
the principle of people's livelihood (Min Shen Chu I).[31] A large portion
of the ideas embedded in San Min Chu I were incorporated into the
constitution of the Republic of China adopted in 1946.[32]

After the government of the ROC moved from mainland China to
Taiwan, counterattacking the mainland or recovering the mainland
became the major political goal of the Chinese Nationalists. In the
first few years of their stay on Taiwan, the Nationalists emphasized
primarily military preparation for a counterattack against the
Communists on the mainland. Nationalist troops and guerrilla forces
made frequent landings on and surprise attacks against the coasts of
Kwangtung and Fukien provinces, which face Taiwan. The Nationalist
navy maintained an effective blockade of the bigger ports of eastern
and southern China. Its air force had regular flights to the mainland
to drop food, propaganda pamphlets, and sometimes intelligence
agents.

As time passed and as the Chinese Nationalists came to realize
that their efforts to recover the mainland would be drawn out, attention gradually shifted from military confrontation to political struggle.
An old slogan, "Thirty percent military action and seventy percent
political struggle," which was used in the anti-Communist campaigns
in the 1930's, was revived and used frequently by the leaders of the
ROC in the 1960's.

Except for a short period in 1962, the Nationalists have refrained
from contemplating large-scale military operations against the
Chinese mainland.[33] This was true even during the height of the
Cultural Revolution, which generated, at least for a while, a chaotic
military and political situation on mainland China. Observing the
internal conflicts within the Chinese Communists during the Cultural
Revolution, President Chiang Kai-shek made the following remarks:

The question of the recovery of the mainland today is
how to tidy up the calamitous situation which Mao has
left behind; when to counter-attack the mainland, and how
to bury Mao have become secondary questions. But by
this so-called secondary question is not meant that, from
now on, our preparations for military counter-attack can
be relaxed even for a moment while we sit and wait for
Mao to exterminate himself; rather, it is to point out that
in the present anti-Mao war, political means are even
more important.[34]

One should not derive from the above statement that the Chinese
Nationalists have given up military means to recover the mainland.
Rather, it reflects a pragmatic policy of exploiting fully the political
situation on the mainland as a prerequisite for a military action
against the Chinese Communists. In other words, the Nationalists
recognized the military imbalance between them and the Communists,
yet they were also convinced that the majority of the people on the
Chinese mainland were not satisfied with Communist rule. The Nationalists believed that sooner or later there would be a large-scale
uprising among the people in mainland China against the Communist
regime.[35] Then a counterattack would be launched by the Nationalist
force to "deliver the people from the Communist yoke."[36]

Since the Chinese Nationalists believe that the recovery of
mainland China does not depend on military force alone, they have
put great emphasis on the construction of Taiwan as the "bastion of
national recovery." In the "Declaration of the Tenth National Congress of the Kuomintang," it was specifically pointed out that "the
recovery of the mainland depends upon our building up Taiwan as a
model province of San Min Chu I."[37] With this in mind, the government of the ROC made great efforts to carry out the programs envisaged by Dr. Sun Yat-sen in the San Min Chu I.

One of the most important and most successful programs carried
out by the government of the ROC has been the land reform. This
program was laid down by Dr. Sun in The Principle of People's Livelihood. But for various reasons the Nationalists had never been able
to carry out this program fully while they were still on the mainland.
It was only after they had retreated to Taiwan that they had the chance
to carry out the ideas of Dr. Sun.* This ideological commitment of

---

*The economic impact of land reform has been discussed pre-
viously in the brief review of history of the ROC on Taiwan. The
sociopolitical consequences of land reform on Taiwan will be presented later in this chapter.

the KMT to improve the lot of the farmers of China and their ability to fulfill this commitment on Taiwan through the land reform has contributed in no small measure to the social and political stability on that island.

Political Structure

Although the Chinese Nationalists have had an impressive record of transforming many of the ideas in San Min Chu I into reality on Taiwan, their devotion to returning to the mainland and their claim to be the sole legitimate government of the whole of China have been a liability for the political system on Taiwan. Among the prices that the Nationalists have paid to keep the "Recovery of the Mainland" slogan alive are a top-heavy governmental structure; a large military budget; limited elite circulation, especially at the national level; and the continuous frustration among the general populace on the island at not being able to fulfill this goal.[38]

Let us first examine the governmental structure at the national level. It is self-evident that if the Chinese Nationalists want to support their claim to be the sole government of the whole of China, they must maintain a political structure that will at least give an impression of a central government. This is exactly what the Chinese Nationalists have been doing ever since they retreated to Taiwan in 1949. To the political leaders of the ROC, the maintenance of a national government on Taiwan is a necessity, not only to support their claim to be the only legitimate government of the whole of China but also to demonstrate to the Chinese people on Taiwan and elsewhere the determination of the government of the ROC to return to the mainland.

Thus one finds on the island province of Taiwan a nearly complete structure of national government that is organized in accordance with a constitution adopted in the winter of 1946. According to the 1946 constitution of the Republic of China, the political power of the people is vested in the National Assembly, which is composed of delegates elected on geographical and occupational bases.[39] Representatives in the National Assembly exercise on the behalf of their constituents political powers that include the election and recall of the president and vice president, amendment of the constitution, and approval of proposed constitutional amendments submitted by the Legislative Yüan or by popular referendum.

The tenure of the delegates to the National Assembly is six years. But since the relocation of the central government to Taiwan in 1949, no national election can have been held on the mainland. As a result, the overwhelming majority of the delegates in the National Assembly on Taiwan are still those who were elected by the people

FIGURE 3.1

Organization Chart of the Government of the Republic of China

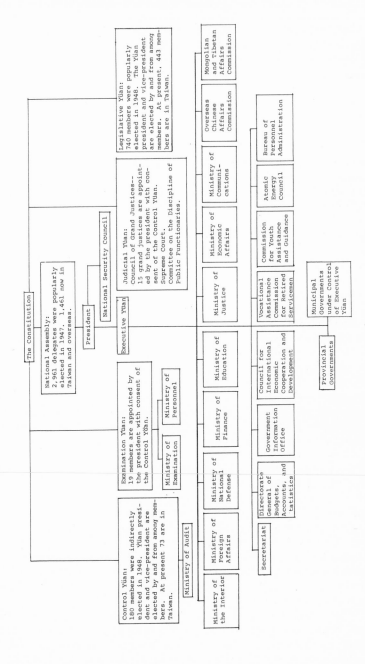

Source: China Yearbook, 1969-70 (Taipei: China Publishing Co., 1970), p. 114.

on the mainland more than 20 years ago. This of course has created serious problems of circulation of political elites.

Of the various functions and powers of the National Assembly, the election of president and vice-president is probably the most important. The president and the vice-president are chosen on separate ballots for a term of six years and, according to Article 47 of the constitution, may be reelected only to a second term. In 1960, however, a temporary provision was introduced and adopted by the National Assembly that stated that during the period of "Communist rebellion," the president and vice-president may be reelected without regard to the original two-term restriction. It is through this special provision that Chiang Kai-shek has been repeatedly elected to the presidency. He is now in his fifth term, which will end in 1978.

One of the special features of governmental structures of the ROC is the Wu-ch'üan (five-power) arrangement. Devised by Dr. Sun Yat-sen, this scheme calls for the separation of governmental powers into five branches: the executive, the legislative, the judicial, the examinational, and the control. A yüan (house) was created to be in charge of each of these five powers. The Examination Yüan performs the functions of the civil-service examination system of traditional China in selecting capable individuals to fill various positions in the administration of the government. The Control Yüan is an organization created to perpetuate the function of the censorate system of imperial China.

Since the members of the Legislative Yüan, Control Yüan, and National Assembly are all elected directly or indirectly by the people, there have been conflicting claims as to which of these three branches is the equivalent of parliament in Western nations. This problem was resolved by a decision made by the Council of Grand Justices in 1957, which held that National Assembly, the Legislative Yüan, and the Control Yüan together constitute the equivalent of the parliament or congress in Western democracies.[40]

According to the 1946 constitution, the president is the head of state of the Republic of China. He represents the state in foreign relations and at all state functions. He is the commander-in-chief of the armed forces. The president promulgates laws and issues mandates with the countersignature of the premier of the Executive Yüan. He also has the powers of declaring war and making peace; appointing and removing, in accordance with law, officials in the civil service and the officers in the armed forces; and granting amnesties.[41]

In February, 1967, the National Security Council was established by adopting an amendment of the temporary provisions of the constitution. With the president as the ex officio chairman, the Council is composed of the vice-president, the presidential secretary-general, the chief-of-staff to the president, the chairman and vice-chairman

of the Strategy Advisory Committee of the Office of the President,
the premier and vice-premier of the Executive Yüan, minister of
national defense, foreign minister, finance minister, minister of economic affairs, the chief of the general staff, the secretary-general
of the National Security Council, and others designated by the president.[42] The major function of the Council is to be in charge of research, design, coordination, supervision, and evaluation of the policy-
making process at the national level, especially in connection with
the "suppression of Communists."

Although the constitution and the outward structure of the central
government of the ROC give one an impression of a presidential
instead of a cabinet system, the head of the Executive Yüan, who is
the equivalent of the prime minister (premier) in Western nations,
actually has the potential of developing into a really powerful figure
in the national government. For example, the constitution requires
that the executive orders of the president have the cosignature of the
premier to become effective. A powerful head of the Executive Yüan
certainly can make good use of the provision to exert his influence
on the president. Furthermore, there is no tenure specification for
the head of the Executive Yüan. All that is needed is nomination by
the president and approval by the members of the Legislative Yüan.
Here again, the head of the Executive Yüan (premier) can become a
powerful figure in the central government if he can command the
support of the majority of the members of the Legislative Yüan. The
fact that the office of the head of the Executive Yüan has not become
more important has been due more to the overwhelming influence
and respect commanded by President Chiang Kai-shek than to the
limitations stated in the constitution.

In regard to political structure at the provincial level, self-
government has been fully practiced on Taiwan since 1951. The most
important development of provincial self-rule was the inauguration
of the Taiwan Provincial Assembly on December 11, 1951, replacing
the Provincial Council. On August 26, 1959, the Executive Yüan
promulgated the Organic Law of the Taiwan Provincial Assembly, and
the Provisional Taiwan Provincial Assembly became the first Taiwan
Provincial Assembly. The current Provincial Assembly was elected
by popular vote on April 21, 1968. Its 71 members have a tenure of
four years. There is no limit on the terms that a member of the
Provincial Assembly may serve.[43]

The Provincial Assembly is the legislative body of the provincial
government. The provincial government, which is headed by a governor
appointed by the national government, is responsible to the Provincial
Assembly. The annual budget of the provincial government must be
approved by the Assembly; so must the laws and bills. While it is
in session, members of the Assembly can call upon officials in the

provincial administration to testify and answer questions in regard
to policies and decisions made by the provincial government.[44]

At the local level, the Province of Taiwan is divided into 16
counties, each having its own county government and council. All
county magistrates and city mayors, with the exception of that of Taipei
which was made into a special municipality under the direct jurisdiction of the Executive Yüan in 1967, are elected by the people. The
term of office is four years, as is that of members of the county and
city councils. The overwhelming majority of the mayors, county
magistrates, and city and county council members are natives of
Taiwan.[45]

Before the city of Taipei became a special municipality in 1967,
its mayor and city assemblymen had been elected by popular vote.
Since it assumed the status of a special municipality, which elevated
it to the level of a province, the mayor has been appointed by the
Executive Yüan, while the city councilmen continue to be elected by
the people. Henry Kao, a Taiwanese who had been repeatedly elected
to the mayoralty as an independent by the residents of Taipei, is now
the mayor of the city.[46]

Political Integration

One of the problems of major concern to the Chinese Nationalists
on Taiwan is that of political integration. According to Karl W.
Deutsch, the term "political integration" refers to the processes that
generate unifying habits and institutions, which in turn produce a
stable expectation of peace among the participating units or groups.[47]
Among the conditions that are needed to reach such an integrative
state are the sharing of a common "memory," mutual interdependence,
and mutual responsiveness among the participating groups.[48]

When the government of the ROC took over Taiwan from Japan
in 1945, it was recovering a former territory of China that had been
ceded to Japan through the Shimonoseki Treaty, signed in 1895. According to most political observers, including those who were critical
of the Chinese Nationalists, the native Taiwanese were longing for
the restoration of Taiwan to China and welcomed the coming of
government officials and armed forces of the ROC.[49]

In terms of cultural heritage, the Taiwanese were still very
much within the Chinese sociocultural system when the island was
restored to China. In Deutsch's term, the Taiwanese still shared a
"common memory" with the mainland Chinese despite 50 years of
Japanese rule. The Japanese had tried very hard to Japanize the
Chinese people on the island, without very much success. Other
than leaving some marks on the food, house construction, and objets

d'art, the Japanese had failed to alter the dominating Chinese socio-cultural pattern on the island.[50]

A recent study conducted by Sheldon Appleton clearly demonstrated that after 50 years of Japanese occupation, the native Taiwanese, as represented by the college students in his survey sample, remained "essentially Chinese in their social and political outlooks as well as in their ancestry."[51] But this is not to say that there have not been provincial feelings between the native Taiwanese and the mainlanders. In fact, 25 years after the restoration of Taiwan to China, there is still provincialism among both the mainlanders and the Taiwanese.

In order to understand the problems between the mainlanders and the Taiwanese, a discussion of the population composition on Taiwan is necessary. Of the 14.8 million people on Taiwan, 210,000 are aborigines of Malay origin.[52] They had settled before the Chinese migrated in large numbers after the 17th century. These aborigines, who live primarily in the mountain regions, have been increasingly sinolized through free but compulsory education, intermarriage with the Chinese, and the opening up of the mountainous regions by the building of the transisland highway.[53] Although the aborigines are full-fledged citizens of the ROC, their political influence is rather limited because of their small percentage in the total population of Taiwan.

Among the people of Chinese (Han) origin, two major groups can be differentiated. The first group, which is generally called the "native Taiwanese," are the offspring of earlier Chinese migrants who came to Taiwan from Fukien and Kwangtung provinces. Though the Chinese started migrating to Taiwan as early as the 14th century, the largest waves of migration occurred after the 17 century.

Of the 14.8 million population on Taiwan, 86.4 percent are identified as "native Taiwanese." Among the Taiwanese, approximately 85 percent are of Fukienese origin and 15 percent are of Kwangtung origin.[54] Though there have been differences and frictions between the Fukien and Kwangtung groups, the Taiwanese generally consider Taiwan their permanent home and have strong ties with the social and economic life of the island.

The "mainlanders," who constitute about 13.6 percent of the population, came to Taiwan after World War II. They arrived in large numbers in 1949, when the Chinese Communists were taking over the mainland. Among them were government officials, industrialists, businessmen, professors and teachers, engineers, and officers, as well as soldiers.[55] Though a burden to the social and economic institutions at first, the mainlanders have made significant contributions to the social, economic, and political development on Taiwan.

There are several discernible differences between the main-landers and Taiwanese. First of all, the overwhelming majority of the mainlanders live in the large urban centers of Taiwan, while the Taiwanese stay mainly in smaller towns and villages. The Taiwanese are engaged in the agricultural, commercial, and fishing sectors of Taiwan's economy, whereas the mainlanders are employed mainly in government, military, and academic circles. In addition, the mainlanders use Mandarin, which is the official spoken language, as their common language, while the Taiwanese speak either a southern Fukienese or Hakka dialect. All of these differences have contributed to the feeling of provincialism between these two groups.

The existence of provincial feelings between the Taiwanese and mainlanders has been exploited by dissenting political groups that advocate an independent Formosa, separate from China. The beginning of the so-called Formosan Independence Movement can be traced to February 28, 1947, when a group of Taiwanese rebelled against the Nationalist authority headed by an incompetent and corrupt governor-general who was later executed for pro-communist activities. Reports on the nature and processes of the Erh Erh Pa [February 28] Incident vary greatly, depending on the political orientation of the writer and the sources used.[56] Nevertheless, all reports have taken note of a single fact, the existence of friction between some Taiwanese and mainlanders and its disastrous manifestation in violent acts during the February 28 Incident.

The Erh Erh Pa Incident and the provincial feelings between the mainlanders and Taiwanese have been used by anti-Nationalist Taiwanese to form the Formosan Independence Movement.[57] Generally speaking, three types of arguments have been offered by the members of the Formosan Independence Movement (henceforth FIM) to support their cause. The first is that the "Formosans," meaning the Taiwanese who had settled on the island before 1945, are the "natives" of Taiwan.* The "Chinese," meaning the mainlanders who came to Taiwan in and after 1945, are "aliens" having conspicuous differences from the Formosans in terms of language, customs, and social and political style.[58] It is, therefore, the natural right and obligation of the Formosan people to arouse their "nationalism" and to overthrow the "alien Chinese rule" on the island.[59]

Among Westerners who have very limited knowledge of the history and the sociocultural background of the Taiwanese society,

---

*Members of the FIM have deliberately tried to avoid using the term "Taiwanese," which is more commonly used in China, to refer to the natives of Taiwan. Instead, they have insisted on using the term "Formosans," which was first used by the Portuguese to name the inhabitants on the island.

this type of argument may be able to win some sympathy. But to any-one who knows the background of the Chinese population on Taiwan and its persistence in maintaining the social structure and cultural heritage inherited from the Chinese mainland, the argument is very weak indeed.

A second argument offered by people in the FIM is that although both the mainlanders and the Taiwanese are of Chinese origin, the 50-year rule of the Japanese on Taiwan has generated enough social, cultural, and political changes on the island to make it a society distinctly different from the one on the mainland. Consequently, a different kind of identity and self-awareness has been developed among the native Taiwanese, which in turn warrants the establishment of an independent political system. This argument is especially appealing to Americans, whose ancestors broke their ties with England through a revolution after they had developed a new identity among the 13 colonies.

The third kind of argument centers on the "undetermined" status of Taiwan under international law. Relying on the opinions of certain Western scholars that the legal status of Taiwan is "undetermined,"[60] many of the participants in the FIM contend that the future status of Taiwan should be decided by a plebescite held among the residents of the island.[61] It has further been asserted that once an "independent" Formosan government is formed after a plebiscite, it would be diffi-cult for Peking to claim Taiwan as part of her territory, thus re-ducing the danger of a Communist invasion.[62]

The idea that the legal status of Taiwan is unsettled has its supporters among a sizable number of officials in the U.S. govern-ment.[63] These officials have hoped that a "two-China" solution, or a "one-China, one-Taiwan" solution, would be made much easier if Taiwan would be accepted as a territory abandoned by Japan but never returned to China. Yet both the Chinese Nationalists and the Chinese Communists have vehemently rejected any questioning of China's sovereignty over Taiwan;[64] they also have repeatedly repudi-ated the "two-China" policy. As for the idea that Communist China would be less hostile to an independent Formosan nation formed through a plebiscite, it probably appeals only to those who are totally uninformed about Mao Tse-tung's firm stand on the territorial integrity of China and his deep distrust of and distaste for "bourgeois democracy."

The real strength and the number of individuals actively involved in the FIM is hard to ascertain, partly because of the diversified nature of its organizations and partly because of the secrecy of their activities. The major areas of their activities are the United States and Japan. In May, 1965, the FIM group in Japan received a crushing blow when its leader, Dr. Thomas Liao, sought and obtained forgiveness from the government of the ROC and returned to Taiwan.[65]

As for the FIM in the United States, its activities seem to have been restricted primarily to college campuses with high concentrations of Taiwanese students. Other than publishing a few magazines advocating their cause and making infrequent demonstrations on special occasions, such as the opening of the U.N. General Assembly, the U.S. branch of the FIM for years took a rather limited, restrained course of action. Yet in recent years, probably because of the impatience with the fruitlessness of the more peaceful methods of promoting their goal, some of the leaders in the FIM movement have begun advocating more violent courses of action.[66] The unsuccessful assassination attempt against Chiang Ching-kuo, vice-premier of the ROC, by a 32-year-old Taiwanese graduate student in New York in April, 1970, seemed to be an indication of this impatience, although FIM spokesmen denied any involvement of their organization in the event.

As the United States is moving toward rapprochement with Communist China, the FIM leaders have found it necessary to reexamine their goals and strategies. One thing has become crystal clear: even if the so-called independent Formosan nation were established, it would not be able to survive without the firm support of the United States. Yet given the fact that the United States is currently eager to improve relations with the Chinese Communists, who probably will tolerate better a hostile but nevertheless Chinese polity on Taiwan than a separatist Formosan state, it is most unlikely that Washington will get entangled in such a new political development on Taiwan.

Most recently, the Chinese Communists have made some efforts to co-opt the FIM leaders into forming a united front against the Nationalists. An indication of this has been the invitation extended to FIM leaders to speak before the pro-Communist Chinese student conferences, such as the so-called Kuo Shih Ta Hui (conferences on the state of the nation), held, respectively, in late August and early September, 1971, at Providence, Rhode Island, and Ann Arbor, Michigan. But most FIM followers, knowing too well of the utilitarian and manipulative nature of the Communist move, have refused to take any part in these conferences. With the diminishing U.S. interest and influence on Taiwan and a concomitant Chinese Communist political and military pressure on the island, it is not entirely improbable for the FIM to seek reconciliation with the Nationalists on Taiwan and to join in a common struggle against a Communist take-over of that island.

Despite the existence of the separatist FIM in the United States and Japan, there are clear signs of increasing assimilation and integration between the mainlanders and Taiwanese. First, there has been increasing penetration of the rural areas of Taiwan by the mainlanders. Between 1955 and 1965 the mainlander population in the cities increased 70.8 percent; but they had a much higher increase, 213.5 percent, in the villages. The percentage of the increase of the mainlanders in the aborigine areas was even higher, reaching 485.2 percent.[67] As a result, the division between the mainlanders and Taiwanese in urban-rural terms was substantially reduced. Moreover, intermarriage between mainlanders and Taiwanese, especially between retired mainlander soldiers and Taiwanese or aborigine girls, has become commonplace, resulting in an increasing number of children of mainlander-Taiwanese parentage.[68] In a survey conducted among college students on Taiwan in June, 1971, it was revealed that the overwhelming majority would not oppose their sisters' and brothers' marrying into either of the major provincial groups on the island.[69]

A third element that has contributed to the goodwill between the mainlanders and Taiwanese has been a highly successful land reform peacefully carried out on Taiwan by the government of the ROC. Despite the accusation by the members of the FIM that the land reform was intended to destroy the power base of the traditional landowning elite on Taiwan, the program has greatly benefited the overwhelming majority of Taiwanese farmers.[70] The Chinese Nationalists' success in the land reform program has been widely accepted as one of the major factors in sustaining political stability on the island.

The last but not least important factor that has promoted political integration on Taiwan is the process of political socialization that the government of the ROC has carried out on the island since 1945.[71] The major instrument of political socialization employed by the Nationalists has been the Kuo-Yü Yün-tung (National Language Movement). This movement consists of teaching standardized Mandarin both to the youth of school age and to the adult Taiwanese population. It also includes intensified courses on Chinese history and geography in schools at all levels. Emphasis is placed on discussion of the process of the Republican Revolution, the role played by Dr. Sun Yat-sen and Generalissimo Chiang Kai-shek in that revolution, the resistance to Japanese aggression, the emergence of the Chinese Communists and their occupation of the Chinese Mainland, and the national goal of counterattack and reunification.

By all indications the National Language Movement has been a great success. The overwhelming majority of the Taiwanese, especially those living in the cities, can now speak, or at least understand, Mandarin, thus eliminating the language barriers between the Taiwanese and the mainlanders. The teaching of Chinese history and geography to Taiwanese students also seems to have produced strong identification with the cultural and political norms of traditional China and significantly to have reduced, if not eliminated, the differences of attitudes between the mainland and Taiwanese youth.[72]

Political Participation

Large-scale political participation by the people of Taiwan in the political process did not occur until after the Chinese Nationalists recovered the island from the Japanese colonial administration. During the 50-year Japanese rule, very few of the Taiwanese had any chance to participate in government and politics. This restrictive policy was applied even to the lowest echelons of the power structure. The Japanese governor-general on Taiwan relied primarily on his own police and administrators to rule the people of the island.[73] Practically all positions of any political significance in the Japanese colonial government, from governor-general down to the headmaster of a village school, were filled by Japanese. "The arbitrary nature of this kind of rule obviously bred contempt and discontent," observed a Japanese scholar.[74]

With the restoration of Taiwan to China in 1945, nearly 480,000 Japanese on the island were repatriated. Of these, 157,000 were military personnel; the remainder were civilians, the overwhelming majority of whom had held positions in the government, transportation, and business.[75] After the departure of the Japanese, their political and occupational positions were largely taken over by the native Taiwanese, especially those in the small cities, counties, and villages.

In addition to transferring the administrative positions originally held by the Japanese to the native Taiwanese, the government of the ROC also made genuine efforts to enlarge the role of Taiwanese participation in politics at the provincial level by holding regular popular elections. Since 1950, with the exception of the governor, who is appointed by the Executive Yüan, all chief executive officials and members of the legislative assemblies at the provincial and local levels have been chosen by direct vote of the people.[76] Nearly all the victors in provincial and local elections have been native Taiwanese.[77]

The Chinese Nationalist Party, Kuomintang (henceforth KMT), the ruling political party on Taiwan, has played an active role in encouraging Taiwanese participation in provincial and local politics.* Efforts have been made by party officials to recruit capable and

---

*Other than the KMT, there are two minor parties in the ROC. One is the Young China Party; the other is the China Democratic Socialist Party. These two parties have representation in the legislative bodies of the ROC at both the national and the provincial level. Members of these two parties have played an active, though minor, role in politics on Taiwan.

popular local leaders into the KMT and later to nominate them as
party candidates to compete with independents and nominees of other
parties. As a result, the party has been able to capture the largest
share of elective offices at all levels. For instance, in 1964 the KMT
controlled 82.43 percent of the seats in the Provincial Assembly and
73.87 percent of those in county and municipal assemblies. Moreover,
in the same year KMT members made up 81 percent of the county
magistrates and mayors of the municipalities, and 92.48 percent of
the heads of towns and villages.[78]

Besides the active encouragement from the KMT, land reform
and its socioeconomic effects on the population have been important
factors in the increasing interest and participation in politics by the
native Taiwanese, particularly those in the rural areas. Before the
land reform, the landlords on Taiwan, like the landlords in most parts
of traditional China, had been the holders of political power in the
rural areas. Their political power was derived both from their wealth
and from their status as an educated elite.[79] After the land was
gradually taken over by the government of the ROC and given to the
farmers, the landlords' dominant social status in the rural areas
began to diminish. With the bulk of their wealth, which was originally
invested in land, converted into government stocks and bonds, the
landlords gradually lost interest in local politics.

The landowning farmers, on the other hand, became increasingly
interested in local affairs for a variety of reasons, such as taxation,
irrigation, construction of roads, and public education for their children. Before long, the political positions previously held by landlords
were gradually passed on to former tenants or their children, who
had received much more education than their parents.[80] A peaceful
transformation of the power structure in rural Taiwan was thus completed.

A third factor that has contributed to the increasing level of
political participation on Taiwan is the emergence of many professional and voluntary associations. Foremost among these associations is the farmers' association. Formed by the Sino-American
Joint Commission on Rural Reconstruction (JCRR) with the support
and assistance of the KMT organizations, the farmers' association
has proved to be a most effective training ground for its members
to start a political career. Many of the former officials of the
farmers' association have won provincial and local elections and
have become members of the provincial assembly, county magistrates,
and city mayors.[81]

Besides the farmers' association, a great number of labor,
business, and other types of professional associations have started
to mushroom on Taiwan as the island becomes an increasingly complex industrial society. The political role of these associations, or

interest groups in the Western sense, is less prominent than the farmers' association. Yet judging by the increasing concern of the Nationalist government over the scandals created by these organizations in their lobbying activities with relation to the Legislative Yüan, Control Yüan, and National Assembly, we have reason to believe that they have played a significant role in the legislative process of these bodies.[82] It will be a matter of time before various business and professional organizations can obtain a major and even legalized role in the political process on Taiwan.

In contrast with the high degree of political participation at the provincial and local levels, the picture at the national level is less impressive. Here one finds that the Chinese Nationalists have been too limited by their political ideology and their two-layer political structure to allow a higher degree of participation.

Ever since their retreat to Taiwan, the Chinese Nationalists have recognized the necessity to broaden the membership of the political elite so as to widen their base of popular support. Yet they have also been painfully aware that the recruitment of a large number of local political leaders, be they mainlanders or Taiwanese, will unavoidably tarnish the image of the Nationalist political elite as the representatives of all the people of China. In short, it is a matter of securing political legitimacy for the government of the ROC to maintain a "national look" for the membership of the highest-level political elite. This naturally has led to a stagnation in the circulation of the political elite at the national level.[83]

The stagnation in elite circulation has been most keenly felt in three representative bodies of the central government of the ROC: the National Assembly, the Legislative Yüan, and the Control Yüan. According to a recent study, of the 2,961 National Assembly members elected by the people on the mainland in 1947, only 1,392 are now in Taiwan.[84] Of the 759 members of the Legislative Yüan elected on the mainland, 434 remain. As for the Control Yüan, its membership has decreased from 180 in 1949 to 69 in April, 1971.[85]

Two major reasons contributed to this decline of the membership in the above-mentioned representative bodies of the central government of the ROC. The first was the failure of a considerable number of members of these organs to come to Taiwan with the Nationalist government. Yet a more important factor was simply loss of the delegates through aging and death. A check of the average age of the members of these three representative organs reveals a rather disquieting picture. For instance, the average age of the members of the National Assembly in April, 1970, was more than 65. That of the members of the Legislative Yüan was approaching 65 in 1970. As for the members of the Control Yüan, their average age was more than 70 in the same year.[86] Looking at these figures, one must agree that as far as members of the national representative bodies are concerned, the Nationalist political leadership is indeed composed of an aging elite.

If the composition of the elite in the legislative bodies is somewhat disturbing, that of the executive branch of the central government in Taiwan is not much better. Until very recently the average age of the members of the cabinet (Executive Yüan) was constantly on the rise. In 1950 their average age was around 50. This figure increased to more than 60 in the early 1960's. In July, 1970, the average age of the cabinet was 63, ranging from 51 to 70.[87] Aside from the executive branch of the government, the age composition of the high-ranking political leaders in the KMT demonstrated a similar trend. By April, 1969, the average age of the members of the Tenth Central Committee of the KMT reached 60, which was only slightly lower than that of the cabinet members.[88]

The Chinese Nationalists are not unaware of the problem of the aging among the political elite at the national level. Serious efforts have been made in recent years to bring capable and younger men into the various branches of the national government as well as of the KMT party echelons. Taking the cabinet as an example, most the appointees to this highest executive decision-making organ after 1969 were substantially younger than those appointed before 1969. The late minister of economic affairs, T'ao Sheng-yang, was only 49 years old when he was appointed. His successor, Chang Chi-cheng, was 50 years old.[89]

A most significant reshuffling of the cabinet occurred when Chiang Ching-kuo became the premier, or the head of the Executive Yüan, in May, 1972. Succeeding C. K. Yen, who was reelected to the post of vice-president along with the reelection of Chiang Kai-shek for a fifth term as president in March, 1972, Premier Chiang Ching-kuo made drastic moves in the appointment of members of the new cabinet. Of the 23 members of the new cabinet, 13 were new appointees. Furthermore, six native Taiwanese were given cabinet positions, including the vice-premiership and the important post of minister of interior affairs. This was indeed an important breakthrough for Taiwanese participation in the decision-making process at the national level.[90]

In addition to the recruitment of a substantial number of native Taiwanese, another significant feature of the new cabinet lies in the age composition of its members. The average age of the members of the newly formed cabinet is 61.19, two years younger than that of the members of the cabinet in 1970. More important, nine of new appointees to the cabinet are younger than 60, with the youngest being 49 years old. Also, none of the members is over 70 years.[91]

Concomitant with the changes in the Executive Yüan, important measures toward party reform were also being taken by the leader of the KMT. On May 15, Dr. Chang Pao-shu, secretary-general of the Central Committee of the KMT, announced the plan for the reorganization of the party structure at the national level. Essentially, the reorganization plan involves a change in the subdivision of the Central Committee, from that of divisions (Tsu) to that of committees (Wei-yuan-hui). The purpose of the reorganization is to make the national party structure more efficient and flexible, so that it can respond quickly to the rapidly changing domestic and international environment. Like the reshuffling of the cabinet, the reorganization of the Central Committee brought more Taiwanese and younger men into the top-ranking positions. As a result of the reorganization process, two of the three deputy secretaries-general of the Central Committee are native Taiwanese; so is the newly appointed head of the Secretariat of the Central Committee.[92]

It must be pointed out, however, that important changes had already taken place in the composition of the elite in the KMT even before the recent reorganization. For instance, there had been a significant decrease in the age average of the KMT party elite. At the Tenth National Congress of the KMT, held in 1969, the average age of the delegates was 46, which compares rather favorably with the average age of 48 of the delegates to the Ninth Party Congress, held in 1963.[93] Moreover, the average age of the members of the Central Standing Committee, the highest ruling echelon of the party hierarchy, dropped from 63 in 1967 to 60 in 1969. The six new members of the Central Standing Committee, who emerged in 1969, had an average age of 56, which was nine years younger than those who retired that year.[94]

In comparison with the problem of elite circulation in the ruling party and in the executive branch of the central government, the problem of rejuvenation of the membership of the National Assembly, the Legislative Yüan, and the Control Yüan is far more difficult for the Chinese Nationalists to resolve. But the leaders of the ROC have become increasingly aware in recent years that decisive measures must be taken to preserve and to revitalize these representative bodies. The first breakthrough in the composition of the membership of the three above-mentioned representative bodies came in 1966, when the National Assembly amended the constitution to authorize the president of the ROC to hold the first supplementary national election of Min-I-Tai-Piao (people's representatives) on Taiwan since the government moved to that island in 1949. The election was held in December 1963 and 15 new members were elected to the National Assembly; 11 new members to the Legislative Yüan; and 2 new members to the Control Yüan.[95]

At the time of this writing, the government of the ROC is in the process of holding another supplementary national election on Taiwan and in other "free areas," meaning other territories under the Nationalist control, as well as in overseas Chinese communities. According to the announcement made by the president on June 30, 1972, an additional 53 members of the National Assembly, 51 members of the Legislative Yüan, and 15 new members of the Control Yüan will be chosen through a supplementary national election to be held toward the end of the year. These newly elected representatives of the people will join the various representative bodies on February 1, 1973.[96] Although this measure taken by the government still falls short of the expectation of those young intellectuals demanding a complete reelection of all members of the national representative bodies, it at least has overcome a problem troubling the Chinese Nationalists ever since they withdrew to Taiwan.[97]

Looking into the future, we may offer several observations in regard to the pattern of political participation on Taiwan. First, the political leaders of the ROC will most likely continue their policy of bringing younger people, especially the Western-trained intellectuals with organizational and technological skills, into the higher echelons of the government and the ruling party. Second, they will also continue bringing large numbers of native Taiwanese into all levels of governmental agencies. In the short run this may even be done in such a way as to restrict temporarily the chances of equally or more qualified mainland youth on Taiwan to enter the political elite.[98] Finally, with mounting demand from all sectors of the population on Taiwan for a greater voice in the operation of the national government, the government of the ROC under the leadership of Chiang Ching-kuo will have to develop skillful yet thorough ways to provide for a complete reelection of the members of the National Assembly, Legislative Yüan, and Control Yüan.*

---

*The new election system adopted by the National Assembly in the spring of 1972 provides that for the original members of the three national representative bodies elected on the Chinese mainland in 1947 and those elected in the 1969 supplementary national election will continue to serve in these bodies. Under the current arrangements these original members of the various representative bodies have in fact lifetime tenure. On the other hand, those members who are to be elected in the December 1972 elections are subject to reelection in accordance with the tenure stipulated in the constitution.

CONCLUSIONS

The purpose of this chapter has been to review and evaluate the process of political development in the ROC on Taiwan. Following a brief review of the history of the ROC since 1949, a discussion of each of the four aspects of political development on Taiwan—political ideology, political structure, political integration, and political participation—has been presented. From these discussions one may obtain some idea of the nature of the political system on Taiwan, its inherent limitations and resultant problems, and the achievements it has made under very trying internal and external circumstances.

It is not easy to come to an objective, detached assessment of the successes or failures of the ROC. Like most of the analyses of the political development of China, discussion on Taiwan has been in most cases colored with emotions and preconceived opinions.[99] Those scholars who are basically antagonistic to the Chinese Nationalists tend to emphasize the failures of the Nationalists before 1949, the "insignificant" size of Taiwan in terms of population and territorial area compared with Communist China, and the authoritarian elements of Nationalist rule on the island. Individuals who are basically sympathetic to the Nationalist cause would stress the land reform, the achievements in economic development, the effort made by the Chinese Nationalists to help the refugees escaping from the Chinese mainland, and the ROC's technical aid to the developing nations.

Whatever orientation a scholar may have, one thing he definitely would like to avoid is evaluating the Chinese Nationalists' political system on Taiwan by a criterion that is usually used for comparable Western democracies. As Lucian W. Pye points out:

> If we were now to review the twentieth-century experi-
> ences of the Chinese in the light of what we currently
> know about the difficulties of achieving advancement in
> the Afro-Asian world we should have to revise many, if
> not most, of the conventional judgements and evaluations
> of the Chinese.[100]

Pye further argues that if we use the measures of progress currently applied to the analysis of the Afro-Asian countries, we will be able to see the significant achievements made by the Chinese Nationalists in the 1930's and 1940's.[101] Obviously, what Pye has to say about the evaluation of political development in non-Western nations and pre-1940 China can also be applied to the problems of assessing the Nationalist experience on Taiwan. Until very recently Taiwan was a traditional or at most a

transitional society. With all the socioeconomic changes that have
taken place on Taiwan, it may be called a "modernizing" society. We
should therefore assess the success or failure of the ROC as a political
system trying to overcome many problems in modernizing the Chinese
society on the island.

With this in mind, we shall be in a better position to appreciate
the efforts made by the Chinese Nationalists to raise the standard
of living on Taiwan; to encourage native Taiwanese, especially those
in the rural areas, to participate in the political process; and to increase the quantity as well as the quality of education. With the exception of Japan, the degree of political stability and economic prosperity
achieved by the Chinese Nationalists on Taiwan compares rather
favorably with most of the nations in East and Southeast Asia.

Needless to say, the Nationalist political system on Taiwan also
has many limitations and problems. Foremost among its limitations
is its commitment to the recovery of the Chinese mainland from the
Chinese Communists. As previously pointed out, this commitment
has led to a two-layer governmental structure, a defense budget ex-
ceeding half of the national budget, and a sense of frustration.

One may suggest, then, that the Chinese Nationalists be satisfied with what they have achieved on Taiwan and give up their seemingly
ambitious goal of recovering mainland China. The crucial question,
however, would be whether the Chinese Communists would leave them
alone if the Nationalists decided to be content to continue as an island
republic. All the existing evidence and available information clearly
show that the answer from the Chinese Communists would be an
emphatic "NO!"

This is the situation in which the Chinese Nationalists find themselves today. Thus the continued adherence to the goal of national
recovery is not necessarily an aggressive posture against a powerful
adversary but very likely is an indispensable defensive position for
the political system to rally the maximum support from the people
on Taiwan to guard the island against a militant and determined enemy
across the Taiwan Straits.

With the increasing contacts between the Chinese Communists
and the Nixon administration, the Chinese Nationalists have found
themselves operating in an increasingly unfavorable international
environment. The political leaders of the ROC on Taiwan have no
illusions about the difficult and crucial situation they are now facing.
But they also believe that their enemy across the Taiwan Straits is
not as strong as many Western observers have claimed.[102]

By all indications the government and the people of the ROC
are determined to defend the fruits of success produced by their
strenuous efforts on Taiwan. The current crisis seems to have
brought the Nationalist government and the people closer than ever

before. In any case, the Chinese Nationalists are going to take a firm stand on no compromise with the Communists for an indefinite period. In the face of an increasing thaw between their arch enemy and a major ally, a strong sense of mission has developed among the Nationalist leaders. As President Chiang Kai-shek pointed out in a message to the nation:

> We do not mind being the only people who still have faith in anti-Communism and who still have the courage to persist in the struggle against Communism for the cause of freedom and justice. This means that in our hands hangs not only the destiny of the nation, but the security or the destruction of all mankind.[103]

It is with this kind of determination that the Chinese Nationalist leaders have managed to overcome the many crises that they have faced in their stormy career. They further hope they can bring these fruits of success on Taiwan to Mainland China to be shared by their compatriots there someday.

NOTES

1. The current figure on the population of Taiwan is 14,833,012, as reported in Chung-yang jih-pao (Central daily news), international ed., Taipei, July 23, 1971, p. 3.

2. See Joyce Kallgren, "Nationalist China's Armed Forces," in Mark Mancall, ed., Formosa Today (New York: Praeger, 1964), p. 95.

3. The term "political development" has not yet had a commonly accepted definition. For this reason the author has decided to leave it undefined and let the discussions on this topic speak for themselves. For various definitions of political development, see Lucian W. Pye, Aspects of Political Development (Boston: Little, Brown & Co., 1966) pp. 31-48; Samuel P. Huntington, "Political Development and Political Decay," World Politics, XVII, 3 (April 1965), 405-10; and Lucian W. Pye, ed., Communication and Political Development (Princeton, N.J.: Princeton University Press, 1963).

4. See A. Doak Barnett, Communist China and Asia, a Challenge to American Policy (New York: Vintage Books, 1960), p. 389; see also Mancall, ed., Formosa Today, p. 5.

5. See Chen Cheng, Land Reform in Taiwan (Taipei: China Publishing Co., 1961), pp. 66-81; and Martin M. C. Yang,

Socio-Economic Results of Land Reform in Taiwan (Honolulu: East-West Center Press, 1970), passim.

6. Industrialization in the Republic of China (Taipei: Council for International Economic Co-operation and Development, 1969), p. 2.

7. See Sheppard Glass, "Some Aspects of Formosa's Economic Growth," in Mancall, ed., Formosa Today, pp. 68-90; Karl Brandt, "Economic Development: Lessons of Statecraft at Taiwan," Orbis, II, 4 (Winter 1968), 1067-80; Barnett, Communist China and Asia, pp. 397-99; and Conference on Economic Development of Taiwan (Taipei: China Council on Sino-American Cooperation in the Humanities and Social Sciences, 1967), passim.

8. Barnett, Communist China and Asia, p. 411.

9. Republic of China Today (Taipei: Overseas Chinese Publishers, 1969), p. 25; Bernard Gallin, Hsin Hsing, Taiwan: A Chinese Village in Change (Berkeley: University of California Press, 1966), pp. 112-17; and Ts'ai Hung-ching, T'ai-wan nung-ti kai-ke tui she-hui ching-chi ying-hsiang ti yen-chiu (The impact of land reform on the society and economy of Taiwan), Chia-Hsin Research Paper No. 94 (Taipei: Chia-Hsin Cultural Foundation Books, 1967), pp. 72-79.

10. For a detailed account of the Quemoy crisis of 1958, especially the diplomatic entanglement among the United States, Communist China, the ROC, and the Soviet Union, see Kenneth T. Young, Negotiating with the Chinese Communists: The United States Experience, 1953-1967 (New York: McGraw-Hill, 1968), pp. 137-62.

11. Industrialization in the Republic of China, pp. 4-5.

12. Ibid., pp. 24-27.

13. Ibid., p. 29.

14. Ibid., p. 3.

15. See Neil H. Jacoby, U.S. Aid to Taiwan, a Study of Foreign Aid, Self-Help, and Development (New York: Praeger, 1966), pp. 227-37; and Melvin Gurtov, "Taiwan in 1966: Political Rigidity, Economic Growth," Asian Survey, VII, 1 (January 1967), 40-45.

16. Essentials of the Taiwan Provincial Administration (Taichung: Taiwan Provincial Government, 1968), p. 3.

17. Ibid., p. 15.

18. Chung-yang jih-pao, international ed., December 21, 1969, pp. 1, 4.

19. Department of International Organizations, Ministry of Foreign Affairs of the Republic of China, ed., Voting Records on the So-called "Chinese Representation Question" in the United Nations, 1950-1969 (Taipei, 1970).

20. Gurtov, "Taiwan in 1966," p. 42.

21. According to data in Essentials of the Taiwan Provincial Administration (Taichung: Taiwan Provincial Government, 1971), p. 19.

22. Ibid., p. 21.

23. See Sheldon L. Appleton, "Taiwan: Portents of Change," Asian Survey, XI, 1 (January 1971), 71.

24. See Richard Nixon, "United States Foreign Policy for the 1970's, Building for Peace" (February 25, 1971), Department of State Bulletin, LXIV, 1656 (March 22, 1971), 382-84.

25. Ibid.

26. For example, see Teng Kung-hsüan, "A Critique of Nixon Doctrine," Tung-fang tsa-chih (Eastern miscellany), IV, 10 (April 1971), 25-33; John Chung Kuan, "A Review of U.S. Policy to China, 1949-1971," Tung-ya chi-kan (Eastern Asia quarterly), II, 4 (April 1, 1971), 83-111; Shih Keh-ming, "New Arrangements in U.S. Foreign Policy," Lien-ho pao (United daily news), March 11, 1971, p. 2; and Tai T'sao-sheng, "The Background of, and the Reactions to Nixon's State of the World Message," Chung-yang jih-pao, March 1, 1971, p. 2.

27. See Newsweek, LXXVII, 12 (April 12, 1971), 16-17; and LXXVII, 14 (April 26, 1971), 14-22.

28. For a full text of Nixon's announcement of his forthcoming trip to Communist China, see U.S. News and World Report, LXXI, 4 (July 26, 1971), 14.

29. For a discussion on the seating of Communist China in the United Nations, see "Why Majority in U.N. Turn on U.S.," U.S. News and World Report, LXXI, 19 (November 8, 1971), 17-19.

30. Hung-chao Tai, "The Kuomintang and Modernization in Taiwan," in Samuel P. Huntington and Clement A. Moore, eds., Authoritarian Politics in Modern Society, the Dynamics of Established One Party Systems (New York: Basic Books, 1970), pp. 409-11.

31. Ibid.

32. For an English text of the constitution, see China Yearbook, 1969-1970 (Taipei: China Publishing Co., 1970), pp. 695-712.

33. On May 1, 1962, the government of the ROC announced a special defense budget totaling $U.S. 60 million to run through June 30, 1963. A number of newspaper editors in Taipei speculated that the budget was to cover military expenses for a counterattack against the mainland. See Sheppard Glass, "Some Aspect of Formosa's Economic Growth," in Mancall, ed., Formosa Today, pp. 88-89.

34. Chung-yang jih-pao, January 1, 1967, p. 1; quoted in Melvin Gurtov, "Recent Developments on Formosa," The China Quarterly No. 31 (July-September 1967), p. 61.

35. "Declaration of the Tenth National Congress of the Kuomintang (Nationalist Party)," Asian Outlook, IV, 4 (April 6, 1969), p. 11.

36. Ibid., p. 12.

37. Ibid.

38. For a critical review of the problem, see Mark Mancall, "Succession and Myth in Taiwan," Journal of International Affairs, XVIII (1964), 12-20.

39. For an official discription of the government structure at the national level, see China Year Book, 1969-1970, pp. 109-59.

40. China Yearbook, 1968-1969 (Taipei: China Publishing Co., 1969), pp. 104-05.

41. China Year Book, 1969-1970, pp. 120-27.

42. Ibid., p. 127.

43. Ibid., p. 160.

44. Ibid., pp. 163-64.

45. Ibid., pp. 165-76.

46. Ibid., p. 167.

47. Karl W. Deutsch, Political Community at the International Level, Problems of Definition and Measurement (Garden City, N.Y.: Doubleday and Co., 1954), p. 33.

48. See ibid., pp. 34-38; see also K. W. Deutsch, Nationalism and Social Communication, an Inquiry into the Foundation of Nationality (Cambridge, Mass.: The M.I.T. Press, 1955), pp. 60-80; and "Communication Theory and Political Integration," in Philip E. Jacob and James V. Toscano, eds., The Integration of Political Communities (Philadelphia and New York: J. B. Lippincott Co., 1964), pp. 46-74.

49. See Barnett, Communist China and Asia, p. 388; Maurice Meisner, "The Development of Formosan Nationalism," in Mancall, ed., Formosa Today, p. 153; and A. T. Steele, The American People and China (New York: McGraw-Hill, 1966), p. 50.

50. Jean T. Burke, A Study of Existing Social Conditions in the Eight Townships of the Shipmen Reservoir Area (Taoyüan, Taiwan: Chinese-American Joint Commission on Rural Reconstruction, 1962), p. 78.

51. Sheldon Appleton, "Taiwanese and Mainlanders on Taiwan: A Survey of Student Attitudes," The China Quarterly, No. 44 (October-December 1970), p. 56.

52. Twenty-five Years After Taiwan's Restoration to China (Taichung, Taiwan: Government Information Service, 1971), Part III, pp. 60-67.

53. Tung-Ming Lee, A Study on Social Increase of Population in Taiwan (Taichung: Taiwan Population Studies Center, 1968), p. 44.

54. Ibid., p. 19.

55. Ibid., pp. 44, 66.

56. For an official report prepared by the Chinese Nationalists, see The Truth About the February 28, 1947 Incident in Taiwan (Taichung: Historical Research Commission of Taiwan Province, 1967). For some opposite and highly critical accounts of the incident, see George H. Kerr, Formosa Betrayed (Boston: Houghton Mifflin, 1965), passim; and Douglas Mendel, The Politics of Formosan Nationalism (Berkeley and Los Angeles: University of California Press, 1970), pp. 31-41.

57. Most of the literature on the Formosa Independence Movement (FIM) is produced either by the activists in the movement or
by Western scholars, journalists, and former diplomats who are highly
sympathetic to the movement. Consequently, opinions expressed in
their work are often one-sided and highly critical of the Nationalist
rule on Taiwan. For example, see Mendel, The Politics of Formosan
Nationalism. Also see Mancall, ed., Formosa Today; pp. 147-170;
Lung-chu Chen and Harold D. Lasswell, Formosa, China and the
United Nations (New York: St. Martin's Press. 1967); and Kerr,
Formosa Betrayed.

58. Chen and Lasswell, Formosa, China and the United Nations,
p. 193.

59. See, for example, Ong Joktik, "A Formosan's View of the
Formosan Independent Movement," in Mancall, ed., Formosa Today,
pp. 163-70.

60. Arthur H. Dean, "United States Foreign Policy and Formosa,"
Foreign Affairs, XXXIII, 3 (April 1955), 360-75; J. P. Jain, "The
Legal Status of Formosa, a Study of British, Chinese and Indian Views,"
American Journal of International Law, LVII, 1 (January 1963), 25-45;
and Quincy Wright, "The Chinese Recognition Problem," ibid., XLIX,
2 (April 1955), 320-38. For a rebuttal of the opinions of the "undetermined" status of Taiwan, see Ch. 4 of this book.

61. For a discussion on a plebiscite on Taiwan, see Robert P.
Newman, Recognition of Communist China (New York: The Macmillan
Company, 1961), p. 270.

62. E.g., ibid., p. 276.

63. Ibid., pp. 276-78; also Ch. 4 of this book.

64. For the position of Nationalist China on the legal status
of Taiwan, see Shih-cheng Chang, O-kuo tui T'ai Peng chu-ch'üan ti
fa-li i-chü (The legal basis of our country's sovereignty over Taiwan
and Penghu) (Taipei: Chung yang wen wu kung yin she, 1971). For
the position of Communist China on the same issue see Hungdah Chiu,
"A Study of Communist China's Position on the Taiwan Problem,"
Jen Wu, No. 9 (December 10, 1968), pp. 1-5.

65. Melvin Gurtov, "Recent Development on Formosa," The
China Quarterly, No. 31 (July-September 1967), p. 88.

66. See Chen and Lasswell, Formosa, China and the United
Nations, p. 187; Frank Ching, "Broad New Group Seeks Independence
for Taiwan," New York Times, April 21, 1970, p. 2. It should be pointed
out, however, that Thomas Liao represented the older generation of
the FIM leaders. There has been a serious "generation gap" between
Liao's generation and the younger FIM leaders in their 20's and 30's.
For a discussion on this, see Thomas J. Weiss, "Taiwan and U.S.
Policy," Orbis, XII, 4 (Winter 1969), 1165-87.

67. Lee, A Study on Social Increase of Population in Taiwan, p. 69.

68. Ibid., p. 70.

69. Yung Wei, "Political Culture and Socialization on Taiwan: Findings from Interviewing College Students" (unpublished research report).

70. Yang, Socio-Economic Results of Land Reform in Taiwan, pp. 419-550.

71. For discussion on "political socialization," see Herbert H. Hyman, Political Socialization (New York: Free Press, 1959); Kenneth P. Langton, Political Socialization (New York and London: Oxford University Press, 1969); and Richard E. Dawson and Kenneth Prewitt, Political Socialization (Boston: Little, Brown and Co., 1969).

72. See Sheldon Appleton, "Taiwanese and Mainlanders on Taiwan"; and Richard W. Wilson, "A Comparison of Political Attitudes of Taiwanese Children and Mainlander Children on Taiwan," Asian Survey, VIII, 12 (December 1968), 980-1000; and "The Learning of Political Symbols in Chinese Culture," Journal of Asian and African Studies, III (July-October 1968), 246-54.

73. Shinkichi Eto, "An Outline of Formosa History," in Mancall, ed., Formosa Today, pp. 43-58.

74. Ibid., p. 57.

75. Lee, A Study on Social Increase of Population in Taiwan, pp. 35, 41-42.

76. Tai, "The Kuomintang and Modernization in Taiwan," p. 419; also see Ch'ang-ch'üan Hsiang, T'ai-wan ti-fang hsüan-chü chih feng-hsi yu chien-tao (An analysis and review of local elections in Taiwan) (Taipei: The Commercial Press, 1971), pp. 61-68.

77. Mark Plummer, "Taiwan: 'The New Look' in Government," Asian Survey, IX, 1 (January 1969), 18-22.

78. Tai, "The Kuomintang and Modernization in Taiwan," p. 417.

79. For a discussion on the social and political roles of the landowning gentry in traditional China, see Hsiao-tung Fei, Chinese Gentry, Essays in Rural-Urban Relations (Chicago: University of Chicago Press, 1953); and Chung-li Chang, The Chinese Gentry, Studies on Their Role in Nineteenth Century Chinese Society (Seattle: University of Washington Press, 1955).

80. For the changes in the power structure in rural Taiwan, see Yang, Socio-Economic Results of Land Reform in Taiwan, pp. 480-505; and Bernard Gallin, Hein Shing, Taiwan: A Chinese Village in Change (Berkeley: University of California Press, 1966), pp. 112-17.

81. Tai, "The Kuomintang and Modernization in Taiwan," p. 423.

82. See Fu Hu, "Interest Groups and the Control Yüan," in Ch'i-Hsüen Fu et al., Chung-hua ming-kuo chien-ch'a yüan chih yen-chiu (A study of the Control Yüan of the Republic of China), 3 vols. (Taipei: College of Law, National Taiwan University, 1957), III, 969-1028; and Mark Plummer, "Taiwan: Toward a Second Generation of Mainland Rule," Asian Survey, X, 1 (January 1970), 18-24.

83. For a theoretically oriented discussion, see Yung Wei, "Elite Recruitment and Political Development," Chung-yang jih-pao, October 18, 1970, p. 2.

84. Tao-chi Chou, "The Problems of Rejuvenation of Political Representatives of the People at the National Level," Tung-fang tsa-chih, IV, 5 (May 1, 1971), 7-10.

85. Ibid., pp. 7-8.

86. Ibid.

87. See J. Bruce Jacob, "Recent Leadership and Political Trends in Taiwan," The China Quarterly, No. 45 (January-March 1971), 129-54.

88. Ibid., p. 135.

89. Ibid.

90. Han Wei, "New Men and New Spirit in the Executive Yüan," Chung-yang-jih-pao, Taipei, May 30, 1972, p. 1.

91. Ibid.

92. Free China Weekly, XIII, 20 (May 21, 1972), 1.

93. Jacob, "Recent Leadership and Political Trends in Taiwan," p. 134; and Plummer, "Taiwan: Toward a Second Generation of Mainland Rule," p. 18.

94. Jacob, "Recent Leadership and Political Trends in Taiwan."

95. For the regulations governing the by-election and election of additional members to the three representative bodies at the national level in 1969, see China Yearbook, 1969-1970, pp. 713-19.

96. Chung-yang-jih-pao, June 30, 1972, pp. 1, 2,

97. For a discussion on the complete overhaul of the representative bodies at the national level, see Shao-t'ing Chen, "The Problem of the Re-Election of the People's Representatives at the National Level," Ta Hsueh (The intellectual), No. 46 (October 1971), pp. 13-16.

98. According to data released by the government of the ROC in May, 1970, native Taiwanese constituted 61.5 percent of governmental employees, who totaled 260,000. Among the successful candidates on the Civil Service examination in recent years, more than 90 percent were Taiwanese (See Chung-yang jih-pao, May 25, 1970, p. 1.). The effort of the Nationalist government to recruit Taiwanese into the government and party organization at all levels has caused concern and even disappointment among the younger mainlanders. Some of them felt that their elders have overcompensated for their "uneasy feelings" by recruiting a disproportionately large number

of Taiwanese into the higher-level political positions at the sacrifice
of the younger mainlanders. For a sample of this kind of feeling,
see Ching-hang Chang, "Removing Three Barriers of Modernization
(on Taiwan)," Ta Hsüen, IV, 1 (January 1971), 8-10.

99. For a discussion on the emotional elements in China
analysis, see A. T. Steele, The American People and China (New
York: McGraw-Hill, 1966), pp. 1-4.

100. Lucian W. Pye, The Spirit of Chinese Politics, A Psycho-
cultural Study of the Authority Crisis in Political Development,
(Cambridge, Mass.: The M.I.T. Press, 1968), p. 2.

101. Ibid. For the achievements made by the Chinese Nation-
alists in the 1930's, see Paul K. T. Sih, ed., The Strenuous Decade:
China's Nation-Building Efforts, 1927-1937 (New York: St. John's
University Press, 1970).

102. The disclosure of a coup organized by Defense minister
Lin Piao and others and the resurgence of a large number of refugees
fleeing the mainland to Hong Kong have generated much speculation
in the government circles in Taipei. See Chung-yang jih-pao, Septem-
ber 26, 1971, p. 1, and September 27, 1971, p. 1; "Maoist Documents
Reveal: Lin, 13 Others Purged in Armed Coup Attempt," Free China
Weekly, XIII, 15 (April 16, 1972), p. 1; "Mainland Secret Document
Disclosed: Mao Exposed for Lies about Lin Piao Death," Free China
Weekly, XIII, 32 (August 13, 1972), p. 2; "Refugees Reach Highest
Level Since 1962," Free China Weekly, XIII, 30 (July 30, 1972), p. 2.

103. See Chiang Kai-shek, "The Stand of Our Nation and the
Spirit of Our People" (a speech delivered at the National Security
Council on June 15, 1971), Free China Weekly, XII, 24 (June 20, 1971),
2. Similar mission-like feelings can also be found in two recent
interviews Western reporters had with Chow Shu-kai, former foreign
minister of the ROC, and James C. H. Shen, the ROC's ambassador
to the United States. See Hugh Sidey, "Asia Feels 'The Nixon Shock,'"
Life, LXXI, 12 (September 17, 1971), p. 4; and "What Now for Nationalist China," U.S. News and World Report, LXXI, 5 (September 2,
1971), 42-45.

4

CHINA,
THE UNITED STATES,
AND THE QUESTION
OF TAIWAN
Hungdah Chiu

INTRODUCTION

Since 1950 the question of Taiwan (Formosa) has been the most difficult issue in Sino-American relations. Both the ROC and the People's Republic of China (PRC) have insisted that Taiwan is an inalienable part of China and have defined their dispute in terms of who should rule China (including Taiwan). To them the question of Taiwan is a domestic problem that should be solved by the Chinese themselves. From the U.S. point of view, however, the question of Taiwan has an international aspect and should not be solved by the use of force because "technical sovereignty over Taiwan has not yet been settled" and the United States is committed to assisting the ROC government in defending Taiwan against "Communist aggression." In the past 20-odd years each government has been adamant and uncompromising. The two Taiwan Straits crises in 1954 and 1958 almost brought the United States into a major armed conflict with the PRC. Therefore, there is little doubt that the question of Taiwan is one of the most important and difficult problems in current world politics.

Despite the importance of the question of Taiwan and the numerous proposals and studies made by various countries and individual scholars, the question has not yet been adequately analyzed and studied. In particular, most of the proposals and studies on the question of Taiwan have not sufficiently taken into consideration the Chinese side of the story. This chapter seeks to provide a more systematic analysis of the Taiwan question, with special consideration of the Chinese view.

THE ORIGIN OF THE TAIWAN QUESTION

Between 1661 and 1895, Taiwan was administered as a part of China. In 1895, after China was defeated in the First Sino-Japanese

War (1894-95), she ceded Taiwan to Japan by the Treaty of Shimonoseki (Doc. 2). On December 9, 1941, the Chinese government made a formal declaration of war against Japan and declared "that all treaties, conventions, agreements, and contracts regarding relations between China and Japan are and remain null and void" (Doc. 9). On November 26, 1943, at the Cairo Conference, President Chiang Kai-shek of the ROC, President Franklin D. Roosevelt of the United States, and Prime Minister Winston Churchill of Great Britain issued a joint communiqué declaring, inter alia, that "all the territories Japan has stolen from the Chinese, such as Manchuria, Formosa, and the Pescadores, shall be returned to the Republic of China" (Doc. 12).* On November 30, 1943, Marshal Stalin of the Soviet Union approved "the communiqué and all its contents" at the Teheran Conference.[1]

On July 26, 1945, the heads of the governments of the United States, China, and the United Kingdom further declared in the Potsdam Proclamation that "the terms of the Cairo Declaration shall be carried out" (Doc. 14). This proclamation was adhered to by the Soviet Union on August 8, 1945, and by France on August 11, 1945.[2] On September 2, 1945, Japan signed the instrument of surrender and accepted the provisions of the Potsdam Proclamation (Doc. 15).

Pursuant to the provisions of the instrument of surrender, the office of the Supreme Commander for the Allied Powers issued General Order No. 1, directing, inter alia, Japanese forces in China and Formosa to "surrender to Generalissimo Chiang Kai-shek."[3] On September 4, 1945, the National government of the Republic of China issued instructions to Japanese officials on Taiwan to wait for the transfer of power to China (Doc. 16); and on October 25, 1945, China formally took over Taiwan for Japan (Doc. 17). After the ceremony of accepting the Japanese surrender was concluded, the Chinese official in charge of the surrender ceremony formally declared, in the presence of representatives of the United States and other countries:

> From this day forward, Taiwan and the Penghu Archipelago are again incorporated into the territory of China. The territory, people, and administration are now placed under the sovereignty of the National government of the Republic of China. I specifically report this fact—so meaningful in history—to all Chinese compatriots and to the whole world. (Doc. 18)

*At the time of drafting the joint communiqué, the Chinese insisted upon the inclusion of the wording ". . . Formosa . . . shall be restored to the Republic of China." See Doc. 11.

On October 26, 1945, the Office of the Taiwan Administrator announced that Taiwan had become a province of China[4]; and since then the ROC has ruled Taiwan as a province of China. It restored Chinese nationality to all inhabitants of Chinese descent in Taiwan and Penghu on January 12, 1946 (Doc. 19),* applied Chinese law on October 25, 1945, and exercised other sovereign rights over the area. For instance, in 1946 the Province of Taiwan elected delegates to participate in the Constitutional National Assembly that enacted the present constitution of the ROC. In 1947 the Province of Taiwan elected 19 delegates to the National Assembly, 8 delegates to the Legislative Yüan, and 5 delegates to the Control Yüan in accordance with the Chinese constitution.[5]

Before 1949 there was virtually no discussion of the so-called question of Taiwan on the international level, and it was generally agreed that it was an internal Chinese question. Moreover, it was widely expected that the peace treaty with Japan would explicitly provide for the return of Taiwan to China.[6] It was not until mid-1949, when the Chinese Communists were about to take over the Chinese mainland, that the so-called question of Taiwan gradually emerged.

In the summer of 1949, Communist forces occupied Foochow and other coastal areas of Fukien Province opposite Taiwan. At that time there were reports by Western news agencies that the United States might occupy Taiwan and support the Taiwan Independence Movement headed by Liao Wen-yi (Thomas Liao).[7] These reports soon drew sharp response from the Chinese Communists. An authoritative commentary in Jen-min jih-pao (People's daily) of September 4, 1949, denounced the alleged American "conspiracy" to occupy Taiwan and pledged that the People's Liberation Army would cross the Taiwan Straits to liberate the Taiwanese people.[8] The president of the leftist Taiwanese organization Taiwan Democratic Self-Government League, Miss Hsieh Hsueh-hung, issued a strong statement supporting the Chinese Communists' determination to "liberate" Taiwan, (Doc. 21).[9]

On October 1, 1949, the Chinese Communists inaugurated the People's Republic of China. Between October 6 and 8, 1949, the U.S. Department of State convened a conference on Far Eastern problems attended by experts and officials. During the discussion the majority of the participants expressed the view that the Chinese government was "finished" and they were no longer interested in its

---

*On June 22, 1946, the ROC Executive Yüan (cabinet) issued a decree governing the procedure for overseas Taiwanese to resume their Chinese nationality. See Doc. 20.

fate. One participant, John K. Fairbank, said that the United States should not prevent the fall of Taiwan into the hands of the Chinese Communists.[10]

By December 1949 the Chinese Communists had virtually conquered the mainland of China, and the Chinese government removed its seat to Taipei. At that time many American political and military leaders, such as ex-President Herbert Hoover, Secretary of Defense Louis Johnson, General Douglas MacArthur, Senators Robert A. Taft, William F. Knowland, and H. Alexander Smith, and Congressman Walter Judd, advocated the protection of Taiwan against Communist invasion.[11] In late December, 1949, the U.S. Joint Chiefs of Staff, under the chairmanship of General Omar Bradley, recommended helping the Chinese government defend Taiwan and the dispatch of a military mission there.[12] A week later, at a meeting of the National Security Council, President Truman rejected the recommendation of the Joint Chiefs of Staff.[13]

On December 23, 1949, the U.S. Department of State sent a secret memorandum on Taiwan to its diplomatic and consular officers in the Far East, informing them of the hands-off policy of the United States toward Taiwan. The memorandum pointed out that the fall of Taiwan to the Chinese Communist forces was widely expected, the island had no special military significance, the island was politically, geographically, and strategically a part of China, and "Formosa is exclusively the responsibility of the Chinese Government" (Doc. 23).

President Truman made a statement on Taiwan at a press conference on January 5, 1950. He pointed out that, in keeping with the terms of the Cairo Declaration, the Potsdam Proclamation, and the terms of Japanese surrender, "Formosa was surrendered to Generalissimo Chiang Kai-shek, and for the past 4 years, the United States and the other Allied Powers have accepted the exercise of Chinese authority over the Island." The United States, Mr. Truman said, "has no predatory design on Formosa, . . . nor does it have any intention of utilizing its armed forces to interfere in the present situation." Specifically, "the United States Government will not provide military aid or advice to Chinese forces on Formosa" (Doc. 24).

On the same day Secretary of State Acheson elaborated on the President's statement by saying that "when Formosa was made a province of China nobody raised any lawyers' doubts about that" (Doc. 25). Furthermore, in Acheson's address before the National Press Club on January 12, 1950, he pointed out that the American defense perimeter in the western Pacific ran along the Aleutians through Japan and the Ryukyus to the Philippines. Taiwan was left out of this defense line.[14]

On February 9, 1950, in a reply to a series of questions on American policy toward China contained in a House resolution, the

Department of State said that it would be unwise for the United States
to establish a non-Chinese administration on Taiwan because the
United States "do[es] not wish to create a Formosa irredenta issue
about which the Chinese Communists could rally support within China"
(Doc. 26).

In Taiwan, President Chiang Kai-shek resumed his office on
March 1, 1950. The Chinese government was preparing for the final
showdown with the Chinese Communists in the last battle of the Chinese
civil war, presumably to be fought sometime in the summer of 1950.
Across the Taiwan Straits, the Chinese Communists were actively
preparing for the invasion of Taiwan. Early in October, 1949, after
capturing Amoy, the victorious Communists forces immediately
launched an amphibious landing on Quemoy (Kinmen); but all Communist
forces that landed were killed or captured by the Nationalist forces.[15]
This defeat caused the Communists to undertake more serious preparation before attempting another large-scale amphibious action. The
Chinese Communist military authorities certainly recognized the
difficulties they would face in attacking the last stronghold of the
Nationalists. For instance, Communist General Su Yu, addressing
the Third Army, assigned to attack the offshore islands of Fukien and
Taiwan, said:

> The liberation of the islands along the southeast coast,
> especially Taiwan, is an extremely big problem and
> will involve the biggest campaign in the history of modern
> Chinese warfare. . . . [Taiwan] cannot be occupied without
> sufficient transport, suitable equipment, and adequate sup-
> plies. Furthermore, a considerable number of Chiang
> Kai-shek land, sea, and air forces are concentrated there.
> . . . They have built strong defense works, depending on
> the surrounding sea for protection. . . . Only when we have
> fully prepared the material and technical conditions for
> overcoming these difficulties can we smoothly carry out
> this tremendous military assignment and eradicate the
> KMT remnants.[16]

In May, 1950, crossing the 20-mile-wide Chiungchow Straits,
Communist forces successfully landed on Hainan and rapidly captured
the whole island. At that time it was widely expected that the Communist forces would soon invade Taiwan. Then, a month later came
the Korean War and the United States suddenly changed its position
on the question of Taiwan. On June 27, 1950, President Truman
declared that he had "ordered the Seventh Fleet to prevent any attack
on Formosa"; and in the meantime he requested the Chinese government on Taiwan to cease military operations against the mainland.

Concerning the status of Taiwan, Truman also drastically changed his January 5 position, saying that "the determination of the future status of Formosa must await the restoration of security in the Pacific, a peace settlement with Japan, or consideration by the United Nations" (Doc. 27).

An aide-mémoire of the United States to this effect was presented to the Chinese government on the same day by the U.S. chargé d'affaires at Taipei. At an Executive Yüan meeting of the Chinese government on June 28, it was decided to accept in principle the proposal of the U.S. government; and an order was immediately issued to Chinese military authorities to suspend operations against the mainland. In the meantime the ROC foreign minister, George K. C. Yeh, made a statement clarifying the Chinese response to the U.S. change of position on the status of Taiwan. Mr. Yeh said that the U.S. proposal "should in no way alter the status of Formosa as envisaged in the Cairo Declaration, nor should it in any way affect China's authority over Formosa." Moreover, the statement said that in accepting the American proposals, the Chinese government "does not intend to depart from its dual policy of resistance against the aggression of International Communism and the maintenance of the territorial integrity of China" (Doc. 28).

Needless to say, the U.S. decision to intervene in the Taiwan situation would compel the PRC to delay its military campaign to "liberate" Taiwan, and therefore the PRC's response to the U.S. action was most unfavorable. On June 28 Mao Tse-tung, referring to Truman's January 5 statement, denounced the U.S. action as an "open exposure" of its "imperialist face" (Doc. 29).

Chou En-lai, premier and foreign minister of the PRC, also declared on behalf of the PRC that Truman's statement and the American action "constitute armed aggression against the territory of China and are a gross violation of the United Nations Charter." Moreover, Chou stated that "no matter what obstructive action U.S. imperialists may take, the fact that Taiwan is part of China will remain unchanged forever" and that "all the people of our country will certainly fight as one man and to the end to liberate Taiwan" (Doc. 30).

Since June 27, 1950, when President Truman changed the American position on Taiwan, the question of Taiwan has become a major issue in international politics. It has affected almost every facet of the PRC's foreign relations.

THE QUESTION OF TAIWAN AT THE
UNITED NATIONS, 1950-51

Soon after the establishment of the PRC on October 1, 1949, it demanded to be seated immediately in the United Nations, especially

the Security Council and the General Assembly. However, at that time
the majority of the members of the United Nations still recognized the
government of the ROC as representing China in this world body. As
a result, when the Korean War broke out, the PRC was not in the United
Nations. Although outside the United Nations, the PRC clearly recognized the importance of that organization in international relations.
Therefore, on July 6, 1950, ten days after Truman's dispatch of the
Seventh Fleet to the Taiwan Straits, PRC Premier and Foreign Minister
Chou En-lai sent a cablegram to U.N. Secretary-General Trygve Lie
saying that the U.S. action constituted "an act of open aggression
which thoroughly violates the principle of the United Nations Charter
forbidding any member to use force against the territorial integrity
or political independence of any other state." The cablegram further
stated that "by keeping silent on this act of open aggression of the
United States government, the Security Council and the Secretary-
General of the United Nations have foregone their functions and duties
of upholding world peace. . . ."[17]

On August 24, 1950, Chou sent another cablegram to the president
of the Security Council and secretary-general of the United Nations,
formally accusing the United States of armed aggression and requesting
the Council to take action against the United States (Doc. 31). On August
29, 1950, the Security Council, at its 592nd meeting, decided to include
the PRC's accusation in its agenda under the title "Complaint of armed
invasion of Taiwan (Formosa)" by seven votes to two (China and Cuba),
with one abstention (Egypt) and one member not participating (Yugoslavia). The representative of the ROC strongly opposed the inclusion
of the item on the agenda, primarily on the ground that the ROC
government, being in effective control and administration of the island
of Taiwan, "knows of no aggression on the part of the United States."[18]

On September 17, 1950, Chou En-lai again cabled the Security
Council, stating that, as "the sole legal government representing the
Chinese people, and being the accuser in the case," his government
had the right and necessity to send its delegation to attend and participate in the proceedings of the Security Council.[19] The Security
Council adopted a resolution on September 29 to invite the representative of the PRC to attend its meetings held after November 15
concerning the discussion of the agenda item "Complaint of armed
invasion of Taiwan (Formosa)."[20]

On October 23, 1950, the PRC accepted the invitation of the
Council.[21] On November 27 the Council decided to consider the agenda
item "Complaint of armed invasion of Taiwan (Formosa)," and on the
same day a representative of the PRC took his seat at the Council
table.[22]

The next day PRC representative Wu Hsiu-chuan made a lengthy
speech denouncing the U.S. aggression against Taiwan. He categorically

rejected the U.S. view that the status of Taiwan "is undetermined." The status of Taiwan as an integral part of China, he stated, was clearly reflected in the Cairo Declaration, the Potsdam Proclamation, and the Japanese instrument of surrender. Therefore, when in 1945 the Chinese government accepted the Japanese surrender of Taiwan and exercised sovereignty over the island, Taiwan had become, not only de jure but also de facto, an inalienable part of China. Wu further pointed out that Article 107 provides that nothing in the charter shall invalidate any action taken by the victorious allies during World War II; therefore, the United Nations "has no right whatsoever to alter the status of Taiwan, all the less as the question of the status of Taiwan does not exist" (Doc. 32).

Since Taiwan is an inalienable part of Chinese territory, Wu said, the dispatch of the U.S. Seventh Fleet to the Taiwan Straits to prevent the Chinese people's "liberation" of the island constituted "armed aggression" against China. At the end of his long speech, Wu submitted a draft resolution calling upon the Security Council to condemn the United States for committing "open and direct aggression against Chinese territory" and "to demand the complete withdrawal by the Government of the United States of its forces of armed aggression from Taiwan."[23] This draft resolution, sponsored by the Soviet Union, was rejected by the Council by nine votes to one (the Soviet Union), with one member not participating.[24]

During the same period, at the fifth session of the General Assembly, the Soviet Union and the United States each sponsored an agenda item concerning Taiwan.

On September 20, 1950, the Soviet Union proposed that the question of U.S. aggression against China should be included in the Assembly's agenda. On September 26 the General Assembly included the item in its agenda under the title "Complaint by the USSR regarding aggression against China by the United States" and referred it to the First Committee.[25] On October 17 the PRC sent a cablegram to the United Nations, claiming its right to participate in the proceedings of the General Assembly, with particular reference to this agenda item. On November 15 the First Committee decided to invite the PRC to participate in the discussion of this item.[26]

On November 26 the PRC replied that it had appointed Wu Hsiu-chuan to participate in the discussion of the Soviets' proposed item in the First Committee, and the next day Wu took part in the committee's 407th meeting.[27] The next meeting of the committee was not held until December 7, and at that meeting it was decided to give priority to the French proposal on the "Intervention of the Central People's Government of the People's Republic of China in Korea"; discussion of the Soviet complaint against the United States was postponed.[28]

On December 16 Wu Hsiu-chuan issued a statement at Lake Success, New York, saying that the PRC firmly opposed and protested the Security Council's rejection of the PRC's proposal calling on the United States to withdraw from Taiwan.[29] He then distributed a speech that he had prepared but was kept from delivering to the First Committee.[30]

On the same day the U.N. Group on Cease-Fire in Korea requested the PRC to instruct Mr. Wu's group to stay on in New York and to discuss with the group the possibility of arranging a cease-fire in Korea.[31] In its reply, dated December 21, the PRC government recalled that its representative had neither participated in nor agreed to the adoption of the General Assembly resolution establishing the group. It also said that after the Security Council had unreasonably voted against the "Complaint of armed invasion of Taiwan (Formosa)" raised by the PRC, it had instructed its representatives to remain in New York for participation in the discussion of the "Complaint by the USSR regarding aggression against China by the United States." However, the PRC's reply said, Mr. Wu had still not been given the opportunity to speak. Under those circumstances it deemed that there was no further necessity for its representatives to remain in New York.[32] On December 19, 1950, Wu's group left New York.

On February 2, 1951, the First Committee resumed consideration of the agenda item proposed by the Soviet Union, and its chairman notified the PRC of the date of the committee's next meeting, February 6. Chou En-lai replied on February 4 that the lengthy speech distributed by Mr. Wu on December 16, 1950, should be read and circulated before the committee's meeting.[33] On February 7 the committee rejected a Soviet draft resolution "to request the Security Council to take the necessary steps to ensure the immediate cessation of aggression against China by the United States."[34]

On September 20, 1950, when the Soviet Union requested the General Assembly to consider the question of U.S. aggression against China, the United States requested that the question of Formosa be included in the agenda of the fifth session of the General Assembly. The United States suggested, inter alia, that the General Assembly study the general situation with respect to Formosa, with a view to formulating appropriate recommendations. The General Committee of the Assembly recommended, on October 5, inclusion of the item on the agenda of the Assembly and its referral to the First Committee. On October 7 the General Assembly accepted the recommendation of the General Committee.[35] During the discussion in the General Committee, the representatives of the ROC, the Soviet Union, and Czechoslovakia strongly opposed inclusion of this item on the agenda of the Assembly. The ROC representative said:

It [is] unprecedented in the United Nations for the government of one Member State to question the right of another
State to its territorial possessions. In so doing, the United
States delegation [has] taken a very grave step. In accordance with principles laid down by the Charter, the Cairo
Declaration and the Potsdam Proclamation, the Chinese
delegation [feels] that it [is] beyond the competence of the
General Assembly to consider the proposed item, and
[will] therefore oppose its inclusion in the agenda."[36]

The PRC also strongly opposed the inclusion of the U.S.-sponsored
item. In a cablegram to the United Nations dated October 17, it stated
that "there exists today only the fact of United States aggression on
Taiwan, the territory of China; there is no such so-called 'question of
Formosa' concerning the status or future of Taiwan."[37]

Meanwhile, the ROC was suspicious of the U.S. intention to
submit the question of Formosa to the United Nations. Therefore,
on October 20 ROC Ambassador to the United States Wellington Koo
asked John Foster Dulles, who was responsible for negotiating the
Japanese peace treaty, what the U.S. intention was. Mr. Dulles said
that the U.S. intention was "to temporarily freeze the status of Taiwan"
and, in so doing, it "was meant to maintain the status of the National
Government of China." He further stated that the United States hoped
that the ROC would not actively oppose the U.S. position at the United
Nations (Doc. 33).

On November 15 the First Committee decided to postpone its
consideration of the U.S.-sponsored item until after the Soviet complaints regarding U.S. aggression against China and the ROC's complaints regarding Soviet aggression against China had been handled.[38]
In early 1951, when the item was recalled, the United States supported
a British move to adjourn consideration of the item "in view of the
unsettled state of the situation in the Far East"; and on February 7
the First Committee decided to adjourn debate on the item.[39] Since
then there has been no further consideration of this item in the United
Nations.

Although U.N. consideration of the Taiwan question has not
produced any substantive result, the positions taken by the ROC and
the PRC toward the Taiwan question at the United Nations need special
attention.

Both the ROC and the PRC consider that the status of Taiwan
as an integral part of Chinese territory has long been settled in
accordance with several wartime agreements among the allies, and
is therefore outside the competence of the United Nations. Moreover,
the PRC believes that the United Nations should deal only with the
question of the "United States armed aggression against the Chinese

territory of Taiwan." It categorically rejects any U.N. consideration of, or interference in, its effort to "liberate" Taiwan, whether by force or by peaceful means. In the past 20-odd years the PRC has consistently maintained this attitude.

In 1950 the PRC's participation in the U.N. proceedings concerning the question of the "aggression against Taiwan" was not conditioned upon expulsion of the representative of the ROC, though the PRC did frequently reiterate its claim to be the sole legal government of China. However, it has changed this attitude since 1955 by insisting that as long as its place in the United Nations was "usurped by the Chiang Kai-shek group," it would be unable to take part in the discussion of questions concerning China in the United Nations.[40]

THE QUESTION OF TAIWAN AND THE JAPANESE PEACE SETTLEMENT

Before the outbreak of the Korean War in mid-1950, the United States at least tacitly adhered to the principle that Taiwan was a part of China and its fate was to be settled by the outcome of the Nationalist-Communist civil war. At that time it was widely expected that the future peace treaty with Japan would explicitly provide for the return of the island to China, in accordance with several wartime agreements among the allies. The Korean War caused the United States to decide that this strategic island should not be controlled by a hostile regime. Therefore the United States had to devise a legal basis to justify its intervention to prevent the Chinese Communists' "liberation" of Taiwan. From the U.S. point of view, if Taiwan's status could be rendered "undetermined," then legally the United States would be in a better position to justify its dispatch of naval forces to the Taiwan Straits.* On the basis of this consideration the United States drafted the provisions concerning the status of Taiwan in the Japanese Peace Treaty.

In 1948 statements made by American officials indicated a strong American interest in Japan as part of the U.S. security system in the Pacific. By the end of 1949, the United States had decided to promote a separate peace with Japan, regardless of objections raised by the Soviet Union and the PRC. John Foster Dulles, appointed as special

---

*For instance, on October 20, 1950, Dulles told ROC Ambassador Koo that "if the United States already regarded Taiwan as purely Chinese territory . . . the United States would lose her grounds for dispatching the Seventh Fleet to protect Taiwan. . . ." (Doc. 33).

adviser to the State Department, was assigned to work on the peace treaty.

After making initial contacts with several wartime allies on the terms of the treaty, Dulles met ROC Ambassador Koo on October 20, 1950, and presented to him a memorandum on the Japanese Peace Treaty. On the question of Taiwan, the memorandum read: "Japan would . . . accept the future decision of the U.K., U.S.S.R., China, and U.S. with reference to the status of Formosa, the Pescadores, South Sakhalin, and the Kuriles. In the event of no decision within a year after the Treaty came into force, the U.N. General Assembly would decide."41

In suggesting such an arrangement of the status of Taiwan in the Japanese Peace Treaty, obviously the United States had in mind that the status of Taiwan would be finally decided by the General Assembly of the United Nations. It was only too obvious that the four powers could not agree on the status of Taiwan. Certainly, in any future negotiation among the four powers on the status of Taiwan, the Soviet Union would insist that the PRC should represent China and both countries would insist that Taiwan should be returned to the PRC. On the other hand, the United States, having recognized the strategic importance of Taiwan after the outbreak of the Korean War, would insist on preventing Communist control of Taiwan. Therefore, if the arrangement suggested by the United States were adopted by the peace settlement, the status of Taiwan would finally be decided by the General Assembly, in which the United States then controlled an absolute majority of the votes.

The ROC was in a dilemma. On the one hand, at that time it badly needed the U.S. naval force in the Taiwan Straits to prevent the Communist attack; and, as stated in the Koo-Dulles talks of October 20, 1950, if Taiwan was openly conceded to be an integral part of China, there would be no sound legal basis for the United States to' intervene, since the "Taiwan question" would be a purely Chinese affair (Doc. 33). On the other hand, if the leaders of the ROC accepted an arrangement that would detach Taiwan from China, they not only would lose their legal basis to govern Taiwan but also would forever be denounced as traitors by all Chinese.

In view of the above considerations, the ROC could not fully accept the U.S. proposal on the status of Taiwan. On December 19, 1950, Ambassador Koo forwarded the ROC's preliminary opinion to Dulles; it stated, inter alia, that Japan was only required to renounce all sovereignty over Taiwan and other territories in the future peace treaty (Doc. 34). On January 22, 1951, Ambassador Koo forwarded another ROC memorandum to Dulles. In this memorandum the ROC pointed out that Taiwan and the Pescadores "constitute historically, ethnically, legally, and in fact a part of Chinese territory, although the formal act of finalization is pending." However, "in view of the unsettled conditions in the Far East and in the interest of promoting the general security of the Pacific region at present," the Chinese government "does not wish to raise objections to the suggestions" for submitting the status of these islands to the decision of the four powers. But, in so doing the ROC "does not wish to be understood as having in any way modified its basic view of Formosa and the Pescadores as Chinese territory." As to the suggestion that, failing a decision on the status of these territories by the four powers, the question should be referred to the U.N. General Assembly for a decision, the ROC government reserved its position. The memorandum concluded that "so far as Japan is concerned, a general renunciation by her in the treaty of her sovereignty over these territories would appear to be sufficient" (Doc. 35).

On March 20, 1951, Dulles informed Ambassador Koo that the United States had decided to simplify the territorial provisions in the draft peace treaty by merely providing for Japanese renunciation of all sovereignty over Taiwan and the other territories.[42] However, in the provisional draft of the peace treaty handed by Dulles to Ambassador Koo on March 28, it was explicitly provided that Japan would return to the Soviet Union South Sakhalin and the Kurile Islands, but merely provided that "Japan renounces all rights, titles and claims to . . . Formosa and the Pescadores. . . ."

The Chinese government was dissatisfied with such a discriminatory arrangement in the peace treaty and proposed revision of this point (Doc. 36). On May 29, Ambassador Koo told Dulles that the Chinese government suggested that the draft peace treaty should also explicitly provide for the restoration of Taiwan and the Pescadores to the ROC. Dulles explained that the difference of treatment in the matter of wording for the two territories (Taiwan and South Sakhalin) was really beneficial to China. If the Soviet Union failed to conclude the peace treaty with Japan, South Sakhalin and the Kurile Islands would still remain with Japan. If the provisions about Taiwan and the Pescadores were alike, the result would be the same should China perchance fail to participate in the treaty, while a simple provision of renunciation would formally detach Taiwan and the Pescadores from Japan (Doc. 37).

The Chinese diplomatic records do not show that the ROC pushed the matter further, but subsequently the United States appeared to accept the Chinese view, Thus, in the final draft of the peace treaty, handed by Dulles to Ambassador Koo on July 6, Taiwan, the Pescadores, South Sakhalin, and the Kuriles were treated identically. Japan was required only to renounce all her rights, titles, and claims to these territories.[43]

The United States initially planned to invite the ROC to the peace conference, but subsequently changed its mind because of the strong objections raised by the United Kingdom and other countries that recognized the PRC as the legitimate government of China.[44] In June, 1951, Dulles finally reached a compromise with the United Kingdom on the question of Chinese participation in the peace conference. According to this compromise, neither the ROC nor the PRC would be invited to the peace conference; after the conclusion of the multilateral peace treaty, Japan would conclude a bilateral peace treaty of similar content with the ROC or the PRC.[45]

Needless to say, the ROC was dissatisfied with such an arrangement. Therefore, on June 18, 1951, President Chiang Kai-shek issued a statement reaffirming the ROC's right to participate in the peace treaty "on an equal footing with the other Allies" (Doc. 38). However, the political situation at that time was not favorable to the ROC's participation in the peace conference.[46] Therefore, the ROC had to accept this compromise and the United States promised to persuade Japan to conclude a bilateral peace treaty with it.[47] On July 11, 1951, the United States published its draft peace treaty with Japan.

While the ROC was pressing its right to participate in the peace conference, the PRC asserted its right to participate in the same conference. On August 15, 1951, Chou En-lai issued a lengthy statement denouncing the American draft peace treaty with Japan. The statement said that the United States had monopolized the task of preparing the draft peace treaty, in violation of the 1942 United Nations Declaration, the 1945 Potsdam Agreement, and other agreements among the allies. It pointed out that the 1942 declaration "provides that no separate peace should be made" and the 1945 agreement "states that the 'preparatory work of the peace settlement' should be undertaken by those states which were signatories to the terms of surrender imposed upon the enemy state. . . ."[48]

Moreover, the statement charged that the U.S. draft peace treaty violated the 1943 Cairo Declaration and the 1945 Potsdam Proclamation by failing to provide for the return of Taiwan and the Pescadores to the People's Republic of China.

Finally, Chou's statement strongly denounced the exclusion of the PRC from the peace conference and said that such an action "completely violates a stipulation in the United Nations Declaration of January 1, 1942, to the effect that each of the signatory Powers pledged itself not to make a separate peace." In conclusion, Chou declared that without the participation of the PRC, the Central People's Government considered the peace treaty "illegal, and therefore null and void" (Doc. 39).

Despite the objections of the ROC and the PRC, the Japanese Peace Treaty was signed on September 8, 1951, at San Francisco.

With respect to the question of Taiwan, Article 2 of the treaty provides: "Japan renounces all right, title and claim to Formosa and the Pescadores." Article 26 provides that Japan prepares to conclude a bilateral treaty with any state which "signed or adhered to the United Nations Declaration of January 1, 1942, and which is at war with Japan."[49]

At the same time the United States continued to try to persuade Japan to conclude a bilateral peace treaty with the ROC. The most difficult problem in U.S. Japan and U.S.-ROC preliminary negotiations on the ROC-Japanese Peace Treaty was whether the peace treaty should be applicable to all China, including those areas under the de facto control of the PRC. According to the understanding of the United States, in the future bilateral peace negotiations between the ROC and Japan, the latter would insist upon the inclusion of a territorial application clause saying that the peace treaty is applicable only to those areas under the control of the ROC. The degree to which the United States could influence Japan to conclude a peace treaty with the ROC depended largely upon whether the ROC would work out an acceptable formula to solve this problem.[50]

The ROC, however, could not accept any proposal in the peace treaty that would impair its claim to the Chinese mainland and its position in the United Nations as the only legal government of China.[51] Subsequently the ROC suggested that it would agree to include the following statement in the agreed minutes when exchanging instruments of ratification of the ROC-Japanese Peace Treaty:

> In respect of the Republic of China, the present Treaty shall be applicable to all the territories which are now, or which may hereafter be, under the control of its Government.

This proposal was handed to Minister Rankin by Foreign Minister Yeh on September 26, 1951.[52] Later the ROC revised its original proposal by suggesting that the contents of the agreed minutes should be applicable to both parties as follows:

> Both Contracting Parties Understand: The present Treaty shall be applicable to all the territories which are now, or which may hereafter be, under the control of either Contracting Party.

This proposal was handed to Minister Rankin by Foreign Minister Yeh on October 24, 1951.[53] On January 19, 1952, American Minister Rankin told Foreign Minister Yeh that, in order to avoid the possible misunderstanding that Japan would expand her territory in future, it would be desirable to use a unilateral clause (i.e., a clause applicable to one of the contracting parties only) for the scope of application of

the Sino-Japanese Peace Treaty.[54] The ROC and the United States
do not appear to have reached an agreement on the form of the territorial clause, and the question was left to the Sino-Japanese peace
negotiations.[55]

 After the ROC accepted the proposal of a territorial clause in
the peace treaty (though the form was still subject to future negotiation), the United States finally persuaded Japan to conclude a peace
treaty with the ROC. On December 24, 1951, Japanese Prime Minister
Yoshida sent a letter to Dulles saying that Japan was willing to conclude
a peace treaty with the ROC based on the principles contained in the
San Francisco Peace Treaty and with a territorial application clause
for the ROC.[56] The letter was communicated to the ROC by the United
States on January 16, 1952, and published in Tokyo on the same day.[57]
On January 18, 1952, ROC Foreign Minister Yeh issued a statement
saying that the ROC was preparing to enter into negotiations with
Japan on the peace treaty.[58]

 In February, 1952, the ROC and Japan started negotiation on the
bilateral peace treaty, which, with accompanying notes and other
documents, was signed on April 28, 1952 (Doc. 40). On the question
of Taiwan, Article 2 of the treaty provides that "Japan has renounced
all right, title and claim to Taiwan and Penghu" in accordance with
Article 2 of the San Francisco Peace Treaty. Article 4 of the treaty
provides that "all treaties, conventions and agreements concluded
before December 9, 1941, between China and Japan have become null
and void as a consequence of the war." It is clear that under Article
4 the 1895 Sino-Japanese Treaty of Shimonoseki, ceding Taiwan to
Japan, was abolished.

 As for the territorial application clause, an exchange of notes
accompanying the treaty provides that "the terms of the present
Treaty shall, in respect of the Republic of China, be applicable to all
territories which are now, or which may hereafter be, under the control of its Government."

 On the same day that the ROC and Japan signed the bilateral
peace treaty, the San Francisco Peace Treaty entered into force.
On May 5, 1952, Chou En-lai again issued a statement declaring that
the San Francisco Peace Treaty was in violation of preceding treaties
agreed upon between the allies and was therefore "completely illegal
and unreasonable."[59] On August 5, 1952, the ROC-Japan Peace
Treaty entered into force.

THE INTERNATIONAL LEGAL
STATUS OF TAIWAN

 Because neither the San Francisco Japanese Peace Treaty nor
the Sino-Japanese Peace Treaty explicitly provides for the return of

Taiwan to China, the question of the legal status of Taiwan has become
a complex and controversial issue among some scholars and several
countries. This part of the chapter attempts to make a concise analysis
of this question, with special emphasis on the Chinese attitude toward
it.

The U.S. position on the status of Taiwan is, as stated by the
late Secretary of State Dulles in a press conference held on December
1, 1954, "that technical sovereignty over Formosa and the Pescadores
has never been settled" and that "the future title is not determined by
the Japanese peace treaty, nor is it determined by the peace treaty
which was concluded between the Republic of China and Japan."[60] On
the other hand, the United States also recognizes that the ROC "effectively controls" Taiwan and the Pescadores.[61]

The British government has taken a similar view. Thus, on
February 4, 1955, British Secretary of State for Foreign Affairs Eden
said in the House of Commons: "Under the Peace Treaty of April,
1952, Japan formally renounced all right, title, and claim to Formosa
and the Pescadores; but again this did not operate as a transfer to
Chinese sovereignty, whether to the People's Republic of China or to
the Chinese Nationalist authorities. Formosa and the Pescadores
are therefore, in the view of Her Majesty's Government, territory,
the de jure sovereignty over which is uncertain or undetermined."[62]

The Anglo-American position appears to suggest that China
could acquire de jure sovereignty over Taiwan only through an explicit
provision on cession in a peace treaty. From the viewpoint of international law, such as assertion is questionable. For instance, in
Lauterpacht's edition of Oppenheim, it is stated:

> Unless the parties stipulate otherwise,the effect of a treaty
> of peace is that conditions remain as at the conclusion of
> peace. . . Thus . . . if nothing is stipulated regarding con-
> quered territory, it remains in the hands of the possessor,
> who may annex it. But it is nowadays usual, although not
> at all legally necessary, for a conqueror desirous of
> retaining conquered territory to secure its cession in the
> treaty of peace.[63] (Emphasis added.)

The above rule is generally referred to as the principle of uti posside-
tis (as you possess, you shall continue to possess).

In 1912 Italy acquired Tripoli and Cyrenaica from Turkey without
going through a formal treaty of cession. On October 15, 1912, three
days before the signing of the formal peace treaty, Turkey and Italy
signed a protocol in which Turkey agreed to grant complete autonomy
to these territories and thereby renounced sovereignty over them.
The peace treaty, signed on October 18, did not provide for the

transfer of these territories to Italy; but after the conclusion of the peace treaty, Italy announced their annexation.[64] No one raised any question about the legality of the Italian title to these territories.[65]

Consequently, the lack of explicit provisions on the transfer of Taiwan to China in the two peace treaties does not necessarily mean that China could not acquire de jure sovereignty over Taiwan. Some Western scholars of international law have expressed a similar view. For instance, D.P. O'Connell of Australia has said that after the Japanese renunciation of the island, it is "doubtful . . . whether there is any international doctrine opposed to the conclusion that China appropriated the terra derelicta of Formosa by converting belligerent occupation into definite sovereignty."[66]

Similarly, F. P. Morello of the United States argued that the ROC could acquire de jure sovereignty over Taiwan through prescription:

> Except for the claims of Red China, it can be said that the occupation of Formosa by the Nationalist Government has been undisturbed. In addition, this de facto exercise of governmental authority has been continuous for nineteen years [up to 1966]. The possession of Formosa by the Nationalist Government has been steadily maintained by an assertion of right. It follows that if the principle of prescription, as interpreted and applied within the framework of international law, is to be accepted in the case of China, then there can be no lawyer's doubts as to the legitimacy of Nationalist China's title to Formosa.[67]

An American authority on international law, Arthur Dean, has also commented on the question of the legal status of Taiwan:

> If Japan in its Treaty of Peace had formally ceded Formosa and the Pescadores to the Republic of China, the legal situation would have been clear. Since this was not done and since Japan renounced all right, title and claim to Formosa and the Pescadores, it is not clear just what would constitute a formal cession of title to the Republic of China. Perhaps an agreement with Japan would still be required. . . . It may well be, however, that from the standpoint of customary international law, at least, no cession is required. Nationalist China may have already acquired legal title to Formosa and the Pescadores by occupation or possibly by subjugation.
>   As pointed out in 1933 by the Permanent Court of International Justice in the Legal Status of Eastern

Greenland Case, acquisition of title by occupation involves
"the intention and will to act as sovereign, and some actual
exercise or display of such authority." The occupation in
order to vest title must be an effective occupation. . . . On
the facts as I know them, Nationalist China has certainly
satisfied the requirement of effective control, and such of
its governmental acts as are known to me, as, for example,
making Formosa a Province of China, clearly indicate an
intention and will to act as a sovereign.

Until the coming into force of the Japanese Peace
Treaty on April 28, 1952, there was a formal obstacle to
Nationalist China's acquiring legal title to Formosa by
occupation, in that technical sovereignty over Formosa
and the Pescadores remained in Japan. They were, accordingly, not terrae nullius capable of being acquired by
occupation. However, when Japan renounced all right,
title and claim to Formosa and the Pescadores this obstacle
was removed, unless the Peace Treaty is regarded as not
merely divesting Japan's title but, in addition, also vesting
in the signatories, or possibly (although I have not seen an
adequate legal justification for this theory . . .) in the
United Nations, the title, or at least the right to cede the
title, to Formosa and the Pescadores. I suppose a case
could also be made for Nationalist China's acquisition of
title to Formosa through subjugation. Certainly there has
been a conquest, but whether or not Nationalist China has
turned the conquest into subjugation through formal annexation is not clear. Moreover, possibly on this theory
Nationalist China did not have a legal right to annex
Formosa without the acquiescence of the other states
which participated in the conquest.[68]

It must be pointed out that to say the San Francisco Peace Treaty
has vested the sovereignty of Taiwan and the Pescadores in its signatories is at least unreal, because it does not say so; and none of
the signatories has ever claimed to exercise a condominium over
Taiwan. Similarly, the theory that sovereignty over Taiwan was
vested in the United Nations as a result of the San Francisco Peace
Treaty is equally unreal. So far no member of the United Nations
has formally made such a claim, nor does the United Nations actually
exercise any sovereignty over Taiwan. Therefore, so far as the ROC
is concerned, it may reasonably be argued that Taiwan has been
incorporated into China in accordance with the principle of occupation
in international law.

As to the theory suggested by Arthur Dean that the ROC may
acquire sovereignty over Taiwan in accordance with the principle of

subjugation, writers have raised two objections. The first, as stated by Dean, is whether China could conquer Taiwan without the acquiescence of the other World War II allies. This argument might be valid if there were no past international agreements and Taiwan had never been a part of China, but everyone knows that Taiwan was a part of China before it was ceded to Japan in 1895. Moreover, the Cairo Declaration of 1943 explicitly stated that Taiwan "shall be restored" to China. The terms of this declaration were incorporated in the 1945 Potsdam Proclamation and accepted by Japan in its instrument of surrender. There is no doubt that the Japanese instrument of surrender is an international agreement binding upon all signatories.[69] Therefore, all the allies who signed the instrument of surrender are legally bound to accept the Chinese claim to Taiwan and are not legally entitled to challenge the Chinese conquest of Taiwan.

Second, one Canadian writer has argued that "whether conquest and annexation are still a legitimate method of obtaining sovereignty over a territory" is open to question.[70] While this principle is true, it certainly cannot be applied to the case of Taiwan. The Cairo Declaration clearly stated that Taiwan, like Manchuria, was "stolen" from China by Japan. The return of Taiwan to China was, like the return of Alsace and Lorraine to France, in accord with international justice.[71] Moreover, the above principle is based primarily upon the 1928 Treaty for the Renunciation of War and the 1945 U.N. Charter, which prohibit the illegal use of force in international relations. However, as pointed out in Lauterpacht's edition of Oppenheim, "the title by conquest remains a valid title . . . when . . . the resort to war . . . is not, in the particular case, unlawful."[72] There is no doubt that China's resistance against Japanese aggression was legitimate under the 1928 Treaty for the Renunciation of War. As to the U.N. Charter, Article 107 of the charter explicitly provides: "Nothing in the present Charter shall invalidate or preclude action, in relation to any State which during the Second World War has been an enemy of any signatory to the present Charter, taken or authorized as a result of that war by the Government having responsibility for such action." The disposition of Taiwan had been decided by the allies during World War II, and Article 107 of the charter certainly precludes the United Nations from dealing with the Taiwan question.

The negotiating history and the content of the ROC-Japan Peace Treaty and accompanying documents also support the ROC's claim to Taiwan. Article 10 of this peace treaty provides: "For the purposes of the present Treaty, nationals of the Republic of China shall be deemed to include all the inhabitants and former inhabitants of Taiwan (Formosa) and Penghu (the Pescadores) and their descendents who are of the Chinese nationality in accordance with the laws and regulations which have been or may hereafter be enforced by the Republic

of China in Taiwan. . . ." Article 3 provides for the disposition of
Japanese properties in Taiwan and Chinese property in Japan. The
territorial application clause contained in the exchange of notes
accompanying the peace treaty merely says that it "shall . . . be
applicable to all the territories which are now, or which may hereafter
be, under the control of [the Republic of China]." The note does not
legally differentiate Taiwan and other territories of China. All these
provisions clearly reject the view that Taiwan has not been assigned
to anyone. It is absurd to say that when Japan agreed to renounce its
claim to Taiwan, it did not know the sovereignty of the island would
go to the ROC. Thus, for instance, in the case of Japan v. Lai Chin
Jung, decided by the Tokyo High Court on December 24, 1956, it was
stated that "Formosa and the Pescadores came to belong to the
Republic of China, at any rate on August 5, 1952, when the Treaty
between Japan and the Republic of China came into force. . . ."[73]

The above discussion clearly indicates that the lack of an explicit
provision on the ceding of Taiwan to China in the two Japanese peace
treaties does not necessarily mean that China could not acquire de jure
sovereignty over Taiwan. However, as stated earlier in this chapter,
the PRC has not recognized either Japanese peace treaty; and therefore
its claim to Taiwan certainly cannot be based upon these two documents.
In view of this, the PRC government and its writers have made various
other arguments to support its claim to Taiwan. On the other hand,
the ROC has considered that Taiwan was legally restored to China on
October 25, 1945, the date of its return to Chinese administration.
In the ROC's view the peace treaty merely confirms the Chinese
restoration, and China had regained her sovereignty over Taiwan long
before the entry into force of the two peace treaties. Therefore, the
ROC government and its writers have also made various arguments
not based on the peace treaties to support the Chinese Nationalist
claim to Taiwan.

According to the ROC, the Cairo Declaration is a legally binding
document. On February 8, 1955, ROC President Chiang Kai-shek
said that the document "was recognized by the Potsdam Proclamation
and accepted by Japan at the time of its surrender" and "its validity
is thus based upon a number of agreements and should not be questioned."
He also severely criticized those who denied the validity of the Cairo
Declaration:

> If one could deny the validity of the Cairo Declaration,
> what about the Potsdam Proclamation and all the inter-
> national treaties and agreements concluded since the
> termination of the Second World War? Could their valid-
> ity be also denied? . . . Those who play fast and loose
> about the status of Taiwan do so against their own

conscience. . . . They do not realize how gravely they
jeopardize world security by arguing from bad law and
false policies. [74]

As to the status of Taiwan, President Chiang said:

When Japan surrendered, the Government of the Republic
of China repossessed Taiwan and Penghu. Since that time,
Taiwan and Penghu have regained their status as an inte-
gral unit of the territory of the Republic of China. In the
San Francisco Peace Treaty and the Sino-Japanese Peace
Treaty, Japan renounced her sovereignty over Taiwan and
Penghu, thereby completing the process of restoring these
areas to our country.[75]

Although Chiang Kai-shek did not say on what legal principles
the ROC repossessed Taiwan, a senior Nationalist Chinese diplomat,
Dr. T'ang Wu, has elaborated President Chiang's view in terms of
international law:

On October 25, 1945, when Japan returned Taiwan to China,
China de facto and de jure recovered her legal right over
Taiwan. In terms of customary international law, the form
of Chinese acquisition of sovereignty resembles occupation,
while the Japanese loss of sovereignty resembles dereliction. This is because the Japanese act of returning was
based on the Instrument of Surrender rather than on a
peace treaty with China in accordance with traditional
precedent in international law.[76]

In addition to Dr. T'ang Wu's argument, the spokesman of the
ROC's Foreign Ministry said in a press conference held on March 3,
1964, that the 1895 Treaty of Shimonoseki ceding Taiwan to Japan
was abrogated by the Chinese declaration of war against Japan on
December 9, 1941, and the abrogation was confirmed by Article 4 of
the Sino-Japanese Peace Treaty, which stated that all Sino-Japanese
treaties before December 9, 1941, "have become null and void."
       The above ROC arguments seem to suggest that since the legal
basis for Japanese occupation of Taiwan was removed on December
9, 1941, China could legally repossess Taiwan on the basis of the
Cairo Declaration and the Japanese instrument of surrender. In the
latter Japan was legally committed to carry out the terms of the
Cairo Declaration and in fact did carry out the commitment on
October 25, 1945, by transferring the administration of Taiwan to
China. Therefore, China did in fact and in law recover her sovereignty
on that date.

The fact that the ROC has been continuously exercising sovereign authority over Taiwan since then appears to support this position. Although Taiwan has constituted the only substantial territory controlled by the ROC since 1950, when the ROC concluded bilateral treaties or multilateral treaties, no state has ever challenged her sovereign right to conclude treaties applicable to Taiwan on the ground that Taiwan is not legally a part of China.

However, a few countries and writers have expressed doubts about the various arguments advanced by the ROC. In the first place, it has been said that the 1895 Treaty of Shimonoseki was in the nature of an "executed" treaty and could not be abrogated by the outbreak of war or a unilateral declaration of China. Thus, in the words of the British government in 1958:

> According to international law, a state cannot merely by unilateral declaration regain rights of sovereignty which it has formally ceded by treaty. China therefore could not, and did not, regain sovereign rights over these territories [Taiwan and the Pescadores] by the unilateral denunciation of this Treaty in 1941.[77]

This argument might be valid if the ROC-Japanese Peace Treaty had not confirmed the unilateral Chinese abrogation of all Sino-Japanese treaties made before December 9, 1941. But, as has been stated, Article 4 of the Sino-Japanese Peace Treaty specifically provides that all those treaties "have become null and void as a consequence of the war." Therefore, so far as the ROC is concerned, the question of whether China could unilaterally abrogate the 1895 Treaty of Shimonoseki in 1941 becomes meaningless, because the contracting parties (China and Japan) agreed that it was abrogated in 1941, and such an arrangement is perfectly valid in international law.[78]

In the second place, it is objected that the Cairo Declaration is not legally binding. For instance, on February 4, 1955, British Foreign Secretary Anthony Eden said that it "was a statement of intention."[79] This view seems questionable. As pointed out in Lauterpacht's edition of Oppenheim, "official statements in the form of Reports of Conferences signed by the Heads of States or Governments and embodying agreements reached therein may, in proportion as these agreements incorporate definite rules of conduct, be regarded as legally binding upon the States in question."[80] The 1943 Cairo Declaration was the result of several serious meetings held among the three heads of government and was carefully drafted (see Doc. 11). To say that the declaration is merely a "declaration of intention" and without legally binding force is certainly contrary to the intention of the three heads of government who signed the declaration.[81]

Moreover, as pointed out by President Chiang, the declaration was confirmed in two other wartime documents; and the legally binding force of at least one of the two documents—the Japanese instrument of surrender—is free from doubt.[82] Furthermore, in the case between Norway and Denmark concerning the status of eastern Greenland, the Permanent Court of International Justice held in 1933 that an oral declaration given by the minister of foreign affairs on behalf of his government in answer to a request by the representative of a foreign state is binding upon the state to which the minister belongs.[83] If a foreign minister's statement is legally binding upon his own state, can we say that the declaration made by three heads of state or government is not binding upon their own states?

Finally, it has been said that the Chinese occupation of Taiwan was in the nature of a military occupation. For instance, the British Joint Undersecretary of State for Foreign Affairs, R. H. Turton, said on May 4, 1955: "The sovereignty was Japanese until 1952. The Japanese treaty came into force, and at that time Formosa was being administered by the Chinese Nationalists, to whom it was entrusted in 1945, as a military occupation."[84] This argument might be valid if there had been no previous commitment among the allies to return Taiwan to China. But, as has been repeatedly pointed out, the United States and Great Britain were committed by several wartime documents to return Taiwan to China. Therefore, the Chinese return to Taiwan certainly was not a purely "military occupation." In the words of American Secretary of State Acheson, "the Island of Formosa was turned over to the Chinese in accordance with the declarations made [at Cairo and Potsdam] and with the conditions of the surrender" (Doc. 25).

Moreover, as previously stated, the Chinese authorities have in fact exercised sovereignty over Taiwan since October 25, 1945, and no state has ever made a diplomatic protest against the Chinese actions there. The situation was, as stated by the Tokyo District Court in the case of Shozo Azuma and Yoshiko Azuma v. Japan, decided on September 11, 1958:

> During the period between the signing of this instrument [of surrender] and the conclusion of the Peace Treaty, Japan was under the control of the Allied Powers and did not exercise its sovereignty over Formosa. Under the Allied policy of control over Japan, the Formosans were treated as a so-called liberated nation and distinguished from the Japanese. Further, Article 2(b) of the Peace Treaty provides that Japan renounces all right, title and claim to Formosa and the Pescadores. Judging from these facts, it is proper to consider that as far as Formosa is

concerned Japan already renounced its sovereignty over that island by accepting the Potsdam Declaration and that the conclusion of the Treaty is the confirmation of this fact."[85]

Similarly, a Japanese scholar, Hirano Yoshitaro, sometime president of the China Problem Research Institute of Japan, is of the opinion that "from the viewpoint of international law, Taiwan became legally a Chinese territory on September 2, 1945, when Japan signed the Instrument of Surrender."[86]

All this evidence clearly rejects the view that the ROC's occupation of Taiwan after October 25, 1945, and until 1952 was in the nature of a military occupation. On the other hand, there is much evidence to support the view that the ROC in fact exercised sovereignty over Taiwan by ruling it as a province of China before 1952.

The view held by the PRC concerning the status of Taiwan has many aspects in common with the position taken by the ROC. Of course, the PRC cannot invoke the 1952 ROC-Japanese Peace Treaty to support its claim that Taiwan is a part of China because the PRC denies the right of the ROC government to conclude any treaty in the name of China after October 1, 1949, the date of the establishment of the Central People's Government of the People's Republic of China. Similarly, as stated before, the PRC has categorically rejected the validity of the San Francisco Peace Treaty and therefore cannot invoke this treaty to its advantage. Moreover, the principles of prescription and occupation that may justify the ROC's claim to Taiwan certainly are not applicable to the PRC because the application of these two principles to the Taiwan situation presupposes the validity of the two peace treaties by which Japan renounced her claim to Taiwan and thus makes the island terra nullius.*

Like the ROC, the PRC's claim to Taiwan is based upon the Chinese abrogation of the 1895 Treaty of Shimonoseki in 1941, several wartime agreements among the allies, and the de facto Chinese control

―――――――――――

*Of course, if Japan in fact renounced the island of Taiwan on October 25, 1945, and the island became terra nullius at that time, then the ROC certainly could acquire sovereignty over the island by occupation. And the PRC, claiming to be the successor of the ROC government, could also invoke the principle of occupation to its advantage. But the PRC certainly could not invoke the principle of prescription to support its claim to Taiwan, because it does not in fact control Taiwan and does not recognize the ROC government as having legal status since October 1, 1949.

over the island since 1945. Thus, for instance, on September 5, 1960, Premier Chou En-lai told British correspondent Felix Greene:

> Taiwan is an inalienable part of China's territory. This is
> a historical fact. The Cairo and the Potsdam Declarations,
> both signed by the U.S. Government, confirm that Taiwan
> is Chinese territory. After the Japanese surrender, Tai-
> wan was formally restored to China on October 25, 1945,
> and was taken over and administered by the then Chinese
> Government (Doc. 69).

A similar view was expressed in many official or authoritative statements of the PRC.[87]

Elaborating the PRC's official position on the status of Taiwan, several PRC writers have made various legal arguments supporting that position. In the first place, the PRC writers insist that the Cairo Declaration is a legally binding document. Thus, in 1955 Dr. Chen T'i-chiang cited passages from Lauterpacht's edition of Oppen-heim[88] to support his view on the validity of the Cairo Declaration and made the following argument:

> The Cairo Declaration doubtless belongs to this category
> of international documents, that is to say, it is an inter-
> national document "legally binding upon the states in
> question." Furthermore, the Potsdam Proclamation
> issued by China, the United States, and Great Britain on
> July 26, 1945 to urge the surrender of Japan reaffirmed
> the obligations of the Cairo Declaration. It was pro-
> vided in the Potsdam Proclamation that "the terms of
> the Cairo Declaration shall be carried out." The phrase
> "shall be carried out" conclusively proves that the Cairo
> Declaration is a document creating international obliga-
> tions, and not merely a statement of the intentions of the
> signatories. Upon the participation of the Soviet Union
> in the Potsdam Proclamation and the acceptance by Japan
> of the terms of the Proclamation by its unconditional
> surrender on September 2, 1945, the obligations of the
> Cairo Declaration became obligations binding upon the
> Four Great Powers as well as Japan.
>
> From a doctrinal view of international law, it is
> impossible to question the binding force of the Cairo
> Declaration as an international treaty.[89]

Another writer, Shao Chin-fu, said:

> Anyone with some legal knowledge realizes that the
> Cairo Declaration, like the Yalta Agreement and

Potsdam Declaration, was neither a unilateral expression of the policy of one allied country nor merely a
statement of general principles between allies. It was
an agreement reached between the heads of governments
of Allied Powers on a specific question in the interest of
joint military operations during the war, having definitely
a legal binding force (Item 4).[90]

As to the view that the return of Taiwan to China must come
about through a peace treaty, Shao Chin-fu rejected the view on the
following grounds:

After the Sino-Japanese War of 1894 the government of the
Ching Dynasty by signing the Treaty of Shimonoseki ceded
Taiwan and Penghu to Japan. With the outbreak of China's
War of Resistance Against Japan in 1937, in accordance
with international law, the treaties between the two countries became null and void. The Treaty of Shimonoseki
was no exception. In 1945 after China's victory in the Anti-
Japanese War, China recovered these two places from
Japan. No question has ever been raised about the legal
status of Taiwan. Since Taiwan has always been Chinese
territory, it is a matter of course for China to take it back
like a thing restored to its original owner. It is not a case
of China taking a new territory from Japan which must be
affirmed by a peace treaty. Particularly since the United
States and Britain signed the Cairo Declaration which
clearly recognizes that Taiwan and the Penghu Islands
are "territories Japan has stolen from the Chinese," and
"shall be restored" to China, they are still less in a position to raise the so-called "question of the legal status of
Taiwan" (Item 4).

Another Communist writer, Mei Ju-ao, former judge of the
International Military Tribunal for the Far East and sometime member
of the Executive Council of the China Political Science and Law Association (Peking) made a similar argument:

Simultaneously with its formal proclamation of war on
Japan on December 9, 1941, China solemnly declared
the abrogation of all treaties between China and Japan.
Since the Shimonoseki Treaty, on the basis of which
Japan occupied Taiwan, was among the treaties abrogated,
Japan's rule over Taiwan naturally became groundless
from that day. It is true that Taiwan was in fact under

Japan's occupation during the war against Japan. But
legally speaking, China has every right to consider that
it had recovered its sovereign rights over Taiwan as
from that day. . . . Taiwan has always been China's
territory. It had been stolen by Japan for 50 years. Following the termination of the Second World War, China
exercised the right conferred on it by international law
as a nation victorious over Japan. On the basis of the
proclamation it issued on December 9, 1941, China recovered Taiwan on October 25, 1945. This action by
China is perfectly lawful. It is consistent with the terms
of the Cairo Declaration and Potsdam Proclamation and
Japan's instrument of surrender.[91]

Both Shao and Mei seem to argue that war will automatically
terminate treaties between the contracting parties or that upon
declaration of war a party may unilaterally abrogate treaties between
belligerents.[92] Some Western scholars do not approve this view.[93]
However, it must be noted that Soviet scholars have expressed the
view that except for those treaties concluded on the contingency of
war or whose texts expressly stipulate that they remain valid during
war, all other treaties terminate ipso facto in wartime.[94]

Moreover, both the PRC and the Soviet doctrines of international
law support the view that all unequal treaties can be abrogated at any
time.[95] There is no doubt that the 1895 Treaty of Shimonoseki was
an unequal treaty and therefore could be abrogated at any time, or
should be void ab initio. In this connection, a Communist Chinese
writer said:

Obviously, according to [the bourgeois theory of international law that the validity of a treaty of cession does
not appear to be affected by the motives which have
impelled the grantor to surrender them,] it was legitimate for Japan to force the Manchu Government of China
to cede Taiwan and Penghu through the unequal Treaty of
Shimonoseki after the 1895 Sino-Japanese war. This is
tantamount to saying that it is legal for a robber to take
property by brandishing a dagger before the owner,
threatening his life, and then forcing him to put his finger-
print on a document indicating his consent. Is that not
absurd? No wonder bourgeois international law has
sometimes been described as the law of bandits.[96]

Mei also takes the position that "the recovery of Taiwan is
China's self-evident and deserving right as a victor." This argument

seems to base the Chinese claim to Taiwan on the international law
principle of conquest or subjugation. The question of applying this
principle to Taiwan has been discussed in connection with the ROC's
claim to Taiwan and will not be repeated here. But it must be pointed
out that both the Soviet and the PRC doctrines of international law
indicate that a state has the right to restore territory unjustly detached
from it or, in other words, to rectify a historical inequity.[97] Recently
the PRC appears to have based its claim to Taiwan on this principle.
Thus, an editorial of the authoritative People's Daily, dated May 12,
1964, stated that the "Cairo and Potsdam Declarations merely confirm
that the Chinese people have the inalienable right to recover their
territory of Taiwan from Japanese militarism" and that "with or
without the Cairo and Potsdam Declarations the Chinese people want
Taiwan restored to China." The same editorial reasoned:

> If Taiwan ceased to be China's territory because it was
> occupied by Japanese militarism for 50 years, then should
> the territories of Asian, African and Latin American coun-
> tries, which have been occupied for scores of years and
> centuries by imperialism—for instance . . . India's Goa
> . . . and Cuba's Guantanamo—eternally be imperialist
> colonies and not be allowed to return to their mother-
> land? If such imperialist logic is allowed to be enforced
> then "might makes right" will become the sole guiding
> principle in international law (Doc. 82).

In addition to the above theories on the international status of
Taiwan, a few countries and scholars have argued that Taiwan has
in fact become a separate state since 1949. The advocates of this
theory argue that as a result of the 1945-49 Chinese civil war,
China has in fact divided into two separate states—the PRC and the
ROC. In early 1960, Chester Bowles, later undersecretary of state
of the United States in the Kennedy administration, suggested that
"two Chinas" already existed and urged a policy that would help
materialize a "Sino-Formosan State" on Taiwan.[98] In the summer
of 1961, there were press reports in the United States of a "successor
states" theory to solve the Chinese representation problem in the
United Nations. Since then this theory has occasionally appeared in
some official statements, press reports, and scholars' opinions.
    In 1966 the Canadian secretary of state for external affairs
said: "We are prepared to accept the reality of the [Communist]
victory in mainland China in 1949. . . . We consider, however, that
the effective political independence of Taiwan is a political reality
too."[99] To elaborate this theory, a Canadian scholar argued in 1968
that Taiwan has in fact become a state:

The island has been completely independent of any foreign control for seventeen odd years [1949-1967]; it has its own government and army; it easily passes all the traditional tests of international law for statehood. The only disabilities are the lack of recognition of a Formosan state, the claims of its own government to be the government of another state of which Formosa is allegedly a part. . . . None of these disabilities, however, are deemed sufficient to override those factors pointing to Formosan statehood.[100]

On the surface this theory seems reasonable and also reflects the reality of the Chinese situation. However, a closer examination reveals two insurmountable difficulties. First, both the PRC and the ROC have maintained that the civil war they have fought since 1945 has not yet been concluded, and therefore the question of succession does not arise. Each side considers the other as an insurgent group rather than a separate political entity having international status, and each has been committed to the elimination of the other. Thus, in the words of President Chiang Kai-shek, "a legitimate government [ROC] and a regime of traitors [PRC] do not exist side by side, just as there is no room for coexistence between justice and evil" (Doc. 81) and "there is no possibility that we in Free China will give up our right and obligation to fight for the freedom of our compatriots and the unification of our country" (Doc. 53).

Similarly, the PRC categorically rejects the theory of succession:

There has only been a revolution in China and there has been no splitting into two states. How then can the question of two "succession states" to China arise? . . . Has or has not the Kuomintang regime of the old China been overthrown? If not, how does the question of "successor states" crop up? If it has been overthrown, how then can the Kuomintang clique which represents nobody become a "successor state" to China? (Doc. 74).

Second, no state in the world has so far maintained diplomatic relations concurrently with the PRC and the ROC. The recognition of the one will automatically lead the severance of diplomatic relations with the other. In this sense the theory of successor states does not reflect the reality of the Chinese situation.

THE QUESTION OF TAIWAN IN
SINO-AMERICAN RELATIONS

Since the U.S. intervention in mid-1950 to prevent the attempted
PRC attack on Taiwan, the question of Taiwan has become the most
difficult aspect of PRC-U.S. relations. Needless to say, the ROC,
being in effective control of Taiwan and certain islands off the mainland
of China, is also intricately involved in the so-called question of
Taiwan. This part of the chapter will deal with the question of Taiwan
in the context of Sino-American relations. Some problems relating
to this question, such as its origin, the PRC accusation in the United
Nations of U.S. aggression against Taiwan, and the legal status of
Taiwan, have been discussed earlier and will not be repeated here.

After the U.S.-imposed "neutralization" of Taiwan in mid-1950,
the PRC temporarily had to delay its attack on Taiwan. Then, in the
winter of 1950, the PRC participated in the Korean War through the
dispatch of the so-called Chinese People's Volunteers to Korea.
The PRC also actively supported the Vietnamese Communists in their
fight against the French.[101] The PRC forces entered Tibet in late
1950, and the PRC also engaged in the ruthless suppression of "counter-
revolutionaries" or "bad elements" in mainland China.[102] Being preoccupied with these activities, it could not engage in an invasion of
Taiwan.

The "neutralization" of Taiwan by the United States gave the
ROC a breathing period. On July 31, 1950, General MacArthur paid a
visit to Taipei to confer with President Chiang Kai-shek concerning
the defense of Taiwan, and a week later the U.S. 13th Air Force set
up liaison offices in Taipei.[103] On February 9, 1951, an agreement
between the United States and the ROC came into force by which the
United States agreed "to make available to the Republic of China . . .
certain military materials for the defense of Taiwan against possible
attack."[104] In May, 1951, the U.S. Military Assistance Advisory
Group was established in Taiwan to aid in training the ROC armed
forces. The United States also increased its economic aid to the ROC
after the outbreak of the Korean War.[105] As a result the ROC government was able to maintain a comparatively stable currency and improve
production in both agriculture and industry. In the military sphere
the 600,000-member ROC forces were reorganized, retrained, and
modernized.

The PRC's entry into the Korean War did not change the U.S.
policy of neutralizing Taiwan, and ROC forces were not permitted to
attack the mainland. However, on February 2, 1953, President Eisenhower, in his first State of the Union message to the Congress,
rescinded this restriction on the ROC forces:

>There is no longer any logic or sense in a condition that
>required the United States Navy to assume defensive
>responsibilities on behalf of the Chinese Communists.
>This permitted those Communists, with greater impunity,
>to kill our soldiers and those of our United Nations allies
>in Korea. I am, therefore, issuing instructions that the
>Seventh Fleet no longer be employed to shield Communist
>China. Permit me to make crystal clear—this order
>implies no aggressive intent on our part.[106]

The decision was hailed in the ROC. However, the ROC did not take
any significant action against the mainland after Eisenhower's statement, though President Chiang Kai-shek reaffirmed the ROC's determination to restore the freedom of the Chinese people on the mainland.[107]

In July, 1953, the Korean Armistice Agreement was signed. On
November 8, 1953, U.S. Vice-President Richard Nixon visited the
ROC and exchanged views on mutual security problems facing the
two countries. In December, 1953, ROC Foreign Minister George
Yeh handed an ROC draft of a proposed Sino-American security treaty
to U.S. Ambassador Rankin.[108] The United States in principle approved
the idea of concluding a security treaty with the ROC, and the two
countries entered into negotiations on the proposed treaty in early
1954.[109]

The Geneva Agreements on Indochina were signed in July, 1954.
Freed from the Korean and the Indochina fronts, the PRC was able to
shift its attention to Taiwan; and it applied strong military pressure
to the ROC-controlled offshore islands in the second half of 1954 and
early 1955.

On August 11, 1954, PRC Premier Chou En-lai said in his report
on foreign affairs that "the people of China and the People's Liberation
Army must redouble their efforts in every field, heighten their vigilance,
avoid the pitfall of conceit, overcome all difficulties, and struggle to the
end to fulfill the glorious task of liberating Taiwan and defending world
peace!"[110] A few days later a joint declaration was issued by 19
parties and mass organizations of the PRC, including the Taiwan
Democratic Self-Government League, which declared, inter alia, that
"the Chinese people are determined to liberate Taiwan."[111] Militarily,
the PRC deployed a force of more than 100,000 to the southern part
of Fukien and assembled a great number of vessels in the vicinity of
Amoy, Foochow, and Swatow. Then, on September 3, 1954, Communist
guns suddenly opened fire on Quemoy, pouring 6,000 rounds onto the
island. This shelling continued for a number of days. The ROC forces
on Quemoy immediately fought back. The ROC air force and navy also
undertook operations against PRC batteries along the coast opposite
Quemoy and PRC gunboats and motor junks near the coast of Fukien.

Occasionally there were air and sea battles between the PRC and
ROC forces.

By September, 1954, the PRC undoubtedly realized that the ROC
and the United States were negotiating a security treaty. Therefore,
in his report to the National People's Congress on September 23,
1954, PRC Premier Chou En-lai pointed out that "any pact signed
between the United States Government and the traitorous Chiang Kai-
shek gang holding on to Taiwan is illegal." He also reaffirmed that
Taiwan is Chinese territory and its "liberation" is not subject to
foreign interference; he also categorically rejected any proposal to
place Taiwan under U.N. trusteeship, to neutralize the island, or to
create an independent state of Taiwan (Doc. 41).

In addition to Quemoy and the Matsu islands off the Fukein coast,
the ROC also controlled the Tachen Islands (250 miles northwest of
Taiwan) and Nanchi Island (140 miles northwest of Taiwan) off the
Chekiang coast. In the middle of October, 1954, the PRC began to fire
on the Tachens; later, sea and air battles were fought between the
PRC and the ROC forces near them. Amid this Communist military
pressure against Quemoy and the Tachen Islands, the ROC and the
United States signed their mutual defense treaty on December 2, 1954
(Doc. 42). Article 6 of the treaty covers, on the part of the ROC,
Taiwan and the Pescadores and "such other territories as may be
determined by mutual agreement." The treaty was accompanied by
an exchange of notes on December 10, 1954, wherein the ROC agreed
not to use force, without "joint agreement," except in a clear case of
self-defense. Naturally, the PRC's reaction to this treaty was most
unfavorable. On December 8, 1954, Chou En-lai issued a lengthy
statement denouncing the treaty as a "treaty of aggression" and
reaffirmed the PRC's determination to "liberate Taiwan" (Doc. 43).
On December 15, 1954, the Soviet Union announced its "full support"
of the PRC position.[112]

Meanwhile, the PRC continued to exert military pressure on the
Tachens; and on January 18, 1955, PRC forces, with air support,
launched an amphibious attack against Yikiangshan, an islet of less
than half a square mile and only eight miles from the Tachens. On
January 20 the Communist forces captured the island, having suffered
heavy casualties in the process; all 720 Nationalist defenders were
killed in the battle. It was clear at that time that the next target of
the Communist forces would be the Tachen Islands. In view of the
gravity of the situation, President Eisenhower sent a message to
Congress on January 24 saying that "Formosa and the Pescadores
should not fall into the control of aggressive Communist forces" and
asked for a congressional resolution authorizing the president to
employ U.S. armed forces promptly and effectively for this purpose.
The message also spoke of "taking into account closely related

localities and actions" that might determine the failure or success of an attack on Formosa and the Pescadores.[113] On January 29, 1955, a congressional resolution to that effect (Doc. 44) was adopted and promptly signed by President Eisenhower.

In order to avoid a major PRC-ROC armed conflict that might involve American forces in the defense of the Tachen Islands, the United States advised the ROC government to evacuate their forces, utilizing American assistance and convoy protection. The ROC government reluctantly accepted the advice, and all 15,000 troops and 17,132 civilians were evacuated to Taiwan in early February. Shortly after this evacuation the ROC government also evacuated its troops and civilians from Nanchi Island.[114] The redeployment left Quemoy and Matsu as the only two island groups off the mainland of China in the hands of the ROC.

During the crisis some countries were afraid that a major armed conflict might break out in the Taiwan Straits and tried to arrange a cease-fire between the PRC and the ROC through the United Nations or through diplomatic channels. Early on October 10, 1954, when the Communist forces resumed their shelling of the Nationalist-controlled offshore islands, the PRC sent a cablegram to the United Nations requesting the ninth session of the General Assembly "to give its most serious attention" to no less than seven "facts relevant to the armed aggression against China's territory of Taiwan by the United States government." The cablegram specifically pointed out that "to liberate Taiwan is a matter of China's internal affairs" and "no foreign intervention will be tolerated."[115] It does not appear that the United Nations took any action on the cablegram, and this document appears to have been the PRC's last resort to the United Nations to protest the U.S. "armed aggression against Taiwan." Subsequently, despite press reports of various cease-fire proposals, no formal action was taken by Western countries until early 1955. On January 19, 1955, President Eisenhower said in a press conference that he would like to see the United Nations try to arrange a cease-fire between the Nationalists and Communists.[116] On January 24, 1955, President Eisenhower, in his message to Congress asking for authorization to use American forces to defend Taiwan and the Pescadores, said that the United States "would welcome any action by the United Nations which might, in fact, bring an end to the active hostilities in the area."[117]

On the same day Chou En-lai issued a statement that rejected any cease-fire proposal, saying that this "is in fact an intervention in China's internal affairs for the alienation of China's territory."[118]

Despite the PRC's objection, New Zealand proposed to the U.N. Security Council, on January 28, 1955, that it consider the situation arising out of the occurrence of armed hostilities between the PRC and the ROC in the area of certain islands off the coast of mainland

China.[119] On January 31 the Council decided to invite the PRC to
participate in the discussion of this question.[120] On February 3, 1955,
Chou En-lai sent a cablegram to the United Nations rejecting the
invitation. The cablegram said that, inasmuch as the liberation of
Taiwan was a sovereign right of the Chinese people and was an entirely
internal affair of China, it was a violation of the U.N. Charter to
suggest, as the New Zealand proposal did, that the Security Council
should consider the question of hostilities between his government and
the "Chiang Kai-shek regime." It further stated that so long as the
PRC's place in the United Nations was usurped by the "Chiang Kai-shek
group," the PRC would be unable to take part in the discussion of
questions concerning China in the United Nations.[121]

The ROC government was not happy about the so-called cease-fire
proposal. On February 8, 1955, President Chiang Kai-shek said that
"it is tantamount to recognition of the fait accompli of the aggressors"
(Doc. 45). The Council decided on February 14 to adjourn discussion
of the New Zealand item.[122]

After the evacuation of the Tachen Islands, some political leaders
in the United Kingdom, India, and the United States felt that Quemoy
and Matsu should be abandoned to the PRC.[123] To clarify the ROC's
position, President Chiang Kai-shek said at a press conference held
on February 14, 1955, that "in no case would they [Quemoy and Matsu]
be abandoned to the enemy"; he also rejected any proposal for "two
Chinas" (Doc. 46). On March 3, 1955, the ROC-U.S. mutual defense
treaty came into force and, after a visit to Taiwan early in March,
U.S. Secretary of State Dulles said in a press conference on March
15 that the president of the United States presumably would order
U.S. air and sea forces into action if there was an attack on the offshore
islands that was a part of the larger assault on Taiwan, and that his
recent discussions with President Chiang had taken account of the
possibility that the United States might have to help defend these
islands.[124] In light of this statement, the PRC quietly dropped its
desultory shelling of Matsu and Quemoy in late March. This, however,
does not mean that the PRC had given up its attempt to "liberate"
Taiwan. It soon turned to "peaceful liberation" tactics to implement
its attempt to seize Taiwan.

In spite of the gradual decrease of armed conflict in the Taiwan
Straits after the spring of 1955, neither side in the conflict has
basically altered its position and the tension remains. In an atmosphere
of tension, the Bandung Conference was held between April 18 and 24,
1955. Chou En-lai led the PRC delegation. His first speech, delivered
on April 19, referred to "the tension created solely by the United
States in the area of Taiwan" and showed little sign of a desire to
compromise. However, after extensive discussions, he dramatically
expressed a more conciliatory attitude at a luncheon given by the
prime minister of Ceylon on April 23. He announced:

The Chinese people are friendly to the American people.
The Chinese people do not want to have a war with the
United States of America. The Chinese Government is
willing to sit down and enter into negotiations with the
United States Government to discuss the question of
relaxing tension in the Far East and especially the question of relaxing tension in the Taiwan area. [125]

This offer was reiterated in Chou En-lai's final speech at the concluding session of the Bandung Conference, held the following day. [126]

The initial U.S. response was negative, but the PRC continued
to keep its offer open and to advocate the "peaceful liberation" of
Taiwan. [127] In a report to the Standing Committee of the PRC's
National People's Congress on May 17, Chou En-lai renewed his offer
and went on to state that the PRC was "willing to strive for the liberation of Taiwan by peaceful means so far as it is possible." [128] But
he reiterated the PRC's claim to Taiwan by saying that "no negotiations
should in the slightest degree affect the Chinese people's exercise of
their own sovereign rights, their just demand and action, to liberate
Taiwan." [129]

Subsequently, through the efforts of the United Kingdom and
India, the United States and the PRC issued a communiqué on July
25, 1955, indicating their agreement to hold ambassadorial talks
beginning on August 1, at Geneva. [130]

The PRC-U.S. communiqué did not say that the talks would
cover the Taiwan question, but this item may have been included in
the "other practical matters now at issue" that were referred to in
the communiqué. [131] At a press conference held on July 26, 1955,
Secretary of State Dulles said that the United States hoped "to find
out in the forthcoming talks whether the Chinese Communists accept
the concept of a cease-fire in accordance with the United Nations
principle of avoiding any use or threat of force which could disturb
the peace of nations" (Doc. 47).

The PRC also explained its position on Taiwan before the opening
of the ambassadorial talks. In a long report entitled "The Present
International Situation and China's Policy," Premier Chou En-lai told
the National People's Congress on July 30, 1955, that the tension in
the Taiwan area was "caused by the United States occupation of
China's territory of Taiwan and its interference with the liberation
of China's coastal island" and that "this is an international issue between
China and the United States." The "liberation" of Taiwan, however,
"is a matter of China's internal affairs." Therefore, "these two questions cannot be mixed up" and only the first question could be subject
to Sino-American negotiation.

Chou went on to say that there were two possible ways for the Chinese people* to "liberate" Taiwan—by war or by peaceful means— and that the Chinese people were ready to use the latter. He also offered to negotiate "with the responsible local authorities of Taiwan to map out concrete steps for Taiwan's peaceful liberation." But he pointed out that "these would be negotiations between the central government and local authorities" and that "the Chinese people are firmly opposed to any ideas or plots of the so-called 'two Chinas.'"[132]

After making an "agreed announcement" on the return of civilians on September 10, 1955,[133] the United States and the PRC entered into negotiations on the Taiwan question in October. The United States proposed that both parties agree to renounce the use of force in the pursuit of their objectives in general and, more specifically, in the Taiwan area. The PRC did not object to the pledge as far as relations between the two countries were concerned. However, it emphasized that this pledge should not be confused with domestic tensions; the status of Taiwan was a domestic matter that the PRC would strive to settle by peaceful means if possible. It made clear that "this internal affair of China's cannot possibly be a subject of the Sino-American talks" and refused to include the nonuse of force in the Taiwan area in any declaration on nonuse of force.[134] Therefore, after prolonged negotiations on the different drafts proposed by each party, it was clear by mid-1956 that no agreement could be reached on this question.[135]

Needless to say, from the very beginning the ROC opposed the PRC-U.S. talks because it feared that these contacts might lead to formal recognition of the PRC.[136] On March 15, 1956, President Chiang Kai-shek commented that even if the Chinese Communists did renounce the use of force in any area, he did not "believe they would live up to their undertaking." He thought that the Chinese Communists' willingness to negotiate with the United States was a plot designed to achieve a foreign ministers' conference that would enhance the prestige of the Communist regime (Doc. 49).

Meanwhile, the PRC had launched a peace offensive to "liberate" Taiwan. Soon after Chou En-lai's July 30, 1955, speech, a letter-writing campaign was launched. Many letters calling for the "peaceful liberation of Taiwan" were sent to the ROC leaders on Taiwan by their relatives, friends, former subordinates, teachers, and students on the mainland through radio broadcasts, newspapers, and other means.[137] On June 28, 1956, Chou En-lai issued a formal appeal to

---

*In PRC terminology "the Chinese people" means the PRC government.

the ROC leaders for "peaceful liberation" in his report to the National People's Congress. After recounting past cooperation between the Nationalists and Communists in the Northern Expedition (1927-28) and the Sino-Japanese War (1937-45), Chou appealed to Chinese patriotism, denounced the United States for playing "its usual splitting tactics to create suspicion and feuds inside Taiwan," and added:

> Now, on behalf of the Government, I formally state: We are willing to negotiate with the Taiwan authorities on specific steps and terms for the peaceful liberation of Taiwan, and we hope that the Taiwan authorities will send their representatives to Peking or other appropriate places,. at a time which they consider appropriate, to begin these talks with us.

He also promised to give those Chinese who had fled to Taiwan "all kinds of convenience and assistance" for a visit to their relatives and friends in mainland China, with a guarantee of "freedom of movement in coming and going" and a promise of clemency as well as appropriate positions for "Kuomintang military and political personnel" on Taiwan "in the motherland." Chou ended his appeal by saying that "the gate of the motherland is always open for all patriots" and that "every Chinese has both the right and the duty to make his contribution to the sacred cause of the unification of the motherland" (Doc. 50).

The ROC immediately rejected Chou En-lai's offer. A government spokesman called it "an insulting gesture" because "what needs liberation" is not Taiwan but the mainland. He regarded the "peace offensive" as an attempt to "bewitch the people of the Free World, wreck the unity among the free countries and isolate the United States."[138] On October 4, 1956, President Chiang Kai-shek told A. T. Steele of the New York Herald Tribune that the Communist "peace offensive" was "worthless."[139]

Despite the ROC's rejection of the peace overture, Chou En-lai continued to spread the idea of peace negotiations between the Nationalists and the Communists in late 1956.[140]

In early 1957 the PRC's propaganda objective became sowing dissension between the ROC and the United States. Therefore, in his March 5, 1957, report to the Chinese People's Political Consultative Conference, Chou En-lai said that the United States had instigated a group of Free China or Independent Taiwan elements to overthrow the ROC authorities so as "to turn Taiwan into a United States dependency like Honolulu" (Doc. 52). Such an attempt was, however, ineffective. On October 4, 1957, President Chiang Kai-shek told Sven Steenberg of West Germany that the ROC government "has already had too many painful experiences in negotiating with Communists";

and he reaffirmed the ROC's rejection of the Communist "peace proposal" and the ROC's determination to restore the freedom of the Chinese on the mainland (Doc. 53).

In early 1958 the PRC had accused the United States of promoting "two Chinas" or other international solutions (such as a plebiscite or U.N. trusteeship) of the Taiwan question (Doc. 54). In April and June of the same year, the PRC criticized the U.S. attitude toward the ambassadorial talks in Geneva. In its June 30 statement on the talks, it announced that unless they were resumed within 15 days, it could not "but consider that the United States" had "decided to break up the talks." The statement carried a threat to the effect that "the Chinese people are perfectly strong enough to liberate their territory Taiwan." It also denounced the United States effort to promote the situation of "two Chinas."[141]

After the period of the PRC's "ultimatum" had expired (it was extended for a few days on July 15), the United States on July 28 informed the PRC of its willingness to continue the talks at Warsaw instead of Geneva. There was no PRC response until September 6. Khrushchev and Mao Tse-tung held a secret meeting in Peking from July 31 to August 3, but they said nothing in their communiqué about Taiwan.[142] Around this time the PRC began a radio and press campaign for "liberating Taiwan." The PRC military movements and other preparations that were evident along the Chinese coast alarmed the ROC government, and a state of emergency was proclaimed in the offshore islands and the Taiwan Straits. On August 11 the United States released a memorandum on nonrecognition of the PRC that had been sent to all U.S. missions abroad. The memorandum explained several reasons for nonrecognition of the PRC, said "communism's rule in China is not permanent and that it one day will pass," and rejected the "two Chinas" solution (Doc. 55).

The PRC immediately denounced the memorandum as "shopworn" and the "occupation" of Taiwan as daydreaming on the part of those who were unaware of their own "impotence," for China had the "determination and strength" to liberate Taiwan.[143] At the same time, a Soviet broadcast in Chinese assured the PRC that it was not isolated in the world but had the support of the Soviet Union and other Communist countries.[144]

During this period it was clear that the PRC was attempting to resort to force to solve the Taiwan question; therefore President Eisenhower and his advisers were considering issuing a strong statement on U.S. intentions before any actual attack could be made by the PRC. However, the warning was not issued until August 23, when the PRC started the second Taiwan Straits crisis.[145]

On August 23, 1958, the PRC suddenly began a massive artillery bombardment of Quemoy in which, from 6:30 to 8:30 P.M., Communist

batteries rained 42,000 rounds of high explosives on the island. PRC
air and navy forces soon joined the action. PRC radios beamed
broadcasts directly to the people on Quemoy, warning them of imminent
landings of the "Liberation Army," demanding surrender of the defenders, and appealing for defectors. The PRC continued to bombard the
island for several weeks and hoped to lay a successful siege so as to
force its surrender. However, the ROC defenders stood firm and fought
back. The United States gave the ROC force some limited logistic
support by escorting the ROC supply ships to the three-mile limit off
Quemoy. But the more significant U.S. reaction was President Eisenhower's statement on August 27, saying that the offshore islands were
more important to the defense of Taiwan than they had been in the
Taiwan Straits crisis of 1955, because there was now a "closer inter-
locking" between the defense system of the islands and Taiwan.[146]

On September 4 the PRC declared it was extending its territorial
waters to 12 miles, thus including all offshore islands within its territorial waters (Doc. 57). The United States refused to recognize this
extension, saying it was an "attempt to cloak aggressive purposes."[147]
On September 7 the U.S. navy continued to escort ROC supply ships
to three miles from Quemoy.[148]

On the same day that the PRC extended its territorial waters,
U.S. Secretary of State Dulles called on the PRC to negotiate and
implied that the United States would not avoid resort to force in the
Taiwan Straits if compelled to use force (Doc. 56). Two days later
Chou En-lai replied, reaffirming the PRC's claim to Taiwan but
expressing willingness to resume the ambassadorial talks with the
United States (Doc. 58). The next day Soviet Premier Khrushchev
sent a letter to President Eisenhower supporting the PRC's claim to
Taiwan.[149] On September 15 the ambassadorial talks were resumed
at Warsaw. 1958

The PRC continued to bomb Quemoy. From August 23 to
October 4, the PRC fired a total of 444,433 rounds to Quemoy.[150]
The United States supplied some new weapons to the ROC, including
eight-inch Howitzers capable of firing tactical atomic shells and air-
to-air "Sidewinder" missiles. The ROC air force also won several
battles and shot down 31 Communist planes. On October 5 the PRC
unilaterally announced a cease-fire and offered to conduct direct
peace talks with the ROC government. On October 20, on the eve of
Dulles' visit to Taipei, the PRC fired on Quemoy again. On October
25 PRC Defense Minister P'eng Teh-huai announced an "even-day"
cease-fire (Doc. 62) This has been the military situation in the Taiwan
Straits up to the present.

During the crisis the tone of the ROC leaders was very conciliatory. On September 15, 1958, President Chiang emphasized in his
answer to questions submitted by the New York Journal-American

that the Communists' shelling and encircling was "in actuality a prelude to an invasion of Taiwan" (Doc. 59). On September 29 President
Chiang told a group of reporters that Quemoy and Matsu "do not
constitute an obstacle to peace" and that every time it was the Communists who started the hostilities in the offshore islands. He said
that the bases of the ROC's counterattack "are not on Quemoy and
Matsu" but "are on the mainland itself." He also warned that if the
Communists "should continue to bomb these islands in an attempt to
re-blockade them," the ROC "shall . . . take retaliatory actions against
Communist bases on the mainland" (Doc. 60).

Despite the conciliatory attitude of the ROC, the U.S. decision
to become involved in the defense of the offshore islands caused much
concern at home.[151] Therefore, when Dulles held his press conference on September 30, he said that the United States had not felt
"that it was sound to make the major commitment of force" by the
ROC to the offshore islands. He further pointed out that "it would be
our judgment, military judgment even, that it would not be wise or
prudent to keep them there,"[152] thus implying that the offshore islands
could be abandoned in exchange for a cease-fire. The ROC's reaction
to Dulles' statement was naturally unfavorable. On October 1 President
Chiang said that "granted that Mr. Dulles made the statement attributed
to him, it would be only a unilateral declaration and my government
would be under no obligation to keep it."[153] On October 15 President
Eisenhower gave an assurance that the United States would not try
to coerce its ally into changing a policy that it regarded, rightly or
wrongly, as essential to its security.[154] Dulles arrived in Taipei on
October 20, and on October 23 the ROC and the United States issued
a joint communiqué in which the ROC, while affirming that "the
restoration of freedom to its people on the mainland is its sacred
mission," nevertheless recognized that "the principal means of
successfully achieving its mission is the implementation of Dr. Sun
Yat-sen's three people's principles and not the use of force" (Doc. 61).
The PRC severely criticized the communiqué as a further attempt by
the United States to create "two Chinas" (Doc. 63). The PRC also
lost no opportunity to sow dissension between the United States and
the ROC. Thus, in P'eng's statement on cease-fire on even-numbered
dates, issued on October 25, he also warned the ROC against being
"thrown into the sea" by the United States (Doc. 62).

At Warsaw the United States and the PRC representatives held
10 talks on Taiwan. But before the 10th meeting on November 7,
PRC Vice-Premier and Foreign Minister Ch'en Yi told Gordon Clark
of the Montreal Star that the PRC would not guarantee anyone the
renunciation of force regarding Taiwan. Certainly realizing the
United States intended to separate the question of the offshore islands
and the question of Taiwan, Ch'en Yi pointed out:

Quemoy, Matsu, Taiwan and the Pescadores must be
liberated as a whole. We will not allow the handing over
of Quemoy in exchange for placing Taiwan under trusteeship. . . . Nor can we accept demilitarization or referring
the matter to the UN or the International Court of Justice.[155]

Thus, in November, 1958, while the military crisis subsided, the
question of Taiwan remained unsolved in PRC-U.S. relations.

Facing the determined effort of the United States and the ROC
to resist the PRC's military action to take over the offshore islands
and Taiwan, the PRC quietly dropped its attempt to "liberate" them
by force and turned to political and long-term strategy. In mid-
September, 1958, Peking Radio said that the PRC would be ready to
wait "five to ten years" to settle the problem of Taiwan.[156] On
October 13 PRC Defense Minister P'eng Teh-huai said that he would
not be surprised if the civil war, which started in 1928, between the
Nationalists and the Communists continued for another "thirty years";
and he rejected any American interference in that civil war.[157]
Moreover, it was reported that Mao Tse-tung said in an interview held
in 1959 that "[the Chinese territory] is spacious, and for the time
being we can get along without these islands [Taiwan and the offshore
islands]" (Doc. 66).

In the meantime Peking did not want to create the impression
that its military inaction toward Taiwan meant that it was tacitly giving
up its claim to the territory or allowing the development of a situation
leading to the detachment of Taiwan from China. Political developments
on Taiwan and abroad during the next three years also gave the PRC
the impression that the United States seemed "actively" to take the
opportunity of its inaction on the "liberation" of Taiwan to promote
the "two Chinas" solution in order to detach Taiwan permanently
from China.

In 1959 Lei Chen, a former high-ranking official of the Nationalist
Party (KMT), began to organize an opposition party in Taiwan.* Dr.
Thomas Wen-yi Liao actively promoted the Taiwan Independence
Movement in Japan.** Many Chinese, whether Communists or not,

---

*Lei was arrested in 1960 by the Nationalist authorities on a
charge of failing to report a Communist agent working closely under
him. He was sentenced to ten years of imprisonment and released in
1970.

**Liao later gave up his movement. See Item 9.

believed that both movements were at least tacitly supported by the
United States and were secretly financed by the U.S. Central Intelligence
Agency. More significantly, on November 1, 1959, the U.S. Senate
Foreign Relations Committee published the "Conlon Report," which
proposed, among other things, the establishment of an independent
Republic of Taiwan as the ultimate solution of the Taiwan question
(Item 5). Furthermore, it was disclosed in 1963 that Soviet Premier
Khrushchev, aware of the danger posed by the 1958 Taiwan Straits
crisis, which might drag the Soviet Union into a major armed conflict
with the United States, suggested to the PRC after his visit to the
United States in October, 1959, that it make a temporary concession
on the Taiwan question and the "two Chinas" issue (Doc. 78). All these
developments alerted the PRC that an "international conspiracy" for
creating "two Chinas" was in the making.

Meanwhile, the PRC realized that such a political atmosphere
would give it a good opportunity to sow dissension between the ROC
and the United States, since all "two Chinas" proposals necessarily
imply the ultimate elimination of the ROC government. Therefore
the PRC's strategy during this period was twofold. It repeated,
elaborated, and emphasized its position on Taiwan in many important
official statements. At the same time it launched subtle psychological
warfare vis-à-vis Taiwan. Unlike its peace offensive after the 1955
Taiwan Straits crisis, this time the PRC did not make an outright
call upon the ROC government to negotiate for the "peaceful liberation"
of Taiwan. On the contrary, it warned the ROC government against being overthrown by the United States and urged the ROC to resist the
"American conspiracy" to create "two Chinas."

Early in February, 1959, a lengthy article entitled "The Absurd
Theory of 'Two Chinas' and Principles of International Law" appeared
in Peking's Kuo-chi wen-t'i yen-chiu (Studies in international problems)
(Item 4). This article was subsequently translated into English and
published, together with other official and unofficial statements
denouncing the "two Chinas" plot, in a widely circulated booklet
entitled Oppose the New U.S. Plots to Create "Two Chinas" (1962).
In addition to arguing in legal terms that Taiwan is de jure and de facto
Chinese territory and the "liberation" of Taiwan is an internal affair
of China that is subject to no foreign interference, the article viewed
the American tactics toward Taiwan as follows:

> Firstly, [American imperialism] appoints the Chiang Kai-
> shek clique as "small China" and stations the Seventh
> Fleet in the Taiwan Strait to separate Taiwan from the
> mainland so as to create the situation of a confrontation
> of "two Chinas." . . . Secondly, [American imperialism]
> will overthrow the Chiang regime . . . at the appropriate

time and then will use the name of the United Nations "trusteeship" or some other to establish a "trusteeship of Taiwan" so as to transform Taiwan into its permanent colony.

The article concluded its study by "exposing" the American "plot" toward Taiwan as follows:

Today the so-called "Republic of China" is . . . also a signboard. The Americans . . . regard the Chiang Kai-shek clique as negligible elements. As the U.S. Vice-President Nixon said that the Americans never intended "to keep the symbol of Chiang Kai-shek on the Taiwan island" but "look beyond Chiang." In other words, if the Chiang Kai-shek clique refuses to act obediently as puppets, the Americans will kick them out. . . . In the last analysis, U.S. imperialists only want to turn Taiwan into an "island of freedom," in other words, seize it as their own, and turn it into a colony of the United States.

At Warsaw the United States and the PRC continued the talks. As stated before, the PRC refused to commit itself to the nonuse of force in the Taiwan Straits and an impasse was reached on this issue. Therefore, in 1959 the United States tried to bypass this issue and to discuss other matters with the PRC. However, the PRC responded by tying every subject under discussion to the question of Taiwan. For instance, when the United States proposed the exchange of correspondents between the two countries, the PRC insisted on including a clause on "the question of withdrawal of all U.S. armed forces from "China's territory Taiwan" in the proposed agreement and therefore made it unacceptable to the United States.[158] On September 5, 1960, Premier Chou En-lai told British correspondent Felix Greene that "so long as the United States continues to occupy Taiwan, there can be no basic improvement in the relations between the United States and China" (Doc. 69). Three days later a People's Daily editorial entitled "100 Meetings of Sino-U.S. Talks" blamed the United States for failure to reach an agreement with the PRC on the question of Taiwan at the talks (Doc. 70). The editorial reiterated the PRC position on Taiwan and denounced the alleged American attempt to create "two Chinas."

Before and after the inauguration of the Kennedy administration, there were numerous reports on the various "two Chinas" proposals that might be adopted by the new administration. In addition to various proposals to detach Taiwan legally from China, there was a suggestion to place it under the "suzerainty" of China while enjoying complete autonomous status and retaining a seat in the U.N. General Assembly.*

In the April 25, 1961, issue of the Bulletin of Activities, a secret, captured publication of the General Political Department of the Chinese People's Liberation Army that was distributed for study only by cadres at or above the regimental level, the proposal of Chinese "suzerainty" over Taiwan as an acceptable solution of the Taiwan question was categorically rejected:

> Recently, most worthy of notice has been [the fact] that from "two Chinas" the United States has changed to seeing "one and half China." It has virtually admitted that China has suzerainty over Taiwan, making Taiwan into a "semi-independent" state. A big China contains a small China and one is added to one half. It seems that there are no more "two Chinas." . . . We are resolved to oppose this firmly.

> . . .

> This method of American imperialism is intended to test our firmness in opposing imperialism, whether we shall yield under pressure or not. China is a new Socialist country, and if it yields or lets an imperialist army occupy our own territory, the international prestige of China will topple over. We need not take back Taiwan at present, so that the United States will continue to be in an equivocal position, criticized but unable to admit the legal status of its occupation. "One and half China" is in reality a crystallization of the plot of "two Chinas"; it is a cup of poisonous wine, sweet in taste but strong poison, which we can never drink.[159] (Emphasis added.)

On July 14, 1961, the People's Daily published a lengthy editorial entitled "There Is Only One China, Not Two" (Doc. 74). It condemned all "two China" proposals, especially the Taiwan Independence Movement headed by Dr. Thomas Wen-yi Liao. It also severely warned those Chinese who participated in the "conspiratorial activities" of "two Chinas" by saying that "they can never escape the severe punishment that will be meted out to them by the Chinese people." At the same time the editorial attempted to sow dissension between the ROC the United States:

---

*This was proposed by Harvard Professor John K. Fairbank on January 20, 1961. See Doc. 76.

If the authorities in Taiwan continue to live under the
thumb and the dictates of others, they will eventually be
thrown overboard by them . . . so long as they consider
their own future and weigh the pros and cons, they will
not fail to see that to follow the "two Chinas" policy of
U.S. imperialism is tantamount to digging their own
graves.

On August 7 the People's Daily published another lengthy article
entitled "A Brief Account of the U.S. 'Two Chinas' Plot" (Doc. 76),
summarizing almost all important American proposals between 1953
and 1961, official or unofficial, for the solution of the question of
Taiwan. It categorically rejected all "these U.S. formulas . . . [that]
have only one aim, i.e., to persist in the forcible occupation of the
Chinese territory of Taiwan." . . . "Opposed by the people of all
China (including those now in Taiwan who do not want to be traitors
to the nation by completely selling Taiwan to the United States) and
the just public opinion of the whole world, the U.S. plot to create 'two
Chinas' by all conceivable means will never succeed," the article
concluded.

On many occasions, the PRC manifested its determination to
"liberate" Taiwan and reasserted its claim to the island. For instance,
on July 17 and 19, 1960, the PRC conducted an "armed demonstration"
by bombing Quemoy to protest President Eisenhower's visit to the
ROC.160 On February 1, 1962, an enlarged celebration of the 300th
anniversary of the recovery of Taiwan by Cheng Ch'en-kung (a
Chinese general who drove the Dutch from Taiwan in 1662) was held
in Peking.161

During the same period the emergence of various proposed
solutions of the Taiwan question also alerted the ROC. Therefore,
on February 20, 1960, President Chiang Kai-shek reaffirmed the
ROC's rejection of any "two Chinas" proposal before the National
Assembly (Doc. 67). As all "two Chinas" proposals presuppose the
handing over of the offshore islands (Quemoy and Matsu) to the
Chinese Communists, on July 9, 1960, Chiang again reaffirmed the
ROC's position that under no circumstance would it be willing to
surrender these islands (Doc. 68). He also reasoned that these islands
are essential to the defense of Taiwan. On June 11, 1961, President
Chiang said that the "two Chinas" theory "would in effect facilitate
the Chinese Communists in their attempt to destroy free China"
(Doc. 72).

Besides the ROC government, many leading non-Communist
Chinese in Taiwan and abroad strongly opposed the "two Chinas"
proposals, especially the creation of an independent Taiwan Republic.
In April, 1960, a critical review of the Conlon Report (Item 5) was

issued by the Sino-American Cultural and Economic Association. It
warned the United States that if the proposal in the Conlon Report
were carried out, Taiwan would most probably "fall into the hands of
the Chinese Communists, because they will take the chance to use the
slogan of 'national united front' again to induce refugee Chinese on
Taiwan to return to the mainland."[162] The famous Chinese writer
Lin Yutang and several Chinese professors in the United States also
issued a statement severely criticizing the Conlon Report (Item 6).
The statement said, among other things, that "should the suggestions
of the Conlon Report be put into effect, it would provide ample reason
for the people on the mainland to hate America because it would have
been the United States that forced Taiwan to become a non-Chinese
state . . . and thereby justify the criticism of 'territorial aggression'
made by the Chinese Communists."

Perhaps to relieve the worry of the ROC about possible changes
in American China policy, Secretary of State Rusk told a BBC representative on March 3, 1961, that the Chinese Nationalist leaders
"were to us and are a much more genuine representation of the China
that we have known" (Doc. 71). But he qualified his statement by
saying that he was "talking in this context about the great cultural
heritage of China," thus leaving the American position on the political
aspect of the question vague. A few months later Vice-President
Ch'en Chen of the ROC was invited by President Kennedy to visit the
United States. A joint communiqué issued on August 2, 1961, reiterated
American support of the ROC and its representation in the United
Nations and continued opposition to the Chinese Communist regime
in the United Nations (Doc. 75).

In late 1958 the PRC began to launch the Great Leap Forward
for "Socialist reconstruction" that later proved to be an economic
disaster. In 1961-62 food shortages and unrest were acute in many
parts of the mainland. Moreover, in the first half of 1962 there were
numerous natural calamities, such as drought, flood, and pestilence
in many provinces of the mainland. In May, 1962, some 100,000
refugees from southern China flooded into Hong Kong, although a substantial number of them were soon rounded up and turned back to the
mainland.[163] Internationally, the PRC was preoccupied with tensions
along its border with the Soviet Union and India and increased American
military involvement in Vietnam.[164]

During this period the ROC obviously saw an opportunity to
"recover" the mainland. In President Chiang's New Year's Day
message to the Chinese people for 1962, he declared:

> Our armed forces have made adequate preparations for
> the counter-offensive, and, therefore, are capable of
> moving into action at any time. Have no fear of being

> alone in rising against the Communists. Have no fear
> of lack or shortage of supplies or help. Both will be
> forthcoming once you take action.[165]

Then additional manpower was conscripted into the ROC armed forces,
and a provisional national defense special assessment was imposed
for the period May 1, 1962, to June 30, 1963.[166] In the early months
of 1962, several high American officials, including Averell Harriman
and Allen Dulles, visited Taiwan. Their purpose was presumably
to discourage the Nationalist eagerness for an invasion of the mainland, but the PRC might have believed just the opposite. The same
applies to the appointment in May of a new American ambassador
to the ROC, Admiral Alan G. Kirk, who had had extensive experience
with amphibious operations during World War II.[167]

As a result, during June, 1962, the PRC heavily reinforced its
forces opposite Taiwan.[168] On June 23 the PRC official news agency
maintained that "the Chiang Kai-shek [clique] . . . with the support
and encouragement of U.S. imperialism, is preparing for . . . an
invasion of the coastal areas of the mainland" (Doc. 77). It said the
Americans wanted "to kill two birds with one stone." If Chiang's
invasion succeeded, it would "deal a blow to the prestige" of the PRC.
On the other hand, if it failed, then his strength would be greatly
weakened, thus facilitating the American imperialists' "kicking him
out" and using a new puppet to take over Taiwan. On the same day,
at a special meeting in Warsaw, American Ambassador to Poland
John Moors Cabot reportedly informed PRC Ambassador Wang that
the United States would not support the Nationalists' attempt to invade
the mainland.[169] This American position was reaffirmed by President Kennedy in his press conference held on June 27. He stressed
the defensive character of the American commitment to the ROC,
but he also strongly reaffirmed his predecessor's statements that
the United States would defend Taiwan and the offshore islands if
necessary.[170] On July 2 Soviet Premier Khrushchev said that "anyone who dares to attack the People's Republic of China will meet a
crushing rebuff from the great Chinese people and the people of the
Soviet Union and the whole socialist camp."[171] A few days later
PRC Vice-Premier and Foreign Minister Ch'en Yi expressed the
PRC's gratitude for Soviet support but again held the United States
responsible for any possible invasion of the mainland "on a big scale
or a small scale."[172]

After the American reaffirmation of the defensive character
of its commitment to the ROC, the possibility of a military confrontation in the Taiwan Straits gradually abated, though the ROC
did launch several commando raids against the mainland coast in
late 1962 and early 1963.[173]

Since 1963 the Taiwan Straits have been relatively quiet; and the so-called even-day cease-fire in the offshore islands, which was initiated by the PRC in late October 1958, has been tacitly observed by both sides. Each side affirms and reaffirms its previous position, but no positive action has so far been taken by either side to upset the status quo in the area. The United States, while affirming and reaffirming its commitment to the defense of Taiwan, has gradually shifted to a de facto "two Chinas" policy, despite vehement opposition from both the ROC and the PRC. It appears that after 1963, each interested party in the Taiwan question adopted a long-range political approach while maintaining its uncompromising position.

To the PRC, a long-range political approach to the Taiwan question necessitates keeping the issue alive; otherwise, a de facto status quo could gradually crystallize into a de jure situation undermining the PRC's ultimate goal of "liberating" Taiwan. Therefore, despite the impasse on the question of Taiwan at the Warsaw talks, the PRC continues the talks as a channel of communication with the United States.[174] At times Peking makes overtures to the ROC leaders, and rumors of Peking-Taipei peace negotiations occasionally appear in the press.[175] The PRC loses no opportunity to announce its determination to "liberate" Taiwan. In international affairs the PRC refuses to participate in any international organization or conference, governmental or nongovernmental, when a delegation from the ROC or Taiwan is also present.[176]

On January 27, 1964, the PRC announced the establishment of diplomatic relations with France and agreed to exchange ambassadors within three months.[177] This time the ROC, perhaps at the suggestion of the United States, did not follow its usual practice of breaking diplomatic relations with any state recognizing the PRC, though it did make a strong protest to the French government.[178] As France also made no move to initiate such a break, the PRC's Foreign Ministry issued a statement on January 28 reminding France that the "government of the People's Republic of China" was the "sole legal government representing all the Chinese people," that "recognition of the new government of a country naturally implies ceasing to recognize the old ruling group overthrown by the people of that country," and that "the Chinese Government deems it necessary to reaffirm that Taiwan is part of China's territory and that any attempt to detach Taiwan from China or otherwise to create 'two Chinas' is absolutely unacceptable to the Chinese Government and people."[179] This statement put France in a difficult position since, prior to its recognition of the PRC, it had hoped to make an arrangement whereby it could recognize "two Chinas."[180] Perhaps under the pressure of the PRC, French President de Gaulle said in a statement on February 10 that France recognized only one China.[181] On the same

day the ROC severed relations with France.[182] In President Chiang
Kai-shek's answer to a question submitted by a Mexican newsman on
March 26, he reaffirmed the ROC's opposition to the "two Chinas"
arrangement (Doc. 81).

During the 1960's the PRC was also very sensitive to the
activities of the Taiwan Independence Movement. On February 25, 1964,
Premier Chou sternly rejected the application of the principle of self-
determination to Taiwan in a press conference held at Dacca, Pakistan
(Doc. 79). An editorial in the People's Daily on May 12, 1964, reaffirmed
the PRC claim to Taiwan in clear-cut legal terms (Doc. 82); and on
May 24, 1964, the secretary-general of the Taiwan Democratic Self-
Government League, Hsu Meng-shan, wrote a long article in the
People's Daily denouncing the "independence movement" in a very
straightforward way (Doc. 83).

> For the sake of realizing its ambition of permanently
> occupying Taiwan, the U.S. bribed a handful of turncoats
> in the motherland and instigated them to clamor for "a
> Taiwan for the Taiwanese" or "Taiwan wants independ-
> ence." This is a scheme, the Taiwan compatriots under-
> stand clearly. The so-called "Taiwan people's Taiwan,"
> to speak frankly, is "America's Taiwan."[183]

The article ends with a threatening pronouncement:

> The strength of the people of China today is unprece-
> dented in history. The people of China have full confi-
> dence in restoring Taiwan province to their motherland.

On October 16, 1964, the PRC announced its first successful
test of a nuclear device.[184] But no pronouncement on the "liberation
of Taiwan" was made in connection with this event. This attitude was
understandable, since the use of nuclear weapons to attack Taiwan
would certainly contradict the alleged purpose of the PRC's "liberation"
of Taiwan—to "save" the inhabitants of Taiwan from the "yoke" of
"the Chiang Kai-shek clique" and "American imperialism."

French recognition and the PRC's entry into the nuclear club
certainly enhanced its international prestige and its chance of replacing
the ROC in the United Nations. Nevertheless, the 19th General Assembly of the United Nations, which opened in the fall of 1964, became
deadlocked over the French and Soviet refusal to make financial
contributions for peace-keeping missions to which they objected.
Therefore, the Assembly adopted a temporary no-voting procedure
to handle business, including the Chinese representation question.
But the ROC certainly realized the adverse nature of the trend in the

international arena on the question of its representation in the United Nations. Accordingly, in his New Year's message for 1965, President Chiang announced that "we are not perturbed by threats to our representation in the United Nations" but "are worried lest the United Nations should repeat the League of Nations' history of more than twenty years ago" (Doc. 84). In May, 1965, the ROC won a significant victory over the Taiwan Independence Movement in Japan. At that time the head of the movement, Dr. Thomas Wen-yi Liao, decided to dissolve his organization, returned to Taiwan (Item 9), and pledged to support President Chiang's anti-Communist struggle (Item 10). In the same month another leader of the Japan-based independence movement, Cheng Wen-fu, president of the Taiwan Democratic-Political Party, also dissolved his organization (Item 11).

On June 27, 1965, the PRC commemorated the 15th anniversary of "the American military occupation" of Taiwan—referring to June 27, 1950, when President Truman decided to send the Seventh Fleet to the Taiwan Straits—with a long editorial in People's Daily entitled "The Chinese People Are Determined to Liberate Taiwan" (Doc. 85). Lin Piao's celebrated article, "Long Live the Victory of People's War," reaffirmed the PRC's determination to "liberate" Taiwan.[185]

On September 26 Li Tsung-jen, the former vice-president of the ROC who had lived in the United States after 1949, appeared in Peking and called for the "reunification of the motherland." Li also warned the Nationalists of being overthrown by the United States: "Even faithful lackeys like Syngman Rhee and Ngo Dinh Diem could not escape the fate of being kicked aside when they were not pliable enough."[186]

However, in a press conference on September 29 Vice-Premier and Foreign Minister Ch'en Yi took advantage of Mr. Li's defection by again making overtures to the ROC leaders (Doc. 86). He did not refer to "liberation" but called for "cooperation" between the Communist Party and the Nationalist Party (Kuomintang). He imposed only one condition for "cooperation": "to break away from U.S. imperialist control and be loyal to the motherland." Ch'en Yi also predicted that "the possibility of Kuomintang-Communist cooperation is great and is moreover increasing."

At the same press conference he unexpectedly announced the following conditions for the PRC's participation in the United Nations:

> Will the present U.N. General Assembly adopt a resolution expelling the elements of the Chiang Kai-shek clique and restoring China's legitimate rights? . . . If things really turn out that way, the question would still remain unresolved.

The United Nations must rectify its mistakes and
undergo a thorough reorganization and reform. It must
admit and correct all its past mistakes. Among other
things it should cancel its resolution condemning China
and the Democratic People's Republic of Korea as aggressors and adopt a resolution condemning the United States
as the aggressor; the U.N. Charter must be reviewed and
revised jointly by all countries, big and small; all independent states should be included in the United Nations; and all
imperialist puppets should be expelled."[187]

Despite such unreasonable conditions for participating in the United
Nations, the result of the voting on the Chinese representation question
in the 20th General Assembly was 47-47.

After the end of the third Taiwan Straits crisis in 1962, the
United States gradually began to reconsider its China policy and made
efforts to test the PRC's willingness to accept a "two Chinas" solution
of the Taiwan problem. On December 13, 1963, the U.S. Assistant
Secretary of State for Far Eastern affairs, Roger W. Hilsman, delivered
a lengthy speech on China policy. In this speech he clearly pointed out
that the United States would "fully honor our close and friendly ties
with the people of the Republic of China on Taiwan and with their
Government" and that "so long as Peiping insists on the destruction
of this relationship as the sine qua non for any basic improvement
in relations between ourselves and Communist China, there can be
no prospect for such an improvement."[188] But he concluded his speech
by saying that "we pursue today toward Communist China a policy of
the open door: We are determined to keep the door open to the possibility of change, not to slam it shut against any developments which
might advance our national good, serve the free world, and benefit
the people of China."[189] This overture for improving relations with
the PRC, together with other similar speeches made by Averell Harriman and Dean Rusk, was rejected by a People's Daily article on
February 19, 1964, which insisted on American withdrawal from
Taiwan and the Taiwan Straits as a precondition for improving relations.[190]

Despite the initial negative response from the PRC, the United
States continued to try to improve relations with it. In the meantime
the United States reassured the ROC of its treaty commitment, but
it no longer explicitly supported the ROC claim to be the "sole legal
government of China." Thus, when Secretary of State Rusk visited
the ROC in April, 1964, he failed to support the ROC claim unequivo-
cally in his statement issued on April 16.[191] The ROC, certainly,
was unhappy with the shift in America's China policy. Its displeasure
was evidenced by the fact that no communiqué was issued at the
conclusion of Rusk's visit.

After the PRC became a nuclear power in the fall of 1964 and
following the 47-47 vote on the Chinese representation in the United
Nations, there were growing pressures in the United States to change
its China policy. Therefore, in March, 1966, hearings on China policy
were held by the Committee on Foreign Relations of the U.S. Senate.192
Many participants in the hearings favored shifting China policy to
"containment without isolation." In this connection Professor A. Doak
Barnett's statement is representative:

> A shift of American policy on the United Nations issue—
> and, in fact, any significant change in our posture toward
> Peking—will inevitably require some modification of our
> policy toward the Nationalist regime on Taiwan. For many
> reasons—political, strategic, and moral—we should con-
> tinue defending Taiwan against attack and should firmly
> support the principle of self-determination in regard to
> the 13 million inhabitants of the island. But we will not be
> able to continue sustaining the fiction that the Nationalist
> regime is the government of mainland China.
>
> Our view of the Nationalist regime should be one in
> which we recognize it as the legal government of the terri-
> tories it now occupies, essentially Taiwan and the Pes-
> cadores, rather than as the government of all China; this,
> one might note, is essentially the position which the
> Japanese Government already maintains in regard to the
> Nationalists. We should do all we can to obtain represen-
> tation for the Taipei regime in the United Nations and to
> urge the international community to accept and support it
> as the government of its present population and territory.
> But we cannot indefinitely sustain the fiction that it is the
> government of all China.193

Officially, Secretary of State Dean Rusk told the Subcommittee
on the Far East and the Pacific of the House Committee on Foreign
Affairs on March 16, 1966, that the United States "do [es] not seek to
overthrow by force the Peiping regime" and announced 10 main elements
in American policy toward Communist China that repeated the U.S.
treaty commitment to the ROC on Taiwan and the continued support
of the ROC's representation in the United Nations, yet indicated a
desire to improve relations with the PRC.194
While the Americans were engaged in a controversial debate
on China policy, the PRC started the "Great Proletarian Cultural
Revolution" in the late spring of 1966 and did not show any interest
in various suggestions made, in the course of the American debate,
to improve PRC-U.S. relations. Thus, on March 29, 1966, the PRC

responded with an article in the People's Daily that again denounced
the "American occupation of Taiwan" and rejected the American
overture.[195] Furthermore, a People's Daily editorial of June 27,
1966, did not compromise on the Taiwan question (Doc. 87). Even at
the height of the Cultural Revolution, the question of Taiwan was still
being mentioned, though in very short but adamant terms. On October
1, 1968, the PRC's national day, Lin Piao, Mao's heir-designate,
said: "We definitely will liberate Taiwan and are ready at all times
to wipe out all enemies who dare to invade us!" Chou En-lai said,
more simply: "We definitely will liberate Taiwan!"[196] The PRC
also maintained its uncompromising position on the "two Chinas"
situation. For instance, when the national emblem of the ROC appeared
in a Soviet publication, the PRC protested strongly to the Soviet
government (Doc. 88). On November 26, 1968, the PRC issued a statement on the Warsaw talks saying that "the Chinese Government will
never barter away principles [i.e., America must withdraw from
Taiwan]" (Doc. 90).

Moreover, all available materials concerning the Cultural
Revolution have indicated that the question of Taiwan, "two Chinas,"
or "one China, one Taiwan" has never been an issue among contending
Communist leaders. As a matter of fact, the attitude of deposed
leaders such as Liu Shao-ch'i[197] and P'eng Chen toward this question
was in no way different from that of other Communist leaders.[198]

The Cultural Revolution created great turmoil on the mainland
and seemingly presented another opportunity for the ROC to "recover"
the mainland. But the ROC seemed to take a very cautious attitude.
In his 1967 New Year's message President Chiang emphasized that
the "counterattack" against the mainland must be political rather
than military.[199] Perhaps to test the American response to the
possibility of ROC action against the mainland, ROC Ambassador
Chow Shu-kai told reporters on January 10, 1967, that because of the
turmoil on the mainland, 1967 might be the decisive year for ROC
recovery of the mainland.[200] But the U.S. response was immediate
and negative. Department of State spokesman Robert J. MacCloskey,
referring to the exchange of notes accompanying the 1954 Sino-
American Defense Treaty (Doc. 42), said that the ROC should not
resort to offensive action against the mainland without prior consultation and agreement with the United States.[201] In May, Vice-
President Yen Chia-ken of the ROC was invited by President Johnson
to visit the United States, but the joint statement issued by them on
May 10 merely said: "They agreed that the struggle for power is far
from over and that developments on the Chinese mainland are closely
related to the peace and security of Asia. They further agreed to
consult on future developments on the Chinese mainland."[202] Probably
as a result of the unfavorable response from the American side,

President Chiang specified in his 1967 National Day (October 10)
message that the "counterattack" should be considered 70 percent
political and 30 percent military.203 Throughout the Cultural Revolution (1966-69) the ROC's attitude was cautious, and no military
action was undertaken against the mainland. However, it did improve
its international status significantly. In January, 1966, 57 states
maintained diplomatic relations with the ROC; by June 1968 it had
increased to 64, while the PRC then had diplomatic relations with only
45 states. In the United Nations the resolution to expel the ROC and
to seat the PRC was defeated in 1968 by a decisive vote of 58-44,
with 23 abstentions.

In early 1969 the Cultural Revolution began to subside, but the
PRC's uncompromising position on the Taiwan question remained.
On April 4, 1969, the PRC insisted that the Japanese agree, in a
trade communiqué, that the PRC "is the only legitimate government
representing the Chinese people, [and] that Taiwan Province is an
inalienable part of China's territory" (Doc. 91). Later, it also expressed great indignation at the alleged support of the United States
and Japan for a leader of the Taiwan Independence Movement who
had escaped from Taiwan (Doc. 92). When it negotiated the establishment of diplomatic relations with other countries, the PRC invariably
insisted on bringing up the question of Taiwan. Negotiations with
Canada on establishing diplomatic relations were deadlocked for more
than a year because the PRC insisted that Canada recognize PRC
sovereignty over Taiwan.204 Finally, Canada and the PRC agreed to
include the following formula on the Taiwan question when they announced the establishment of diplomatic relations on October 13, 1970:
"The Chinese Government reaffirms that Taiwan is an inalienable
part of the territory of the People's Republic of China. The Canadian
Government takes note of this position of the Chinese Government."205
A few weeks later the same formula was followed in Italian recognition
of the PRC.206 However, with respect to countries not directly allied
with the United States, such as Kuwait, Cameroon, and Austria, the
PRC showed flexibility by not including the Taiwan clause in the
communiqué announcing the establishment of diplomatic relations,
though it did insist on being recognized as "the sole legal Government
which represents the entire Chinese people"207 or "the sole legal
Government of China."208

Despite its uncompromising position on the question of Taiwan,
since 1969 the PRC has been very active in trying to end its international isolation. At the time of this writing, August 1972, diplomatic
relations have been established or resumed with some thirty countries
during the past two years—Argentina, Austria, Belgium, Burundi,
Cameroon, Canada, Chile, Cyprus, Ecuador, Equatorial Guinea,
Ethiopia, Ghana, Greece, Guyana, Iceland, Iran, Italy, Kuwait, Lebanon,

Malta, Mauritius, Mexico, Nigeria, Peru, Rwanda, San Marino, Senegal, Sierra Leone, Southern Yemen, Tunisia, and Turkey.* The PRC has also shown more interest in participating in the United Nations by refraining from mentioning its 1965 conditions for participating in this organization, except the one on expelling the ROC or Taiwan.

On the part of the United States, the Nixon administration, inaugurated in January, 1969, undertook cautious steps to improve relations with the PRC. First, it withdrew the Seventh Fleet from periodic patrol in the Taiwan Straits.209 Then certain trade and travel restrictions applied to China in the early 1950's were removed.210 Furthermore, though the United States voted against the Albanian-sponsored resolution to expel the ROC and to seat the PRC at the 25th session of the U.N. General Assembly, it did soften its attitude toward admission of the PRC. The U.S. representative to the General Assembly, Christopher H. Phillips, said:

> The fact of the matter is, the United States is as interested as any in this room to see the People's Republic of China play a constructive role among the family of nations. . . .
>
> But let us also remember . . . that the Charter nowhere confers upon states the right to make their own conditions for membership in the United Nations. Neither in the Charter nor in any resolution is it written that a state may say "we will join, but only if you expel member x."211

The above statement clearly implied that if the ROC were not to be expelled, then the United States would no longer oppose the seating of the PRC at the United Nations.

President Nixon and other high administration officials have made a series of statements since early 1969 on the American desire to improve relations with the PRC.212 The most significant was President Nixon's foreign policy message to Congress on February 25, 1971, in which he said:

> We are prepared to establish a dialogue with Peking. We cannot accept its ideological precepts, or the notion that Communist China must exercise hegemony over Asia. But neither do we wish to impose on China an international position that denies its legitimate national interests.
>
> The evolution of our dialogue with Peking cannot be at the expense of international order or our own commitments. Our attitude is public and clear. We will continue to honor our treaty commitments to the security of our

---

*Togo and Libya have recognized the PRC but still maintain diplomatic relations with the ROC.

Asian allies. An honorable relationship with Peking cannot
be constructed at their expense.

. . .

In that connection, I wish to make it clear that the
United States is prepared to see the People's Republic of
China play a constructive role in the family of nations.
The question of its place in the United Nations is not, how-
ever, merely a question of whether it should participate.
It is also a question of whether Peking should be permitted
to dictate to the world the terms of its participation. For a
number of years attempts have been made to deprive the
Republic of China of its place as a member of the United
Nations and its Specialized Agencies. We have opposed
these attempts. We will continue to oppose them.213

The PRC's official response to this Nixon overture was negative;
an article in the authoritative Peking Review denounced Nixon for
"still . . . engaging in his criminal 'two Chinas' plot."214 Unexpectedly,
in April, the PRC's team agreed to participate in the 31st World Table
Tennis Championships held at Nagoya, Japan. While there, the Chinese
invited the American team to visit mainland China and, as a result,
started "Ping Pong Diplomacy."215 The PRC also admitted several
American reporters to mainland China. These gestures have produced
a widely favorable reaction in the United States and elsewhere.
Nevertheless, there is not the slightest hint that the PRC might make
concessions to the United States on the question of Taiwan.216 Thus,
when the U.S. State Department said on April 28, 1971, that the legal
status of Taiwan is undetermined (Doc. 95), the PRC categorically
rejected such an assertion (Doc. 97).217 The PRC also made it clear
that no seat for the ROC or Taiwan in the United Nations would be
tolerated.218 However, amid its intransigent pronouncements on the
Taiwan question, the PRC again made overtures to the ROC leaders
on Taiwan. Thus Chou En-lai told visiting American reporters that
no vengeful action would be taken against the people of Taiwan if the
island yielded to Peking's control. He also said that high-ranking
officers of the defeated Chinese Nationalist armies had been living
in Peking since 1949 and "were well looked after." Apparently
realizing that the inhabitants of Taiwan now enjoy a rather high living
standard, Chou also said that the economic well-being of the people
on Taiwan would improve (after unification), since income levels
would be maintained and the present income tax would be rescinded.219
On July 15, 1971, President Nixon suddenly announced that he
had reached agreement with Premier Chou En-lai to visit the PRC
at an appropriate date before May, 1972, for the purpose of seeking

"the normalization of relations between the two countries and also
to exchange views on questions of concern to the two sides."220
Although Nixon said that "our action in seeking a new relationship
with the People's Republic of China will not be at the expense of our
old friends [ROC]," such a move certainly shatters the ROC's claim
to the mainland and its position in the United Nations.

With the gradual subsiding of the Cultural Revolution on the
mainland, the ROC's diplomatic crisis has been increasing. In the
25th session of the U.N. General Assembly, which opened in the fall
of 1970, the resolution to seat the PRC and oust the ROC for the first
time received a simple majority (51-49) but was not adopted because
the United States sponsored a resolution that made the Chinese
representation question an important question requiring a two-thirds
majority.221 On October 25, 1971, the ROC was compelled to announce
its withdrawal from the United Nations before the 26th session of the
U.N. General Assembly passed the Albania-sponsored resolution to
seat the PRC and to oust the ROC by a decisive vote of 76-35, with 17
abstentions.222 On November 15, 1971, the PRC delegation took its
place in the United Nations.223

Moreover, as stated before, at least 30 countries established
diplomatic relations with the PRC between 1970 and early 1972, and
more are expected to do so. The greatest threat to the international
status of the ROC, however, comes from the shift of U.S. policy toward
the PRC. Therefore, on July 16, 1971, the ROC strongly protested to
the United States Mr. Nixon's decision to visit the PRC. Many Chinese
in Taiwan were afraid that the Nixon visit would lead to the establishment of diplomatic relations between the PRC and the United States.
Vice-President and Premier Yen Chia-kan said Nixon's move "could
lead to a tragedy far more serious than involved in the fall of the
Chinese mainland [in 1949]." He also said that "we have the faith and
determination to recover the Chinese mainland and to resist any adverse
tide" and that "under no circumstance shall we relax or weaken our
stand."224

On February 27, 1972, when President Nixon concluded his visit
to mainland China, a joint communiqué was issued at Shanghai in which
the United States declared:

> The United States acknowledges that all Chinese on either
> side of the Taiwan Strait maintain there is but one China
> and that Taiwan is a part of China.
>
> The United States Government does not challenge
> that position. It reaffirms its interest in a peaceful settle-
> ment of the Taiwan question by the Chinese themselves.
> With this prospect in mind, it affirms the ultimate objective
> of the withdrawal of all U.S. forces and military instal-
> lations from Taiwan.

In the meantime, it will progressively reduce its
forces and military installations on Taiwan as the tension
in the area diminishes (Doc. 99).

It is beyond doubt that the ROC's response to the communiqué
was most unfavorable. An ROC Foreign Ministry statement declared
that any agreement reached between the United States and the "Chinese
Communist regime" was "null and void" and reaffirmed the ROC's
efforts "in striving for the sacred tasks of the early restoration of
freedom to our compatriots on the Chinese mainland" (Doc. 100).
This relatively moderate public reaction was understandable, since
the ROC leaders know that angry words will not serve their purpose
of keeping the maximum possible level of American support.
      Although the U.S.-PRC joint communiqué does not mention the
1954 ROC-U.S. Mutual Defense Treaty, the United States, before and
after President Nixon's visit, repeatedly assured the ROC that the
treaty remains unaffected. On March 3, 1972, U.S. Assistant Secretary
of State Marshall Green brought President Nixon's message of re-
assurance to the ROC leaders, pledging that "faithfully honoring all
our commitments remain[s] a cornerstone of U.S. policy."[225]
      Despite the American assurance of its defense commitment to
the ROC, the joint communiqué certainly has, and will continue to
have, an unfavorable impact on the ROC's international status. On
March 13, 1972, the United Kingdom announced that it recognizes the
PRC as "the sole legal Government of China" and "acknowledge[s] the
position of the Chinese Government that Taiwan is a province of the
People's Republic of China,"[226] thus relinquishing its long-held view
that the status of Taiwan was "undetermined." Then, on September 29,
1972, Japan and the PRC issued a joint communiqué announcing their
establishment of diplomatic relations in which Japan "fully understands
and respects" the stand of the PRC that "Taiwan is an inalienable part
of the territory of the People's Republic of China."[227]
      The Taiwan part of the joint communiqué is a major change in
America's China policy, because the United States in fact recognizes
Taiwan as a part of China and thus virtually rules out American support for an independent Taiwan,[228] as advocated by some dissident
elements indigenous to the province. This is a major concession
made by the United States, which has so far maintained that the
status of Taiwan "is undetermined." On the other hand, the PRC
also made a major concession by agreeing to shelve, at least in the
foreseeable future, its dispute with the United States over Taiwan
for the sake of improving relations on other fronts. Previously the
PRC had made a settlement of the Taiwan question a precondition for
improved relations with the United States.[229]

Compared with the gradual erosion of the ROC's international status, its economic prospects appear much brighter. The volume of foreign trade reached $U.S. 4 billion in 1971,[230] compared with approximately the same volume of foreign trade on the mainland during the same year. The ROC still maintains a high rate of economic growth, and per capita income reached $U.S. 329 in 1971,[231] compared with the $U.S. 100 or less per capita income on the mainland. While the ROC's political relations with other states are at a low ebb, its economic relations with them continue to grow, including its trade with states maintaining diplomatic relations with the PRC (such as Canada and Italy).[232]

CONCLUDING OBSERVATIONS

There is little doubt that the Chinese claim to Taiwan is supported by well-documented historical records and reasonable legal arguments. As one knowledgeable commentator stated:

China's claim to Taiwan is not a Cold War tactic but has a good deal of legitimacy. After World War II, it was as strong as her claim to Manchuria, which no nation in principle disputed. . . . It is far stronger than China's ancient and long-inactive claims to such surrounding areas as Korea, Indochina and Outer Mongolia, and than her claim to Tibet. None of these territories was ever part of China proper, as Taiwan was, and none is populated by [Han] Chinese people.[233]

The so-called question of Taiwan in fact was settled in 1945 when the ROC took over Taiwan—a Chinese province forcibly detached from it in 1895—from Japan. The question was revived in mid-1950 solely because of the unexpected eruption of the Korean War. After the outbreak of the Korean War, the United States decided that Taiwan is strategically important to the defense of East Asia and should be denied to Communist control; but the United States does not want to be involved in any Nationalist attempt to "recover" the lost mainland. Under the circumstances, the United States deemed it expedient to shift its previous position by resorting to certain niceties on which it could plausibly be claimed that Taiwan's status was "undermined." The ideal arrangement, from the American point of view, is gradually to transform Taiwan into an independent state in alliance with the United States. This arrangement, if accomplished, would have the benefit of providing the United States with an important base in East Asia while disengaging Washington from the "hazardous" Nationalist goal of mainland "recovery." While the United States has not yet explicitly announced such a policy objective, many of its policy statements certainly imply that it is moving in this direction.

From the very beginning the implementation of the above arrangement has met several almost insurmountable difficulties because it is in direct conflict with the basic interest of both the ROC and the PRC. The ROC government is committed to the "recovery" of the mainland, and it is in effective control of Taiwan. The establishment of an independent Taiwan republic necessitates the ultimate elimination of the ROC government from the political scene on Taiwan; therefore, the United States hardly expects the ROC to cooperate in carrying out this American plan. President Chiang Kai-shek and other ROC leaders are Chinese nationalists, and they are proud of their success in recovering Taiwan from Japan. Regardless of their uncertain political future, they will always be remembered in Chinese history and admired by all Chinese as patriots who restored a lost province to China. To allow Taiwan to become independent would not only destroy their political power but would also put them in the position of being forever denounced as "traitors" in Chinese history. Consequently, regardless of what political pressure and legal technicalities the United States has invoked to justify the claim that the status of Taiwan is "undetermined," the ROC has never agreed to the American view.

It is true that the United States may subvert the ROC government (as it did the South Vietnamese in 1963[234]) and organize a so-called Taiwanese government to carry out such a plan. But the situation of Taiwan is different from that of South Vietnam. The ROC's control of Taiwan is well entrenched, and there appears to be no reasonable and viable alternative to ROC rule on the island.[235] Moreover, in case of an American-sponsored open or covert coup against the ROC government, some ROC leaders may be compelled to cooperate with Peking in order to keep China united. Under that circumstance U.S. intervention would most probably risk a major armed conflict with both ROC and PRC forces—a risk no American administration would care to take.

Even if the United States could topple the ROC government and set up a puppet Taiwan republic, the situation would not be a stable one. Such a development would increase, rather than decrease, both PRC hostility toward the United States and tension in East Asia. The PRC's position on Taiwan is well known—it regards Taiwan as an inalienable part of China. Its tactics to "liberate" Taiwan are cautious and flexible. Whenever its "liberation" campaign has risked a major armed conflict with the United States, the PRC has retreated to political tactics. This is because the PRC feels that time is in its favor. As long as Taiwan is legally a part of China and is controlled by a government holding the same view, there is always the possibility of peaceful unification. As one writer points out:

> The Communist Chinese leaders may have reason to
> believe that other factors will prevail over the anticom-
> munism of the Nationalists to persuade them to accept
> reunification on Peking's terms.[236]

It is perhaps because of this consideration and other internal and
external problems that the PRC has been unwilling to pay the high
cost of armed conflict to launch its campaign to "liberate" Taiwan.
The emergence of an independent Taiwan would change the whole
situation.

If that should happen and the PRC did not take swift action to
crush the new republic, then the latter might be gradually accepted by
the international community as an independent state vis-à-vis China.
This in turn would make it legally and politically more difficult for
the PRC to reunite Taiwan with the mainland. Therefore, the emergence of an independent Taiwan republic would be a great inducement
to the PRC to take military action against Taiwan and would thus lead
to direct armed conflict between the United States and the PRC.[237]

Besides practical difficulties, the moral grounds for creating
an independent Taiwan republic are not convincing. Some Americans
have argued that the principle of self-determination should be applied
to the people of Taiwan.[238] But, as pointed out in a recent study on
China policy: "Problems such as Taiwan are difficult because they
are laced with opposing principles and values, for example the principle
of self-determination as opposed to the principle of upholding the
territorial integrity of other countries."[239] If in 1861 the American
government was unwilling to grant the right of self-determination to the
Confederate states, can it expect the Chinese (Communist or non-
Communist) to grant self-determination to a province? Moreover,
if the principle of self-determination should be applied to the people
of Taiwan, should not the same principle be applied to other Chinese
provinces under Communist rule, where the people enjoy far less
political freedom and economic well-being than the people of Taiwan?

In contrast with a policy of independence for Taiwan, some
Americans advocate total disengagement from the Taiwan question,
i.e., leaving the question of Taiwan to be settled by the two contending
Chinese factions without outside interference.[240] The main argument
to support this policy is that the PRC will not improve or establish
relations with the United States unless the United States agrees to
withdraw from Taiwan; by disengaging from the Taiwan question, the
United States would remove the main obstacle to establishing relations
with the PRC. However, carrying out this policy would, as in the case
of a policy of independence for Taiwan, meet several serious difficulties.

The United States is committed by treaty to assist the ROC to
repel any armed attack against Taiwan and the Pescadores; a

disengagement policy would necessitate the termination of this treaty. This, if carried out, would produce far-reaching, undesirable political consequences for the United States. If the United States were to repudiate the defense treaty with the ROC—its oldest and most faithful ally in Asia—would other states in alliance with the United States, especially Asian states, continue to have faith in American treaty commitments?* The likely result would be the bankruptcy of American credibility in the world. This is a price that no American administration, at least in the foreseeable future, would be willing to pay for improving relations with the PRC.

Today there are more than 14 million overseas Chinese, the great majority of them residing in Southeast Asia. Their attitude toward the Chinese Communists is an important factor in maintaining the stability of these areas.241 The ROC still attracts the allegiance of a substantial number of them, and its destruction (since this would very likely follow the U.S. repudiation of its treaty commitment to

---

*Even the American President's visit to the PRC caused considerable suspicion among America's Asian allies. For instance, after President Nixon announced his decision to visit the PRC, President Marcos of the Philippines said: "If this can happen to Nationalist China, there is no assurance that this won't happen to us." "Manila Reviews Its Ties with U.S.," The New York Times, July 25, 1971, p.10.

Compare the following United Press International report on Western European reaction to the Nixon-Chou communiqué of February 27, 1972:

> President Nixon's policy of withdrawal from Asian commitments revived fears among Western allies today that the United States will loosen its links also with Europe before too long.
>   . . .
> Nixon consulted European leaders before leaving on his Peking tour and gave them assurances, with an eye to the forthcoming Moscow round of talks, that European interests will not be sold out in these vital encounters.
>
> But, looking at the Peking developments, European diplomats frankly feared the consequences to Europe of any possible accommodation Nixon might reach with the Kremlin chiefs later this spring ("Withdrawal Pledge Arouses Fear in Europe," London, February 28, 1972, UPI, in The China News [February 29, 1972], p. 8).

the ROC) would most probably shift the allegiance of these overseas Chinese to the Communist side and make it more difficult for the local governments to maintain stability. In this connection the present American ambassador to the ROC, Walter P. McConaughy, told a U.S. Senate subcommittee on November 24, 1969:

> The overseas Chinese, who will look to a free Chinese
> Government, many of them, for spiritual and moral
> leadership, and the interests of these overseas Chinese
> all around the world would require us to do what we can
> to keep in existence a free China with all of the values
> and with all of the disposition to work with us that we see
> manifested in the government of China on Taiwan. I think
> of the Republic of China as a big plus in this vital area of
> traditional Chinese values as well as from the strategic
> standpoint, rather than being a minus.[242]

Therefore, the destruction of the ROC would not only cause the Asian allies of the United States to lose confidence in the United States, but would also contribute significantly to the instability of Southeast Asia.

Moreover, it would be immensely naive to think that by sacrificing the ROC on Taiwan the United States could solve all its problems with the PRC. The U.S. conflict with that regime (at least for the period under Mao) is global in nature.[243] Taiwan is not the only area in which the U.S. interest is in direct conflict with that of the PRC. Consequently, whether it is worthwhile to sacrifice the ROC on Taiwan to reach a limited accomodation with the PRC under Mao is a matter that should be seriously considered by American policy makers.

The Taiwan question is a difficult problem in international politics, and this author does not pretend to have a solution that would satisfy all parties concerned. However, there are certain steps that the United States certainly can take, which, while they cannot solve the problem now, will make the situation more tolerable and less dangerous.

The first and most important step for the United States is to continue its recently announced policy of recognizing Taiwan as an integral part of China. This step has in fact removed a major and basic friction between the United States and both the ROC and the PRC.

Second, although the United States has made it clear that it will not oppose any negotiation between the Nationalists and the Communists concerning the settlement of the Taiwan question, it should not push the ROC to the negotiating table. The unhappy experience of the American effort to sponsor Nationalist-Communist peace negotiations in 1945-46 should have taught the United States one lesson at least—if an American-sponsored negotiation fails, both sides blame the United States.

Third, the United States should dissociate from any activities
in connection with the Taiwan separatist (or independence) movement.
The Chinese on the mainland and Taiwan are very suspicious of the
origin of and the support received by this movement. Many believe
that it is financed by American intelligence funds. The movement
vividly reminds the Chinese, especially those over 40 (and these are
the people who are in power both on the mainland and on Taiwan), of
the puppet Manchukuo. Most of them look upon this movement as
nothing but a new Manchukuo plot, directed by a foreign power, to steal
a piece of Chinese territory. Moreover, the existence of this movement can only do more harm than good to the people of Taiwan. As
long as the movement is active and is believed to be secretly supported by the United States, the Chinese government on Taiwan will
be reluctant to grant more political freedoms to the people there
for fear that elements of this movement would abuse these freedoms
to promote their cause of destroying the territorial integrity of
China. Even if this movement could succeed in overthrowing the ROC
government on Taiwan, it could only make the situation more dangerous,
as has already been explained.* In any case, internal violence on Taiwan will necessarily invite PRC intervention and, if that happens, the
people of Taiwan will be the first to suffer.

NOTES

1. Foreign Relations of the United States, Diplomatic Papers:
The Conferences at Cairo and Tehran 1943 (Washington, D.C.: U.S.
Government Printing Office, 1961), pp. 565-66.
2. Foreign Relations of the United States, Diplomatic Papers:
The Conference of Berlin (The Potsdam Conference) 1945, II (Washington, D.C.: U.S. Government Printing Office, 1960), 1474 (Soviet Union),
1555-56 (France).
3. Majorie M. Whiteman, Digest of International Law, III
(Washington, D.C.: U.S. Government Printing Office, 1964), 487-88.
4. Lien Chen-tung, Chiang tsung-t'ung yü T'ai-wan sheng ti
kuang-fu ch'ung-chien (President Chiang and the restoration and

---

*Ironically, the emergence of an independent Taiwan will provide
a legal justification for the United States to withdraw its treaty commitment to defend Taiwan and the Pescadores. Under international
law a political treaty terminates upon the disappearance of a contracting party; therefore, if the ROC disappears, the United States
could legally consider the ROC-U.S. Mutual Defense Treaty terminated.

reconstruction of Taiwan province), I (Taipei: Chung-yang wen-wu kung-ying she, 1967), 82.

5. Min-kuo ssu-shih nien Chung-hua min-kuo nien-chien (Yearbook of the Republic of China, 1951) (Taipei: Chung-hua min-kuo nien-chien she, 1951), p. 99.

6. For instance, D. Barry Kirkham wrote that "had the Communists not come to power on the mainland, Formosa undoubtedly would have been ceded to China by express terms of [the San Francisco Peace] Treaty." See his "The International Legal Status of Formosa," in Canadian Yearbook of International Law, VI (Vancouver: The Publication Center, University of British Columbia, 1968), 147.

7. For instance, a Hsinhua (official news agency of the Chinese Communists) news dispatch of August 30, 1949, citing an Associated Press dispatch of August 12, 1949, from Washington said that American Secretary of State Acheson told the U.S. Senate Committee on Foreign Affairs that before the signing of the Japanese Peace Treaty Taiwan technically remained a part of Japan. Kuang-min Jih-pao (Enlightenment daily), Peking, September 1, 1949. See also Doc. 22.

8. See also other statements, reports, or articles concerning the liberation of Taiwan contained in Kuang-min jih-pao tzu-liao she, T'ai-wan wen-t'i (The question of Taiwan) (rev. ed.; Peking: Hsin-hua shu-tien, 1950).

9. See also the statements of other leftist Taiwanese, ibid., pp. 9, 14-29.

10. See U.S. Department of State, Transcript of Proceedings: Conference on Problems of United States Policy in China (Washington, D.C.: Division of Central Services, 1949). For Fairbank's statement, see pp. 138-39.

11. See Tang Tsou, America's Failure in China 1941-50 (Chicago: University of Chicago Press, 1963), pp. 528-31. Senator Taft even suggested the establishment of an independent republic of Formosa and forcing the Nationalists to accept such a solution. See ibid., p. 534.

12. See Time, LX, 1 (January 2, 1950), 11-12.

13. Ibid., No. 2 (January 9, 1950), 9-10.

14. Department of State Bulletin, XXII, 551 (January 23, 1950), 116.

15. A. Doak Barnett, China on the Eve of Communist Takeover (New York: Praeger, 1963), p. 310.

16. Allen S. Whiting, China Crosses the Yalu: The Decision to Enter the Korean War (New York: Macmillan, 1960), p. 21.

17. Hsinhua News Agency, Daily News Release, No. 427 (Peking: China Information Bureau, Press Administration, July 7, 1950), p. 51.

18. Yearbook of the United Nations 1950 (New York: Columbia University in cooperation with the United Nations, 1950), pp. 288-89.

19. Ibid., p. 289.

20. Ibid., p. 291.

21. Ibid., p. 292.

22. Ibid.

23. Ibid., p. 293.

24. Ibid., p. 294.

25. Ibid.

26. Ibid.

27. Ibid., p. 295

28. Ibid., pp. 296-97.

29. See Hsinhua News Agency, Daily News Release, No. 576 (December 19, 1950), pp. 133-34.

30. Ibid., No. 577 (December 20, 1950), pp. 143-52.

31. Yearbook of the United Nations 1950, p. 250.

32. Ibid., pp. 250-51.

33. See "Foreign Minister Chou En-lai Replies Arbelaez's Cable," NCNA-Peking, February 5, 1951, in Hsinhua News Agency, Daily News Release, No. 617 (February 9, 1951), p. 21.

34. Yearbook of the United Nations 1951 (New York: Columbia University Press, 1952), pp. 259, 261.

35. Yearbook of the United Nations 1950, pp. 297, 298.

36. U.N. General Assembly, Official Records, 5th session, General Committee, 71st Meeting, October 5, 1950, A/BUR/SR. 71 (1950), p. 11.

37. Hsinhua News Agency, Daily News Release, No. 523 (October 18, 1950), pp. 143-44. See also Wu Hsiu-chuan's statement at the Security Council on November 28 (Doc. 43).

38. Yearbook of the United Nations 1950, p. 298.

39. Yearbook of the United Nations 1951, p. 262.

40. See Chou En-lai's cablegram to the secretary-general of the United Nations dated February 3, 1955, U.N. Doc. S/3358 (1955).

41. Chung-hua min-kuo wai-chiao wen-t'i yen-chiu hui, Chin-shan ho-yüeh yu Chung-jih ho-yüeh ti kuan hsi (The relationship between the San Francisco peace treaty and the Sino-Japanese peace treaty) (Taipei: Chung-hua min-kuo wai-chiao wen-t'i yen-chiu hui, 1966), pp. 9-11. English text in "U.S. Sets Forth Principles for Japanese Peace Treaty," Department of State Bulletin, XXIII, 596 (December 4, 1950), 881.

42. Chung-hua min-kuo wai-chiao wen-t'i yen-chiu hui, Chin-shan ho-yüeh yu Chung-jih ho-yüeh ti kuan-hsi, p. 17.

43. Ibid., pp. 41, 43.

44. See ibid., pp. 76-82, for Anglo-American negotiation on the question of Chinese participation in the peace conference. The Chinese records show that the United Kingdom insisted that the PRC be invited to the peace conference and that the peace treaty should provide for "ceding Taiwan to China." Ibid., pp. 76-77.

45. Information conveyed by Dulles to Ambassador Koo on June 15, 1951, at U.S. Department of State. Ibid., p. 78.

46. See record of conversation between Foreign Minister George Yeh and Minister Rankin, dated August 23, 1951, Ibid., pp. 155-58.

47. See the statement read by American Minister Rankin to ROC Foreign Minister George Yeh on August 23, 1951. Ibid., p. 155. See also the Chinese note to U.S. Minister Rankin, dated September 26, 1951. Ibid., pp. 166-67.

48. The Potsdam Agreement did not mention the Japanese Peace Treaty. See U.S. memorandum to the Soviet Union on Japanese Peace Treaty, dated May 19, 1951. Department of State Bulletin, XXIV, 621 (May 28, 1951), 852-56.

49. United Nations Treaty Series, CXXXVI, (New York: The United Nations, 1955), 48, 76.

50. Statement read by American Minister Rankin to ROC Foreign Minister Yeh on August 23, 1951. Chin-shan ho-yüeh yu Chung-jih ho-yüeh ti kuan-hsi, p. 156.

51. See record of conversation between Foreign Minister Yeh and Minister Rankin, August 30, 1951. Ibid., p. 160.

52. Ibid., pp. 166-67. Quoted portion was translated from the Chinese.

53. Ibid., pp. 167-68.

54. Ibid., p. 189.

55. See ROC Foreign Minister Yeh's statement at the eighth informal meeting of the Sino-Japanese peace negotiations, held on March 19, 1952, in Chung-hua min-kuo wai-chiao wen-t'i yen-chiu hui, Chung-hua min-kuo tui-jih ho-yüeh (Peace treaty between the Republic of China and Japan) (Taipei: Chung-hua min-kuo wai-chiao wen-t'i yen-chiu hui, 1966), p. 137.

56. Chinese translation of the letter in Chin-shan ho-yüeh yu Chung-jih ho-yüeh ti kuan-hsi, pp. 185-87.

57. Ibid., pp. 185, 187.

58. Ibid., p. 187.

59. Chung-hua jen-min kung-ho kuo tui-wai kuan-hsi wen-chien chi (Compilation of documents relative to the foreign relations of the People's Republic of China), II, 1951-1953 (Peking: Shih-chieh chih-shih ch'u-pan she, 1958), p. 66.

60. Whiteman, Digest of International Law, III, 564. See also Doc. 64.

61. E.g., see the exchange of notes accompanying the 1954 ROC-U.S. Mutual Defense Treaty in Doc. 42. See also Doc. 95.

62. Whiteman, Digest of International Law, III, 565.

63. L. Oppenheim, International Law, II (7th ed., H. Lauterpacht, ed., London: Longmans, Green and Co., 1952), 611.

64. Ibid.

65. Diena, regarded this as a dereliction of these territories by Turkey and Italy's occupation of them as the occupation of a no man's land. Ibid.

66. D. P. O'Connell, "The Status of Formosa and the Chinese Recognition Problem," American Journal of International Law, L, 2 (April 1956), 415.

67. Frank P. Morello, The International Legal Status of Formosa (The Hague: Martinus Nijhoff, 1966), p. 92.

68. Arthur Dean, "International Law and Current Problems in the Far East," Proceedings of the American Society of International Law, XLIX (1955), 86, 95, 96-97; cited in Whiteman, Digest of International Law, II (1963), 1230.

69. Doc. 24. The instrument's treaty character seemed beyond doubt, in that, as in the case of other treaties concluded by the United States, it was printed in the United States Statutes at Large.

70. Kirkham, "The International Legal Status of Formosa," p. 149.

71. E.g., see Doc. 13 for President Roosevelt's statement. He said that the principles contained in the Cairo Declaration "are as simple as they are fundamental" and that "they involve the restoration of stolen property to its rightful owners. . . ."

72. Oppenheim, International Law, I (8th ed., H. Lauterpacht, ed.; London: Longmans, Green and Co., 1955), 574-75.

73. Materials on Succession of States, U.N. Doc. ST/LEG/SER. B/14 (New York: The United Nations, 1967), p. 70. Similarly, in the case of Chang Fukue v. Chang Chin Min, decided by the Osaka District Court on June 7, 1960, the court said: "The determination as to whether the parties have lost the Japanese nationality they had once held should be made on the basis of the Formosan Register of Personal Status established for the Formosans as a special category, separately from the Family Register of Japan, ever since the establishment of Japanese sovereignty over Formosa. It is therefore proper to understand that those who held such personal status in the Register referred to above have lost Japanese nationality and acquired the nationality of the Republic of China with the establishment of permanent sovereignty of the Republic of China, i.e., with the entry into force of the Peace Treaty in 1952 when the de jure change of sovereignty over that territory. . . ." Ibid., p. 71.

74. See Doc. 45.

75. Ibid.

76. T'ang Wu, Chung-kuo yu kuo-chi-fa (China and international law), II (Taipei: Chung-hua wen-hua ch'u-pan shih-yeh wei-yuan hui, 1957), 436.

77. United Kingdom, Parliamentary Debates, House of Lords, CCXII, 5th Series (London: Her Majesty's Stationery Office, 1958),

p. 497. Cited in Kirkham, "The International Legal Status of Formosa," p. 147.

78. See Oppenheim, International Law, II, 7th ed., p. 304, where it is said: "Political and other treaties concluded for the purpose of setting up a permanent condition or thing . . . are not ipso facto annulled by the outbreak of war; but nothing prevents the victorious party from imposing by the treaty of peace alterations in, or even the dissolution of, such treaties." (Emphasis added.)

79. Great Britain, Parliamentary Debates, . . . House of Commons, Official Report, DXXXIX, February 4, 1955, col. 159.

80. Oppenheim, International Law, I, 8th ed., p. 873.

81. Both the Cairo Declaration and the Potsdam Proclamation were included in Charles I. Bevans, Treaties and Other International Agreements of the United States of America, 1776-1949, III, Multilateral, 1931-1945 (Washington, D.C.: U.S. Government Printing Office, 1969), 858 (Cairo), 1204-05 (Potsdam).

82. Ibid.

83. See Oppenheim, International Law, I, 8th ed., p. 898.

84. Great Britain, Parliamentary Debates, . . . House of Commons, DXL, May 4, 1955, cols. 1870-71.

85. Materials on Succession of States, pp. 69-70. In the same judgment, when the Court dealt with the determination of the nationality of Formosans, it referred to the contents of paragraph 3 of the Cairo Declaration (Doc. 12) and took the view that "the Formosans are those who would have had Chinese nationality if Japan had not annexed Formosa. . . . Accordingly, it must be concluded that the Formosans have lost their Japanese nationality as a result of the signing of the Instrument of Surrender. . . ." Ibid., p. 70.

Many Japanese scholars and court decisions have expressed the view that Article 2(b) of the Sino-Japanese Peace Treaty "may be construed to restore the status of Formosa which existed before its acquisition by Japan, i.e., the status before the [1894-95] Sino-Japanese War." Yoshio Tameike, "Nationality of Formosans and Koreans," The Japanese Annual of International Law, No. 2 (1958), p. 58.

86. See his "Refuting the Absurd Theory of 'One-China, One-Taiwan' by International Law," Ta-kung Pao (Impartial daily), Hong Kong, May 30, 1964.

87. E.g., see Docs. 30, 31, 32, 54, 79, and 82.

88. See Oppenheim, International Law, I, 8th ed., p. 873,.

89. See his "Sovereignty of Taiwan Belongs to China," People's Daily, February 8, 1955, p. 4; English translation entitled "Taiwan— A Chinese Territory", in Law in the Service of Peace (Brussels), No. 5 (1956), pp. 39-40.

90. He also cited the same passage from Lauterpacht's edition of Oppenheim, see International Law, I, 8th ed., p. 873.

91. See his "Strip the Aggressor of Its Legal Cloak," People's Daily, January 31, 1955, p. 3; English translation under the title "The Aggressor and the Law," People's China, No. 5 (March 1, 1955), p. 10.

92. President Chiang Kai-shek seems to take the same view. On October 25, 1950, he said: "In 1941, our Government declared war on Japan, thus automatically abolishing the Treaty of Shimonoseki and legally restoring Taiwan and Penghu to China." Selected Speeches and Messages of President Chiang Kai-shek, 1949-1952 (Taipei: Office of the Government Spokesman, 1952), p. 65.

93. E.g., see Oppenheim, International Law, II, 7th ed., p. 304.

94. V. M. Shurshalov, Osnovnye voprosy teorii mezhdunarodnogo dogovora (Basic questions of the theory of the international treaty) (Moscow: Izd-vo Akademiia Nauka USSR, 1959), p. 191; cited in D. W. Wainhouse, et al., Alternative Methods for Dealing with Breaches of Arms Control Agreements, ACDA/IR-107 (Washington, D.C., Johns Hopkins University, mimeographed material, 1968), p. 178. A Soviet textbook published under the auspices of the Institute of State and Law of the Academy of Sciences of the U.S.S.R. said: "Among the treaties concluded between the belligerents some (political, economic) become completely inoperative. . . ." F. I. Kozhevnikov, ed., International Law (Moscow: Foreign Languages Publishing House, [1961]), p. 421. The English edition was a slightly revised version of the 1957 Russian edition. The Russian edition, translated into Chinese in 1959, was used for some time as a textbook in the PRC.

95. E.g., a Soviet textbook said: "[Unequal] treaties' repudiation cannot be considered a violation of the principle that international treaties must be observed." Kozhevnikov, ed., International Law, p. 248. A PRC article also said: "Unequal treaties . . . undermine the most fundamental principles of international law—such as the principle of sovereignty; therefore they are illegal and void, and states have the right to abrogate this type of treaty at any time." Shih Sung, Yu Ta-hsin, Lu Ying-lui, Tsao K'o, "An Initial Investigation into the Old Law Viewpoint in the Teaching of International Law," Chiao-hsueh yü yen-chiu (Teaching and research), No. 4 (April 1958), p. 14.

96. Hsin Wu, "A Criticism of the Bourgeois International Law on the Question of State Territory," Kuo-chi wen-t'i yen-chiu (Studies in international problems), No. 7 (1960), p. 46.

97. E.g., a Soviet textbook observed: "The return of territory as restitution of the historic rights of States from whom territory was previously forcibly detached has received international recognition recorded in important international agreements. . . . The Cairo Agreement of 1943 and the Potsdam Declaration of July 26, 1945 reestablished China's right to the Taiwan and the Penghulieh [Pescadores] Islands, seized by Japan in 1895." Kozhevnikov, ed., International Law,

pp. 188, 189. A PRC article said: "It is clearly recognized in the practice of modern international law that in order to correct historical inequities, sovereignty over national territory must be restored." Shih Sung et al., "An Initial Investigation into the Old Law Viewpoint in the Teaching of International Law," p. 16.

98. See his "The 'China Problem' Reconsidered," Foreign Affairs, XXXVIII, 3 (April 1960), 476-86.

99. See External Affairs, No. 18 (1966), p. 431.

100. Kirkham, "The International Legal Status of Formosa," pp. 162-63.

101. King Chen, Vietnam and China, 1938-1954 (Princeton, N.J.: Princeton University Press, 1969), ch. 4.

102. See Richard L. Walker, China Under Communism: The First Five Years (New Haven, Conn.: Yale University Press, 1955), pp. 11-17, 214-32.

103. China Handbook 1951 (Taipei: China Publishing Co., 1951), p. 494.

104. Ministry of Foreign Affairs, ed., Treaties Between the Republic of China and Foreign States 1927-1961 (rev. ed.; Taipei: The Commercial Press, Ltd., 1963), pp. 794-98.

105. See China Handbook 1952-53 (Taipei: China Publishing Co., 1952), pp. 142-43.

106. American Foreign Policy, 1950-1955, Basic Documents, II (Washington, D.C.: U.S. Government Printing Office, 1957), 2475.

107. E.g., see President Chiang's statement issued on March 1, 1953, as summarized in China Handbook 1953-54 (Taipei: China Publishing Co., 1953), p. 483. The ROC did increase its coastal raids against the Communists in 1953. See China Handbook 1954-55 (Taipei: China Publishing Co., 1954), pp. 263-65.

108. See Chang Chun and Huang Shao-ku, Chiang tsung-tung wei tzu-yu cheng-i yu ho-ping erh fen-tou shu-lueh (President Chiang's fight for freedom, justice and peace) (Taipei: Chung-yang wen-wu kung-ying she, 1968), pp. 369-71.

109. Ibid., pp. 371-72.

110. Important Documents Concerning the Question of Taiwan (Peking: Foreign Languages Press, 1955), p. 126.

111. For the whole text, see New China News Agency, Daily News Release, No. 1717 (August 23, 1954), pp. 243-45.

112. "Soviet Backs Chou in Formosa Stand," The New York Times, December 16, 1954, pp. 1, 3.

113. See Keesing's Contemporary Archives, X, 1955-1956 (London: Keesing's Publications, Ltd.,), pp. 14017-18.

114. See China Handbook, 1955-1956 (Taipei: China Publishing Co., 1955), pp. 7-11.

115. New China News Agency, Daily News Release, No. 1758 (October 11, 1954), pp. 117-19.

116. Keesing's Contemporary Archives, X, p. 14017.

117. Ibid., p. 14018.

118. Chinese People's Institute of Foreign Affairs, ed., Oppose U.S. Occupation of Taiwan and "Two Chinas" Plot (Peking: Foreign Languages Press, 1958), p. 29.

119. Yearbook of the United Nations 1955 (New York: Columbia University Press, 1956), p. 55. The Soviet Union also proposed on January 30, 1955, that the Security Council consider the question of acts of aggression committed by the United States against Communist China in the area of Taiwan and other Chinese islands. Ibid.

120. Ibid., p. 57.

121. Ibid., p. 58.

122. Ibid. The Council also rejected a Soviet proposal to discuss the item submitted by the Soviet Union on January 30. Ibid.

123. E.g., Adlai Stevenson of the United States questioned whether Quemoy and Matsu were essential to the security of the United States or even to the defense of Formosa. See Geoffrey Barraclough and Rachel F. Wall, Survey of International Affairs, 1955-1956 (London: Oxford University Press, 1960), p. 12.

124. American Foreign Policy, 1950-1955, Basic Documents, II (Washington, D.C.: U.S. Government Printing Office, 1957), 2491-93.

125. Kenneth T. Young, Negotiating with the Chinese Communists (New York: McGraw-Hill, 1968), p. 44.

126. Ibid., p. 45.

127. See ibid.

128. Ibid., pp. 46-47.

129. Ibid., p. 47.

130. See ibid., pp. 47-50, 52.

131. See ibid., pp. 52-53.

132. Oppose U.S. Occupation of Taiwan and "Two Chinas" Plot, pp. 35-36.

133. For the text of the "agreed announcement," see Young, Negotiating with the Chinese Communists, pp. 412-13.

134. See ibid., pp. 94-95.

135. See Docs. 48 and 50. See also Young, Negotiating with the Chinese Communists, pp. 95-110.

136. See Young, Negotiating with the Chinese Communists, pp. 58, 113.

137. See Lewis Gilbert, "Peking and Taipei," in Mark Mancall, ed., Formosa Today (New York: Praeger, 1964), pp. 112-20.

138. The New York Times, June 30, 1956, p. 2.

139. President Chiang Kai-shek: Selected Speeches and Messages in 1956 (Taipei: Government Information Office), p. 61.

140. In a press conference held at Madras on December 6, 1956, Chou En-lai said: "We are making every effort to bring about a peaceful liberation of Taiwan." Hsinhua News Agency, Daily News Release, No. 2481 (December 7, 1956), p. 59. Similarly, in his press conference held at Calcutta on December 9 of the same year, Chou said: "If Taiwan is restored to China then Chiang Kai-shek would have made a contribution and he could stay in any part of his fatherland according to his wish. You have mentioned an offer of a government position to Chiang Kai-shek would be offered a minister's post. I said a minister's post is too low." Survey of China Mainland Press, No. 1430 (Hong Kong, December 13, 1956), p. 31.

141. "Chinese Government's Statement on Sino-American Ambassadorial Talks," Peking Review, I, 19 (July 8, 1958), 21-22.

142. See Young, Negotiating with the Chinese Communists, pp. 139-41.

143. Ibid., p. 142.

144. Donald S. Zagoria, The Sino-Soviet Conflict, 1956-61 (Princeton, N.J.: Princeton University Press, 1962), p. 210.

145. Young, Negotiating with the Chinese Communists, p. 143.

146. Ibid., p. 144.

147. See G. Barraclough, Survey of International Affairs, 1956-1958 (London: Oxford University Press, 1962), p. 568.

148. Ibid., p. 569.

149. Soviet News, No. 3911 (London: Press Department of the Soviet Embassy, September 9, 1958), pp. 193-95. For President Eisenhower's reply, see Department of State Bulletin, XXXIX, 1005 (September 29, 1958), 498. Khrushchev again sent a letter to Eisenhower on September 19, 1958. See Soviet News, No. 3917 (September 22, 1958), pp. 221-23.

150. China Yearbook 1958-1959 (Taipei: China Publishing Co., 1959), pp. 2-3.

151. See Barraclough, Survey of International Affairs, 1956-1958, p. 572.

152. Ibid.

153. Ibid., p. 573.

154. Ibid.

155. China and U.S. Far East Policy, 1945-1967 (Washington, D.C.: Congressional Quarterly Service, 1967), p. 90.

156. Young, Negotiating with the Chinese Communists, p. 161.

157. See P'eng's message to compatriots on Taiwan, October 13, 1958. Chung-hua jen-min kung-ho kuo tui-wai kuan-hsi wen-chien chi (Compilation of documents relating to the foreign relations of the People's Republic of China), V, 1958 (Peking: Shih-chieh chih-shih ch'u-pan she, 1959), p. 176.

158. See the statement issued by the spokesman for the Information Department of the PRC Foreign Ministry on the question of exchanging correspondents between China and the United States, September 13, 1960. Peking Review, III, 37 (September 14, 1960), 29-31.

159. J. Chester Cheng, et al., eds., The Politics of the Chinese Red Army: A Translation of the Bulletin of Activities of the People's Liberation Army (Stanford, Calif.: Hoover Institute on War, Revolution, and Peace, 1966), p. 487.

160. See "Message of the Fukien Front Command of the Chinese People's Liberation Army to Compatriots in Taiwan, Penghu, Quemoy and Matsu, June 17, 1960," Peking Review, III, 25 (June 21, 1960), 3-4.

161. People's Daily, February 2, 1962, p. 4.

162. "A Critical Review of the Conlon Report by the SACEA," Chung-mei yueh-k'an (West and East), V, 4 (April 1960), inside cover, 1-6.

163. Frank Robertson, "Refugees and Troop Moves—a Report from Hong Kong," The China Quarterly, No. 11 (July-September, 1962), pp. 111-15.

164. See Harold C. Hinton, Communist China in World Politics (Boston: Houghton Mifflin Co., 1966), pp. 296, 324, 350.

165. China Yearbook 1962-63 (Taipei: China Publishing Co., 1963), p. 1012.

166. Ibid., p. 342.

167. See Hinton, Communist China in World Politics, p. 271.

168. Max Frankel, "Red China Building up Troops and Jet Units Opposite Quemoy," The New York Times, June 21, 1962, pp. 1, 5.

169. Young, Negotiating with the Chinese Communists, p. 250.

170. Ibid., p. 251.

171. Hinton, Communist China in World Politics, p. 272.

172. "Ch'en Yi Condemns U.S. Imperialism," Peking Review, V, 29 (July 20, 1962), 21.

173. China Yearbook, 1963-64 (Taipei: China Publishing Co., 1964), pp. 2-4; "Guerrilla War Hits Red China," U.S. News and World Report, March 4, 1963, pp. 40-44.

174. Kenneth T. Young, Diplomacy and Power in Washington-Peking Dealings: 1953-1967 (Chicago: The University of Chicago Center for Policy Study, 1967), p. 18.

175. E.g., see Edgar Snow, The Other Side of the River: Red China Today (New York: Random House, 1961), pp. 765-66.

176. E.g., see "No 'Two Chinas' in Gymnastics," Peking Review, VII, 32 (August 7, 1964), 5, 27; and Item 12. Peking maintained the same attitude in the 1950's. See Item 4.

177. Stephen Erasmus, "General de Gaulle's Recognition of Peking," The China Quarterly, No. 18 (April-June 1964), p. 195.

178. Ibid., p. 197.

179. Hinton, Communist China in World Politics, pp. 150-51.

180. Drew Middleton, "De Gaulle Tries to Retain Tie with Nationalist China," The New York Times, January 26, 1964, pp. 1, 4.

181. Hinton, Communist China in World Politics, p. 151.

182. On February 15 a PRC chargé d'affaires arrived in Paris; on February 23 a French chargé d'affaires took up residence in Peking. In April ambassadors were exchanged. Erasmus, "General de Gaulle's Recognition of Peking," p. 197.

183. On May 24, 1957, Taipei rioters destroyed the American embassy in protest against the unjust acquittal by an American military tribunal of an American who killed a Chinese. See Grey MacGregor, "U.S. Acts Annoy Taiwan's People," The New York Times, May 28, 1957, p. 5. Each year the Chinese Communists celebrated this event as the Anti-American Patriotic Demonstration Day. Hsu's article was written to commemorate the seventh anniversary of this event.

184. See Hungdah Chiu, "Communist China's Attitude Towards Nuclear Tests," The China Quarterly, No. 21 (January-March 1965), p. 96.

185. Lin Piao, "Long Live the Victory of the People's War!," Peking Review, VIII, 36 (September 3, 1965), 29.

186. "Li Tsung-jen's Press Conference," ibid., No. 40 (October 1, 1965), p. 26.

187. "Vice-Premier Ch'en Yi's Press Conference," ibid., No. 41 (October 8, 1965), p. 12.

188. American Foreign Policy, Current Documents, 1963 (Washington, D.C.: U.S. Government Printing Office, 1967), p. 759.

189. Ibid., p. 761.

190. See excerpts of the Article in American Foreign Policy, Current Documents, 1964 (Washington, D.C.: U.S. Government Printing Office, 1967), pp. 876-77.

191. Ibid., p. 878.

192. U.S. Policy with Respect to Mainland China, Hearings before the Committee on Foreign Relations, U.S. Senate, 89th Congress, 2nd sess., March 8, 10, 16, 18, 21, 28, 30, 1966 (Washington, D.C.: U.S. Government Printing Office, 1966).

193. Ibid., pp. 14-15.

194. See American Foreign Policy, Current Documents, 1966 (Washington, D.C.: U.S. Government Printing Office, 1969), pp. 650-59.

195. Observer, "Old Tune, New Plot," English translation in Peking Review, IX, 14 (April 1, 1966), 13-15.

196. Peking Review, XI, 40 (October 4, 1968), 14, 15.

197. See Doc. 51.

198. See P'eng Chen's speech at mass rally in Peking welcoming Brazilian Vice-President Goulart, August 17, 1961. Oppose the New U.S. Plots to Create "Two Chinas" (Peking: Foreign Languages Press, 1962), pp. 9-10.

199. China Yearbook 1967-68 (Taipei: China Publishing Co., n.d.), p. 653. See also "General Chiang Termed Wary on Red China," The New York Times, January 19, 1967, p. 2.

200. Associated Press, Washington, January 10, 1967, in Chung-yang jih-pao (Central daily news), international ed., January 11, 1967, p. 1.

201. United Press International, Washington, Tsing-tao jih-pao (Hong Kong), January 12, 1967, p. 2.

202. Department of State Bulletin, LVI, 1458 (June 5, 1967), 849.

203. Free China Review, XVII, 11 (November 1967), 88.

204. See Jay Walz, "Canada's Talks on Ties to Peking Appear Stalled," The New York Times, August 3, 1969, p. 15.

205. "Canada Establishes Diplomatic Relations with the Chinese People's Republic," External Affairs (Ottawa), XXII, 11 (November 1970), 378.

206. See "joint Communiqué of the Government of People's Republic of China and the Government of the Republic of Italy on Establishment of Diplomatic Relations Between China and Italy," Peking Review, XIII, 46 (November 13, 1970), 6.

207. E.g., see joint communiqué on the establishment of Diplomatic relations between the People's Republic of China and the Federal Republic of Cameroon, March 26, 1971. Peking Review, XIV, 15 (April 9, 1971), 9.

208. E.g., see joint communiqué of the government of the People's Republic of China and the government of the state of Kuwait on the establishment of diplomatic relations between the two countries, March 22, 1971. Ibid., XIV, 14 (April 2, 1971), p. 16.

209. "7th Fleet Cut Seen in the Taiwan Straits," UPI, Tokyo, December 24, 1969, in The New York Times, December 25, 1969, p. 8. See also The New York Times, March 19, 1970, p. 14.

210. In April, 1970 the United States authorized the selective licensing of goods for export to the PRC. During 1970 the United States validated passports for 270 Americans to visit the PRC. See Nixon's message to the Congress on February 25, 1971, "U.S. Foreign Policy for the 1970's, Building for Peace," Department of State Bulletin, LXIV, 1656 (March 22, 1971), 384.

211. Ibid., LXIII, 1642 (December 14, 1970), 734.

212. E.g., Marshall Green, assistant secretary of state for East Asian and Pacific affairs, told the Subcommittee on Asian and Pacific Affairs, Committee on Foreign Affairs of the House of Representatives, on October 6, 1970: "For our part, we will continue to reiterate our willingness to remain responsive to any indications of reduced hostility from Peking, to cooperate in removing tensions and to enter into a constructive dialogue eventually leading to more relations. We will attempt to convince Peking that we are not seeking to 'contain and isolate' China and that we favor China's emergence from isolation. . . ." Excerpt in Current Scene (Hong Kong), IX, 3 (March 7, 1971), 23. For excerpts of similar statements by Nixon, Secretary of State Rogers, and Green, see ibid., pp. 22-24.

213. "U.S. Foreign Policy for the 1970's," p. 383.

214. "A Look at Nixon's Foreign Policy Report, Big Exposure of U.S. Imperialism's World Hegemony Ambition," Peking Review, XIV, 11 (March 12, 1971), 27.

215. See "Chinese Table Tennis Team in Nagoya," ibid., No. 16 (April 16, 1971), pp. 11-12.

216. See Tillman Durdin, "China's U.S. Policy, a Chasm Still Separates Two Governments," New York Times News Service, Asahi Evening News, Tokyo, May 8, 1971, p. 4.

217. The ROC also took strong exception to the American view on the status of Taiwan. See Doc. 96, See also Docs. 89 and 94.

218. See Takashi Oka, "Chou Ties U.N. Seat to Taipei's Ouster," The New York Times, July 1, 1971, pp. 1, 32.

219. Seymour Topping, "Chou Says U.S. Shield at Taiwan Is a Main Bar to Diplomatic Ties," The New York Times, June 23, 1971, pp. 1, 2. There is no personal income tax in the PRC. The ROC government categorically rejected the overtures of the PRC and made it clear that it would not negotiate with the PRC authorities. See "President Chiang Kai-shek's New Year's Day Message, January 1, 1972," Free China Weekly, XIII, 1, January 2, 1972, p. 2.

220. "Transcript of the President's Statement", The New York Times, July 17, 1971, p. 4.

221. UN Monthly Chronicle, VII, 11 (December 1970), 39-40.

222. Resolution 2758 (XXVI), ibid., VIII, 10 (November 1971), 61. For President Chiang's message on the ROC's withdrawal from the United Nations, see Doc. 98.

223. UN Monthly Chronicle, VIII, 11 (December 1971), 26.

224. "Nationalist Chinese React with Dismay to Nixon's Decision," The New York Times, July 17, 1971, p. 3.

225. Lee Lescaze, "U.S. Aide Reassures Taiwan with Pledge Backing Treaty," International Herald Tribune, Paris, March 4-5, 1972, p. 2.

226. "Britain and China to Exchange Ambassadors," South China Morning Post, Hong Kong, March 14, 1972, p. 1. British authorities soon notified the ROC government of the closure of its consulate at Tamsui, Taiwan.

227. "Text of the Chinese-Japanese Accord Signed by Chou and Tanaka," The New York Times, September 30, 1972, p. 12. Japan immediately informed the ROC ambassador at Tokyo of the termination of diplomatic relations between the two countries. Richard Halloran, "Tokyo Informs Envoy," ibid.

228. See "Harvard Expert's View [J. A. Cohen], U.S. Stand on Taiwan Is Seen As Peril to Nixon-Chou Accord," International Herald Tribune, Paris, March 6, 1972, p. 2.

229. See "U.S., Peiping Agree To Shelve Taiwan," London, March 11, 1972, Associated Press, in The China News, Taipei, March 12, 1972, p. 7; Max Frankel, "Close Bargaining Seen on U.S.-China Paper," International Herald Tribune, March 3, 1972, pp. 1-2.

230. Chung-hua ming-kuo tung-chi yüeh-pao (Monthly statistics of the Republic of China), No. 74 (February 1972), p. 42. In 1971 the ROC enjoyed a favorable trade balance of $U.S. 151,843,000. See also United States Foreign Policy 1971, a Report of the Secretary of State, p. 66.

231. Chung-hua ming-kuo tung-chi yüeh-pao, No. 74, p. 118.

232. Ibid., pp. 43-44, 45. See also United States Foreign Policy 1971, a Report of the Secretary of State, p. 66.

233. Thomas J. Weiss, "Taiwan and U.S. Policy," Orbis, XII, 4 (Winter 1969), 1179.

234. See "U.S. and Diem's Overthrow: Step by Step," The New York Times, July 1, 1971, pp. 1, 12-14.

235. Weiss, "Taiwan and U.S. Policy," pp. 1173, 1180.

236. Gregory Clark, In Fear of China (Melbourne: Lansdowne Press, 1967), p. 70.

237. Compare the following comment by a Western correspondent from Peking: "In the short range, Peking wants Taiwan; it is more worried about a Taiwanese independence movement than about Chiang Kai-shek or America's troops on that island." James Reston, "A View from Peking" (Peking, August 7, 1971), The New York Times, August 8, 1971, Sec. 4, p. 11.

238. E.g., see Lung-chu Chen and Harold D. Lasswell, Formosa, China, and the United Nations (New York: St. Martin's Press, 1967). Chen and Lasswell suggest that the United States should take military action against the ROC so as to establish an independent Taiwan republic.

239. Richard Moorsteen and Morton Abramowitz, Remaking China Policy (Cambridge, Mass.: Harvard University Press, 1971), p. 11.

240. E.g., Edgar Snow, "China Will Talk from a Position of Strength," Life, LXXI, 5 (July 30, 1971), 24, 26.

241. See Doc. 55. See also Walter H. Judd's statement before the U.S. Senate Committee on Foreign Relations on March 28, 1966. U.S. Policy with Respect to Mainland China, p. 441.

242. United States Security Agreements and Commitments Abroad, Republic of China, Hearings before the Subcommittee on U.S. Security Agreements and Commitments Abroad of the Committee on Foreign Relations, U.S. Senate, 91st Cong., 2nd Sess., Pt. 4, November 24, 25 and 26, 1969, and May 8, 1970 (Washington, D.C.: U.S. Government Printing Office, 1970), p. 942.

243. E.g., see Tad Szulc, "China Said to Want Accord on Key Issues Before Ties," The New York Times, August 7, 1971, pp. 1, 2. Szulc wrote: "A principal Chinese requirement for formal relations with the United States was described as a global political concept and not simply geographical concessions such as withdrawal from Taiwan." Ibid., p. 2.

PART

II

**DOCUMENTS
AND
MATERIALS**

Compiled by
Hungdah Chiu
George Po-chung Chen
Lung-sheng Tao
John Chung Kuan

5

**OFFICIAL DOCUMENTS
CONCERNING THE QUESTION
OF TAIWAN, 1662-1950**

DOCUMENT 1: KOXINGA-DUTCH TREATY, FEBRUARY 1, 1662[1]

Treaty made and agreed upon; from the one side, by His Highness the Lord Teibingh Tsiante Teysiancon Koxin, who has besieged Castle Zeelandia on Formosa since 1st May 1661 up till this first day of February 1662; and from the other side, as representing the Dutch Government, by the Governor of the said Castle, Frederick Coyett and his Council, consisting of the undernoted eighteen Articles:

I. All hostilities committed on either side to be forgotten.

II. Castle Zeelandia, with its outworks, artillery, remaining war-materials, merchandise, money, and other properties belonging to the Honourable Company, to be surrendered to Lord Koxinga.

III. Rice, bread, wine, arack, meat, pork, oil, vinegar, ropes, canvas, pitch, tar, anchors, gunpowder, bullets, and linen, with such other articles as may be required by the besieged during their voyage to Batavia, to be taken on board the Company's ships in keeping with instructions from the before-mentioned Governor and Council.

IV. All private movable property inside the Castle or elsewhere belonging to officers of the Dutch Government, shall first be inspected by Koxinga's delegates, and then placed on board the said ships.

V. In addition to these goods, each of the twenty-eight Councillors shall be permitted to take with him two hundred rijksdaalders, and twenty chosen civilians an aggregate sum of one thousand rijksdaalders.

VI.   After inspection, the Dutch soldiers may come forth with flying banners, burning fusees, loaded rifles, and beating drums, marching thus for embarkation under command of the Governor.

VII.   The names of all Chinese debtors or lease-holders in Formosa, with particulars of claims against them, shall be copied out from the Company's books, and handed to Lord Koxinga.

VIII.   All the Government archives may be taken to Batavia.

IX.   Every servant of the Company, now imprisoned by the Chinese in Formosa, shall be liberated within eight or ten days, and those who are in China, as soon as possible. Servants of the Company who are not imprisoned in Formosa shall be granted a free pass to reach the Company's ships in safety.

X.   The said Lord Koxinga shall now return to the Company the four captured boats, with all their accessories.

XI.   He shall also provide a sufficient number of vessels to take the Honourable Company's people and goods to their ships.

XII.   Vegetables, flesh-meat, and whatever else may be necessary to sustain the Company's people during their stay, shall daily be provided by his Highness's subjects at a reasonable price.

XIII.   So long as the Honourable Company's people remain on land before embarkation, no soldier or other subject of Lord Koxinga shall be permitted to enter the Castle (unless . . . on service for the Company), to approach the outworks nearer than the gabions, or to proceed further than the palisades erected by order of His Highness.

XIV.   No other than a white flag shall float from the Castle until the Honourable Company's people have marched out.

XV.   Those who guard the stores shall remain in the Castle two or three days after the other people and goods have been taken on board, and thereafter they shall proceed themselves to the vessels.

XVI.   As soon as this Agreement is signed, sealed, and sworn to on both sides, each according to his own country's customs, Lord Koxinga shall deliver to one of the Dutch ships two hostages, viz. the Mandarin or Captain Moor Ongkun and Pimpan Jamoosje of the political Council. On the other side, and as representing the Company, Lord Koxinga shall receive custody of Mr. Jan Oetgens van Waveren, an official second in rank to the Governor, and Mr. David Harthouwer, also a member of the Formosa Council. Each of these hostages shall remain in a previously fixed place until everything has been carried out in accordance with the terms of this contract.

XVII.   Chinese prisoners at present in the Castle or on the Company's ships shall be released in exchange for any of our people who have been seized by the subjects of Lord Koxinga.

XVIII.   All misunderstandings, and every important matter overlooked in this Agreement, shall immediately be dealt with to the satisfaction of both parties, upon notice having been given from either side.

DOCUMENT 2: TREATY OF SHIMONOSEKI, APRIL 17, 1895[2]

His Majesty the Emperor of Japan, and His Majesty the Emperor of China, desiring to restore the blessings of peace* to their countries and subjects and to remove all cause for future complications, have named as their Plenipotentiaries for the purpose of concluding a Treaty of Peace. . . .

. . .

ARTICLE II

Territorial Cessions by China to Japan.

China cedes to Japan in perpetuity and full sovereignty the following territories, together with all fortifications, arsenals, and public property thereon:

. . .

Island of Formosa

(b) The island of Formosa, together with all islands appertaining or belonging to the said Island of Formosa.

---

*War was declared by Japan against China on August 3, 1894.

Pescadores Group

(c) The Pescadores Group, that is to say, all islands lying between the 119th and 120th degrees of longitude east of Greenwich, and the 23rd and 24th degrees of north latitude.

. . .

ARTICLE V

Right of Inhabitants to Emigrate from Territory Ceded to Japan

The inhabitants of the territories ceded to Japan who wish to take up their residence outside the ceded districts shall be at liberty to sell their real property and retire. For this purpose a period of two years from the date of the exchange of the ratifications of the present Act shall be granted. At the expiration of that period those of the inhabitants who shall not have left such territories shall, at the option of Japan, be deemed to be Japanese subjects.

DOCUMENT 3: TELEGRAM FROM GOVERNOR OF TAIWAN, T'ANG CHING-SUNG, TO THE CHÜN WU-CH'U DEPARTMENT OF MILITARY AFFAIRS, APRIL 28, 1895[3]

. . . I have received a blood oath from the gentlemen and people of Taiwan which states: "All the people are pledged that they will not surrender to Japan. Death is inevitable regardless of whether we obey the order to surrender the territory or resist. We would prefer death at the hands of violent rebels to that at the hands of the Japanese. Now that we have learned that the empress [dowager], the emperor and the officers before the court would not take the opportunity to cancel the article in the Treaty concerning ceding Taiwan, they would be deliberately giving up the people of Taiwan. If the people of Taiwan are given up, the empire will lose popular support. With what, then, can it administer the country? According to Chapter 286 of Kung-fa hui-tung, "it is necessary to consider whether the inhabitants are willing to cede a territory," and "only when the inhabitants express their willingness, can the territory be considered transferred."[4]

We urge that the treaty must be abolished and that opinions be sought from foreign countries. We also beg the emperor to say a word in our favor, to comfort the people and to prevent disruptions of the social order. This is urgent, and we cry and await orders from the

government. Please memorialize on our behalf." Please memorialize
the telegram to the emperor.

DOCUMENT 4: TELEGRAM FROM GOVERNOR
OF TAIWAN, T'ANG, TO THE CHIEF OFFICERS
OF ALL THE PROVINCES, MAY 25, 1895[5]

Japan asked for and took Taiwan. The people of Taiwan do not
succumb to this situation and I have telegraphed to memorialize about
it repeatedly, asking the government not to agree to the cession.
However, the situation is not remediable. The people of Taiwan are
loyal and patriotic, and they pledge not to succumb to the Japanese.
As a result, after I received the order to go back to the mainland, and
while I was packing, these people unexpectedly took an official seal and
announcement to the Governor's Office [on May 25, 1895]. The seal is
inscribed with the words "The Seal of the President of the Republic of
Taiwan." The flag has a yellow tiger over a blue ground. I have no
alternative but to agree to serve temporarily as the president. This
is done under the pressure of popular will, and we shall still use the
mandate of the empire as our sovereign. We will use Taiwan as a
frontier line for the defense of the empire. Meanwhile, we are engaged
in discussions with foreign states, asking for foreign support to settle
the present situation. The whole thing has happened unexpectedly, and
I have not had much freedom of action. I have telegraphed to memorialize the throne, and have announced to the respective foreign states
the present situation in Taiwan. As to whether the republic will be
able to survive, no one can predict. I hope that you will sympathize
with us and help us. Ching-sung.

DOCUMENT 5: STATEMENT OF T'ANG
CHING-SUNG, PRESIDENT OF THE REPUBLIC
OF TAIWAN, MAY [25?], 1895[6]

Japan has insulted China and made many demands of China. This
time, the Treaty of Shimonoseki consists of not only clauses for
monetary reparation to Japan, but also a clause in which Japan demands
the cession of the island of Taiwan. The people of Taiwan are loyal
and patriotic and do not succumb to the future Japanese rule. The
people have asked for a decision not to let go the territory, and this
president has repeatedly memorialized for them. Yet China desires
to keep promises and she therefore does not agree to alter the treaty.
As a result, the whole population on Taiwan has been in great sorrow
and indignation. At this moment, when we cannot call for help from

heaven and we have no master to rely upon, the people of Taiwan decide to express the public will to establish an independent democratic republic. Since the inauguration of this republic will inevitably concern the establishment of a government and the setting up of military forces for its defense, there must be people to take the leadership.

Thus, [on May 16] the people assembled in this office to submit their request that I take charge of the state affairs temporarily. Despite my repeated declination to do so, [on May 21] these people surrounded me and urged me to take the presidency. [On May 25] they inscribed a seal, and the inscription states "The Official Seal of the President of the Republic of Taiwan." Also they suggested a new national flag, on which was a yellow tiger over blue ground. They brought all these and came forward to present them to me. It was my personal opinion that the popular will was determined, and that it was impossible to disobey this popular will. Having no alternatives, and for the purpose of protecting the people, I finally agreed to the request and promised to take charge of governmental affairs temporarily.

On the same day we reached the decision to establish a democratic state on Taiwan. The first thing for the new administration of this country would be to set up a parliament composed of publicly elected members. Also, laws and ordinances would be enacted, and the rules ought to be simple. The territory of Taiwan has been cultivated by the great Ch'ing for more than 200 years. Now that we must establish an independent state, we are grateful to the emperor for his benevolence. For this reason we ought to respect the empire as the sovereign, and our government shall serve as a unit of national defense for the empire. The culture, however, is still the same; and Taiwan does not differ from the mainland.

Moreover, we shall be as careful as usual and shall never neglect our duty. If there is any person among the people who would falsely establish a cause, for the purpose of gathering people to make trouble, or to commit homicide, he shall be punished as a bandit. From now on, Taiwan shall eliminate corruption and solicit foreign support, exploit natural resources and get rid of undesirable customs. It will also build railways and make ships, and gradually develop industries. The objectives of strength and wealth will be achieved. It will also be a strong state on the southeast frontier of China. If this goal is finally achieved, it will be to the benefit of the people of Taiwan. I hereby announce the policy to the people of Taiwan.

DOCUMENT 6: DECLARATION OF THE PEOPLE OF TAIWAN, MAY 25, 1895[7]

Taiwan has belonged to the territory of the Ch'ing Empire for over 200 years. Recently, it was made a province, and since then it has become prosperous and a strong point in the southeast part of China. However, last year Japan made trouble and took issue with China, and peace was finally disrupted. In order to preserve military force and to protect the people, the emperor sent representatives to Japan to sign a treaty. Under the Japanese demands there is a clause in the treaty calling for China's cession of Taiwan to Japan. This was entirely beyond the expectation of the people of Taiwan; and when they received the information, they were angry and indignant. . . . their cry even shocked the heavens. Although Governor T'ang repeatedly telegraphed to memorialize the emperor for alteration of the treaty, and high officials in and out the court were also indignant and rose to dispute about the appropriateness of the treaty, yet the situation has been such that no remedy is possible.

The gentlemen and people then turned to Britain for help. However, Britain was restrained by being a neutral and, for this reason, has ignored the request. The people again asked the governor to telegraph and memorialize, suggesting that the Tsungli Yamen negotiate with . . . Russia, France, and Germany, and ask them to prevent the Japanese from annexing Taiwan. Nevertheless, no agreement has been reached. Alas, what a lamentable situation!

The Island of Taiwan contains a mountainous area of 2,000 li* and has thousands of people. Moreover, virtually every family possesses weapons for hunting animals and resisting aborigines. There are a million warriors and people who can be called to fight. Moreover, there are 40,000 military personnel. How can all these people succumb to the enemy's rule? Now that we have neither heaven to appeal to, nor persons who would give us help, the people of Taiwan have no alternatives but to establish an independent state and to elect a man of excellent virtues to take charge of political matters. After the turmoil ceases to exist, they will request a decree from the emperor to decide what should be done.

If Japan has a conscience and feels it improper to coerce the people of Taiwan, the latter would be willing to make peace with the Japanese and agree to grant benefits to Japan. However, the land and administration of Taiwan can never be interfered with by foreign people. If, on the other hand, Japan uses force against Taiwan, the people of Taiwan can do nothing but gather together for its defense. They prefer to lose Taiwan after everyone has died in defending it rather than give up Taiwan voluntarily.

We also hope the extraordinarily talented people on the mainland will come eastward to Taiwan and fight with us for a new world and

---

*One li is approximately one-third of a mile.

a meritorious cause. As to subsistence and food, Taiwan can provide for the troops temporarily. However, it will rely on financial support from the mainland. Also, in the near future we will set up companies in ports such as Shanghai, Canton, and those along the southeast coast. Rules shall be fixed for these corporations, and the purpose will be to raise money. Considering the sorrowful situation in which the people of Taiwan have been put, the people on the mainland will certainly render whatever help they can afford to. Only in so doing can the great hatred be revenged and the endangered island be saved.

We will again announce to foreign countries that if any of them will recognize the independence of Taiwan, and render support, all the gold and coal mines, together with land suitable for housing and farming, are open for rent and cultivation. Thus, every state will equally enjoy the benefits. In accordance with public [international] law, if the subjects [gentlemen and people] of the ceded territory do not agree to give up the land, then the treaty has no effect. There are precedents available to be invoked. If foreign countries will, for the sake of justice, raise the issue and decide to return Taiwan to China, the people of Taiwan will respond to their goodwill with all profits available in Taiwan.

All people in Taiwan are from Fukien and Kwangtung. Thus, those overseas Chinese who are from Fukien and Kwangtung are expected to show concern and sympathy with people from their provinces. If they will come to Taiwan with money, the people on Taiwan will protect them with great prudence. Of those who are poor but willing to come to Taiwan, this is a place for them to make a good living; and there is also the opportunity for them to get even with our common enemy. All this is not due to the obstinacy of the people of Taiwan. It is, rather, due . . . to the fact that, for the people of Taiwan, cession of this island without first engaging in a war of resistance would be a strange thing in history. If we abandon our families and farms and go back to the mainland, we shall have no means of survival. If we want to survive regardless of the humiliation . . ., we shall have no face to live together with other people under the heavens. For these reasons we are sorrowful and thus make a blood pledge, and all with one heart, to fight against the Japanese take-over until death. If the heroes in China and foreign states have a sense of pity, they ought come to our aid. This is precisely what the whole population on Taiwan awaits. We hereby issue the declaration to the world.

DOCUMENT 7: TELEGRAM FROM GOVERNOR OF TAIWAN, T'ANG CHING-SUNG, TO THE TSUNG-SHU,* MAY 27, 1895[8]

The whole population of Taiwan does not accept Japan as their sovereign, because they want to be the people of the holy Ch'ing Empire. The independence today is for the purpose of fighting Japan and eliminating the possibility of providing Japan with an excuse it might use to raise complaints against China. If there is an opportunity, Taiwan will return to China. I have been compelled to stay, and have therefore postponed the trip to the capital to see the emperor. In the past few days, I have felt very frightened. However, since there will still be documents and memorials to be issued, it is proposed that they be authorized under my previous title, from which I should have resigned, and under the "Official Seal of the Taiwan Governor." As long as I live, I dare not go beyond the confines that an officer should obey. I hereby respectfully explain this.

DOCUMENT 8: PRESIDENT CHIANG KAI-SHEK'S SPEECH TO THE PROVISIONAL NATIONAL CONVENTION OF THE KUOMINTANG, APRIL 1, 1938[9]

Taiwan is the key to China's survival. Taiwan cannot be left under the control of the Japanese imperialists if China desires to establish a genuine national defense and to preserve permanent peace in East Asia. For thousands of years China has been a leading state in East Asia. To preserve the independence of the nations in East Asia and to establish peace in this area are China's duty and responsibility. We must cope with Japan's intricate plots and set free the people of Taiwan in order to accomplish the goals of our national revolution and prevent ambitious foreign states from disturbing the peaceful order of East Asia. This was made plain by the late director-general of our party [Dr. Sun Yat-sen] when he was alive. What the late director-general meant was that only when freedom was restored to the people of Taiwan could China's national defense be strengthened and the foundation for a peaceful East Asia be consolidated.

---

*Abbreviation of "Tsung-li Ko-Kuo shih-wu ya-men." This was a Chinese Government's department dealing with foreign relations between 1861 and 1901.

DOCUMENT 9: CHINA'S DECLARATION OF
WAR ON JAPAN, DECEMBER 9, 1941[10]

Japan's national policy has always aimed at the domination of
Asia and mastery of the Pacific. For more than four years China has
resolutely resisted Japan's agression, regardless of suffering and
sacrifice, in order not only to maintain her national independence and
freedom but also to uphold international law and justice and to promote
world peace and human happiness.

China is a peace-loving nation. In taking up arms in self-defense,
China entertained the hope that Japan might yet realize the futility of
her plans of conquest. Throughout the struggle all the other powers
have shown the utmost forebearance likewise in the hope that Japan
might one day repent and mend her ways in the interest of peace in the
entire Pacific region.

Unfortunately Japan's aggressive capacities prove to be incor-
rigible. After her long and fruitless attempt to conquer China, Japan,
far from showing any sign of penitence, has treacherously launched
an attack on China's friends, the United States and Great Britain, thus
extending the theater of her aggressive activities and making herself
the archenemy of justice and world peace.

This latest act of aggression on the part of Japan lays bare her
insatiable ambitions and has created a situation that no nation which
believes in international good faith and human decency can tolerate.

The Chinese Government hereby formally declares war on Japan.
The Chinese Government further declares that all treaties, conventions,
agreement, and contracts regarding relations between China and Japan
are and remain null and void.

(signed) Lin Sen
President of the
Republic of China

DOCUMENT 10: DECLARATION BY THE
UNITED NATIONS, JANUARY 1, 1942[11]

A Joint Declaration by the United States of America, the
United Kingdom of Great Britain and Northern Ireland, the Union
of Soviet Socialist Republics, China, Australia, Belgium, Canada,
Costa Rica, Cuba, Czechoslovakia, Dominican Republic, El
Salvador, Greece, Guatemala, Haiti, Honduras, India, Lux-
embourg, Netherlands, New Zealand, Nicaragua, Norway, Panama,
Poland, South Africa, Yugoslavia

The Governments signatory hereto,

Having subscribed to a common program of purposes and principles embodied in the Joint Declaration of the President of the United States of America and the Prime Minister of the United Kingdom of Great Britain and Northern Ireland dated August 14, 1941, known as the Atlantic Charter.[12]

Being convinced that complete victory over their enemies is essential to defend life, liberty, independence and religious freedom, and to preserve human rights and justice in their own lands as well as in other lands, and that they are now engaged in a common struggle against savage and brutal forces seeking to subjugate the world, DECLARE:

(1) Each Government pledges itself to employ its full resources, military or economic, against those members of the Tripartite Pact and its adherents with which such Government is at war.

(2) Each Government pledges itself to cooperate with the Governments signatory hereto and not to make a separate armistice or peace with the enemies.

The foregoing declaration may be adhered to by other nations which are, or which may be, rendering material assistance and contributions in the struggle for victory over Hitlerism.

Done at Washington
January First, 1942

The United States of America
   by Franklin D. Roosevelt

The United Kingdom of Great
   Britain & Northern
   Ireland
     by Winston S. Churchill

On behalf of the Government of the Union of Soviet Socialist Republics

Maxim Litvinoff
Ambassador

DOCUMENT 11: THE CAIRO CONFERENCE:
THE CHINESE RECORD OF THE
NOVEMBER 26, 1943,
MEETING[13]

At the Cairo Conference, President Franklin D. Roosevelt fully understood and supported our will to recover the lost territories. Therefore, the draft of the conference communiqué, prepared in accordance with the conclusion reached at the Sino-American consultation, stated that "such as Manchuria, Taiwan and the Pescadores shall be restored to China." However, Britain took a different view on this matter and proposed to change the phrase "shall be restored to China" into "shall be renounced by Japan." On November 26, when the representatives of the three countries discussed the draft of the conference communiqué, the Chinese representative, Wang Chung-hui, strongly opposed the British proposal. It is worthwhile to describe the details of the discussions:

Alexander Cadogan, the British undersecretary of state, stated that the proposed amendment was made because the British Parliament might ask the British government to explain why the communiqué should specify the return of Manchuria, Taiwan, and others to China while mentioning no countries to whom other occupied territories should be restored. Certainly these areas belonged to China, so it was unnecessary to specify their disposition. At that time British Secretary of State Sir Anthony Eden was also present, but he did not say anything on this problem. Secretary-General Wang of China replied that such an amendment would not only be opposed by China but also would cause suspicion among other countries. The phrase "shall be renounced by Japan" was correct, but it would cause doubts and suspicions throughout the world if the communiqué did not specify to whom the territories should be restored after Japanese renunciation. All countries of the world realized that this world war was initiated by Japan's aggression against China's Northeastern Provinces [Manchuria]. The goal of China's prosecution of the war was to eliminate aggression totally. If the matter was so ambiguously stipulated in the communiqué, the Chinese people, as well as people throughout the world, would be greatly confused. Therefore, the Chinese side could hardly accept this amendment to the draft.

Alexander Cadogan further stated that since the first part of the sentence had referred to "the territories Japan had stolen from the Chinese," these territories would naturally be restored to China after Japan's renunciation; and it would not be necessary to specify them. Secretary-General Wang replied that if the wording was so ambiguous, then the conference communiqué would become totally meaningless and perhaps would be of no value at all. Mr. Wang further stated that although Mr. Cadogan indicated that these territories should naturally be restored to China without special mention in the communiqué, he certainly was not unaware of the various absurd claims to Manchuria, Taiwan, and other Chinese territories made by foreigners. Thus, if the communiqué did not specify that these territories should be restored to China, then the goal of the United Nations to fight this war and to resist aggression would be too obscure. Mr. Wang therefore insisted on retaining the wording of the original draft.

Ambassador Averell Harriman [of the United States] supported Secretary-General Wang's view and said that if we adopted the ambiguous wording, the countries of the world would suspect the principles long held by our United Nations; he therefore supported the retention of the original wording and proposed that the last sentence of that paragraph ("Japan will also be expelled from all other territories which she has taken by violence and greed.") be placed after the third paragraph as a new paragraph. All other paragraphs should remain unchanged. Secretary-General Wang agreed with Ambassador Harriman's proposal. However, Alexander Cadogan said that, although such a proposal would be better than the original wording, he still could not be relieved of his original worry. Due to the insistence of both China and United States, the original draft of the conference communiqué was retained.

DOCUMENT 12: THE CAIRO DECLARATION, NOVEMBER 26, 1943[14]

Press Communiqué

President Roosevelt, Generalissimo Chiang Kai-shek and Prime Minister Churchill, together with their respective military and diplomatic advisers, have completed a conference in North Africa. The following general statement was issued:

"The several military missions have agreed upon future military operations against Japan. The three great Allies expressed their resolve to bring unrelenting pressure against their brutal enemies by sea, land and air. This pressure is already rising.

"The three great Allies are fighting this war to restrain and punish the aggression of Japan. They covet no gain for themselves and have no thought of territorial expansion. It is their purpose that Japan shall be stripped of all the islands in the Pacific which she has seized or occupied since the beginning of the First World War in 1914, and that all the territories Japan has stolen from the Chinese, such as Manchuria, Formosa, and the Pescadores, shall be restored to the Republic of China. Japan will also be expelled from all other territories which she has taken by violence and greed. The aforesaid three great powers, mindful of the enslavement of the people of Korea, are determined that in due course Korea shall become free and independent.

"With these objects in view the three Allies, in harmony with those of the United Nations at war with Japan, will continue to persevere in the serious and prolonged operations necessary to procure the unconditional surrender of Japan."

DOCUMENT 13: U.S. PRESIDENT ROOSEVELT'S ADDRESS, DECEMBER 24, 1943[15]

I have just returned from extensive journeyings in the region of the Mediterranean and as far as the borders of Russia. I have conferred with the leaders of Britain and Russia and China on military matters of the present—especially on plans for stepping up our successful attack on our enemies as quickly as possible and from many different points of the compass.

. . .

At Cairo, Prime Minister Churchill and I spent four days with . . . Generalissimo Chiang Kai-shek. It was the first time that we had an opportunity to go over the complex situation in the Far East with him personally. We were able not only to settle upon definite military strategy but also to discuss certain long-range principles which we believe can assure peace in the Far East for many generations to come.

Those principles are as simple as they are fundamental. They involve the restoration of stolen property to its rightful owners and the recognition of the rights of millions of people in the Far East to build up their own forms of self-government without molestation. . . .

DOCUMENT 14: POTSDAM PROCLAMATION, JULY 26, 1945[16]

Proclamation by the Heads of Governments,
United States, China and the United Kingdom

(1) We, the President of the United States, the President of the National Government of the Republic of China and the Prime Minister of Great Britain, representing the hundreds of millions of our countrymen, have conferred and agree that Japan shall be given an opportunity to end this war.

. . .

(4) The time has come for Japan to decide whether she will continue to be controlled by those self-willed milita[r]istic advisers whose unintelligent calculations have brought the Empire of Japan to the threshold of annihilation, or whether she will follow the path of reason.

(5) Following are our terms. We will not deviate from them. There are no alternatives. We shall brook no delay.

. . .

(8) The terms of the Cairo Declaration shall be carried out and Japanese sovereignty shall be limited to the islands of Honshu, Hokkaido, Kyushu, Shikoku and such minor islands as we determine.

. . .

(13) We call upon the Government of Japan to proclaim now the unconditional surrender of all the Japanese armed forces, and to provide proper and adequate assurances of their good faith in such action. The alternative for Japan is prompt and utter destruction. POTSDAM July 26, 1945

> HARRY S. TRUMAN
> WINSTON CHURCHILL
> by H. S. T.
> PRESIDENT OF CHINA
> by wire

DOCUMENT 15: JAPANESE INSTRUMENT OF SURRENDER, SEPTEMBER 2, 1945[17]

1. Instrument of Surrender

We, acting by command of and in behalf of the Emperor of Japan, the Japanese Government, and the Japanese Imperial General Headquarters, hereby accept the provisions in the declaration issued by the heads of the Governments of the United States, China, and Great Britain on July 26, 1945, at Potsdam, and subsequently adhered to by the Union of Soviet Socialist Republics, which four Powers are hereafter referred to as the Allied Powers.

. . .

We hereby undertake for the Emperor, the Japanese Government, and their successors to carry out the provisions of the Potsdam declaration in good faith, and to issue whatever orders and take whatever action may be required by the supreme commander for the Allied Powers or any other designated representative of the Allied Powers for the purpose of giving effect to that declaration.

. . .

The authority of the Emperor and the Japanese Government to rule the state shall be subject to the supreme commander for the Allied Powers, who will take such steps as he deems proper to effectuate these terms of surrender.

2. Proclamation of the Japanese Emperor

PROCLAMATION

Accepting the terms set forth in the Declaration issued by the heads of the Governments of the United States, Great Britain and China on July 26, 1945, at Potsdam and subsequently adhered to by the Union of Soviet Socialist Republics, We have commanded the Japanese Imperial Government and the Japanese Imperial General Headquarters to sign on Our behalf the Instrument of Surrender presented by the Supreme Commander for the Allied Powers and to issue General Orders to the Military and Naval Forces in accordance with the direction of the Supreme Commander for the Allied Powers. We command all Our people forthwith to cease hostilities, to lay down their arms and faithfully to carry out all the provisions of the Instrument of Surrender and the General Orders issued by the Japanese Imperial Government and the Japanese Imperial General Headquarters hereunder.

This second day of the ninth month of the twentieth year of Syōwa.

Signed: HIROHITO [Countersignatures omitted.]

DOCUMENT 16: PROCLAMATION OF THE
NATIONAL GOVERNMENT OF
THE REPUBLIC OF CHINA,
SEPTEMBER 4, 1945[18]

On August 14 of this year, Japan replied to China, the United States, Great Britain, and the Soviet Union, accepting the provisions set forth in the Potsdam Proclamation of July 26, and announced unconditional surrender. According to these provisions, the whole territory of Taiwan and the Penghu [Pescadores] Islands should be returned to the Republic of China. This government will immediately send administrative and military officials to Taiwan to govern the territory. The people on Taiwan must live in peace and continue their business, preserve the social order, and must not disturb the peace or make trouble. All the Japanese armed forces and police in Taiwan should keep quiet and wait for transference of power, and should not

disobey ordinary rules and injure the life and property of the people.
They should also be responsible for the local order. The Japanese
administrative and judicial officials and members of the transportation,
manufacturing, and educational organs should continue to go to their
offices as usual. . . . They must not destroy or damage public property, usurp or embezzle public funds. Anyone who disobeys these
instructions shall definitely be punished. It is so announced!

DOCUMENT 17: JAPANESE INSTRUMENT OF SURRENDER ON TAIWAN, OCTOBER 25, 1945[19]

I. Administrator Ch'en I's Statement

On September 9, 1945, the Japanese forces on Taiwan surrendered
[to China] at Nanking. On the order of the supreme commander of the
China War Theater, Generalissimo Chiang, transferred to me by the
commander-in-chief of the Chinese Army, General Ho, I have been
designated the chief officer to accept the surrender on Taiwan. I hereby
issue my No. 1 order to the Japanese governor of Taiwan and the
commander of the 10th Area forces, General Kikichi Ando. It is
expected that this order will followed and complied with.

II. Ch'en I's Order No. 1

1. In accordance with the order of the Japanese imperial government and the Japanese Imperial General Headquarters, General
Yasutsugu Okamura, commander of the Japanese forces in China,
signed the document of surrender at Nanking on September 9, 1945,
for all Japanese ground, sea, and air forces within China (excluding
Manchuria), Vietnam north of 16 degrees north latitude, and Taiwan
and Penghu Archipelago, surrendering unconditionally to General Ho
Ying-chin, commander-in-chief of the Chinese Army and special
representative designated by the supreme commander of the China War
Theater, Generalissimo Chiang Kai-shek.

2. In accordance with the orders issued by the supreme
commander of the China War Theatre and president of the national
government of the Republic of China, [Generalissimo] Chiang, and
Commander-in-Chief Ho and the Chung tzu memoranda issued by
Commander-in-Chief Ho to General Yasutsugu Okamura, I, and the
forces and administrative personnel named by me, have been designated to accept the surrender of Japanese ground, sea, air, and
auxiliary forces on Taiwan and the Penghu Archipelago and to accept
the territory, people, administrative power, military and civil
arrangements, and assets on Taiwan and the Penghu Archipelago.

3. After receiving this order, you should cancel your titles, such as governor of Taiwan and commander of the 10th Area forces, and assume the title of director of coordination for rehabilitation of Japanese officers and soldiers in the Taiwan area, subject to my command. Aside from transmitting my orders, instructions, rules, and directives, you should not issue any orders to your subordinate personnel in administrative, military, and any other organs and forces. Your subordinates should only execute or transmit the orders, rules, and directives of military officers and civilian officials designated by me. They should not dispose of any matter without prior instructions.

. . .

III. Japanese Document of Acceptance

I hereby receive a copy of Order No. 1 issued by the administrator and commander-in-chief of the Garrison Headquarters of Taiwan Province in the China War Theater, which should be complied with and executed. I shall immediately transmit the order to my subordinates and on behalf of the respective political and military organs and officers and soldiers of various ranks, comply with this order. With respect to this order and all subsequent orders, rules, or directives, I and all my subordinates and all the officials and soldiers whom I represent, assume the responsibility of full execution.

Japanese Governor of Taiwan and
Commander of the 10th Area Forces
Army, General   Kikichi Ando

[October 25, 1945]
at Taipei Public Hall*

DOCUMENT 18: TAIWAN ADMINISTRATOR CHEN I'S STATEMENT AT THE JAPANESE SURRENDER CEREMONY, TAIPEI, OCTOBER 25, 1945[20]

On the order of the supreme commander of the China War Theater, Generalissimo Chiang, which was transferred to me by Commander-in-Chief of the Chinese Army Ho, I have been designated the chief officer to accept the Japanese surrender on Taiwan. The

---

*The hall was renamed Chung shan t'ang in late 1945.

ceremony for accepting the Japanese surrender was held in the Taipei
Public Hall at 10 o'clock on the morning of October 25, 1945. Now the
ceremony has been successfully concluded. From this day forward,
Taiwan and the Penghu Archipelago are again incorporated into the
territory of China. The territory, people, and administration are now
placed under the sovereignty of the National government of the Republic
of China. I specifically report this fact—so meaningful in history—to
all Chinese compatriots and to the whole world. Now that Taiwan has
been recovered, we should be grateful to the revolutionary martyrs,
officers, and soldiers of this war of resistance against Japan, who
sacrificed themselves for the restoration of Taiwan. We should also
thank our allied states for assisting us in recovering Taiwan. Moreover, we should engrave in our hearts forever the images of Dr. Sun
Yat-sen, founder and leader of the Chinese National Revolutionary
Movement and Father of the Republic, and President Chiang, Dr. Sun's
successor, who has brought the revolution to a successful conclusion.

DOCUMENT 19: DECREE ON THE RESUMPTION OF CHINESE NATIONALITY FOR THE TAIWANESE PEOPLE, JANUARY 12, 1946[21]

The people of Taiwan are people of our country. They lost their
nationality because the island was invaded by an enemy. Now that the
land has been recovered, the people who originally had the nationality
of our country shall, effective on December 25, 1945, resume the
nationality of our country. This is announced by this general decree
in addition to individual orders.

DOCUMENT 20: MEASURES CONCERNING THE NATIONALITY OF OVERSEAS TAIWANESE, JUNE 22, 1946[22]

1. Effective on October 25, 1945, overseas Taiwanese shall
resume the nationality of the Republic of China. The Ministry of
Foreign Affairs shall telegraph the embassies of all the friendly countries to notify the respective governments for reference, and to ask
these governments to inform their subordinate administrative units
in the places or areas concerned.

As to Japan, the representative of our government to Japan shall
notify the Headquarters of the Allied Forces, and ask them to inform
the Japanese government for reference.

As to Korea, the representative of our government to Japan shall notify the Headquarters of the Allied Forces, and the representative of our Ministry of Foreign Affairs to Korea shall also notify the military governments established by the United States and the Soviet Union in Korea for reference.

2. The embassies or consulates (or representatives) to foreign countries shall make a registry of the overseas Taiwanese in accordance with the Measures for the Registration of Overseas Chinese. A certificate of registration shall be issued to an overseas Taiwanese who has registered himself, and a report of such registration shall be submitted to the Ministry of Interior Affairs for reference.

The certificate of registration provided for in the preceding provision shall have the effect of a certificate of nationality.

3. When an overseas Taiwanese makes the registration, he shall present two overseas Chinese to prove that he is truly a native of Taiwan. Those who are unwilling to resume the nationality of the Republic of China may submit an announcement of the decision not to resume the nationality to our embassies or consulates (or representatives) in the countries concerned.

The aforementioned announcement should be made prior to December 31, 1946.

4. The embassies or consulates (or representatives) shall give permission to an overseas Taiwanese who announces an unwillingness to resume the nationality of the Republic of China. They shall also submit the case to the Ministry of Interior Affairs for reference and notify the government of the country where the overseas Taiwanese resides. As to Japan, our representative to Japan shall notify the Headquarters of the Allied Forces and ask them to inform the Japanese government of the case. As to Korea, our representative to Japan shall notify the Headquarters of the Allied Forces, and the Ministry of Foreign Affairs shall also notify our representative to Korea, who shall let the case be known to the American and Soviet military governments in Korea.

5. The legal status and treatment of the overseas Taiwanese who has resumed the nationality of the Republic of China shall be exactly the same as an overseas Chinese. As to those who reside in the territory of Japan, they shall be entitled to the same treatment as is given to the aliens of other allied countries.

6. The measures are effective as of the day of proclamation.

DOCUMENT 21: STATEMENT OF PRESIDENT
HSIEH HSUEH-HUNG OF THE TAIWAN
DEMOCRATIC SELF-GOVERNMENT
LEAGUE,* SEPTEMBER 3, 1949[23]

On behalf of the 6,700,000 people of Taiwan, I declare strong
opposition against conspiratorial attempts of American imperialism
to annex Taiwan. . . . Any conspiracy for aggression against Taiwan
will be resolutely opposed by all the people of Taiwan, and of all
China. Today the Chinese people possess the strength to crush any
American imperialistic conspiracy of aggression.

For almost a hundred years, American imperialism has engaged
in aggression against Taiwan. In 1847 the United States sent troops
to assist the Japanese attack on Taiwan, and supplied ammunition
and ships to Japanese forces massacring the people of Taiwan. In
1857 the commander of the American naval fleet in Hong Kong . . .
attempted to establish a colonial "independent state" on Taiwan. In
1895, when China was negotiating the Treaty of Shimonoseki with
Japan, the American government supported the Japanese demand to
annex Taiwan from China. Since the Japanese surrender American
imperialism has deliberately attempted to take the place of the
Japanese on Taiwan. On the one hand, American imperialism has
colluded with the Kuomintang gang for the acquisition of naval and
air bases in Taiwan, and for the control of Taiwan's industrial and
mining enterprises and important economic sectors. . . . On the
other hand, it has actively instigated a disgraceful handful of Taiwanese,
like Liao Wen-yi, to conduct the activities of the so-called "Taiwan
independence movement" so as further to transform Taiwan into an
American colony. However, the Taiwanese people and the Chinese
people have already seen through the villainy of American imperialism;
and therefore the activities of . . . Liao Wen-yi, for example, have
not brought about the result their American master expected.
Recently, in view of the rapid development of the Chinese revolutionary
war, and the fact that the liberation of Taiwan by the People's Liberation Army is day by day drawing nearer, American imperialism is
growing impatient, and openly cries for "occupying Taiwan." . . .

---

*The League was established by Hsieh Hsueh-hung and other
leftist Taiwanese on November 12, 1947. In 1949 the League participated in the Chinese People's Political Consultative Conference held
at Peking. Since 1949 it has been a Communist Chinese front organization to promote the cause of "liberating Taiwan."

We don't know on what grounds the American government dares to make such foolish and frantic attempts to occupy the Chinese territory of Taiwan.

American imperialism's conspiracy to occupy Taiwan is doomed to failure. For 300 years the Taiwanese people have repeatedly struggled against aggressors. Presently the People's Liberation Army is advancing to southern China and has already liberated Foochow. Taiwan's liberation is not far off. The Taiwanese people, all the people of the country, and the People's Liberation Army, combined, are determined to wipe out the remnants of the Kuomintang gang, to drive out American imperialism's aggressive force on Taiwan, and to build a people's democratic new Taiwan and new China.

DOCUMENT 22: "AMERICAN SCHEME OF
AGGRESSION AGAINST TAIWAN IN
THE PAST FOUR YEARS"24

. . .

In 1945, accompanying the Kuomintang reactionaries' plunder [acceptance] of Taiwan, American imperialism also sent a liaison group headed by Colonel [Evans*] to Taiwan. [Evans] not only participated in the plunder of Taiwan, but also blackmailed the Bank of Taiwan for 120 kilograms of gold. When the "[Evans] case" was exposed, Taiwan public opinion was greatly disturbed. However, under the protection of American imperialism and the Kuomintang reactionaries, [Evans] was declared innocent and safely returned to the United States.

Thereafter, American imperialism formally established a consular office and a [United States Information Service] on Taiwan. Three notorious special agents took charge of these organs: [Bragg**] was consul, [George] Kerr was vice-consul, and [Robert J.] Catto was director of the [United States Information Service]. Before the outbreak of the Pacific War, Kerr was doing intelligence work in Taiwan under the cover of being a teacher; in wartime he was an American naval intelligence officer. He was considered a "Taiwan expert" among American imperialism's special agents.

---

*The editor is unable to locate the correct English name from the Chinese transliteration Ai-wen-ssu.

**The editor is unable to locate the correct English name from the Chinese transliteration Pu-lai-ke.

At that time, their primary role was sowing discord in the relations between the people of Taiwan and the people from mainland [China] so as to pave the way for the American Scheme [against Taiwan].

During the "February 28" incident, Kerr conspired to transform growing anger of the Taiwan people against the corrupt Kuomintang reactionary rule into a movement separating Taiwan from China. He engaged in various inciting and fomenting activities. He personally drove a jeep to meet the masses who surrounded the Monopoly Bureau and shouted: "Go ahead! Go ahead!" Moreover, the American consulate convened a "People's Representative Assembly" and attempted to use the running dogs Liao Wen-i, Liao Wen-k'uei and others to take that opportunity to declare Taiwan's independence. These acts were too exposed and, therefore, Washington expressed great dissatisfaction over them. As a result, both [Bragg] and Kerr were recalled to the United States.

After returning to the United States, Kerr used his teaching opportunities to spread all-out propaganda of "how the people of Taiwan like the United States." He continued to conduct conspiratorial activities. [Bragg] later became a political adviser of MacArthur and in Tokyo he openly advocated the idea of American occupation of Taiwan. He also bribed some Taiwanese traitors to organize "The Formosan League for Re-emancipation."

Catto remained in Taiwan and used the signboards of the United States Information Service to conduct the separatist movement until the spring of 1948, when . . . Wei Tao-ming in a press conference openly uncovered the activities of Catto. Then the American government had no other choice but to recall him.

. . .

DOCUMENT 23: U.S. DEPARTMENT OF STATE'S POLICY MEMORANDUM ON FORMOSA, DECEMBER 23, 194925

Department of State
Policy Information Paper—Formosa. Special Guidance No. 28, December 23, 1949.

I. Problem
To formulate information policy which will minimize damage to United States prestige and others' morale by the possible fall of Formosa to the Chinese Communist forces.

II. Background

A. Comment on Formosa is on the increase as the Communist advances on the Chinese mainland leave the island as the last substantial part of China under Nationalist control. Attention is focused by three principal elements:

1. Communists, world-wide, who charge the United States with conspiring to build the island into a fortress to be taken over by the United States (if it does not already control it), thereby trying to brand the United States with the mark of aggressive imperialism, and also hoping to get us involved in a risky and unpromising venture;

2. Pro-Nationalists (principally in the United States) who consider Formosa a redoubt in which the Government could survive, and who tend to create an impression the United States is delinquent if it fails to "save Formosa";

3. Groups in the United States who are inclined to be critical of the United States for failure to act to prevent loss of the island to the Communists, largely because of [the] mistaken popular conception of its strategic importance to United States defense in the Pacific.

B. Loss of the island is widely anticipated, and the manner in which civil and military conditions there have deteriorated under the Nationalists adds weight to the expectation. Its fall would threaten:

1. Loss of United States prestige at home and abroad to the extent we have become committed in the public mind to hold it;

2. Damage to the morale of other nations, particularly in the Far East, which are disturbed by the Communist gains and fear its possible further advances.

C. Formosa, politically, geographically, and strategically, is part of China in no way especially distinguished or important. Although ruled by the Japanese (as "Taiwan") for 50 years, historically it has been Chinese. Politically and militarily it is a strictly Chinese responsibility.

It is true that the technical status of the island remains to be determined by the Japanese peace settlement, but the Cairo agreement and the Potsdam declaration and the surrender terms of September 2, 1945, looked to its return to China and the United States facilitated its take-over by Chinese troops shortly after V-J Day.

Even the small United States military advisory group sent there at Chinese Government request was completely withdrawn a year ago. Merely a handful of military attaché personnel with diplomatic status remains. The United States never has had military bases there, and never has sought any special concessions there.

ECA [Economic Cooperation Administration] work done on the island, particularly through the Joint Commission on Rural Reconstruction, has been of purely economic and technical nature for assistance in improvement of conditions, and no quid pro quo has been sought.

D. United States public opinion has concerned itself primarily with the question of the island's strategic importance; there has been insistent demand from a few sources for military action by the United States, but it has not assumed significant proportions. Rather, public opinion obviously is divided and uncertain, and there is no apparent consensus for a particular course of active intervention.

III. Treatment

A. If rising public interest warrants it, gradually increasing attention may be paid Formosa, to establish publicly the facts indicated below. Overseas use should be made of unofficial materials in public analysis and comment appearing both at home and abroad, as well as official statements as they may appear. Label conflicting public statements properly as "individual expressions of opinion," as "unofficial," etc.

B. All material should be used best to counter the false impressions that:

1. Formosa's retention would save the Chinese Government;

2. The United States has a special interest in or "designs on" the island or any military bases on Formosa;

3. Its loss would seriously damage the interests of either the United States or of other countries opposing communism;

4. The United States is responsible for or committed in any way to act to save Formosa.

C. Without evidencing undue preoccupation with the subject, emphasize as appropriate any of the following main points:

1. Formosa is exclusively the responsibility of the Chinese Government:

(a) Historically and geographically a part of China;

(b) The national government has run the island's affairs since the take-over and is responsible for present conditions there;

(c) The United States has assumed no responsibilities or obligations, actual or moral.

2. Formosa has no special military significance:

(a) It is only approximately 100 miles off the China coast;

(b) Other potential objects of Communist aggression are closer to points on the Chinese mainland than to Formosa;

(c) China has never been a sea power and the island is of no special strategic advantage to the Chinese Communist armed forces.

3. Economic assistance in Formosa has been for economic and social purposes, has been consistent with demonstrated United States concern for the welfare of the Chinese generally, and has involved no thought of special concessions for the United States.

4. In areas of insistent demand for United States action, particularly in the United States itself, we should occasionally make clear that seeking United States bases on Formosa, sending in troops, supplying arms, dispatching naval units, or taking any similar action would:

(a) Accomplish no material good for China or its Nationalist regime;

(b) Involve the United States in a long-term venture producing at best a new area of bristling stalemate, and at worst possible involvement in open warfare;

(c) Subject the United States to a violent propaganda barrage and to reaction against our "militarism, imperialism, and interference" even from friendly peoples, and particularly from Chinese, who would be turned against us anew;

(d) Eminently suit purposes of the U.S.S.R., which would like to see us "substantiate" its propaganda, dissipate our energies and weaken effectiveness of our policies generally by such action.

5. In reflecting United States unofficial demands for action of various kinds in Formosa, avoid giving them prominence unwarranted by their limited (usually individual) source, and make clear that the total of such demands evidences concern and frustration in some quarters but does not add up to a consensus on any particular position different from that officially taken.

D. Avoid:

1. Speculation which would show undue concern with whether Nationalists can hold the island or when Communists may take it;

2. References which would indicate important strategic significance, or that the island is a political entity;

3. In output to China, any emphasis on bad conditions in Formosa under the Nationalists, although to other areas reference can be made among reasons why Nationalists are vulnerable there as elsewhere;

4. Statement that Formosa's final status still is to be determined by the Japanese peace treaty;

5. Name "Taiwan"; use "Formosa."

DOCUMENT 24: PRESIDENT TRUMAN'S STATEMENT
ON U.S. POLICY RESPECTING THE STATUS
OF FORMOSA (TAIWAN), JANUARY
5, 1950[26]

The United States Government has always stood for good faith in international relations. Traditional United States policy toward China, as exemplified in the open-door policy, called for international respect for the territorial integrity of China. This principle was recently reaffirmed in the United Nations General Assembly resolution of December 8, 1949, which, in part, calls on all states—

[''] To refrain from (a) seeking to acquire spheres of influence or to create foreign controlled regimes within the territory of China; (b) seeking to obtain special rights or privileges within the territory of China.['']

A specific application of the foregoing principles is seen in the present situation with respect to Formosa. In the joint declaration at Cairo on December 1, 1943, the President of the United States, the British Prime Minister, and the President of China stated that it was their purpose that territories Japan had stolen from China, such as Formosa, should be restored to the Republic of China. The United States was a signatory to the Potsdam declaration of July 26, 1945, which declared that the terms of the Cairo declaration should be carried out. The provisions of this declaration were accepted by Japan at the time of its surrender. In keeping with these declarations, Formosa was surrendered to Generalissimo Chiang Kai-shek, and for the past 4 years, the United States and the other Allied Powers have accepted the exercise of Chinese authority over the Island.

The United States has no predatory designs on Formosa or on any other Chinese territory. The United States has no desire to obtain special rights or privileges or to establish military bases on Formosa at this time. Nor does it have any intention of utilizing its armed forces to interfere in the present situation. The United States Government will not pursue a course which will lead to involvement in the civil conflict in China.

Similarly, the United States Government will not provide military aid or advice to Chinese forces on Formosa. In the view of the United States Government, the resources on Formosa are adequate to enable them to obtain the items which they might consider necessary for the defense of the Island. The United States Government proposes to continue under existing legislative authority the present ECA [Economic Cooperation Administration] program of economic assistance.

DOCUMENT 25: SECRETARY OF STATE ACHESON'S
REMARKS ELABORATING THE POLICY RE-
SPECTING THE STATUS OF FORMOSA
(TAIWAN), JANUARY 5, 1950[27]

I am having this conference this afternoon at the request and at the direction of the President for the purpose of going into the background of the statement which he made this morning on the subject of Formosa.

. . .

It is important that our position in regard to China should never be subject to the slightest doubt or the slightest question.

Now, what has that position been? In the middle of the war, the President of the United States, the Prime Minister of Great Britain, and the President of China agreed at Cairo that among the areas stolen from China by Japan was Formosa and Formosa should go back to China.

As the President pointed out this morning, that statement was incorporated in the declaration at Potsdam and that declaration at Potsdam was conveyed to the Japanese as one of the terms of their surrender and was accepted by them, and the surrender was made on that basis.

Shortly after that, the Island of Formosa was turned over to the Chinese in accordance with the declarations made and with the conditions of the surrender.

The Chinese have administered Formosa for 4 years. Neither the United States nor any other ally ever questioned that authority and that occupation. When Formosa was made a province of China nobody raised any lawyers' doubts about that. That was regarded as in accordance with the commitments.

Now, in the opinion of some, the situation is changed. They believe that the forces now in control of the mainland of China, the forces which undoubtedly will soon be recognized by some other countries, are not friendly to us, and therefore they want to say, "Well, we have to wait for a treaty." We did not wait for a treaty on Korea. We did not wait for a treaty on the Kuriles. We did not wait for a treaty on the islands over which we have trusteeship.

Whatever may be the legal situation, the United States of America, Mr. Truman said this morning, is not going to quibble on any lawyers' words about the integrity of its position. That is where we stand.

Therefore, the President says, we are not going to use our forces in connection with the present situation in Formosa. We are not going to attempt to seize the Island. We are not going to get involved militarily in any way on the Island of Formosa. So far as I know, no responsible person in the Government, no military man has ever believed that we should involve our forces in the island.

DOCUMENT 26: REVIEW OF U.S. POLICY IN
RELATION TO CHINA[28]

The Committee on Foreign Affairs, to whom was referred the resolution (H. Res. 452) requesting the State Department to furnish

full and complete answers to certain questions relating to the foreign
policy of the United States in the Far East, having considered the
same, report adversely thereon and recommend that the resolution . . .
not pass.

The recommendation of the committee is based on the fact that
answers to the questions contained in the resolution have been
furnished the committee by the Department of State. With the exception
of portions of two answers, the publication of which portions is felt
by the Department of State would be incompatible with the public
interest, the answers are included in this report for the information
of the Members of the House, and are as follows:

Question 1
    With respect to the President's statement of January 5, 1950,
on policy regarding Formosa—

. . .

Question 1 (d)
    Have the following been considered by the Executive as alterna-
tives to the policy enunciated in said statement?
    (1) Insistence on the execution of the terms of the Cairo
Declaration, which provided for the return of Formosa to the Republic
of China.
    Comment.—This cannot properly be considered an alternative
to the policy enunciated by the President. The President's statement
of January 5, 1950, contained a re-affirmation of the Cairo Declaration
on the part of the United States in respect to the disposition of
Formosa. Formosa has been administered since 1945 by China, the
surrender of Japanese forces on Formosa having been made to the
Generalissimo Chiang Kai-shek.
    (2) Consideration of Formosa as a possession of Japan to be
administered by the victor powers until eventual disposition under a
peace settlement with Japan.
    (3) A plebiscite in Formosa, under the auspices of the Far
Eastern Commission or a special commission of the UN, to determine
whether the inhabitants desire—
(a) to continue as a province of and the seat of government of the
Republic of China; (b) to be placed under a United Nations trusteeship;
or (c) to become an independent nation.
    Comment.—These alternatives were considered. As has been
noted under (1) above, Formosa has been administered by China
since 1945, when Japanese forces on the island surrendered to
Generalissimo Chiang Kai-shek. It was incorporated into China as
a province. It is now the seat of the Chinese Government. The

Allied Powers associated in the war against Japan have not questioned
these steps. The United States Government has not questioned these
steps because they were clearly in line with its commitments made
at Cairo and reaffirmed at Potsdam. In other words, the Allied
Powers including the United States have for the past 4 years treated
Formosa as a part of China.

For the United States Government, at this date, to seek to
establish a non-Chinese administration on Formosa, either through
SCAP or a United Nations or FEC-sponsored plebiscite, would be
almost universally interpreted in mainland China and widely interpreted
throughout Asia as an attempt by this Government to separate Formosa
from China in violation of its pledges and contrary to its long-standing
policy of respecting the territorial integrity of China. The important
point from the standpoint of our interests in Asia, including mainland
China, is not the technical justifications which we might urge for
taking such steps but rather the way such action on our part would
be viewed by the people of Asia. In this connection we do not wish
to create a Formosa irredenta issue about which the Chinese Communists could rally support within China and with which they could
divert attention from Soviet actions in the North. We must not place
ourselves in the unenviable position of the U.S.S.R. with regard to
the integrity of China and must remain free to take the position that
anyone who violates the integrity of China is the enemy of China and
is acting contrary to our own interests.

These are compelling reasons for rejecting alternatives stated
above. There are, of course, additional practical difficulties. The
seat of the Chinese Government is now on Formosa and that island,
with Hainan, is the only remaining substantial territory now under
its control. There is no evidence that the Chinese Government would
willingly accomplish its own demise by acquiescing in either of the
proposed alternatives. There is likewise the question of military
force to carry out the course of action proposed if the Chinese Government refuses its consent, and to defend the island if either proposal
were effected. The United Nations, of course, has no forces and it
seems clear that any defense of the island would finally rest upon the
United States.

In any case the conduct of a plebiscite for the purpose of
determining the wishes of the inhabitants on the future disposition of
Formosa is beyond the competence of the Far Eastern Commission.
The Far Eastern Commission by its terms of reference is "to formulate the policies, principles, and standards in conformity with which
the fulfillment by Japan of its obligations under the terms of surrender
may be accomplished." The terms of reference also provide that
"the Commission shall not make recommendations with regard to
the conduct of military operations nor with regard to territorial
adjustments."

NOTES

1. William Campbell, Formosa Under the Dutch (London: Kegan Paul, Trench, Trubner, 1903), pp. 455-56.

2. Excerpts from Hertslet's China Treaties, I (London: His Majesty's Stationery Office, 1908), 362, 363, 364. The treaty entered into force on May 8, 1895.

3. Translated from Tai-wan yin-hung ching-chi yen-chiu shih, ed., Ch'ing-chi wai-chiao shih-liao hsün chi (Selections from historical materials on late Ch'ing diplomacy), III (Taipei: Chung hua shu chü, 1964), 278.

4. The quoted part was summarized from Kung-fa hui-tung, III (Peking, 1880), p. 3. This is a Chinese translation of M. Bluntschli, Le Droit international codifié, translated from the German by M. C. Lardy (Paris: Librairie de Guillaumin, 1874). The original French text says: "Pour qu'une cession de territoire soit valable, il faut: . . . c) Comme minimum, la reconnaissance de la cession par les personnes qui, habitant de territoire cédé et y jouissant de leurs droits politiques, pussent au nouvel état. . . ." Pp. 174-75.

5. Translated from Tsai Erh-k'ang and Chi Fu, eds., Chung-tung chan-chi pan-mo (History of Sino-Japanese War), IV (Shanghai: Kuang hsueh hui, 1897), pp. 58-59.

6. Translated from ibid., p. 59.

7. Translated from ibid., pp. 59-60.

8. Translated from Tai-wan yin-hung ching-chi yen-chiu shih, ed., Ch'ing-chi wai-chiao shih-liao hsün chi (Selections from historical materials on late Ch'ing diplomacy), III (Taipei; Chung hua shu chü, 1964), p. 317.

9. Excerpt translated from Huang Shun-ch'ing, Lin Hsiung-hsiang and Kuo Hai-ming, eds., Tai-wan sheng t'ung-chih kao (Draft history of Taiwan Province), X, Kuang-fu chih (History of restoration) (Taipei: Tai-wan sheng wen-hsien wei-yuan hui, 1952), p. 2.

10. Contemporary China. A Reference Digest, I, 15 (December 15, 1941), [p. 1]. Japan began an undeclared war on China on July 7, 1937, and China resisted that undeclared war without technically announcing the existence of a state of war until December 9, 1941.

11. U.S. Executive Agreement Series, No. 236. Cooperative War Effort, Declaration by United Nations, Washington, January 1, 1942 and Declaration Known as the Atlantic Charter, August 14, 1941, Washington: U.S. Government Printing Office, 1942, pp. 1-3.

12. The Atlantic Charter provides, inter alia, the following principles: "First, their countries [the United States and Great Britain] seek no aggrandizement, territorial or other; Second, they desire to see no territorial changes that do not accord with the freely

expressed wishes of the people concerned; Third, they respect the right of all peoples to choose the form of government under which they will live; and they wish to see sovereign rights and self-government restored to those who have been forcibly deprived of them. . . ." For the complete text of the Charter, see Department of State Bulletin, V, 112 (August 16, 1941), 125-26.

13. From the archives of the ROC Presidential Office, reprinted in Chang Chun and Huang Shao-ku, Chiang Tsung-tung wei tzu-yu cheng-i yu ho-p'ing erh fen-tou shu-lüeh (On President Chiang's fight for freedom, justice and peace) (Taipei: Chung-yang wen-wu kung-ying she, 1968), pp. 439-40.

14. Foreign Relations of the United States, Diplomatic Papers: The Conferences at Cairo and Tehran 1943 (Washington, D.C.: U.S. Government Printing Office, 1961), pp. 448-49. The communiqué was released to the press by the White House on December 1, 1943, and was printed, with slight editorial variations, in the Department of State Bulletin, IX, 232 (December 4, 1943), 393.

15. Excerpt from Department of State Bulletin, X, 236 (January 1, 1944), 3, 4.

16. Excerpt from Foreign Relations of the United States, Diplomatic Papers: The Conference of Berlin (The Potsdam Conference) 1945, II (Washington, D.C.: U.S. Government Printing Office, 1960), 1474-76.

17. Excerpt from United States Statutes At Large, LIX, Part II (Washington, D.C.: U.S. Government Printing Office, 1946), 1734-35, 1738-39.

18. Translated from T'ang Wu, Chung-kuo yü kuo-chi-fa (China and the international law), II (Taipei: Chung-hua wen-hua ch'u-pan shih-yeh wei-yuan-hui, 1957), 435.

19. Translated from Huang Shun-ch'ing, Lin Hsiung-hsiang and Kuo Hai-ming, eds., T'ai-wan sheng t'ung-chih kao, X, Kuang-fu chih, 39, 40-41.

20. Translated from ibid., p. 39.

21. Translated from Ssu-fa hsing-cheng pu, ed., Chung-hua min-kuo ssu-fa fa-ling hui pien (Compilation of laws and decrees on administration of justice of the Republic of China), II (Taipei: Ssu-fa hsing-cheng pu, 1954), p. 985.

22. Translated from Huang Shun-ch'ing, Lin Hsiung-hsiang, Kuo Hai-ming, eds., T'ai-wan sheng t'ung-chi kao, X, Kuang-fu chih, pp. 43-44.

23. Excerpt translated from T'ai-wan wen-t'i (The Taiwan problem) (rev. ed., Peking: Hsin-hua shu-tien, 1950), pp. 4-5.

24. Excerpt from Kwang-min jih-pao (Enlightenment daily), Peking, September 4, 1949, p. 1.

25. Military Situation in the Far East, hearings before the Committee on Armed Services and the Committee on Foreign Relations, United States Senate, 82nd Congress, 1st Sess., Part III (Washington, D.C.: U.S. Government Printing Office, 1951), pp. 1667-69.

26. American Foreign Policy, 1950-1955, Basic Documents, II (Washington, D.C.: U.S. Government Printing Office, 1957), 2448-49.

27. Excerpt from ibid., pp. 2449, 2451.

28. "Replies by the U.S. Department of State to a Series of Questions Contained in House Resolution 452, Eighty-First Congress, Second Session): Report of the House Committee on Foreign Affairs, February 9, 1950." (Excerpt from American Foreign Policy, 1950-1955, Basic Documents, II (Washington, D.C.: U.S. Government Printing Office, 1957), 2456-58.

6

OFFICIAL DOCUMENTS
CONCERNING THE QUESTION
OF TAIWAN, 1950-58

DOCUMENT 27: PRESIDENT TRUMAN'S STATEMENT
ON THE MISSION OF THE U.S. SEVENTH FLEET
IN THE FORMOSA AREA, JUNE 27, 1950[1]

The attack upon Korea makes it plain beyond all doubt that communism has passed beyond the use of subversion to conquer independent nations and will now use armed invasion and war. It has defied the orders of the Security Council of the United Nations issued to preserve international peace and security. In these circumstances, the occupation of Formosa by Communist forces would be a direct threat to the security of the Pacific area and to United States forces performing their lawful and necessary functions in that area.

Accordingly, I have ordered the Seventh Fleet to prevent any attack on Formosa. As a corollary of this action, I am calling upon the Chinese Government on Formosa to cease all air and sea operations against the mainland. The Seventh Fleet will see that this is done. The determination of the future status of Formosa must await the restoration of security in the Pacific, a peace settlement with Japan, or consideration by the United Nations.

DOCUMENT 28: ROC'S SUSPENSION OF MILITARY
OPERATIONS AGAINST THE CHINA
MAINLAND, JUNE 27-28, 1950[2]

1. U.S. Aide-Mémoire of June 27, 1950 to the ROC. (excerpt)
The attack of the North Korean forces against the Republic of Korea raises problems with respect to the security of the Pacific area with which the United States is deeply concerned. The United

States Government wishes to inform the Chinese Government of the mission assigned to the United States Seventh Fleet with reference to Taiwan, and requests the full cooperation of the Government of the Republic of China in the issuance of necessary orders to effect the termination of air and sea operations by Chinese Government forces against the Chinese mainland or against shipping in Chinese waters or on the high seas.

2. ROC Foreign Minister George K. C. Yeh's Statement, June 28, 1950 (complete text)

The Government of the Republic of China, having accepted in principle the proposals of the Government of the United States of America regarding the defense of Taiwan as set forth in the latter's aide mémoire of June 27, 1950, has issued orders to its naval and air forces to suspend such air and sea operations as requested. In so doing, the Government of the Republic of China was prompted by the following considerations:

First, pending the conclusion of the treaty of peace on Japan, the Government of the United States of America may share with the Government of the Republic of China the responsibility for the defense of Taiwan.

Secondly, that Taiwan is a part of the territory of China is generally acknowledged by all concerned Powers. The proposals of the United States of America as contained in the above-mentioned aide mémoire should in no way alter the status of Formosa as envisaged in the Cairo Declaration, nor should it in any way affect China's authority over Formosa.

Thirdly, the aforesaid proposals and the policies outlined in President Truman's statement dated June 27 are emergency measures adopted to cope with the critical situation as existing on the mainland and in the Pacific region where a number of states have been threatened by or become the victims of aggressive International Communism. The Chinese Government may succeed in the suppression of the aggression of International Communism within a reasonably short time, but should these measures prove to be inadequate, the Chinese Government, in conjunction with other governments concerned, will have to seek for more effective measures in resisting such aggression.

Fourthly, in accepting the American proposals, the Government of the Republic of China does not intend to depart from its dual policy of resistance against the aggression of International Communism and the maintenance of the territorial integrity of China.

DOCUMENT 29: PRC CHAIRMAN MAO TSE-TUNG'S
ADDRESS AT THE EIGHTH MEETING OF THE
CENTRAL PEOPLE'S GOVERNMENT,
JUNE 28, 1950[3]

. . .

The Chinese people . . . long ago declared that the affairs of all
countries of the world should be run by the peoples of the respective
countries themselves, and the affairs of Asia should be run by the
peoples of Asia themselves and not by the United States. United
States aggression in Asia will only arouse the extensive and resolute
resistance of the peoples of Asia.

Only on January 5 this year Truman stated that the United
States would refrain from interfering in Taiwan. Now he himself
proves that his statement was false and he has torn to shreds all
international agreements regarding U.S. non-interference in the
internal affairs of China. This open exposure by the United States
of its true imperialist face is beneficial to the people of China as
well as the peoples of Asia.

. . .

DOCUMENT 30: PRC FOREIGN MINISTER CHOU
EN-LAI'S STATEMENT REFUTING TRUMAN'S
STATEMENT OF JUNE 27, 1950, JUNE 28, 1950[4]

After instigating the puppet government of Syngman Rhee in
South Korea to provoke civil war in Korea, President Truman of the
United States of America made a statement on June 27, declaring
that the United States Government had decided to prevent by armed
force our liberation of Taiwan.

On Truman's order, the U.S. Seventh Fleet has moved to the
coast of Taiwan.

On behalf of the Central People's Government of the People's
Republic of China, I declare that Truman's statement of June 27 and
the action of the U.S. navy constitute armed aggression against the
territory of China and are a gross violation of the United Nations
Charter. This violent, predatory action by the United States Government comes as no surprise to the Chinese people but only increases
their wrath, because the Chinese people have, over a long period,
consistently exposed all the conspiratorial schemes of U.S. imperialism
to commit aggression against China and seize Asia by force. In his

statement, Truman merely discloses his premeditated plan and puts it into practice. In fact the attack by the puppet Korean troops of Syngman Rhee on the Korean Democratic People's Republic at the instigation of the United States Government was a premeditated move by the United States, designed to create a pretext for the United States to invade Taiwan, Korea, Vietnam and the Philippines. It is nothing but a further act of intervention by U.S. imperialism in the affairs of Asia.

On behalf of the Central People's Government of the People's Republic of China, I declare that, no matter what obstructive action U.S. imperialists may take, the fact that Taiwan is part of China will remain unchanged forever. This is not only a historical fact; it has also been confirmed by the Cairo and Potsdam Declarations and the situation since the surrender of Japan. All the people of our country will certainly fight as one man and to the end to liberate Taiwan from the grasp of the U.S. aggressors. The Chinese people, who have defeated Japanese imperialism and Chiang Kai-shek, the hireling of U.S. imperialism, will surely succeed in driving out the U.S. aggressors and in recovering Taiwan and all other territories belonging to China.

. . .

DOCUMENT 31: PRC FOREIGN MINISTER CHOU EN-LAI'S CABLE TO THE PRESIDENT OF THE SECURITY COUNCIL AND THE SECRETARY-GENERAL OF THE UNITED NATIONS, AUGUST 24, 1950[5]

Mr. Yakov Malik, President of the Security Council, and Mr. Trygve Lie, Secretary-General of the United Nations, Lake Success, New York:

On June 27 this year, President Truman of the United States of America announced the decision of the United States Government to prevent with armed forces the liberation of Taiwan by the Chinese People's Liberation Army. Meanwhile, the United States Seventh Fleet moved toward the Straits of Taiwan, followed by the arrival in Taiwan of contingents of the United States Air Force, in an open encroachment on the territory of the People's Republic of China. This action on the part of the United States Government is direct armed aggression on the territory of China, and a total violation of the United Nations Charter.

Taiwan is an integral part of China. This is not only a fact based on history, confirmed by the situation since the surrender of

Japan, but it is also stipulated in the Cairo Declaration of 1943 and
the Potsdam Communiqué of 1945 as binding international agreements
which the United States Government has pledged itself to respect and
observe.

The people of China cannot tolerate this action of armed aggression by the United States Government on the territory of China, and
are determined to liberate from the tentacles of the United States
aggressors Taiwan and all other territories belonging to China. On
behalf of the Central People's Government of the People's Republic
of China, I now lodge this accusation with the United Nations Security
Council and propose that, for the maintenance of international peace
and security and for the upholding of the dignity of the United Nations
Charter, the United Nations Security Council is obliged by its inalienable
duties to condemn the United States Government for its criminal act
in the armed invasion of the territory of China, and to take immediate
measures to bring about the complete withdrawal of all the United
States armed invading forces from Taiwan and from other territories
belonging to China.

> Chou En-lai,
> Minister for Foreign Affairs
> of the Central People's Government
> of the People's Republic of China

Peking, August 24, 1950

DOCUMENT 32: PRC DELEGATE WU HSIU-CHUAN'S STATEMENT AT THE UNITED NATIONS SECURITY COUNCIL, NOVEMBER 28, 1950[6]

People with any common sense know that Taiwan is an inseparable part of the territory of China. Long before Christopher Columbus
discovered America, the Chinese people were already in Taiwan.
Long before the United States achieved its own independence, Taiwan
had already become an inseparable part of the territory of China.
Precisely because of this irrevocable historical fact that Taiwan is
part of China, civilized nations of the whole world have never conceded
that the occupation of Taiwan by imperialist Japan during the fifty-
year period from 1895 to 1945 was justifiable. Moreover, the people
of Taiwan have always opposed the rule of Japanese imperialism.
During the fifty years under Japanese imperialist rule, the people of
Taiwan lived like beasts of burden and underwent all the sufferings
of a subject people. But during these fifty years the people in Taiwan
never ceased conducting a dauntless struggle against the alien rule of

Japanese imperialism and for their return to the motherland. In
their heroic struggle against Japanese imperialism, the people in
Taiwan have written with blood and fire into the pages of history that
they are a member, an integral part, of the great family of the Chinese
nation. Even the White Paper, United States Relations with China,
compiled by the United States Department of State, has to admit that:

"The Native population for fifty years had been under the rule
of a foreign invader and therefore welcomed the Chinese forces as
liberators. During the Japanese occupation the principal hope of
the people had been reunion with the mainland."

Precisely because Taiwan is an inseparable part of China, the
Cairo Declaration jointly signed on 1 December 1943 by the Governments of China, the United States of America and the United Kingdom
explicitly stipulated that "it is their"—the three Great Powers'—
"purpose . . . that all territories Japan has stolen from the Chinese,
such as Manchuria, Formosa and the Pescadores, shall be restored
to the Republic of China."

Taiwan is an integral part of China. This is not only an unshakable historical fact, but also one of the main aims for which the
Chinese people fought unitedly against imperialist Japan. The Cairo
Declaration signed on 1 December 1943 by the United States, the
United Kingdom and China clearly reflected this aim of the people of
China. Moreover, the Cairo Declaration is a solemn international
commitment which the United States Government has pledged itself
to observe. As one of the principal provisions concerning the unconditional surrender of Japan, this solemn international commitment
was again laid down in the Potsdam Declaration which was signed
jointly on 26 July 1945 by China, the United States and the United
Kingdom, and was subsequently adhered to by the Soviet Union.
Section 8 of the Potsdam Declaration, which provides the terms of
the unconditional surrender of Japan, states:

The terms of the Cairo Declaration shall be carried out
and Japanese sovereignty shall be limited to the islands
of Honshu, Hokkaido, Kyushu, Shikoku and such minor
islands as we determine.

On 2 September 1945, Japan signed the Instrument of Surrender,
the first article of which explicitly provided that Japan "accepts"—I
am quoting from the original wording—"the provisions set forth in
the Declaration issued by the heads of the Governments of the United
States, China and Great Britain on July 26, 1945, at Potsdam, and
subsequently adhered to by the Union of Soviet Socialist Republics."
When the Chinese Government accepted the surrender of the Japanese
armed forces in Taiwan and exercised sovereignty over the island,

Taiwan became, not only de jure, but also de facto, an inalienable part of Chinese territory, and this has been the situation as regards Taiwan since 1945. For this reason, during the five post-war years from 1945 to 27 June 1950, no one has ever questioned the fact that Taiwan is an inseparable part of Chinese territory, de jure or de facto.

This state of affairs was so clear that on 5 January 1950, even President Truman of the United States could not but admit the following:

> In the joint Declaration at Cairo on December 1, 1943, the President of the United States, the British Prime Minister and the President of China stated that it was their purpose that territories Japan had stolen from China, such as Formosa, should be restored to the Republic of China.
>
> The United States was a signatory to the Potsdam Declaration of July 26, 1945, which declared that the terms of the Cairo Declaration should be carried out. The provisions of this Declaration were accepted by Japan at the time of its surrender. . . .
>
> . . . for the past four years the United States and the other allied Powers have accepted the exercise of Chinese authority over the island.
>
> The United States has no predatory designs on Formosa or on any other Chinese territory. . . . Nor does it have any intention of utilizing its armed forces to interfere in the present situation. The United States Government will not pursue a course which will lead to involvement in the civil conflict in China.

Thus, even President Truman admitted that Taiwan is Chinese territory.

. . .

There is not the slightest justification for the United States Government's invasion and occupation of Taiwan. Yet, to carry out that aggression, the United States Government had somehow to find a justification. Thus, we have the story that "the status of Taiwan is not yet determined" and that, therefore, the armed occupation of Taiwan by the United States cannot be regarded as invasion and occupation of Chinese territory by the United States. Can you call this a "justification"? Did not President Truman declare, at the time the order for armed aggression against Taiwan was issued, that:

> The determination of the future status of Formosa must await the restoration of security in the Pacific, a peace

settlement with Japan, or consideration by the United
Nations?

Let us first of all deal with the question of the status of Taiwan
and the peace treaty with Japan. Does it hold water to say that, since
the status of Taiwan is not yet determined, the invasion of Taiwan by
United States armed forces constitutes no aggression against China?
No, it does not. Here we have in the first place the Truman of 5
January 1950 contradicting the Truman of 27 June 1950. On 5 January,
this year Mr. Truman stated:

> The United States and the other Allied Powers have ac-
> cepted the exercise of Chinese authority over the island.

Surely, at that time, Mr. Truman could not consider that a
peace treaty with Japan had already been signed. Then, we have
President Roosevelt contradicting President Truman. On 1 December
1943, President Roosevelt solemnly declared, in the Cairo Declaration,
that:

> All the territories Japan has stolen from the Chinese
> such Manchuria, Formosa and the Pescadores, shall be
> restored to the Republic of China.

Surely, neither President Roosevelt nor anyone else considered
at that time that, in the absence of a peace treaty with Japan, the
Cairo Declaration would be invalid and that Manchuria, Taiwan and
the Penghu Islands would remain in the possession of Japan.

The facts of history in the course of the past several centuries
and the situation during the last five years, since the surrender of
Japan, also contradict Mr. Truman, because the facts of history and
the situation following the Japanese surrender have long determined
the status of Taiwan to be an integral part of China. The status of
Taiwan was determined long ago; there is no such question as that
of Taiwan's status.

Article 107 of the Charter of the United Nations clearly provides
that: "Nothing in the present Charter shall invalidate or preclude
action, in relation to any State which during the Second World War
has been an enemy of any signatory to the present Charter, taken or
authorized as a result of that war by the Governments having responsibility for such action." Therefore, the United Nations has no right
whatsoever to alter the status of Taiwan, all the less as the question
of the status of Taiwan does not exist.

President Truman declared that the so-called question of the
status of Taiwan must await consideration by the United Nations.

However, after the People's Republic of China had charged the United States before the United Nations with armed aggression against Taiwan, the United States Government indicated that it would welcome consideration by the United Nations of the question of Taiwan and investigation by the United Nations. The United States representative at the fifth session of the United Nations General Assembly introduced the so-called "Question of Formosa," and made use of its voting machine in the General Assembly to put this matter on the agenda. All these moves of the United States Government aim at stealing the name of the United Nations to legalize its illegal acts of armed aggression against Taiwan and to consolidate its actual occupation of Taiwan.

My government has protested in strong terms to the United Nations General Assembly, resolutely opposing the inclusion of the so-called "Question of Formosa"—concerning the status of Taiwan—in the agenda of the fifth session of the General Assembly. Whatever decision the United Nations General Assembly may take on the so-called question of the status of Taiwan, whether it be to hand over the island to the United States so that it might administer it openly under the disguise of "trusteeship," or "neutralization," or whether it be to procrastinate by way of "investigation," thereby maintaining the present state of actual United States occupation, it will, in substance, be stealing China's legitimate territory and supporting United States aggression against Taiwan in opposition to the Chinese people. Any such decision would be unjustifiable and unlawful. Any such decision would in no way shake the resolve of the Chinese people to liberate Taiwan, nor would it prevent action by the Chinese people to liberate Taiwan.

DOCUMENT 33: RECORD OF THE CONVERSATION
BETWEEN AMBASSADOR KOO AND DULLES
CONCERNING THE JAPANESE PEACE
TREATY, OCTOBER 20, 1950[7]

Mr. Dulles said that . . . concerning the territorial question of the peace treaty, the United States was of the opinion that Japan could keep her four original islands and the adjacent minor islands in accordance with the Cairo Declaration and the provisions concerning Japanese surrender. Other islands such as the Ryukyu and Bonin islands should be placed under United Nations trusteeship and the United States should be the administering state. The status of Taiwan, Penghu, the southern half of Sakhalin and the Kurile Islands should be decided by China, Britain, the United States and the Soviet Union in future; and if the question could not be settled within one year after the implementation of the peace treaty, it should be submitted to the decision of the United Nations General Assembly. . . .

. . .

Dr. Koo inquired as to the intention and expection of the United
States for submitting the so-called question of Taiwan to the discussion
of the United Nations General Assembly.

Mr. Dulles replied that he could answer the question only after
consultation with Secretary of State Acheson on the next morning.
However, the intention of the United States was temporarily to freeze
the status of Taiwan. Although the United States earnestly hoped that
a world war would not break out, it was not very sure about this. The
United States certainly did not wish Taiwan to fall into hands hostile
to the United States and particularly did not want Taiwan to be used
by Soviet Russia. The United States did not have enough manpower.
With respect to the defense of the Pacific, the United States could
use only naval and air forces to establish a strong defense line. Thus,
if something happened, the United States could control the Asian mainland coast; and Taiwan was just within this defense line.

The freezing of the status of Taiwan was meant to maintain the
status of the national government of China. Therefore, the United
States earnestly expected that the representative of China would not
actively oppose the United States position toward Taiwan at the meetings
of the United Nations. If the government of China declared Taiwan to
be the territory of China for the purpose of clarifying the Chinese
position, the United States certainly could understand. However, if
China strongly opposed the United States position toward Taiwan at
the meetings and tried to argue with the United States, then such
actions would increase the difficulties of the United States and would
frustrate the United States intention to keep Taiwan [out of Communist
control] and to maintain the international status of the Chinese Government. If the United States already regarded Taiwan as purely Chinese
territory, not only must the question of the representation of the
Chinese government be solved immediately, but the United States
would lose her grounds for dispatching the Seventh Fleet to protect
Taiwan and for taking the initiative to sponsor this case [at the United
Nations]. . . .

DOCUMENT 34: RECORD OF THE CONVERSATION
BETWEEN AMBASSADOR KOO AND DULLES
CONCERNING THE JAPANESE PEACE
TREATY, DECEMBER 19, 1950[8]

Dr. Koo said that he had submitted for consideration of his
government the opinions of the United States Government concerning
the Japanese Peace Treaty expressed in the October conversation.

Now he wished to make a preliminary general reply on his government's opinion; a more detailed reply would follow later. The opinion was:

(A) Concerning the Taiwan and other territorial questions, his government considered that Japan was required only to declare renunciation of all sovereignty over those territories in accordance with the condition of surrender prescribed by the Potsdam Proclamation. The territories would be handled by the Allies themselves and it should not require Japan to confirm to whom each of the territories should be ceded.

Mr. Dulles replied that this was also the view of the United States. However, the Taiwan question should, perhaps, first be discussed in the United Nations; the communiqué of the Truman-Attlee conference also referred to this point. Otherwise, there would be no basis for the United States to dispatch a fleet to protect Taiwan. In the meantime, in order to respond to the demand of some members of the United Nations who asserted that Taiwan should be returned to the Chinese Communists, it could not but retain this question on the agenda of the United Nations.

Dr. Koo said that the question did not require one-by-one discussion.

Mr. Dulles said yes.

. . .

DOCUMENT 35: MEMORANDUM CONTAINING
GENERAL OBSERVATIONS OF THE CHINESE
GOVERNMENT ON THE U.S. TENTATIVE
PROPOSALS REGARDING THE PEACE
TREATY WITH JAPAN, JANUARY 22, 1951[9]

In a conversation held at the State Department on December 9, 1950, the Chinese Ambassador pursuant to instructions of his Government communicated to Hon. John Foster Dulles the general observations of the Chinese Government on the tentative proposals of the United States Government regarding a treaty with Japan which "would end the state of war, restore Japanese sovereignty and bring back Japan as an equal in the society of free peoples." These observations are recapitulated in this memorandum together with supplemental comments. They are, however, not intended to be final or exhaustive. Fuller statements will be made as further study of the United States memorandum may suggest them or when the views of the other Governments concerned are known.

3. The Chinese Government considers that express recognition of the independence of Korea by Japan is essential. The creation of United Nations trusteeship of the Ryukyu and Bonin Islands with the United States as administering authority is in principle agreeable to the Chinese Government. With reference to the so-called status of Formosa and Pescadores, it is the considered view of the Chinese Government that these islands constitute historically, ethnically, legally, and in fact a part of Chinese territory, although the formal act of finalization is pending. For these reasons their status is really different from that of South Sakhalin and the Kuriles. But in view of the unsettled conditions in the Far East and in the interest of promoting the general security of the Pacific region at present, the Chinese Government does not wish to raise objections to the suggestion that the status of these four groups of islands be made subject to the future decision of the United Kingdom, the Union of Soviet Socialist Republics, China and the United States. In refraining from objecting to it the Chinese Government does not wish to be understood as having in any way modified its basic view of Formosa and Pescadores as Chinese territory. It also considers the period of one year after the conclusion of the treaty within which such a decision should be made as too short and suggests at least two years or longer. It is assumed that though the character of the four groups of territory is not identical, as explained above, they would be decided at the same time and in accordance with a uniform procedure. Failing a decision within the suggested period, the advisability of referring the question to the General Assembly of the United Nations might be considered in the light of the conditions then prevailing. So far as Japan is concerned, a general renunciation by her in the treaty of her sovereignty over these territories would appear to be sufficient. As regards Japan's former special rights and interests in China, an express renunciation of them by her would be necessary and proper.

. . .

DOCUMENT 36: RECORD OF THE CONVERSATION
BETWEEN AMBASSADOR KOO AND DULLES
CONCERNING THE JAPANESE PEACE
TREATY, APRIL 24, 1951[10]

Dr. Koo said that the Chinese government paid special attention to the territorial question. However, the United States draft used different language to deal with Taiwan, Penghu, and the other two islands (i.e., the southern part of Sakhalin and the Kurile Islands). That was discriminatory, so the Chinese reply proposed revision [on this point].

Mr. Dulles replied that in principle these islands should be treated equally. But the United States discovered practical difficulties after consideration of the matter.

The language concerning the Kurile Islands and the southern part of Sakhalin Island used in the United States draft was taken from the Yalta Agreement. Although the language was not accurate and proper, the United States did not want to change the text of the agreement so as to give the Soviet Union a pretext for refusal to participate in the Japanese Peace Treaty. The United States, however, did know that the Soviet Union would definitely not participate in the Japanese Peace Treaty.

. . .

Dr. Koo inquired about the United States reply to a British note which called for (a) invitation of the Chinese Communists to participate in the Japanese Peace Treaty and (b) a prescription for the return of Taiwan to China.

Mr. Dulles said that the United States had made a written reply. The reply generally said that the United States recognized only the national government, so it had no intention to invite the Chinese Communists for consultation. With respect to Taiwan, it should be returned to the Republic of China in accordance with the minutes of the Cairo Declaration. In the meantime, he personally informed the British Ambassador that the national government insisted upon Taiwan as a part of Chinese territory, and such a position was the same as the Chinese Communists'; thus both regarded Taiwan as an internal question of China. If [the peace treaty] explicitly provided for the return of Taiwan [to China], then the United States dispatch of its Seventh Fleet to protect Taiwan would lose its basis. This would provide the Chinese Communists and the Soviet Union more grounds to condemn United States intervention. Therefore, at this stage, the United States had to keep the Taiwan question as a pending case so as to facilitate its handling. This was a top secret and he hoped the Chinese government would . . . keep the secret.

DOCUMENT 37: RECORD OF THE CONVERSATION BETWEEN AMBASSADOR KOO AND DULLES CONCERNING THE JAPANESE PEACE TREATY, MAY 29, 1951[11]

. . . the Ambassador said that . . . he would bring out for the consideration of the United States authorities two points which were regarded to be of special importance to his Government.

First, as regards the articles on territorial settlement in the Provisional Draft of the United States, there was a difference between the wording in Article 3 about Formosa and the Pescadores and that in Article 5 about Southern Sakhalin and the Kurile Islands. The Chinese Government desired that the United States Government would not bring up any more the proposal that the status of Formosa and the Pescadores would be decided in the future following the conclusion of the Japanese Peace Treaty, (here implied reference was made to Point 3 of the Memorandum of the United States, dated October 20, 1950—received [in advance] on September 11, 1950) and that it would be stipulated in the Peace Treaty that Formosa and the Pescadores should be restored to the Republic of China. If the word "renounce" was to be used, it should then be specified that such territories should be renounced by Japan in favor of the Republic of China. The Chinese people had suffered so heavily and so long from Japanese aggression that it would be a great blow to them morally [and would have a demoralizing effect on them concerning the security guarantee of the future of the two islands] if the provisions about Formosa and the Pescadores were different from those about Southern Sakhalin. Such a discrepancy of treatment would have a tremendous demoralizing effect on the Chinese people as a whole, particularly on those on the mainland of China.

Mr. Dulles expressed that it was a little too apprehensive to assume that such provisions would have great demoralizing effect on the people. The difference of treatment in the matter of wording for the two territories was really beneficial to China. The United States, he continued, did not want the Soviet Union to get Southern Sakhalin and the Kurile Islands, unless it would sign and ratify the treaty (here implied reference was made to Article 19 of the Provisional U.S. Draft); and if it failed to conclude the peace treaty with Japan, such territories would still remain with Japan. If the provisions about Formosa and the Pescadores were alike, the result would be the same should China perchance fail to participate in the treaty; while a simple provision of renunciation would formally detach Formosa and the Pescadores from Japan. [The former result was certainly not the wish of China.]

Secondly, continued the Ambassador, the National Government's right to participate in the treaty should be recognized by all. The Chinese Government would appreciate it if the United States Government would persist in this view and prevail on the other governments concerned that the National Government should take part in the treaty. In view of the tremendous losses and sufferings of the Chinese people throughout the long period of Japanese aggression, it would be too flagrant a denial of justice if the treaty would be concluded without the participation of the Chinese Government. Besides, the Chinese

Government is physically in possession of Formosa and the Pescadores in addition to other legal leases; and the status of these territories could not be legitimately settled without the participation of the National Government in the treaty. [Thirdly, if the National Government was refused participation in the peace treaty because of the existence of Chinese Communists, then it was like confusing black with white and treating the National Government the same as the Chinese Communists. Such an act was like imposing a penalty of non-participation in the peace treaty upon the National Government. If so, where was the justice?]

Mr. Dulles then said that no doubt the Ambassador could see the United States point of view and the practical circumstances. Of all the member countries of the Far Eastern Commission not more than two were in favor of the participation by the National Government. Several others of such countries still recognized the National Government and wanted to deal with it in many matters, but not for the purpose of the treaty. They felt that the ratification of the treaty by the National Government would have no effect on the mainland of China. The United States Government was quite sympathetic toward the point of view just expressed by the Ambassador, but, nevertheless, it must find a practical way to bring about the treaty.

The Ambassador observed that Russia would probably not take part in the treaty, and if that were the case, the treaty even duly consummated would still be a partial one only.

To this remark by the Ambassador Mr. Dulles replied that he was quite aware of the Soviet position but the United States would like to have some, preferably a majority, of the Far Eastern Commission countries, like Great Britain, Canada, New Zealand, India, etc. to go along; otherwise it would be meaningless for the United States to conclude the peace treaty with Japan alone, and it would put the United States at a disadvantageous position while other countries would still be in a state of war with Japan and could even take up occupation duties in that country. [In the course of the controversy, if Japan went red, Formosa and the Pescadores could hardly be defended. Such a situation would not be beneficial to China.]

The Ambassador said that it was beyond doubt that legitimately the National Government had the right to sign the Japanese peace treaty for China, while the actual effect of the ratification on the mainland would have to depend on future international developments, which, so far as it could be ascertained, might point to a more favorable direction.

DOCUMENT 38: ROC PRESIDENT CHIANG KAI-SHEK'S STATEMENT ON THE PEACE TREATY WITH JAPAN, JUNE 18, 1951[12]

World War II was heralded by the aggression of Japan against the Republic of China. Of all the Allies, we fought the longest. Our losses in lives and property were the greatest. In the defeat of the aggressors China made a significant contribution. A treaty of peace with Japan without the participation of China is at once unrealistic and unjust.

The USSR, through the agency of her protégé, the Chinese Communists, took advantage of the weakened condition of China to make further inroads of aggression. In spite of these circumstances, certain powers still chose to recognize the puppet regime at Peiping and even to question and oppose the right of participation of the Republic of China in the conclusion of a treaty of peace with Japan. From a purely legal point of view, such doubts and opposition are entirely without justification. First, the Government of the Republic of China is the Government recognized by the United Nations. Secondly, the majority of the fifty-odd governments which declared war or a state of belligerency against Japan recognize the Government of the Republic of China. Thirdly, allied bodies dealing with Japan, such as the Allied Council in Tokyo, accept the representatives of the Republic of China among its [sic] members. It is therefore obvious that the right of participation of the Republic of China in the conclusion of the treaty of peace with Japan is not subject to challenge by any one allied power or any small group of such powers.

Only through the sincere cooperation of the two neighboring Asiatic countries, China and Japan, may the future security of Asia be assured. Since V-J Day I have repeatedly stated that China would not adopt an attitude of vengeance against Japan. On various occasions, I have, both directly and indirectly, stressed the necessity of the early conclusion of a treaty of peace with Japan on the basis of a reasonably generous policy. The recent efforts of the U.S. Government, despite the obstructionist tactics of the USSR, in promoting the early conclusion of peace with Japan are timely and are in accord with the policy of the Chinese Government. In its discussions with the U.S. Government, the Government of the Republic of China has exercised considerable restraint and demonstrated unstintedly its willingness to cooperate on such important questions as reparations and the security of Japan. Should the Republic of China be denied the right of equal participation in the conclusion of the treaty of peace with Japan, it would not only dishearten the people now living in Free China, but also dim the hopes of millions of mainlanders who await emancipation from Communist rule. The ultimate effect of such an unjust act will not be limited to the effectiveness of the peace treaty, but may seriously damage the traditional friendship between the Chinese and American peoples.

In view of the foregoing considerations I wish to reaffirm that the right of participation of the Republic of China in the conclusion of the treaty of peace with Japan is undeniable and that the Republic of China can only participate in the conclusion of such a treaty on an equal footing with the other Allies. Any discriminatory treatment would not be acceptable.

Any instrument of peace concerning Japan concluded in violation of the position of the Government of the Republic of China would certainly be lacking in both moral force and legal justification, and leave an indelible blot on the history of Allied cooperation in resisting aggression. Such an unrealistic peace treaty will not only fail to terminate the state of belligerency of World War II, but will also add confusion to the Far Eastern situation and sow the seeds for further world disaster.

DOCUMENT 39: PRC FOREIGN MINISTER CHOU
EN-LAI'S STATEMENT ON THE U.S. PROPOSAL
OF THE JAPANESE PEACE TREATY,
AUGUST 15, 1951[13]

The Central People's Government of the People's Republic of China considers that the Draft Peace Treaty with Japan as proposed by the United States and British Governments is a draft which violates international agreements and is therefore basically unacceptable and that the conference which has been scheduled to meet on September 4 at San Francisco, under the compulsion of the United States Government, and which audaciously excludes the People's Republic of China is a conference which repudiates international commitments and therefore basically cannot be recognized.

Whether considered from the procedure through which it was prepared or from its contents, the United States-British Draft Peace Treaty with Japan flagrantly violates those important international agreements to which the United States and British Governments were signatories, viz, the United Nations Declaration of January 1, 1942, the Cairo Declaration, the Yalta Agreement, the Potsdam Declaration and Agreement, and the Basic Post-Surrender Policy for Japan which was adopted by the Far Eastern Commission on June 19, 1947. The United Nations Declaration provides that no separate peace should be made. The Potsdam Agreement states that the "preparatory work of the peace settlements" should be undertaken by those states which were signatories to the terms of surrender imposed upon the enemy state concerned. . . .

[T]he United States has monopolized the task of preparing the Draft Peace Treaty with Japan as now proposed, excluding most of the states that had fought against Japan and particularly the two principal Powers in the war, China and the Soviet Union, from the preparatory work for the peace treaty. . . .

[I]n violation of the agreement under the Cairo Declaration, the Yalta Agreement and the Potsdam Declaration, the Draft Treaty only provides that Japan should renounce all right to Taiwan and the Pescadores as well as to the Kurile Islands, the southern part of Sakhalin and all islands adjacent to it, without mentioning even one word about the agreement that Taiwan and the Pescadores be returned to the People's Republic of China and that the Kurile Islands be handed over to, and the southern part of Sakhalin and all islands adjacent to it be returned to, the Soviet Union.

With a view to expediting the concluding of a separate peace treaty with Japan, the United States Government, in its notification for the convocation of the San Francisco Conference, openly excludes the People's Republic of China—the principal Power which had fought against Japan—and thus completely violates a stipulation in the United Nations Declaration of January 1, 1942, to the effect that each of the signatory Powers pledged itself not to make a separate peace. . . .

Now, the Central People's Government of the People's Republic of China once again declares: If there is no participation of the People's Republic of China in the preparation, drafting and signing of a peace treaty with Japan, whatever the contents and results of such a treaty, the Central People's Government considers it all illegal, and therefore null and void.

DOCUMENT 40: TREATY OF PEACE BETWEEN THE REPUBLIC OF CHINA AND JAPAN, APRIL 28, 1952[14]

Article I

The state of war between the Republic of China and Japan is terminated as from the date on which the present Treaty enters into force.

Article II

It is recognized that under Article 2 of the Treaty of Peace with Japan signed at the city of San Francisco in the United States of America on September 8, 1951 (hereinafter referred to as the San Francisco Treaty), Japan has renounced all right, title and claim to

Taiwan (Formosa) and Penghu (the Pescadores) as well as the Spartly Islands and the Paracel Islands.

Article III

The disposition of property of Japan and of its nationals in Taiwan (Formosa) and Penghu (the Pescadores), and their claims, including debts, against the authorities of the Republic of China in Taiwan (Formosa) and Penghu (the Pescadores) and the residents thereof, and the disposition in Japan of property of such authorities and residents and their claims, including debts, against Japan and its nationals, shall be the subject of special arrangements between the Government of the Republic of China and the Government of Japan. The terms nationals and residents whenever used in the present Treaty include juridical persons.

Article IV

It is recognized that all treaties, conventions and agreements concluded before December 9, 1941, between China and Japan have become null and void as a consequence of the war.

. . .

Article X

For the purposes of the present Treaty, nationals of the Republic of China shall be deemed to include all the inhabitants and former inhabitants of Taiwan (Formosa) and Penghu (the Pescadores) and their descendants who are of the Chinese nationality in accordance with the laws and regulations which have been or may hereafter be enforced by the Republic of China in Taiwan (Formosa) and Penghu (the Pescadores); and juridical persons of the Republic of China shall be deemed to include all those registered under the laws and regulations which have been or may hereafter be enforced by the Republic of China in Taiwan (Formosa) and Penghu (the Pescadores).

. . .

Protocol

At the moment of signing this day the Treaty of Peace between the Republic of China and Japan (hereinafter referred to as the present Treaty), the undersigned Plenipotentiaries have agreed upon the following terms which shall constitute an integral part of the present Treaty:

. . .

2. The commerce and navigation between the Republic of
China and Japan shall be governed by the following Arrangements:

. . .

(d) In the application of the present Arrangements, it is
understood:
(i) that vessels of the Republic of China shall be deemed
to include all those registered under the laws and regulations
which have been or may hereafter be enforced by the Republic
of China in Taiwan (Formosa) and Penghu (the Pescadores);
and products of the Republic of China shall be deemed to
include all those originating in Taiwan (Formosa) and Penghu
(the Pescadores); and

. . .

The Arrangements set forth in this paragraph shall remain
in force for a period of one year as from the date on which
the present Treaty enters into force.

. . . . .

Exchange of Notes

(I) Note from the Japanese Plenipotentiary to the Chinese Plenipotentiary
No. 1.

Taipei, April 28, 1952

Excellency,

In regard to the Treaty of Peace between Japan and the Republic
of China signed this day, I have the honor to refer, on behalf of my
Government, to the understanding reached between us that the terms
of the present Treaty shall, in respect of the Republic of China, be
applicable to all the territories which are now, or which may hereafter
be, under the control of its Government.
I shall be appreciative, if you will confirm the understanding
set forth above.
I avail myself of this opportunity to convey to Your Excellency
the assurance of my highest consideration.

(signed) Isao Kawada

His Excellency
    Monsieur Yeh Kung Chao,
        Plenipotentiary of the Republic of China

(II) Note from the Chinese Plenipotentiary to the Japanese Plenipotentiary
No. 1.

                                        Taipei, April 28, 1952

Excellency,

    In connection with the Treaty of Peace between the Republic of China and Japan signed this day, I have the honor to acknowledge receipt of Your Excellency's Note of to-day's date reading as follows:
                [Text of Japanese note]
    I have the honor to confirm, on behalf of my Government, the understanding set forth in Your Excellency's Note under reply.
    I avail myself of this opportunity to convey to Your Excellency the assurance of my highest consideration.

                                    (signed) Yeh Kung Chao

His Excellency
    Mr. Isao Kawada,
        Plenipotentiary of Japan

                        . . .

                Agreed   Minutes

                        I

Chinese Delegate:
    It is my understanding that the expression "or which may hereafter be" in the Notes No. 1 exchanged to-day can be taken to mean "and which may hereafter be." Is it so?
Japanese Delegate:
    Yes, it is so. I assure you that the Treaty is applicable to all the territories under the control of the Government of the Republic of China.

                        . . .

                            (signed) Yeh Kung Chao

                            (signed) Isao Kawada

DOCUMENT 41: PRC PREMIER CHOU EN-LAI'S
REPORT ON THE WORK OF THE GOVERNMENT
TO THE FIRST SESSION OF THE FIRST NATIONAL
PEOPLE'S CONGRESS, SEPTEMBER 23, 1954[15]

The Government of the People's Republic of China has repeatedly stated that Taiwan is China's sacred and inviolable territory and that no United States infringement or occupation will be tolerated. Our compatriots on Taiwan, including the Kaoshan people, have always been members of the great Chinese family of nationalities and their enslavement by the United States will never be tolerated. The liberation of Taiwan is China's sovereign right and internal affair and no interference by any foreign country will be tolerated. Both the Cairo Declaration and the Potsdam Declaration, to which the United States is a signatory, affirm that Taiwan is Chinese territory; no perfidious violation of these solemn international agreements by the United States is permitted. Any pact signed between the United States Government and the traitorous Chiang Kai-shek gang holding on to Taiwan is illegal. In this connection it must be pointed out that all proposals to place Taiwan under United Nations trusteeship or under neutral mandate, or to "neutralize" Taiwan or to create a so-called "independent Taiwan state," are attempts to carve up China's territory, enslave the Chinese people on Taiwan and legalize United States occupation of Taiwan. None of this will be tolerated by the Chinese people.

The Chinese people are determined to liberate Taiwan. As long as Taiwan is not liberated, China's territory is not intact, China cannot have a tranquil environment for peaceful construction, and peace in the Far East and throughout the world is not secure. On August 11, 1954, the Central People's Government Council passed a resolution urging all Chinese people and the Chinese People's Liberation Army to redouble their efforts in all fields of work and strive to liberate Taiwan and eliminate the traitorous Chiang Kai-shek gang, so as to complete our people's sacred task of liberation. On August 22, all the democratic parties and groups and people's organizations of China issued a joint declaration on the liberation of Taiwan in response to this call of the Central People's Government. This is a manifestation of the unshakable common will of the six hundred million people of China.

DOCUMENT 42: MUTUAL DEFENSE TREATY
BETWEEN THE UNITED STATES AND THE
REPUBLIC OF CHINA, DECEMBER 2, 1954[16]

The Parties to this Treaty,

Reaffirming their faith in the purposes and principles of the
Charter of the United Nations and their desire to live in peace with
all peoples and all Governments, and desiring to strengthen the
fabric of peace in the West Pacific Area,

Recalling with mutual pride the relationship which brought their
two peoples together in a common bond of sympathy and mutual ideals
to fight side by side against imperialist aggression during the last war,

Desiring to declare publicly and formally their sense of unity
and their common determination to defend themselves against external
armed attack, so that no potential aggressor could be under the illusion
that either of them stands alone in the West Pacific Area, and

Desiring further to strengthen their present efforts for collective
defense for the preservation of peace and security pending the development of a more comprehensive system of regional security in the
West Pacific Area,

Have agreed as follows:

Article I

The Parties undertake, as set forth in the Charter of the United
Nations, to settle any international dispute in which they may be involved by peaceful means in such a manner that international peace,
security and justice are not endangered and to refrain in their international relations from the threat or use of force in any manner
inconsistent with the purposes of the United Nations.

Article II

In order more effectively to achieve the objective of this
Treaty, the Parties separately and jointly by self-help and mutual
aid will maintain and develop their individual and collective capacity
to resist armed attack and communist subversive activities directed
from without against their territorial integrity and political stability.

Article III

The Parties undertake to strengthen their free institutions and
to cooperate with each other in the development of economic progress
and social well-being and to further their individual and collective
efforts toward these ends.

Article IV

The Parties, through their Foreign Ministers or their deputies, will consult together from time to time regarding the implementation of this Treaty.

Article V

Each Party recognizes that an armed attack in the West Pacific Area directed against the territories of either of the Parties would be dangerous to its own peace and safety and declares that it would act to meet the common danger in accordance with its constitutional processes.

Any such armed attack and all measures taken as a result thereof shall be immediately reported to the Security Council of the United Nations. Such measures shall be terminated when the Security Council has taken the measures necessary to restore and maintain international peace and security.

Article VI

For the purposes of Articles II and V, the terms "territorial" and "territories" shall mean in respect of the Republic of China, Taiwan and the Pescadores; and in respect of the United States of America, the island territories in the West Pacific under its jurisdiction. The provisions of Articles II and V will be applicable to such other territories as may be determined by mutual agreement.

Article VII

The Government of the Republic of China grants, and the Government of the United States of America accepts, the right to dispose such United States land, air and sea forces in and about Taiwan and the Pescadores as may be required for their defense, as determined by mutual agreement.

Article VIII

This Treaty does not affect and shall not be interpreted as affecting in any way the rights and obligations of the Parties under the Charter of the United Nations or the responsibility of the United Nations for the maintenance of international peace and security.

Article IX

This Treaty shall be ratified by the Republic of China and the United States of America in accordance with their respective constitutional processes and will come into force when instruments of ratification thereof have been exchanged by them at Taipei.

Article X

This Treaty shall remain in force indefinitely. Either Party may terminate it one year after notice has been given to the other party.

IN WITNESS WHEREOF, the undersigned Plenipotentiaries have signed this Treaty.

DONE in duplicate, in the Chinese and English languages, at Washington on this Second day of the Twelfth month of the Forty-third Year of the Republic of China, corresponding to the Second day of December of the Year One Thousand Nine Hundred and Fifty-four.

For the Republic of China:
(signed) George K. C. Yeh
For the United States of America:
(signed) John Foster Dulles

Exchange of Notes

I
The Secretary of State to the Chinese Minister
of Foreign Affairs
Department of State
Washington

December 10, 1954

Excellency:

I have the honor to refer to recent conversations between representatives of our two Governments and to confirm the understandings reached as a result of those conversations, as follows:

The Republic of China effectively controls both the territory described in Article VI of the Treaty of Mutual Defense between the Republic of China and the United States of America signed on December 2, 1954, at Washington and other territory. It possesses with respect to all territory now and hereafter under its control the inherent right of self-defense. In view of the obligations of the two Parties under the said Treaty and of the fact that the use of force from either of these areas by either of the Parties affects the other, it is agreed that such use of force will be a matter of joint agreement, subject to action of an emergency character which is clearly an exercise of the inherent right of self-defense. Military elements which are a product of joint effort and contribution by the two Parties will not be removed from the territories described in Article VI to a degree which would substantially diminish the defensibility of such territories without mutual agreement.

Accept, Excellency, the assurances of my highest consideration.

John Foster Dulles
Secretary of State of the United States of America
His Excellency George K. C. Yeh
Minister of Foreign Affairs of the Republic of China

II

December 10, 1954

Excellency:

I have the honor to acknowledge the receipt of Your Excellency's Note of today's date, which reads as follows:

[See note I]

I have the honor to confirm, on behalf of my Government, the understanding set forth in Your Excellency's Note under reply.

I avail myself of this opportunity to convey to Your Excellency the assurances of my highest consideration.

George K. C. Yeh
Minister for Foreign Affairs
of the Republic of China

His Excellency John Foster Dulles
Secretary of State of the United States of America

DOCUMENT 43: PRC FOREIGN MINISTER CHOU EN-LAI'S STATEMENT ON U.S.-CHIANG KAI-SHEK "MUTUAL SECURITY TREATY," DECEMBER 8, 1954[17]

On December 2, 1954, the United States Government, disregarding the repeated protests and warnings of the Chinese people, concluded a so-called Mutual Security Treaty with the Chiang Kai-shek traitor gang fugitive on Taiwan. The United States Government is trying, by means of this treaty, to legalize its armed seizure of Chinese territory of Taiwan, and make Taiwan a base for further aggression against China and the preparation for a new war. This act is a grave warlike provocation against the People's Republic of China and the Chinese.

On behalf of the Government of the People's Republic of China, I hereby declare: Taiwan is China's territory, and Chiang Kai-shek is the public enemy of the Chinese people. To liberate Taiwan and liquidate the Chiang Kai-shek gang of traitors is entirely within the purview of China's sovereignty and a purely internal affair of China, and no interference by any foreign country will be tolerated. Threats of war cannot shake the determination of the Chinese people to liberate Taiwan but can only heighten their indignation. The Chiang Kai-shek traitor gang has no authority whatsoever to conclude any treaty with any country. The "Mutual Security Treaty" concluded between the United States and Chiang Kai-shek has no legal basis whatsoever and is null and void. This treaty is a betrayal of China's sovereign and territorial rights and the Chinese people oppose it resolutely. If the United States Government does not withdraw all its armed forces from Taiwan, the Penghu Islands and the Taiwan Straits, and persists in interfering in China's internal affairs, it must take upon itself all the grave consequences.

. . .

The "Mutual Security Treaty" between the United States and Chiang Kai-shek cannot be called defensive in any sense; it is a treaty of naked aggression. The aggressive circles of the United States and those who follow them pretend that the treaty is defensive in character; but such a pretense cannot hide its aggressive nature in any way. Taiwan is China's territory. This is a fact which the United States Government has recognized in such international agreements as the Cairo and Potsdam Declarations and the Instrument of Japanese Surrender, all of which bear its own signature. For the Chinese people to liberate Taiwan is an internal affair of China. Here too the United States Government, in January 1950, acknowledged China's exercise of her sovereign rights over Taiwan and declared its intention not to become involved in the civil conflict in China.

. . .

[Now the United States Government] is endeavoring to prevent the Chinese people from liberating their own territory of Taiwan. In so doing, the United States Government is committing flagrant violations of international good faith, seizing Chinese territory, infringing upon China's sovereignty and interfering in China's internal affairs—acts which can in no way be described as defensive. It is a genuine act of defense, on the other hand, for the Chinese people to liberate their own territory of Taiwan and to safeguard their national sovereignty and the territorial integrity of their country. The Japanese militarists, in their time, also represented their seizure of North-east China in 1931 as an act of self-defense. But nobody believed them.

Everyone knows that to seize another country's territory, to infringe
upon another country's sovereignty and to interfere in another country's
internal affairs is to commit acts of aggression. The Chinese people,
tempered in victorious struggle against the Japanese militarist
aggression, will never tolerate United States aggression, undertaken
under the name of "defense," against China's Taiwan and Penghu
Islands.

. . .

By this treaty, the United States Government now attempts to
legalize the occupation of Taiwan by its naval and air forces, and to
secure the right to dispose its ground forces "in and about Taiwan
and the Pescadores" with a view to strengthening its military base
in Taiwan. By this treaty the United States Government openly
attempts to use the threat of war to hinder the Chinese people from
liberating Taiwan; and at the same time provides for further aggression
against "other territories" of China. There can be no doubt that the
signing of the "Mutual Security Treaty" between the United States and
Chiang Kai-shek has increased the danger of the extension of the United
States aggression against China.

. . .

All that has been said above shows that the aim pursued by the
United States Government in this "Mutual Security Treaty" is not
peace, but war. The aggressive circles of the United States are in
fact copying the old tactics used by Japanese militarism in its aggression against China. Nevertheless, there are some who want the
Chinese people to forget the lessons of history and accept as the
status quo the U.S. occupation of Taiwan. . . . But the Chinese people
will never forget the calamities that ensued from the Mukden Incident
of 1931; nor will they forget that the Lukouchiao Incident of 1937 was
a sequel to the Mukden Incident. The peoples of Asia and of the
Pacific, whose memory of the attack on Pearl Harbor in 1941 is still
fresh, will also never forget how disastrous were the consequences
of the policy of appeasing Japanese militarist aggression. Similarly,
the peoples of Europe will never forget that the Munich policy of
giving rein to German militarist aggression was precisely the thing
that led to the Second World War. The mistakes of history must not
be repeated. The Chinese people are firmly opposed to this U.S.-
Chiang Kai-shek treaty for war which endangers the security of
China and the peace of Asia.

The United Nations Charter categorically forbids any infringement of the territorial integrity and political independence of any nation. This principle constitutes the basis of peace between nations. The treaty the United States Government has concluded with the Chiang Kai-shek traitor gang, like other so-called treaties of defense engineered by the United States, includes a reaffirmation of faith in the purposes and principles of the United Nations Charter. But all these so-called treaties of defense are in their essence diametrically opposed to the purposes and principles which the United Nations Charter proclaims. These treaties can only lead to war. They cannot possibly promote peaceful co-existence between nations. These treaties make a mockery of the United Nations Charter. They cannot possibly contribute to the realization of the purposes and principles of the United Nations Charter or the safeguarding of international peace.

. . .

To this end, the Chinese people make the following declaration solemnly before the world:

Taiwan is China's territory. The Chinese people are determined to liberate Taiwan. Only by liberating Taiwan from the tyranny of the Chiang Kai-shek gang of traitors can the Chinese people achieve the complete unity of their motherland and further safeguard the peace of Asia and the world. All proposals to set up a so-called "independent state" of Taiwan, to "neutralize" Taiwan or to place Taiwan under "trusteeship" mean, in practice, dismemberment of China's territory, infringement upon China's sovereignty and interference in China's internal affairs. All are therefore utterly unacceptable to the Chinese people.

In order to ease the situation in the Far East, eliminate the threat of war against China and safeguard peace in Asia and the world, the U.S. Government must withdraw all its armed forces from Taiwan, the Penghu Islands and the Taiwan Straits. There is no justification whatsoever for the action of the United States in crossing vast oceans to occupy China's territory of Taiwan.

The Chinese people are resolutely opposed to war, but no threats of war will ever frighten them into submission. Should anybody insist on imposing war on the Chinese people, the Chinese people will, without fail, deal determined counter-blows to those who commit such acts of intervention and provocation.

The Chinese people fervently desire peace, but they will never beg for peace at the expense of their territory and sovereignty. To sacrifice territory and sovereignty can only lead to further aggression; it cannot possibly bring about genuine peace. The Chinese people understand that only by resisting aggression can peace be defended.

DOCUMENT 44: U.S. CONGRESSIONAL AUTHORIZATION
FOR THE PRESIDENT TO EMPLOY THE ARMED FORCES
OF THE UNITED STATES TO PROTECT FORMOSA, THE
PESCADORES, AND RELATED POSITIONS AND
TERRITORIES OF THAT AREA[18]

Whereas the primary purpose of the United States, in its relations
with all other nations, is to develop and sustain a just and enduring
peace for all; and

Whereas certain territories in the West Pacific under the jurisdiction of the Republic of China are now under armed attack, and
threats and declarations have been and are being made by the
Chinese Communists that such armed attack is in aid of and in
preparation for armed attack on Formosa and the Pescadores,

Whereas such armed attack if continued would gravely endanger the
peace and security of the West Pacific Area and particularly of
Formosa and the Pescadores; and

Whereas the secure possession by friendly governments of the
Western Pacific Island chain, of which Formosa is a part, is
essential to the vital interests of the United States and all friendly
nations in or bordering upon the Pacific Ocean; and

Whereas the President of the United States on January 6, 1955, submitted to the Senate for its advice and consent to ratification a
Mutual Defense Treaty between the United States of America and
the Republic of China, which recognizes that an armed attack in
the West Pacific Area directed against territories, therein described,
in the region of Formosa and the Pescadores, would be dangerous
to the peace and safety of the parties to the treaty: Therefore be it
Resolved by the Senate and House of Representatives of the
United States of America in Congress assembled, That the President
of the United States be and he hereby is authorized to employ the
Armed Forces of the United States as he deems necessary for the
specific purpose of securing and protecting Formosa and the Pescadores against armed attack, this authority to include the securing
and protection of such related positions and territories of that area
now in friendly hands and the taking of such other measures as he
judges to be required or appropriate in assuring the defense of
Formosa and the Pescadores.

This resolution shall expire when the President shall determine
that the peace and security of the area is reasonably assured by
international conditions created by action of the United Nations or
otherwise, and shall so report to the Congress.

DOCUMENT 45: ROC PRESIDENT CHIANG KAI-SHEK'S
REVIEW OF THE INTERNATIONAL SITUATION,
FEBRUARY 8, 1955[19]

After the occupation of the Chinese mainland, these habitual criminals [i.e., Chinese Communists] against international peace are again invading the territories of Free China under the instigation of the Russian imperialists. Under such circumstances, the United Nations should have little choice but to impose severe sanctions against the aggressors. Surprisingly, the Security Council has adopted a resolution aimed at bringing about a cease-fire between a Member State and the aggressors. Even if an agreement could be reached for a cease-fire, it would only bear resemblance to the ones concluded for Korea and Indo-China, in which the injured party would be forced to recognize the fait accompli of the aggressors. If this should be the case, where are the dignity, authority and righteousness of the United Nations? If there is any sense for the Security Council to invite a representative of the Chinese Communist regime to a conference sponsored by the United Nations, it should be for the purpose of the trial of, and imposing a sanction against, this habitual international criminal for its aggression on the Chinese mainland, in Korea, in Indo-China and now again against the Republic of China. Otherwise, the United Nations will be acting against its own principles, with the possible consequence of sealing its own fate.

The preamble to the New Zealand resolution states that the question of hostilities in the area of certain islands off the coast of the mainland of China endangers international peace and the maintenance of security. We must realize that the present hostilities around our offshore islands were all started by the Chinese Communists through their shelling of the Kinmen Islands. They are a continuation and an extension of Soviet Russian aggression in China. The Republic of China, in continuing her resistance against aggression, had to hit back. The United Nations should do the proper thing by imposing sanctions against the aggressors instead of wasting its time on a cease-fire proposal. This should be so for two reasons. First, the aggression of the international Communist bloc will never stop. Second, the United Nations should not impose equal responsibility for the cease-fire on the invader and a Member State which is being invaded.

Furthermore, if the cease-fire arranged by the United Nations follows the line of similar arrangements in Korea and Indo-China, it is tantamount to recognition of the fait accompli of the aggressors. In the end, it will encourage them to start aggression on a larger scale and create far more serious faits accomplis to force recognition from the United Nations.

When the United Nations disregards the fact that one of its Member States is invaded and fails to impose sanctions against the aggressors, when it accords recognition to the fait accompli of the aggressors in the form of a cease-fire, when it invites the aggressors to attend triumphantly a meeting sponsored by itself, and when in addition it imposes on a Member State the equal obligation of a cease-fire to compel it to sacrifice its sovereignty, territory and people taken away from it as a result of aggression, the United Nations will one day follow the path of the defunct League of Nations.

. . .

The cease-fire resolution involves another unreasonable argument which resulted from a mistaken notion of some foreign observers about Taiwan. Without justification, these people say that the status of Taiwan has not been determined and that they want to find a solution for it after the conclusion of the cease-fire agreement. This argument is contrary to fact, and its proponents obviously have an ax to grind. There may be some countries who wish to resort to the secret diplomacy of the Geneva Conference. If this is true, then they will ignore the existence of the United Nations. They will not only betray a Member State of the United Nations but also betray the United Nations which they themselves had a hand in organizing.

I recall that in 1943, the late American President Roosevelt and the present British Prime Minister Churchill and I held a conference at Cairo to discuss problems relating to the prosecution of war against Japan and its aftermath. In the communiqué issued at the conclusion of the conference, we announced that all the territories "stolen" by Japan from China, including the Northeast provinces and Taiwan and Penghu, should be returned to the Republic of China. This announcement was recognized by the Potsdam Declaration and accepted by Japan at the time of her surrender. Its validity is thus based on a number of agreements and should not be questioned.

Therefore, when Japan surrendered, the Government of the Republic of China repossessed Taiwan and Penghu and constituted them as Taiwan Province. Since that time, Taiwan and Penghu have regained their status as an integral unit of the territory of the Republic of China. In the San Francisco Peace Treaty and the Sino-Japanese Peace Treaty, Japan renounced her sovereignty over Taiwan and Penghu, thereby completing the process of restoring these areas to our country. The people I mentioned above must all know the bases of law and history about Taiwan and Penghu. That they purposely choose to misinterpret them shows that they have an ax to grind.

Some people deny the validity of the Cairo Declaration in order to justify their distorted view about the status of Taiwan. If one could deny the validity of the Cairo Declaration, what about the Potsdam

Declaration and all the international treaties and agreements concluded since the termination of the Second World War? Could their validity be also denied? If the Democracies repudiate the Cairo Declaration, which they signed themselves, how, either now or in the future, can they criticize the Communist aggressive bloc for tearing up treaties and agreements? Those who play fast and loose about the status of Taiwan do so against their own conscience. In their eagerness to appease the aggressors they have their eyes fixed on a transient state of affairs. They do not realize how gravely they jeopardize world security by arguing from bad law and false policies. Some countries, taking a very dim view of international faith, have recognized the . . . Peiping regime. . . . Simply because they recognize the phenomenon created by Soviet aggression through their Chinese stooges, they do not regard the Chinese mainland as the territory of the Republic of China. In order to please Soviet Russia and the Chinese Communist regime by placing more interests of the Republic of China on the platter, they further deny the sovereignty of the Republic of China over the offshore islands now defended by our forces. I wish to declare most solemnly to the whole world: The United Nations Charter has expressly laid down the injunction against any Member State encroaching upon the territorial integrity and political independence of another. Although our mainland is at present under the occupation of that instrument of Soviet aggression, the Communist puppet Peiping regime, it is nevertheless a part of the territory of the Republic of China. No one can deny this. Our Government has naturally the responsibility to drive out the aggressors and recover our lost territories. Elected by the people and charged with responsibility, the Government can under no circumstance renounce it. Furthermore, we have to help our mainland compatriots in their struggle for freedom. . . .

DOCUMENT 46: ROC PRESIDENT CHIANG KAI-SHEK'S REPLIES TO QUESTIONS ASKED IN A PRESS CONFERENCE, FEBRUARY 14, 1955[20]

. . .

3. Question: What is the view of the Government of the Republic of China about certain talks in international circles that Kinmen, Matsu and other offshore islands should belong to the Chinese Communists?

Answer: The territory of the Republic of China is not to be carved up. Although the Chinese mainland has been stolen by the Peiping . . . regime . . . it is still a part of the territory of the

Republic of China, which the people and Government of the Republic of China are determined to recover. Kinmen and Matsu have not been stolen by the Chinese Communists. They constitute parts of the bastion where our people and Government are withstanding the aggression of the international Communist bloc. In no case would they be abandoned to the enemy.

. . .

5. Question: What is the view of the Government of the Republic of China about the proposal for "two Chinas"?

Answer: Such a proposal is absurd. The four-thousand-year-old Chinese history shows that although there have been rebellions staged by traitors at the instigation of and supported by foreign enemies, the Chinese nation always has been a unified State. "The loyal and the traitorous cannot co-exist." This has always been accepted by all Chinese as a basic concept of loyalty toward the country. To recognize the rule of traitors goes against all teachings of our history. Besides, the cruelty practiced by the Chinese Communists is such as we have never witnessed in history. If we recognized the fruit of Soviet aggression in China, we would be abandoning the four hundred and fifty million of our people to the tyranny of imperialistic Russia and the Chinese Communists. We would be watching the enslavement and butchering of our own people without raising a finger. Then we would be committing the most grievous crime in the whole course of human history. It goes without saying that the people and government of the Republic of China cannot renounce the sacred mission of liberating their compatriots on the mainland. Furthermore, I do not think that the free world as a whole will tolerate the transition into fact of such an absurd theory against all principles of righteousness and justice.

DOCUMENT 47: U.S. SECRETARY OF STATE DULLES'
STATEMENT ON NEGOTIATIONS WITH COMMUNIST
CHINA FOR A CEASE-FIRE ARRANGEMENT IN THE
FORMOSA AREA, JULY 26, 1955[21]

Last April at the Bandung conference Mr. Chou En-lai suggested that there should be bilateral talks with the United States. He said, "The Chinese people do not want to have war with the United States. We are willing to settle international disputes by peaceful means."

Immediately (on April 23, 1955) the Department of State responded by stating that "the United States always welcomes any efforts, if sincere, to bring peace to the world." Then at my subsequent press conference (April 26, 1955) I referred to Mr. Chou En-lai's statement and said, "Whether or not that was a sincere proposal remains to be seen. Perhaps the Chinese Communists are merely playing a propaganda game. But we intend to try to find out. In doing so we shall not, of course, depart from the path of fidelity and honor to our ally, the Republic of China."

. . .

. . . the United States proposed on July 11 to Mr. Chou En-lai that the talks that had been going on at Geneva, recently at the consular level, should be somewhat raised in level and enlarged in scope. This proposal was made through the intermediary of the United Kingdom, which represents the interests of the United States in Communist China. There was prompt acceptance of this proposal and, after the date was agreed to, a mutually agreed communiqué with reference to it was arrived at and simultaneously issued in Peiping and in Washington yesterday morning.

It was made clear that the offer of the United States did not imply any diplomatic recognition whatsoever. It was also made clear that we were not prepared in any way in these talks to make arrangements which would prejudice the rights of our ally, the Republic of China.

. . .

The United States believes that whatever may be the differences which now divide countries, these differences should not be settled by recourse to force where this would be apt to provoke international war. The United States has itself consistently acted on that belief. Wherever we give any military assistance, it is under the explicit condition that it will not be used for aggressive purposes. There is no doubt but what East Germany is part of Germany, but Chancellor Adenauer has given solemn assurance that he will not use force to unite his country. There is no doubt that North Korea is a part of Korea, but the security treaty which we made with the Republic of Korea makes clear that the United States will not extend its protection other than to areas which we recognize as having been lawfully brought under the jurisdiction of the Republic of Korea, and we do not believe that aggressive force is such a lawful means. There is no doubt but that North Viet-Nam is part of Viet-Nam, but we stated in connection with the Indo-China armistice that we were opposed to any renewal of aggression to bring about the unification of Viet-Nam.

Both the Republic of China and the Chinese People's Republic claim that the area held by the other is part of China. But in connection with the mutual security treaty which the United States made with the Republic of China, it was agreed that the Republic of China would not use force except as a matter of joint agreement, subject to action of an emergency character which was clearly an exercise of the inherent right of self-defense.

We believe that the principle of nonrecourse to force is valid not merely for the United States and its allies but that it is valid for all.

We shall hope to find out in the forthcoming talks whether the Chinese Communists accept the concept of a cease-fire in accordance with the United Nations principle of avoiding any use or threat of force which could disturb the peace of nations.

. . .

DOCUMENT 48: PRC FOREIGN MINISTRY
STATEMENT ON SINO-AMERICAN TALKS
AT GENEVA, JANUARY 18, 1956[22]

The Sino-American ambassadorial talks have been going on for more than four months without any agreement being achieved on the second item of the agenda, ever since agreement was reached on September 10, 1955, on the return of civilians of both sides. . . .

. . .

(1) As soon as agreement was reached at the Sino-American talks on the return of civilians of both sides, our side put forward under the second item of the agenda two subjects for discussion— the question of embargo and the question of preparations for Sino-American negotiations at a higher level. But the American side refused to proceed to any substantive discussion of these two subjects. It was not until October 8, 1955, that the American side suggested that both China and the United States should first of all make a declaration on the renunciation of the use of force.

If the so-called renunciation of the use of force means that China and the United States should, in accordance with the purposes and principles of the United Nations Charter, settle peacefully disputes between the two countries without resorting to force, then it is precisely what China has advocated consistently. It was precisely for the purpose of realizing the principle of non-use of force in international relations that China proposed at Bandung that China and the United States should sit down and enter into negotiations. It was for this same purpose that in the Sino-American ambassadorial talks China proposed the holding of Sino-American negotiations at a higher level. However, the question of non-use of force in the

international relations between China and the United States should in
no way be mixed up with the domestic matters of either China or the
United States. So far as the question of Taiwan is concerned, the
occupation of China's territory of Taiwan by the United States is an
international dispute between China and the United States, while the
liberation by the Chinese people of their own territory of Taiwan is
China's sovereign right and internal affair. The Chinese Government
has repeatedly declared that it would strive for the liberation of Taiwan
by peaceful means so far as it is possible. But this internal affair
of China's cannot possibly be a subject of the Sino-American talks.

(2) After making clear in the talks its above-mentioned stand.
the Chinese side put forward on October 27, 1955, a draft agreed
announcement of the Ambassadors of China and the United States on
the question of renunciation of the use of force as raised by the
American side. The text of the draft announcement reads as follows:

"Ambassador Wang Ping-nan, on behalf of the Government of
the People's Republic of China, and Ambassador U. Alexis Johnson,
on behalf of the Government of the United States of America, jointly
declare:

"In accordance with Article 2, paragraph 3 of the United Nations
Charter, 'All Members shall settle their international disputes by
peaceful means in such a manner that international peace and security,
and justice, are not endangered';

"And in accordance with Article 2, paragraph 4 of the United
Nations Charter, 'All Members shall refrain in their international
relations from the threat or use of force against the territorial
integrity or political independence of any state, or in any other manner
inconsistent with the Purposes of the United Nations';

"The People's Republic of China and the United States of America
agree that they should settle disputes between their two countries by
peaceful means without resorting to the threat or use of force;

"In order to realize their common desire the People's Republic
of China and the United States of America decide to hold a conference
of Foreign Ministers to settle through negotiations the question of
relaxing and eliminating the tension in the Taiwan area."

If there is sincerity on both sides, there should not be any
difficulty in reaching an agreement on the basis of this draft announcement submitted by the Chinese side. The United States is a member
of the United Nations. It should not have any objection to the explicit
provisions of the United Nations Charter. The United States has
resorted to the use and threat of force against China in the Taiwan
area, thus creating tension there. In order that the principle of non-
use of force stipulated in the United Nations Charter may be realized
in Sino-American relations, it is obvious that only through a Sino-
American conference of the Foreign Ministers will it be possible to

settle the question of the relaxation and elimination of the tension in
the Taiwan area.

(3) However, in the course of the talks, the American side
expressed unwillingness to have particular stipulations of the United
Nations Charter specifically mentioned in the announcement, or to
have the announcement explicitly provide for the holding of a Sino-
American conference of the Foreign Ministers. It was not until
November 10, 1955, that is, two whole months after both sides reached
agreement on the first agenda item, that the American side for the
first time put forward in concrete form its own draft announcement
concerning the renunciation of the use of force. The substantive
part of the draft announcement put forward by the American side
reads as follows:

"Ambassador U. Alexis Johnson, on behalf of the United States
of America, informed Ambassador Wang Ping-nan that:

"In general, and with particular reference to the Taiwan area,
the United States of America renounces the use of force, except in
individual and collective self-defense.

"Ambassador Wang Ping-nan, on behalf of the People's Republic
of China, informed Ambassador U. Alexis Johnson that:

"In general, and with particular reference to the Taiwan area,
the People's Republic of China renounces the use of force, except in
individual and collective self-defense."

Just as the Chinese side has pointed out in the talks, the draft
announcement put forth by the American side is in substance an
attempt to confuse the international dispute between China and the
United States in the Taiwan area with the domestic matter between
the Chinese Government and the Chiang Kai-shek clique, and a demand
that China accept the status quo of the United States occupation of
China's territory Taiwan and give up its sovereign right to liberate
Taiwan. That is absolutely unacceptable to China. Taiwan is China's
territory; there can be no question of defense, so far as the United
States is concerned. The United States has already used force and
the threat of force against China in the Taiwan area. Therefore,
should one speak of defense, it is precisely China which should exercise
its right of defense to expel such force and threat. Yet the United
States has demanded the right of defense in the Taiwan area. Is this
not precisely a demand that China accept continued United States
occupation of Taiwan and that the tension in the Taiwan area be maintained forever?

(4) Nevertheless, in order that the talks may progress step by
step, the Chinese side made another effort, and on December 1, 1955,
put forward the following new draft:

"Ambassador Wang Ping-nan, on behalf of the Government of
the People's Republic of China, and Ambassador U. Alexis Johnson,

on behalf of the Government of the United States of America, agree
to announce:

"The People's Republic of China and the United States of
America are determined that they should settle disputes between
their two countries through peaceful negotiations without resorting
to the threat or use of force;

"The two Ambassadors should continue their talks to seek
practical and feasible means for the realization of this common
desire."

The Chinese side holds that the only practical and feasible
means for settling disputes between China and the United States,
particularly a serious question such as the tension in the Taiwan
area, is a Sino-American conference of the Foreign Ministers.
However, in order to promote the progress of the talks, the Chinese
side has agreed to issue first the above announcement and then the
Ambassadors of the two sides will discuss and decide upon the
specific question of holding a Sino-American conference of the
Foreign Ministers. At the same time, it should be pointed out that
since the United States has already used force and threat of force
against China in the Taiwan area, it would not be possible to realize
that desire expressed in the above announcement if agreement is
not reached at the Sino-American ambassadorial talks on the holding
of a Sino-American conference of the Foreign Ministers.

It can be seen that if the United States Government really has
the sincerity to renounce the use or threat of force, it has no reason
whatsoever to continue to drag out the talks instead of entering into
agreement on our new draft.

(5) However, in three consecutive meetings following our
putting forward of this new draft, the American side refused to
make any specific comments, expressing neither opposition nor
agreement to it. It was not until January 12, 1956, that the American
side put forward a counter-proposal. The full text of it reads as
follows:

"Ambassador U. Alexis Johnson, on behalf of the Government
of the United States of America, and Ambassador Wang Ping-nan, on
behalf of the Government of the People's Republic of China, agree to
announce:

"The United States of America and the People's Republic of
China are determined that they will settle disputes between them
through peaceful means, and that, without prejudice to the inherent
right of individual and collective self-defense, they will not resort
to the threat or use of force in the Taiwan area or elsewhere;

"The two Ambassadors should continue their talks to seek
practical and feasible means for the realization of this common
desire."

It is obvious that in substance there is no difference whatsoever between this counter-proposal of the American side and its November 10 draft announcement which the Chinese side . . . firmly rejected long ago. The American side continues to demand that our side accept that the United States has "the inherent right of individual and collective self-defense" in China's Taiwan area. That is what our side absolutely cannot accept.

. . .

(7) The tension in the Taiwan area is the key issue between China and the United States, and the root of the tension is United States armed occupation of China's territory. Nevertheless, the Chinese side still advocates settlement of this dispute between China and the United States through negotiation, and has been striving constantly in the Sino-American ambassadorial talks to find a practical and feasible means to achieve this aim. The American side, however, has deliberately dragged out the Sino-American talks and refused to enter into agreement on the means for the relaxation and elimination of the tension in the Taiwan area, and on the contrary demands that China accept the status quo of United States armed occupation of Taiwan. In the meantime, United States Secretary of State Dulles again openly cried out recently that in order to hold on to China's territory and infringe upon China's sovereignty, he would not scruple to start an atomic war. The United States aggressors imagined that this would frighten the Chinese people into giving up their own sovereign rights. But this attempt will never succeed. In . . . recent years, the armistice in Korea, the restoration of peace in Indo-China and the withdrawal from the Tachen Islands have successively demonstrated the strength of the world people who fight for peace and uphold justice, and declared the bankruptcy of the policy of positions-of-strength and atomic intimidation. Should the United States aggressors still want to carry on such a policy of atomic intimidation, they would inevitably encounter greater and more disastrous defeats.

The Chinese Government holds that the Sino-American talks should seek practical and feasible means for the relaxation and elimination of the tension in the Taiwan area. The Chinese side has already put forward a reasonable proposal completely acceptable to both sides. The Sino-American talks should speedily reach an agreement on the basis of this reasonable proposal and proceed to settle the question of abolishment of the embargo and the question of preparations for a Sino-American conference of the Foreign Ministers. To drag out the talks and carry out threats will settle no question.

DOCUMENT 49: ROC PRESIDENT CHIANG KAI-SHEK'S
REPLIES TO QUESTIONS SUBMITTED BY WILLIAM
RANDOLPH HEARST, JR., MARCH 15, 1956[23]

. . .

10. Q. Why in your opinion has the Communist Peiping regime refused to renounce use of force in respect to the question of the settlement of what is called the problem of Formosa?

A. In the first place, even if the Communists did renounce the use of force in any area, I do not believe they would live up to their undertaking. When have the Communists ever lived up to their promises? At present the Chinese Communists know that the United States attaches importance to a renunciation of the use of force in the Taiwan area by the Chinese Communists. They are holding out in order to bargain for a United States agreement to hold a foreign ministers' conference. Such a conference would further enhance the prestige of the [bogus] regime. To the Asian peoples such a conference may look very close to being the recognition of the Peiping regime by the United States. We should know that even if the Communists should agree to renounce the use of force in the Taiwan area for the time being, it will be only to trade for political gains from the United States. It will in addition deal a severe blow to America's leadership and prestige among the free Asians. It is tantamount to the thorough destruction of the confidence of the anti-Communist Asians.

11. Q. What would you do if the United States should decide to have Communist China as well as your government represented in the United Nations?

A. It is impossible for me to believe that the United States would make such a decision.

DOCUMENT 50: PRC PREMIER CHOU EN-LAI'S
SPEECH TO THE THIRD SESSION OF THE FIRST
NATIONAL PEOPLE'S CONGRESS, JUNE 28, 1956[24]

The strenuous efforts of the United States to exclude New China from participation in international affairs have not caused China any harm. On the contrary, by obstructing the restoration to the People's Republic of China of its legitimate position and rights in the United Nations, the United States has damaged the prestige of the United Nations and made it impossible for that organization to play effectively the role envisaged by its Charter.

The United States has also aroused the dissatisfaction of many countries by forcing them to refrain from establishing diplomatic relations
with China, and accelerated their tendency to fall away from the United
States. As for China, regardless of recognition or non-recognition
by the United States, it will all the same exist and develop with growing
strength, its contacts with other countries will further increase, and
its international position will further rise.

In the face of such undeniable and powerful facts, certain people
are hatching a plot to create "two Chinas." They are vainly attempting
to describe Taiwan as another China or as a separate independent
state. But these vain attempts can only be interpreted as a sign of
losing one's senses in the face of powerful facts. Taiwan has always
been a part of China. Solemn international agreements have also long
affirmed that Taiwan belongs to China. Even the Chiang Kai-shek
clique . . . admits that Taiwan belongs to China. All Chinese people,
including those on Taiwan, will never tolerate the detachment of
Taiwan from their motherland.

Those who vainly seek to create "two Chinas" recognize that it
is becoming more and more difficult to continue to exclude the People's
Republic of China from international organizations and conferences.
Therefore, they are attempting to create beforehand a state of "two
Chinas" in international organizations and conferences. The Chinese
people long ago saw through this plot. It is futile to hope that China
will fall into this trap. International organizations and conferences
are only one means of effecting international exchanges and contacts.
China will not find it . . . difficult to expand its contacts and connections
with other countries because of its being excluded from international
organizations and conferences.

Only one China exists in the world. Only the Government of the
People's Republic of China can represent the Chinese people. We
believe that sooner or later this fact will receive general recognition
in the world. The sooner this day arrives, the sooner will normal
international relations be restored.

Now, I should like to report to the Congress on the situation in
the Sino-American talks.

After agreement was reached on the return of civilians of both
sides at the Sino-American ambassadorial talks in Geneva on September
10, 1955, the two sides entered into discussions on the question of
renunciation of force. . . .

The Chinese side is not against the issuance jointly with the
United States of an announcement on mutual renunciation of the use
and threat of force in Sino-American relations. In fact, as early as
during the Bandung Conference, China declared that the Chinese people
do not want war with the United States and that the Chinese Government
is willing to sit down and enter into negotiations with the United States

Government on the question of easing and eliminating the tension in the Taiwan area. However, it must be pointed out that the tension in the Taiwan area was entirely created by the U.S. occupation by force of China's territory of Taiwan. Therefore, any announcement concerning the renunciation of the use of force between China and the United States must be capable of leading to the relaxation and elimination of the tension, and must not imply acceptance of the U.S. occupation of Taiwan. At the same time, the question as to what means will be used by China to liberate Taiwan is entirely a matter of China's sovereignty and internal affairs, in which no outside interference will be tolerated. Therefore, a Sino-American announcement should in no way allow interference in this matter.

. . .

Finally, I wish to say something on the question of the liberation of Taiwan, about which we are all concerned.

The Chinese people are determined to liberate Taiwan. This is the unshakable common will of the 600 million people of China.

The Chinese Government has repeatedly pointed out that there are two ways for the Chinese people to liberate Taiwan, that is, by war or by peaceful means, and that the Chinese people would seek to liberate Taiwan by peaceful means so far as it is possible. There is no doubt that if Taiwan can be liberated peacefully, it would be best for our country, for all the Chinese people and for Asian and world peace.

At present, the possibility of peacefully liberating Taiwan is increasing. This is first of all because the international situation is now definitely tending toward relaxation, and the United States armed occupation of Taiwan and interference in China's internal affairs are opposed by more and more peace-loving countries and peoples. As regards our internal situation, our great motherland has grown even stronger and become even more consolidated. It is inspiring more pride in all patriotic Chinese than ever before. At present, our compatriots on Taiwan, who have a revolutionary tradition, are unwilling to suffer any longer their bitter life of slavery, and want to return as soon as possible to the embrace of the motherland; and even among the Kuomintang military and political personnel who have fled to Taiwan from the mainland, more and more people have come to realize that their only future lies in the peaceful reunification of their motherland. Since we issued the call to strive for the peaceful liberation of Taiwan, many Kuomintang military and political personnel in Taiwan and abroad have expressed their patriotic aspirations. We believe that those who wish to bring about the peaceful liberation of Taiwan and the complete unification of our motherland will certainly grow in number from day to day. This will be an inexorable trend.

The trends are very clear. The situation of the Taiwan authorities maintaining a feeble existence by following the behest of the
United States cannot possibly last long. The foreign forces on which
they depend are by no means reliable. On the contrary, by inviting
the wolf into the house, they will not only lose everything they have,
but also be in constant danger of being treacherously bitten in the
back or abandoned. An important lesson can be drawn from a comparison of the contrasting attitudes taken by China and the United
States in the Geneva talks. The Chinese Government has consistently
maintained that only the international dispute between China and the
United States in the Taiwan area can be discussed and settled by
China and the United States; as for the question of the return of
Taiwan to the motherland, regardless of the means by which it is
realized, this is a question which can only be settled and definitely
can be settled by us Chinese people, and no foreign interference will
be tolerated. The United States, however, has adopted a totally
different attitude in the talks. It regards Taiwan as its colony and
makes use of it to bargain with China. It can also be seen that the
United States has not only occupied Taiwan and extended its control
into every sphere in Taiwan—political, military, economic and cultural—
but is also playing its usual splitting tactics to create suspicion and
feuds inside Taiwan, attempting thus to strengthen its control and to
profit thereby. However, these tactics of the U.S. aggressive forces
to make fools of the Chinese people, interfere in China's internal affairs and disrupt China's national unity, have aroused even stronger
dissatisfaction among the Kuomintang military and political personnel
on Taiwan. Many of them have indicated that they will suffer no longer
their life of abject dependence, at the beck and call of others. They
want to enhance national self-respect, defend national dignity, free
themselves from U.S. control and handle domestic matters in an
independent spirit. We welcome this patriotic stand of theirs.

We have consistently stood for national solidarity and united
resistance against external enemies. In the interest of our great
motherland and our people, the Chinese Communists and the Kuomintang
members have twice fought shoulder to shoulder against imperialism.
After the conclusion of the War of Resistance to Japanese Aggression,
we also made efforts to bring about internal peace. Even during the
Chinese War of Liberation, when the Chinese people were forced to
take up arms, and even after the mainland was liberated, we have
never given up our efforts for peaceful negotiations. Although in the
past few years, owing to U.S. armed intervention, we and the Kuomintang
military and political personnel on Taiwan have taken different paths,
yet so long as we all hold supreme the interests of our nation and
motherland, we can still link arms again and unite. We believe that
our great nation, which experienced long years of suffering, will

certainly be able through our own efforts to accomplish the complete unity of our motherland.

Now, on behalf of the Government, I formally state: We are willing to negotiate with the Taiwan authorities on specific steps and terms for the peaceful liberation of Taiwan, and we hope that the Taiwan authorities will send their representatives to Peking or other appropriate places, at a time which they consider appropriate, to begin these talks with us.

In order to unite all patriotic forces to realize at an early date the complete unification of our motherland, I wish here to declare once again that all patriotic people, regardless of whether they joined the patriotic ranks earlier or later, and regardless of how great the crimes they committed in the past may have been, will be treated in accordance with the principle that "patriots belong to one family" and the policy of no punishment for past misdeeds; they are all welcome to perform meritorious service for the peaceful liberation of Taiwan, and will be duly rewarded according to the degree of their merit and provided with appropriate jobs.

Our compatriots in Taiwan have always been an inseparable part of the Chinese people. We not only have constant concern for them and support them in various ways in their struggle against foreign rule, but also stand ready to welcome them at any time to participate in the socialist construction of the motherland and to share the glory of our nation.

We appreciate the situation in which all the Kuomintang military and political personnel on Taiwan whose homes are on the mainland find themselves, and we hope that they may soon realize their desire of reuniting with their families. They can communicate with their relatives and friends on the mainland; they can also return to the mainland for short visits to their relatives and friends. We are prepared to give them all kinds of convenience and assistance.

We hope the responsible Kuomintang military and political personages on Taiwan will play an important role in the cause of the peaceful liberation of Taiwan. So long as they work in this direction, their future position will be definitely assured. If they still harbor doubts, they can obtain clarification through their relatives and friends on the mainland or send people to the mainland to ascertain what the situation is. We guarantee the latter's freedom of movement in coming and going.

We hope the Kuomintang military personnel on Taiwan will actively expedite the peaceful liberation of Taiwan. If they do so, they will surely earn the confidence and care of the motherland and the people. The treatment accorded to those commanders and soldiers who came over peacefully on the mainland is a precedent.

We also hope that all Kuomintang military and political personnel who are abroad will work for the peaceful liberation of Taiwan. Only thus can they escape the fate of leading the life of exiles in foreign lands, looked down upon by others.

We attach great importance to the positive role played by the broad mass of patriotic overseas Chinese in promoting the cause of the peaceful liberation of Taiwan. We hope that those few overseas Chinese who used to maintain or still maintain a hostile attitude toward the motherland will distinguish between right and wrong, see the direction in which events are moving, and, together with the broad mass of patriotic overseas Chinese, contribute toward the patriotic cause of the peaceful liberation of Taiwan.

The gate of the motherland is always wide open for all patriots. Every Chinese has both the right and the duty to make his contribution to the sacred cause of the unification of the motherland. With the unity of the entire nation and the efforts of all our people, the liberation of Taiwan will certainly be consummated.

DOCUMENT 51: LIU SHAO-CHI'S POLITICAL REPORT OF THE CENTRAL COMMITTEE OF THE CHINESE COMMUNIST PARTY TO THE EIGHTH NATIONAL CONGRESS OF THE PARTY, SEPTEMBER 15, 1956[25]

Except in Taiwan, which is still occupied by the U.S. aggressors, all the forces of foreign imperialism, which sat on the backs of the Chinese people for the last hundred years, have been driven out. China has become a great independent and sovereign country.

. . .

Our motherland's territory Taiwan is still under the occupation of the U.S. imperialists. This is a most serious threat to the security of our country. The liberation of Taiwan is purely China's internal affair. We are willing to bring Taiwan back to the embrace of the motherland through the peaceful means of negotiation, and avoid the use of force. If force has to be used, it would only be when all possibilities for peaceful negotiation have been exhausted or when peaceful negotiations have failed. Whatever means we adopt, we shall win the ultimate victory in the just cause of liberating Taiwan.

. . .

Our policy of peaceful co-existence based on the five principles does not exclude any country. We have the same desire for peaceful co-existence with the United States. But the United States has been consistently hostile to our country. It has occupied our territory Taiwan, sent spies into our country to engage in subversive activities, imposed an embargo on our country, done its best to bar us from international affairs, and insolently deprived us of our country's rightful place in the United Nations. Despite all this, our government has made efforts to settle our disputes with the United States by peaceful negotiation. We have repeatedly proposed a conference between the foreign ministers of China and the United States to settle the question of easing as well as eliminating the tension in the Taiwan area. Our efforts in this connection are made solely for the purpose of easing international tension, and by no means signify acquiescence in aggression. As the whole world knows, the Chinese people will not hesitate to make sacrifices to safeguard the independence and security of their motherland. But even now, the attitude of the United States government toward us is far from realistic or reasonable. And what is the result? Despite the fact that the U.S. imperialists have resorted to all vicious means to disrupt our country and attempted to isolate us, the great New China is firm on its feet in this world. Justice is on our side; world-wide sympathy is with us. It is not we that stand isolated in the world, but precisely the U.S. imperialists themselves. If the U.S. imperialists do not want to suffer further setbacks, their only way out is to adopt a realistic, reasonable attitude toward our country. This fact is no longer a secret even to the Americans themselves.

. . .

DOCUMENT 52: PRC PREMIER CHOU EN-LAI'S
REPORT TO THE CHINESE PEOPLE'S POLITICAL
CONSULTATIVE CONFERENCE, MARCH 5, 1957[26]

Taiwan is China's territory. Its inhabitants, including all Kuomintang military and administrative personnel, are Chinese. The liberation of Taiwan is China's internal affair, a question which the Chinese can settle by themselves. Since our call for a peaceful liberation of Taiwan, more and more people among the Kuomintang military and administrative personnel in Taiwan are willing to bring this about and the possibilities for peaceful liberation have been growing. However, this development is greatly feared by the United States Government, which does not scruple to adopt any means to sabotage it. Recently, the United States has instigated a group of people claiming to represent so-called Free China or so-called Independent Taiwan to overthrow the Taiwan authorities in an attempt to turn Taiwan into a United States dependency like Honolulu. Indeed, such means employed by the United States Government will only enable all patriotic Chinese to see all the more clearly the true colors of the United States Government which attempts to enslave China. If the United States can launch today a movement to overthrow the authorities in Taiwan, why could it not abandon tomorrow the self-termed Free China or Independent Taiwan elements? Those who seek after glory by selling out their own country will not win any glory, but only gain ill fame for thousands of years to come. All decent Chinese should unite as patriotic members of one big family, and together fight against and crush the schemes of United States imperialism.

The United States Government's policy of hostility toward the Chinese people cannot affect in the least China's existence and development. The People's Republic of China not only stands in the world as firm as a rock, but will develop and grow continuously along the road of socialism. The attempt of the United States Government to turn Taiwan into a United States dependency not only is firmly opposed by all patriotic Chinese, but also will not be allowed by the peace-loving countries and peoples the world over. The return of Taiwan to the embrace of the motherland cannot be prevented. No force on earth can forever separate Chinese from Chinese.

DOCUMENT 53: ROC PRESIDENT CHIANG KAI-SHEK'S REPLIES TO QUESTIONS SUBMITTED BY SVEN STEENBERG, OCTOBER 4, 1957[27]

1. Q. What does Free China think of the . . . "proposal" of Chou En-lai?

A. . . . [T]here can be no doubt that Chou's utterances about "peaceful liberation" of Taiwan were acts of deception. The Chinese Government has already had too many painful experiences in negotiating with the Communists, and shall not even consider these lies.

2. Q. Suppose the United States is to ask Free China to agree to a . . . "compromise" with the Chinese Communists under the condition that the territory of Free China would be guaranteed by the United Nations, what would be the reaction of Free China?

A. From Russian indulgence in brutalities and recent attitudes exhibited by the Chinese Communists, it can be seen that the democratic world and the aggressive bloc of international Communism are absolutely incompatible with each other. Unless the free world willingly lets itself to be defrauded, there can be no compromise between the two. There is absolutely no possibility of any "compromise" between Free China and the Chinese Communists. It is also my belief that the

United States, as leader of the democratic camp and ally of this country, understands the situation perfectly and will not fall into such a Communist trap.

. . .

4. Q. Is there any possibility for the hypothetical situation in which Free China may give up the intention of liberating the Chinese mainland?

A. There is no possibility that we in Free China will give up our right and obligation to fight for the freedom of our compatriots and the unification of our country. Just as the German people will not give up their intention to reunify Germany, we in Free China shall not stand still and watch our compatriots on the mainland suffer endlessly from Communist oppression and enslavement.

DOCUMENT 54: PRC PREMIER CHOU EN-LAI'S
REPORT TO THE FIFTH SESSION OF THE FIRST
NATIONAL PEOPLE'S CONGRESS,
FEBRUARY 10, 1958[28]

. . .

However, it should also be pointed out that the United States is not without followers in its plots to create "two Chinas." There are some who attempt to invite representatives of the People's Republic of China to participate in certain international organizations and conferences while retaining the representatives of the Chiang Kai-shek clique, thus creating a situation of "two Chinas." Of course, among these are also people who are truly friendly to China but who naively think that by so doing they are introducing New China into international organizations and activities, not knowing that they are in fact duped by the U.S. scheme to create "two Chinas." There are also some who deliberately spread the absurd contentions that the status of Taiwan is as yet undetermined and that the people in Taiwan are not Chinese (Han), and so they advocate a so-called plebiscite in Taiwan, autonomy for Taiwan, or putting Taiwan under trusteeship, all of which are methods to pave the way for the U.S. plot of creating "two Chinas." Taiwan is Chinese territory. Both the Cairo and Potsdam Declarations affirmed that Taiwan should be restored to China, and Taiwan was indeed returned to China after the Japanese surrender. The Chiang Kai-shek clique itself cannot deny these facts. Even the United States Government, which is now bent on creating "two Chinas," acknowledged these facts on more than one occasion.

The great majority of the people in Taiwan are of Han nationality, while the national minorities there, like other national minorities on the Chinese mainland, are also members of the big family of nationalities making up China. The absurdities concerning the status of Taiwan and the nationality of Taiwan are completely groundless. No scheme to separate Taiwan from the motherland through the fabrication of these absurdities can ever be realized.

. . .

The Chinese Government and people are firmly opposed to the scheme to create "two Chinas." We absolutely will not allow this scheme to materialize in any form or on any occasion. There is only one China—the People's Republic of China. The crucial issue in Sino-American relations today is not that China wants American recognition but that the United States antagonizes the Chinese people, occupies Chinese territory and even wants China to accept this occupation as lawful. This is a great issue between right and wrong which is not to be obscured. Taiwan is an inalienable part of Chinese territory. The Chinese people are determined to liberate Taiwan. All the Chinse people are opposed to the U.S. scheme to create "two Chinas." Even members of the Chiang Kai-shek clique in Taiwan, provided they are patriotic, would not like to see a situation of "two Chinas." Of course, the United States would not scruple to rear a more pliant puppet regime in Taiwan in order to realize its schemes. But our great nation has never yielded to foreign oppression and our compatriots in Taiwan have also a glorious revolutionary tradition. So long as all patriotic Chinese persist in their struggle for the complete unification of their motherland and will not permit U.S. occupation of Taiwan to be legalized, Taiwan will certainly return to the bosom of the motherland. Recognition or no recognition by the United States, China will forever exist and go on developing. Exclusion of China with its 600 million population from the United Nations only hurts the United Nations itself. We will never allow a state of "two Chinas" to arise in any international organization, conference or on any occasion. Such is our firm and unshakable stand.

DOCUMENT 55: THE U.S. POSITION ON THE QUESTION OF RECOGNITION OF THE CHINESE COMMUNIST REGIME [29]

In the case of China there are special considerations which influence United States policy with regard to recognition. For one thing, although the Chinese Communists have seized the preponderant bulk of China, they have not completed their conquest of the country. The generally recognized legitimate Government of China continues to exist and in Taiwan is steadily developing its political, economic, and military strength. The Government of the Republic of China controls the strategic island of Taiwan and through its possession of a sizable military force—one of the largest on the side of the free world in Asia—presents a significant deterrent to renewed Chinese Communist aggression. Recognition of Communist China by the United States would seriously cripple, if not destroy altogether, that Government. On the other hand, continued United States recognition and support of the Republic of China enables it to challenge the claim of the Chinese Communists to represent the Chinese people and keeps alive the hopes of those Chinese who are determined eventually to free their country of Communist rule.

. . .

Another special consideration in the case of China is that large and influential "overseas" Chinese communities exist in most of the countries of Southeast Asia. The efforts of these countries to build healthy free societies and to develop their economies would be seriously retarded if these communities were to fall under the sway of the Chinese Communists, and a grave threat of Communist subversion through these overseas communities would arise. Recognition of Communist China by the United States and the decline in the fortunes of the Republic of China which would inevitably result would have such a profound psychological effect on the overseas Chinese that it would make inevitable the transfer of the loyalties of large numbers to the Communist side. This in turn would undermine the ability of the host countries to resist the pressures tending to promote the expansion of Chinese Communist influence and power.

. . .

In public discussions of China policy one of the proposals that has attracted widest attention is that known as the "two Chinas solution." Briefly, advocates of this arrangement propose that the Chinese Communist regime be recognized as the government of mainland China while the Government of Taipei remains as the legal government of Taiwan. They argue that this approach to the Chinese problem has the merit of granting the Communists only what they already control while retaining for the free world the militarily strategic bastion of Taiwan. However, it overlooks or ignores certain facts of basic importance. The Republic of China would not accept any diminution of its sovereignty over China and could be expected to resist such an arrangement with all the means at its disposal. If a "two Chinas solution" were to be forcefully imposed against its will, that Government's effectiveness as a loyal ally to the free-world cause would be destroyed. Peiping, too, would reject such an arrangement. In fact, over the past year Chinese Communist propaganda has repeatedly and stridently denounced the "two Chinas" concept and, ironically, has been accusing the United States Government of attempting to put it into effect. Peiping attaches great importance to the eventual acquisition of Taiwan and has consistently reserved what it calls its "right" to seize Taiwan by force if other means fail. There is no prospect that it would ever acquiesce in any arrangement which would lead to the permanent detachment of Taiwan from China.

The "two Chinas" concept is bitterly opposed by both Peiping and Taipei. Hence, even if such a solution could be imposed by outside authority, it would not be a stable one. Constant policing would be required to avert its violent overthrow by one side or the other.

DOCUMENT 56: U.S. SECRETARY OF STATE DULLES' STATEMENT, SEPTEMBER 4, 1958[30]

I have reviewed in detail with the President the serious situation which has resulted from aggressive Chinese Communist military actions in the Taiwan (Formosa) Straits area. The President has authorized me to make the following statement.

1. Neither Taiwan (Formosa) nor the islands of Quemoy and Matsu have ever been under the authority of the Chinese Communists. Since the end of the Second World War, a period of over 13 years, they have continuously been under the authority of Free China, that is, the Republic of China.

2. The United States is bound by treaty to help to defend Taiwan (Formosa) from armed attack and the President is authorized by Joint Resolution of the Congress to employ the armed forces of the United States for the securing and protecting of related positions such as Quemoy and Matsu.

3. Any attempt on the part of the Chinese Communists now to seize these positions or any of them would be a crude violation of the principles upon which world order is based, namely, that no country should use armed force to seize new territory.

4. The Chinese Communists have, for about 2 weeks, been subjecting Quemoy to heavy artillery bombardment and, by artillery fire and use of small naval craft, they have been harassing the regular supply of the civilian and military population of the Quemoys, which totals some 125 thousand persons. The official Peiping radio repeatedly announces the purpose of these military operations to be to take by

armed force Taiwan (Formosa), as well as Quemoy and Matsu. In virtually every Peiping broadcast Taiwan (Formosa) and the offshore islands are linked as the objective of what is called the "Chinese People's Liberation Army."

5. Despite, however, what the Chinese Communists say, and so far have done, it is not yet certain that their purpose is in fact to make an all-out effort to conquer by force Taiwan (Formosa) and the offshore islands. Neither is it apparent that such efforts as are being made, or may be made, cannot be contained by the courageous, and purely defensive, efforts of the forces of the Republic of China, with such substantial logistical support as the United States is providing.

. . .

7. The President and I earnestly hope that the Chinese Communist regime will not again, as in the case of Korea, defy the basic principle upon which world order depends, namely, that armed force should not be used to achieve territorial ambitions. Any such naked use of force would pose an issue far transcending the offshore islands and even the security of Taiwan (Formosa). It would forecast a widespread use of force in the Far East which would endanger vital free world positions and the security of the United States. Acquiescence therein would threaten peace everywhere. We believe that the civilized world community will never condone overt military conquest as a legitimate instrument of policy.

8. The United States has not, however, abandoned hope that Peiping will stop short of defying the will of mankind for peace. This would not require it to abandon its claims, however ill-founded we may deem them to be. I recall that in the extended negotiations which the representatives of the United States and Chinese Communist regime conducted at Geneva between 1955 and 1958, a sustained effort was made by the United States to secure, with particular reference to the Taiwan area, a declaration of mutual and reciprocal renunciation of force, except in self-defense, which, however, would be without prejudice to the pursuit of policies by peaceful means. The Chinese Communists rejected any such declaration. We believe, however, that such a course of conduct constitutes the only civilized and acceptable procedure. The United States intends to follow that course, so far as it is concerned, unless and until the Chinese Communists, by their acts, leave us no choice but to react in defense of the principles to which all peace-loving governments are dedicated.

DOCUMENT 57: PRC'S DECLARATION ON THE TERRITORIAL SEA, SEPTEMBER 4, 1958[31]

The Government of the People's Republic of China declares:

1. The breadth of the territorial sea of the People's Republic of China shall be twelve nautical miles. This provision applies to all territories of the People's Republic of China, including the Chinese mainland and its coastal islands, as well as Taiwan and its surrounding islands, the Penghu Islands, the Tungsha Islands, the Hsisha Islands, the Chungsha Islands, the Nansha Islands and all other islands belonging to China which are separated from the mainland and its coastal islands by the high seas.

2. China's territorial sea along the mainland and its coastal islands takes as its baseline the line composed of the straight lines connecting base-points on the mainland coast and on the outermost of the coastal islands; the water area extending twelve nautical miles outward from this baseline is China's territorial sea. The water areas inside the baseline, including Pohai Bay and the Chiungchow Straits, are Chinese inland waters. The islands inside the baseline, including Tungyin Island, Kaoteng Island, the Matsu Islands, the Paichuan Islands, Wuchiu Island, the Greater and Lesser Quemoy Islands, Tatan Island, Erhtan Island and Tungting Island, are islands of the Chinese inland waters.

3. No foreign vessels for military use and no foreign aircraft may enter China's territorial sea and the air space above it without the permission of the Government of the People's Republic of China.

While navigating Chinese territorial sea, every foreign vessel must observe the relevant laws and regulations laid down by the Government of the People's Republic of China.

4. The principles provided in paragraphs 2 and 3 likewise apply to Taiwan and its surrounding islands, the Penghu Islands, the Tungsha Islands, the Hsisha Islands, the Chungsha Islands, the Nansha Islands, and all other islands belonging to China.

The Taiwan and Penghu areas are still occupied by the United States by armed force. This is an unlawful encroachment on the territorial integrity and sovereignty of the People's Republic of China. Taiwan, Penghu and such other areas are yet to be recovered, and the Government of the People's Republic of China has the right to recover these areas by all suitable means at a suitable time. This is China's internal affair, in which no foreign interference is tolerated.

DOCUMENT 58: PRC PREMIER CHOU EN-LAI'S
STATEMENT, SEPTEMBER 6, 1958[32]

On September 4, 1958, United States Secretary of State Dulles, authorized by United States President Eisenhower, issued a statement openly threatening to extend United States aggression in the Taiwan Straits area against the People's Republic of China and carrying out war provocation, thereby aggravating the tension in this area created by the United States and seriously jeopardizing the peace of the Far East and the world. Regarding this, I have been authorized by the Government of the People's Republic of China to make the following statement.

1. Taiwan and the Penghu Islands have been China's territories from ancient times. Following the Second World War, they were restored to China after being occupied by Japan for a period of time. It is entirely China's internal affair for the Chinese people to exercise their sovereign right to liberate these areas. This is the Chinese people's sacred and inviolable right. The United States Government itself also declared formally that it would not get involved in China's civil conflict in the Taiwan area. Were it not for the fact that the United States Government later went back on its own statement and carried out armed intervention, Taiwan and the Penghu Islands would have long been liberated and placed under the jurisdiction of the Government of the People's Republic of China. These are undeniable facts unanimously recognized by fair-minded world public opinion.

2. United States support of the Chiang Kai-shek clique entrenched on Taiwan and the Penghu Islands, which has long been repudiated by all the Chinese people, and its direct armed occupation of Taiwan and the Penghu Islands constitute unlawful interference in China's internal affairs and infringement on China's territorial integrity and sovereignty, and are in direct conflict with the United Nations Charter and all codes of international law. All so-called treaties concluded between the United States and the Chiang Kai-shek clique and all related resolutions adopted by the United States Congress are null and void as far as the Chinese people are concerned. They can never legalize United States aggression. Much less can they be used as pretexts by the United States for extending its aggression in the Taiwan Straits area.

. . .

4. The Chinese people's determination to liberate their own territory of Taiwan and the Penghu Islands is unshakable. . . .

6. The Sino-American dispute in the Taiwan Straits area and the Chinese people's internal matter of liberating their own territory are two matters entirely different in nature. The United States has all along tried to confuse these two matters so as to cover up its aggression and intervention in China. This is absolutely not to be allowed. The Chinese people have every right to liberate their own territory by all suitable means at a suitable time, and will not tolerate any foreign interference. Should the U.S. Government, brazenly disregarding the Chinese people's repeated warnings and the desire of the people of the world for peace, persist in their aggression and intervention against China and impose war on the Chinese people, it must bear the responsibility for all the serious consequences.

DOCUMENT 59: ROC PRESIDENT CHIANG KAI-SHEK'S REPLIES TO QUESTIONS SUBMITTED BY THE NEW YORK JOURNAL-AMERICAN, SEPTEMBER 15, 1958[33]

. . .

4. Q. Is any invasion of offshore islands or Taiwan possible during the presence in the Taiwan Straits of the U.S. Seventh Fleet?

A. . . . The U.S. Seventh Fleet in the Taiwan Straits is a powerful deterrent against the threat of Communist invasion. We cannot, however, take it for granted that during the presence of the Seventh Fleet in the Taiwan Straits, the Chinese Communists will for that reason not venture to invade the offshore islands or even Taiwan itself.

. . .

7. Q. Is the impression in the U.S. correct that the bombardments are partly to demonstrate to the world that the Chinese Communists cannot be ignored as a major power?

A. The Chinese Communists have always considered the seizure of Taiwan as a condition precedent to the consolidation of their domination of the mainland. In addition, Taiwan is the key to Southeast Asia and the West Pacific. Before the Communists can accomplish their Russian-assigned mission of conquering Southeast Asia, they must first seize Taiwan. But before they can seize Taiwan, they must first invade and occupy the offshore islands of Kinmen and Matsu. Recent Communist broadcasts have bragged repeatedly that their landing on Kinmen was imminent and that their objective was the seizure of Taiwan. These facts have proved that their shelling and encircling of Kinmen are not merely a demonstrative action, but in actuality a prelude to an invasion of Taiwan.

DOCUMENT 60: ROC PRESIDENT CHIANG KAI-SHEK'S
REPLIES TO QUESTIONS SUBMITTED BY CHINESE
AND FOREIGN PRESS, BROADCASTERS, AND
CAMERAMEN, SEPTEMBER 29, 1958[34]

. . .

3. Q. What policy would your government take if the United
States and the Chinese Communists should reach in the Warsaw talks
an agreement not satisfactory to the Republic of China? Do you think
it is possible to arrive at results in the talks that are practicable and
acceptable to all three parties concerned?
A. The talks now under way at Warsaw are only between the
United States and the Chinese Communists. They, therefore, cannot
be described as involving three parties. Moreover, we are opposed
to these talks as a matter of principle. If, however, the present talks
should prove helpful in stopping the Chinese Communists' war of
aggression, I will not object. If, on the other hand, the Chinese
Communists should refuse to stop shelling nor agree to abandon
armed aggression, then what is there to talk about? It is hardly
conceivable that the talks would result in anything acceptable to all
parties concerned.
The Quemoy and Matsu islands do not constitute an obstacle to
peace. During the past nine years, Chinese Communists, operating
from bases on the mainland coast and on adjacent islands, have
repeatedly disturbed peace in the Taiwan Straits. From September 3,
1954, to August 23 of this year, the Chinese Communists shelled the
Quemoy islands 504 times. Every time it was they who started the
hostilities while our garrison troops merely returned fire to stop the
bombardment. This fact clearly shows that it is the Communist bases
on the mainland coast and on the adjacent islands that have been "a
thorn in the side of peace" in the Taiwan Straits, and not our Quemoy
and Matsu islands.
Since August 23, the Chinese Communists, by their indiscriminate
bombardment of the Quemoy islands, have destroyed numerous civilian
houses, schools and hospitals. Our troops have only returned fire.
Either on the land, on the sea, or in the air, our forces have exercised
the utmost self-restraint without taking further retaliatory action.
The course of the fighting for the past month or so is enough to show
who is the provocateur and who is disturbing the peace. But if the
Chinese Communists should continue to bombard these islands in an
attempt to re-blockade them and to starve out our 130,000 troops and
civilians there, we shall at the crucial moment exercise our inherent
right of self-defense and take retaliatory actions against Communist

bases on the mainland. Whether it is for the maintenance of our sovereignty, or for the sake of safeguarding security in the Taiwan Straits area, and to save the lives of our troops and civilians, we shall have no alternative but to discharge our responsibility toward our people there. However, we are not willing to take such a step until and unless we come to the crucial moment.

. . .

5. Q. What will be the attitude and standpoint of the Republic of China, should the Taiwan Straits incident be raised in the United Nations?

A. The Republic of China is one of the founding members of the United Nations. Adherence to the U.N. Charter is clearly stipulated in China's Constitution, and a precedent for this is seldom found in other countries. According to its Charter, the United Nations is an organization formed to protect world peace and security and to maintain justice and humanity. Therefore, wherever in the world there is danger of aggression, the United Nations has the right to discuss it. It is the opinion of our government, however, that the timing and the way to refer the Taiwan Straits problem to the United Nations have to be further examined.

The Battle of Quemoy is the result of the Chinese Communist provocation and is indeed the result of Soviet Russia's instigation. Besides, the Soviet imperialists, threatening the United States with a nuclear war, are encouraging the Chinese Communists in their armed aggression and political blackmail. The Republic of China will bring up the matter before the United Nations at a proper time so that condemnation and sanction can be involved.

6. Q. Is the Republic of China using the Quemoy and Matsu islands as bases for its projected counter-attack on the mainland? What are the main conditions for the counter-attack on the mainland?

A. No, we are not using Quemoy and Matsu for this purpose. The bases for our counter-attack against the mainland are on the mainland itself. The principal condition for our national recovery is the loyalty of the people on the mainland. Therefore, the bases for our counter-attack are not on Quemoy and Matsu.

I must emphasize that all provinces on the Chinese mainland as well as Taiwan, Penghu, Quemoy and Matsu are the territory of the Republic of China. The People on the mainland, like the people on Taiwan, Quemoy and Matsu, are our people. . . .

. . .

As to the question whether Quemoy can ever serve as a base in our counter-attack against the mainland, one must consider it from the standpoint of policy and strategy.

During World War II, when the Allies planned to open a second front in Europe, why was it that they did not simply cross the English Channel at Dover and instead made a detour to Normandy? We are defending Quemoy and Matsu because these islands constitute a shield for Taiwan and not because we intend to use them as springboards for our counter-attack against the mainland. We certainly have no wish to storm positions opposite Quemoy which the Chinese Communists have prepared during the past nine years. Besides, the Communists have concentrated in that area troops three times the size of our garrison forces on Quemoy. The coastal area literally bristles with defense works. To suggest that we begin our counter-attack at Quemoy is merely a conjecture on the part of those who do not understand the strategy involved in our plan for such a counter-attack. Of course, what I have just said has bearing only on our policy and for national recovery.

. . .

DOCUMENT 61: ROC—U.S. JOINT COMMUNIQUÉ OCTOBER 23, 1958[35]

Consultations have been taking place over the past three days between the Government of the United States and the Government of the Republic of China pursuant to Article IV of the Mutual Defense Treaty. These consultations had been invited by President Chiang Kai-shek. The following are among those who took part in the consultations:
For the Republic of China:
President Chiang Kai-shek
Vice-President—Premier Chen Cheng
Secretary-General to the President Chang Chun
Minister of Foreign Affairs Huang Shao-ku
Ambassador to the United States George K. C. Yeh
For the United States of America:
Secretary of State John Foster Dulles
Assistant Secretary of State Walter S. Robertson
Ambassador to the Republic of China Everett F. Drumright.
The consultations had been arranged to be held during the two weeks when the Chinese Communists had declared they would cease fire upon Quemoy. It had been hoped that, under these circumstances, primary consideration could have been given to measures which would

have contributed to stabilizing an actual situation of nonmilitancy.
However, on the eve of the consultations, the Chinese Communists,
in violation of their declaration, resumed artillery fire against the
Quemoys. It was recognized that under the present conditions the
defense of the Quemoys, together with the Matsus, is closely related
to the defense of Taiwan and Penghu.

The two Governments recalled that their Mutual Defense Treaty
had had the purpose of manifesting their unity "so that no potential
aggressor could be under the illusion that either of them stands alone
in the West Pacific Area." The consultations provided a fresh occasion
for demonstrating that unity.

The two Governments reaffirmed their solidarity in the face of
the new Chinese Communist aggression now manifesting itself in the
bombardment of the Quemoys. This aggression and the accompanying
Chinese Communist propaganda have not divided them, as the Communists have hoped. On the contrary, it has drawn them closer together.
They believe that by unitedly opposing aggression they serve not only
themselves but also the cause of peace. As President Eisenhower said
on September 11, the position of opposing aggression by force is the
only position consistent with the peace of the world.

The two Governments took note of the fact that the Chinese
Communists, with the backing of the Soviet Union, avowedly seek to
conquer Taiwan, to eliminate Free China and to expel the United States
from the Western Pacific generally, compelling the United States to
abandon its collective security arrangements with free countries of
that area. This policy cannot possibly succeed. It is hoped and
believed that the Communists, faced by the proven unity, resolution
and strength of the Governments of the United States and the Republic
of China, will not put their policy to the test of general war and that
they will abandon the military steps which they have already taken to
initiate their futile and dangerous policy.

In addition to dealing with the current military situation, the
two Governments considered the broad and long-range aspects of
their relationship.

The United States, its Government and its people, have an abiding
faith in the Chinese people and profound respect for the great contribution which they have made and will continue to make to a civilization
that respects and honors the individual and his family life. The United
States recognizes that the Republic of China is the authentic spokesman
for Free China and of the hopes and aspirations entertained by the
great mass of the Chinese people.

The Government of the Republic of China declared its purpose
to be a worthy representative of the Chinese people and to strive to
preserve those qualities and characteristics which have enabled the
Chinese to contribute so much of benefit to humanity.

The two Governments reaffirmed their dedication to the principles of the Charter of the United Nations. They recalled that the
treaty under which they are acting is defensive in character. The
Government of the Republic of China considers that the restoration
of freedom to its people on the mainland is its sacred mission. It
believes that the foundation of this mission resides in the minds and
the hearts of the Chinese people and that the principal means of
successfully achieving its mission is the implementation of Dr. Sun
Yat-sen's three people's principles (nationalism, democracy and
social well-being) and not the use of force.

The consultations which took place permitted a thorough study
and reexamination of the pressing problems of mutual concern. As
such, they have proved to be of great value to both Governments. It
is believed that such consultations should continue to be held at appropriate intervals.

DOCUMENT 62: PRC DEFENSE MINISTER P'ENG TEH-HUAI'S SECOND MESSAGE TO COMPATRIOTS IN TAIWAN, OCTOBER 25, 1958[36]

Compatriots, military and civilian, in Taiwan, Penghu, Quemoy
and Matsu:

We are fully aware that the overwhelming majority of you are
patriots, and only extremely few among you are willing slaves of the
Americans. Compatriots! Chinese problems can only be settled by
us Chinese. If they are difficult to settle for the time being, things
can be talked over at length. The American political broker Dulles
likes to poke his nose into other people's business. He wants to take
a hand in the matter of the long-standing dispute between the Kuomintang and the Communist Party, and order Chinese to do this or that,
to harm the interests of the Chinese and serve the interests of the
Americans. That is to say: step one, to isolate Taiwan; step two,
to place Taiwan under trusteeship. If things do not turn out to their
liking, they can resort to the most sinister measures. Do you know
how General Chang Tso-lin met his death? There is a place called
Huangkutun in northeast China, and it was there that he was done to
death. No imperialist in the world has any conscience. And the
American imperialists are especially vicious, at least no better than
the Japanese who did Chang Tso-lin to death. Compatriots! I advise
you to be a little more careful. I advise you not to depend too much
on other people, lest all your rights and authority be taken away. To
arrange things between our two Parties is very easy. I have already
ordered our troops at the Fukien front not to shell the airfield in
Quemoy and the wharf, beach and ships at Liaolo Bay on even days of

the calendar, so that the compatriots, both military and civilian, on
the big and small islands of Greater Quemoy, Lesser Quemoy, Tatan,
Erhtan and others may all get sufficient supplies, including food, vegetables, edible oils, fuels and military equipment, to facilitate your
entrenchment for a long time to come. If you are short of anything,
just say so and we will give it to you. It is time now to turn from foe
into friend. Your ships and aircraft should not come on odd days.
We will not necessarily conduct shelling on odd days. But you should
refrain from coming, to avoid possible losses. In this way, half of
each month will be free for transportation, and supplies would not
be lacking. Some of you suspect that we want to undermine the unity
between your troops and civilians and between your officers and men.
No, compatriots! We hope you will strengthen your unity, so as to
act in unison in facing up to the foreigners. Fight-fight-stop-stop,
half-fight, half-stop: this is no trick but a normal thing in the present
specific circumstances. Our refraining from shelling the airfield,
the wharf, the beach and the ships is still conditional on not introducing
American escorts. Exception will be taken if there should be escorts.
In the Chiang-Dulles talks, you have suffered a little loss. Now you
have only the right of speaking for "Free China"; in addition, you are
still permitted to represent a small part of the overseas Chinese.
The Americans have conferred upon you the title of a small China.
On October 23, the U.S. Department of State published an interview
Dulles had given to a correspondent of a British broadcasting company
which was recorded in advance on October 16. The interview was
made public as soon as Dulles took off from Taiwan. Dulles said that
he saw a China of the Communists, that, since this country actually
exists, he was willing to deal with it, and so on. Thank heaven, our
country is seen by an American lord. This is a big China. Under the
force of circumstances, the Americans have changed their policy and
treated you as a "de facto political unit," that is to say, in fact, not as
a country. Such a "de facto political unit" is still needed by the
Americans at the initial stage starting from the present time. That
means isolating Taiwan. In the second stage, Taiwan is to be placed
under trusteeship. Friends of the Kuomintang! Do you not yet sense
this danger? Where is the way out? Please think it over. The document issued after the Chiang-Dulles talks this time was only a communiqué devoid of legal force. It is easy to shake yourselves free,
depending on whether you have the determination or not. There is
only one China, not two, in the world. On this we agree. All Chinese
people, including you and compatriots abroad, absolutely will not
allow the American plot forcibly to create two Chinas to come true.
The present age is an age full of hope. All patriots have a future and
should not be afraid of the imperialists. Of course, we are not advising
you to break with the Americans right away. That would be an

unrealistic idea. We only hope that you will not yield to American pressure, submit to their every whim and will, lose your sovereign rights, and so finally be deprived of shelter in the world and thrown into the sea. These words of ours are well-intentioned and bear no ill-will. You will come to understand them by and by.

> Peng Teh-huai
> Minister of National Defense

DOCUMENT 63: "ON THE CHIANG KAI-SHEK—DULLES TALKS," PEOPLE'S DAILY, OCTOBER 30, 1958[37]

Not long ago, U.S. Secretary of State Dulles went to Taiwan and held talks with Chiang Kai-shek. Now the United States is ballyhooing these talks as marking a change in U.S. policy toward China, as having strengthened the unity between the United States and Chiang Kai-shek and as a manifestation of U.S. peaceful intentions. There is indeed a change in U.S. policy toward China—its plot to create "two Chinas" is coming out into the open. This change, however, merely amounts to the implementation in another form of its policy of aggression and war against China. There are no peaceful intentions whatsoever about it. Dulles' aim in these talks was to force Chiang to accept the "two Chinas" scheme. He has actually made some gains in this respect. However, his dream is far from being realized. As to the lip service paid to greater unity, that is just so much eyewash.

. . .

On the eve of publication of the communiqué on the Chiang-Dulles talks, U.S. Vice-President Richard Nixon declared publicly that there was a "need for an independent Chinese government to which both the twelve million people on Formosa and the millions more of overseas Chinese can owe allegiance." In the Chiang-Dulles joint communiqué of October 23, Dulles forced the Taiwan authorities to accept the so-called principle of no recourse to the use of force, and granted the Chiang Kai-shek clique the right to represent only "free China." This appeared to be an agreement between Chiang Kai-shek and Dulles.

. . .

The creation of the "two Chinas," it must be pointed out, is merely a matter of expediency for the United States. The United States wants first to separate Taiwan from China and isolate it completely, so as to facilitate its control over the Chiang Kai-shek

clique and strengthen its occupation of Taiwan. But this is only a
first step. Once Taiwan should become a "de facto political unit"
independent of China, the United States could then use some pretext
or other to place it under trusteeship. In this way, the United States
would make a double gain: on the one hand, it would legalize its
seizure of Taiwan and turn that island into a U.S. colony; at the same
time, by involving certain other countries, it would get them to share
its responsibility for aggression. The Chiang Kai-shek clique clearly
has no place in this sinister U.S. scheme. Nixon declared that the
aim of the United States in the Far East was to make Taiwan an "island
of freedom" rather than "to tie the United States policy to Chiang Kai-
shek." Isn't the meaning of these words clear enough?

It is very absurd for the United States to abuse the principle
of no recourse to the use of force in international relations, by trying
to apply it to China's internal affairs. By so doing, the United States
aims to tie the hands of the Taiwan authorities and make them completely subservient to the U.S. The Taiwan authorities are not unaware
of this. That is why, after the release of the Chiang-Dulles joint
communiqué, they made such a hullabaloo about there being reservations to their declaration on renunciation of the use of force. However,
the United States featured this same declaration as its major victory.
Both parties are clinging to their own interpretation and making a
big fuss about it. It was in these circumstances that, at his press
conference on October 28, Dulles, as if handing down a verdict, came
out bluntly with the remark that, despite all their reservations, the
Taiwan authorities "didn't have much chance of winning by force."
Coming from Dulles, isn't this a deliberate attempt to make it difficult
for the Taiwan authorities even to drag on their miserable existence?

We stated long ago that it is absolutely impossible for the U.S.
to carry through its plot of creating "two Chinas" so as to occupy
Taiwan indefinitely. The Chinese people who have stood up are
confident that they can smash this U.S. plot. There is only one China
in the world, not two. Every patriotic Chinese opposes the "two
Chinas" scheme. The masses of overseas Chinese oppose it. Even
the Taiwan authorities do not agree to it. On October 24, Chiang Kai-
shek said that Taiwan and the mainland were part of the same entity,
with a flesh and blood relationship, sharing the common weal and
woe. We believe that the U.S. scheme to split China and create "two
Chinas" will be utterly defeated if the whole Chinese people unite and
face the foreign foe.

. . .

The United States realizes that a direct proposal of the "two Chinas"
scheme just will not work. That is why it is employing a series of

crafty devices such as demands for a cease-fire, renunciation of
the use of force, reduction of Chiang Kai-shek's troops on the offshore
islands, and so on and so forth. But no patriotic Chinese will permit
the U.S. to use such devices to meddle in the internal affairs of China
and realize its aim of creating "two Chinas."

The U.S. is purposely confusing public opinion in order to sell
the world its scheme for the creation of "two Chinas." The U.S. says:
just as there can be two Koreas, two Viet-nams, two Germanys, why
can't there be "two Chinas"? But this is absolutely ridiculous. The
existence of two Germanys is an outcome of the Second World War.
The division of Korea and Vietnam into northern and southern parts
is a temporary state of affairs provided for by the relevant international agreements. They provide no basis for comparison with the
forcible U.S. occupation of Taiwan and its obstruction of the unification
of China. The U.S. has used every possible means and done its utmost
to obstruct the unification of Germany, Korea and Viet-nam, and now
it is trying to turn division of these three nations into a justification
for creating "two Chinas" and perpetuating its occupation of Taiwan.
Not only is this an utterly untenable position; it exposes the U.S.
crimes of aggression all over the world.

. . .

Faced by the resolute opposition of the Chinese people, the U.S. is
planning to implement its "two Chinas" plot by means of a so-called
international settlement. It is trying to get the question of the situation
in the Taiwan Straits area submitted to the United Nations. It is true
that U.S. aggression against and interference in China have created
tension in the Taiwan Straits area and the United Nations should have
dealt with it, but since the People's Republic of China is deprived
of its legitimate place in the United Nations, the United Nations has
lost its competence to handle this question. As to the Chinese people's
liberation of Taiwan, Penghu, Quemoy and Matsu to complete the
unification of their motherland, this is an internal matter and the
U.N. has no right to interfere in it at all. No Chinese with any sense
of self-respect will ever agree to the submission of this question to
the U.N. The U.S. is also trying to interfere in China's internal affairs
and obstruct the Chinese people's liberation of Taiwan, Penghu, Quemoy
and Matsu through some sort of international court, referendum,
international mediation or other kind of so-called international settlement. The Chinese people will tolerate none of this. We are convinced
that no fair-minded nation or people will fall into these U.S. traps.

. . .

DOCUMENT 64: ELY MAURER, "LEGAL PROBLEMS REGARDING FORMOSA AND THE OFFSHORE ISLANDS."[38]

International Legal Problems

On the international front it is best to examine the problem of Formosa separately from the problem of the offshore islands [Quemoy and Matsu in the vicinity of the coast of Fukien Province].

In giving the historical background of Formosa it has been pointed out that at Cairo the Allies stated it was their purpose to restore Formosa to Chinese sovereignty and that at the end of the war the Republic of China receive the surrender of Japanese forces on Formosa. It has also been pointed out that under the Japanese Peace Treaty Japan renounced all right, title, and claim to Formosa. However, neither in that treaty nor in any other treaty has there been any definitive cession to China of Formosa. The situation is, then, one where the Allied Powers still have to come to some agreement or treaty with respect to the status of Formosa. Any action, therefore, of the Chinese Communist regime to seize Formosa constitutes an attempt to seize by force territory which does not belong to it. Such a seizure is prohibited by international law and the United Nations Charter as an attempt to settle claim to territory by force. It would thus appear that the United States is within its legal rights in taking action to defend Formosa.

With respect to the offshore islands the situation is admittedly somewhat different. There is no question that these islands are a part of the state of China. It may be admitted further that these islands are close to the mainland of China. However, the offshore islands have been in the possession and effective control of the Government of the Republic of China since its inception, except for the period of the Japanese war. Since 1949 a status quo has come into existence vis-à-vis the Peiping regime. It is this status quo which the Chinese Communists have threatened with the menace of armed force. It is our view that we have here in fact a situation comparable to that which obtained in Korea preceding the invasion of south Korea by north Korea. In other words, the action of the Chinese Communists in taking warlike measures is an effort to change the status quo and to gain additional territory by force in violation of the prohibitions of the United Nations Charter.

It has been urged that this is essentially a civil war and therefore it is improper for the United States to participate with the Government of the Republic of China in defense of the offshore islands. It should first be pointed out that it is too narrow to look upon the conflict merely as a civil war. Even as early as the end of the war with Japan the Soviet Union, in violation of its treaty with the Chinese Nationalists, turned over large stores of equipment and in other ways furnished material aid to the Chinese Communists. Since that time the Soviet Union has continued giving large assistance to the Chinese Communist regime. Thus much of the ammunition, artillery, and planes that are at present being used by that regime derive from Russian sources. And the Soviet Union is allied by military treaty with the Chinese regime. On the other hand the United States has vital interests in the Formosa area and is allied with the Republic of China in a Mutual Defense Treaty and has agreements to supply arms for defensive purposes. In the circumstances it seems fair to say that we are here involved in what is realistically an international dispute which the Communist regime is attempting to settle by force.

Further with respect to the argument that this is a civil war, it will be recalled that this was the same argument that was made by Vishinsky regarding the north Korean invasion of south Korea. It was an argument however which the United Nations paid no heed to but, instead, viewed the action of the north Koreans as one of aggression which came under the ban of the United Nations Charter.

. . .

On this phase of the matter it is our view, then, that the United States would be justified from an international standpoint in cooperating with the Republic of China in the defense of the offshore islands and Formosa.

NOTES

1. Excerpt from American Foreign Policy, 1950-1955, Basic Documents, II (Washington, D.C.: U.S. Government Printing Office, 1957), 2468.

2. Excerpt from China Handbook 1951 (Taipei: China Publishing Co., 1951), p. 115.

3. Excerpt from Chinese People's Institute of Foreign Affairs, ed., Oppose U.S. Occupation of Taiwan and "Two Chinas" Plot (Peking: Foreign Languages Press, 1958), p. 3.

4. Excerpt translated in ibid., pp. 5-6.

5. United Nations Document S/1715 (August 24, 1950).

6. Excerpt from United Nations Security Council, Official Records, (S/P.V.527), 5th Year, 527th Meeting, No. 69, August 29, 1950, pp. 5-7, 9-10.

7. Translated from Chung-hua min-kuo wai-chiao wen-t'i yen-chiu hui, Chin-shan ho-yüeh yu chung-jih ho-yüeh ti kuan-hsi

(The relationship between the San Francisco peace treaty and the Sino-Japanese peace treaty) (Taipei: Chung-hua min-kuo wai-chiao wen-t'i yen-chiu hui, 1966), pp. 5-7.

8. Excerpt translated from ibid., pp. 11-12.

9. Excerpt translated from ibid., pp. 14-15, 16; English text supplied by the ROC Ministry of Foreign Affairs.

10. Excerpt translated from ibid., pp. 28-29.

11. Excerpt translated from ibid., pp. 29, 30-32; English version supplied by the ROC Ministry of Foreign Affairs. The English version does not conform entirely to the Chinese text. The underlined part does not appear in the Chinese text and the part in brackets does not appear in the English version.

12. Excerpt from Selected Speeches and Messages of President Chiang Kai-shek, 1949-1952 (Taipei: Office of the Government Spokesman, 1952), pp. 87-89.

13. Excerpt from Hsinhua News Agency, Daily News Release, No. 777 (Peking: China Information Bureau, Press Administration, August 16, 1951), pp. 75-78.

14. Excerpt from United Nations Treaty Series, CXXXVIII, pp. 38, 40, 42, 44, 46, 48, 50, 52. The treaty came into force on August 5, 1952.

15. Excerpt from Oppose U.S. Occupation of Taiwan and "Two Chinas" Plot, pp. 16-17.

16. United Nations Treaty Series, CCXLVIII (New York: The United Nations, 1958), pp. 214-216, 226, 228. The treaty came into force on March 3, 1955.

17. Excerpt from Oppose U.S. Occupation of Taiwan and "Two Chinas" Plot, pp. 18-23, 25-27.

18. House Joint Resolution 159, 84th Congress, 1st Session, January 29, 1955. United States Statutes at Large, LXIX (Washington, D.C.: U.S. Government Printing Office, 1955), p. 7.

19. Excerpt from President Chiang Kai-shek: Selected Speeches and Messages in 1955 (Taipei: Government Information Office), pp. 20-21, 22-23.

20. Excerpt from ibid., pp. 26, 27-28.

21. Excerpt from American Foreign Policy, 1950-1955, Basic Documents, II, pp. 2504-06.

22. Excerpt from Hsinhua News Agency, Daily News Release, No. 2158 (January 19, 1956), pp. 188-91.

23. Excerpt from President Chiang Kai-shek: Selected Speeches and Messages in 1956 (Taipei: Government Information Office), p. 21.

24. Excerpt from Oppose U.S. Occupation of Taiwan and "Two Chinas" Plot, pp. 41-44, 46-51.

25. Excerpt from Hsinhua News Agency, Daily News Release, No. 2398, Supplement (September 15, 1956), pp. 1, 42, 48.

26. Excerpt from ibid., No. 2570 (March 6, 1957), p. 62.

27. Excerpt from President Chiang Kai-shek: Selected Speeches and Messages in 1957 (Taipei: Government Information Office), pp. 45-46.

28. Excerpt from Oppose U.S. Occupation of Taiwan and "Two Chinas" Plot, pp. 55-56, 57-58.

29. Memorandum of the Department of State sent to all U.S. overseas missions as Circular Instruction 1452, August 12, 1958; excerpt from American Foreign Policy, Current Documents, 1958 (Washington, D.C.: U.S. Government Printing Office, 1962), pp. 1138, 1139, 1143.

30. Excerpt from Department of State Bulletin, XXXIX, 1004 (September 22, 1958), 445-46.

31. Peking Review, I, 28 (September 9, 1958), 21.

32. Excerpt from ibid., pp. 15-16.

33. Excerpt from President Chiang Kai-shek: Selected Speeches and Messages in 1958 (Taipei: Government Information Office), pp. 55, 57-58.

34. Excerpt from ibid., pp. 66-73.

35. American Foreign Policy, Current Documents, 1958, pp. 1184-85.

36. Peking Review, I, 35 (October 28, 1958), 5.

37. Excerpt from ibid., No. 36 (November 4, 1958), pp. 9-11.

38. Excerpt from Department of State Bulletin, XXXIX, 1017 (December 22, 1958), 1009-10. Maurer was assistant legal adviser for Far Eastern affairs. This was an address made before the Washington chapter of the Federal Bar Association on November 20, 1958.

**OFFICIAL DOCUMENTS
CONCERNING THE QUESTION
OF TAIWAN, 1959-72**

DOCUMENT 65: U.S. PRESIDENT EISENHOWER'S
REPLY TO A QUESTION AT A NEWS
CONFERENCE, OCTOBER 22, 1959[1]

. . . When the subject of Red China was brought up between Mr.
Khrushchev and me [at the Camp David talks], there was no further
discussion other than the statement of our two separate positions,
And it was then agreed only one thing, which was [that] there was no
sense in pushing the discussion any further because our viewpoints
were so far apart.

On the other hand, I notice that as quickly as he went out to
China, he made one or two speeches in which he put forth the generali-
zation that all international disputes should be solved by peaceful
means, in negotiation.

Now, I think that both China and Russia argue that the Formosa-
Red China dispute is from their viewpoint an internal one and not
international. But, after all, I believe there are 42 or more nations—
I forget how many, but a great number of nations—that recognize the
independence of Formosa, so I think certainly the rest of the world
would take it as a threat to international peace.

DOCUMENT 66: FROM A 1959 MAO INTERVIEW[2]

The Words and Deeds of the Leaders of the Communist Party
of China.—Concerning an Interview With Mao Tse-tung. (By Eduardo
Mora Valverde, member of the leadership of the People's Vanguard
Party of Costa Rica. Izvestia, June 19, p. 2. 2,000 words. Condensed
text:) . . . [At a meeting of leaders of a number of Latin American

Communist and Workers' Parties with Comrade Mao Tse-tung on
March 3, 1959, he declared:|
    "We have thrown out the North American imperialists from the
continent, but they are holding out on Taiwan. We have warned them
to get out of there, but they refuse. Perhaps you can suggest some
means to us. You know about the events of last year. The island of
Quemoy has a population of only 80,000, but it is now known to the
entire world. The U.S.A. does not object to the islands of Quemoy
and Matsu being given back to us, but in return it wishes to retain
Taiwan for itself. This would be an unprofitable deal. We had better
wait; let Chiang Kai-shek stay on Quemoy and Matsu, and we shall
get them back later, together with the Pescadores and Taiwan. Our
territory is spacious, and for the time being we can get along without
these islands."
    But Mao Tse-tung continued developing his idea, and in the course
of the interview another Mao Tse-tung, quite unlike the one we had
known before, gradually began to appear before us. His words
astonished us. He said: "We do not want conciliation with the U.S.A.
The United States must submit to us. Otherwise we do not wish to
enter into negotiations with them. It is unimportant if they do not
return Taiwan to us for another 100 years. If they do not recognize
us, then we have no desire to recognize them either." . . .
    During the conversation Mao Tse-tung spoke quite disdainfully
about the opportunities provided by the U.N. for the peoples' struggle
for peace. Holding to entirely different views, our parties have for
many years mobilized their peoples in order to achieve the admission
of the Chinese People's Republic into the U.N. But, as it turned out,
the C.P.C. leaders viewed these efforts with scorn. The government
headed by Mao Tse-tung was willing to examine "the possibilities of
joining or refusing to join" this important organization only if the
puppet government of Taiwan were expelled from the U.N. Mao Tse-
tung told us then: "China has no legal status in the international arena.
The Western countries consider China an outlaw state. And that is
why we can act without regard for laws that restrict us. We act in
whatever way we please. This is why we are in no hurry to join the
U.N. We shall not poke our nose into this cesspool. . . ."

DOCUMENT 67: ROC PRESIDENT CHIANG KAI-SHEK'S
ADDRESS AT THE OPENING OF THE THIRD SESSION
OF THE FIRST NATIONAL ASSEMBLY,
FEBRUARY 20, 1960[3]

    If the Free World, in the face of a double game of political
chicanery and military threat alternately played by Soviet Russia and

the Chinese Communists, should continue to entertain absurd illusions and to endure Communist insults and deceptions without waking up, it will only sink deeper into the pit of fear of war. In the end, it will be so helplessly bewildered that it will cease to think of the proper way to remove the threat of war at its very source. The situation will necessarily deteriorate until the Free World fails to distinguish disaster from blessing, harm from benefit, and even mistakes what is easy for what is difficult, and mistakes a foe as a friend. At the same time, it will neglect what is near at hand and seek what is beyond reach, and forsake the fundamentals in favor of the trivialities. This is how the present abnormal psychology vis-à-vis the Communist bloc has come into being in the Free World. Thus, today some of the free nations no longer dare to assert that territorially the Chinese mainland comes under the sovereignty of the Republic of China. Instead they argue speciously that Kunmen and Matsu are islands off the mainland. They dare not say that the Free World should respect the legitimate continuity of the Republic of China and its authority to unify its own territory. The United Nations has also failed to discharge its obligations toward its member states in defending international justice and in asserting the power of moral principles. Moreover, some of the nations, being anxious to avert the dangers of war, are freely talking about "two Chinas." This cowardly and selfish attitude is like pacifying the tiger with one's own flesh, and inviting the robber to become master of the house. This being the case, how will it ever be possible to stop the Communist bloc from asking for a foot when it is given an inch and from going on endlessly from aggression to aggression, from expansion to expansion? In their present state of mind, these nations naturally regard our holy mission of recovering the mainland and delivering our compatriots there from Communist tyranny as an act that will touch off another world war. They do not seem to realize that their fear of the Communists and their appeasing policy will eventually plunge the whole of mankind into the abyss of a disastrous war. Herein lies the greatest danger for the Free World today!

Of course, the recovery of the mainland and the deliverance of our compatriots there from Communist tyranny are the sacred missions from which we are morally bound never to fall back. However, we cannot ask any of the friendly countries in the Free World to provide us military forces in our effort to recover our own territory, nor can we act in disregard of our obligations which we have undertaken in international agreements. Consequently, although the troubles caused by the aggression of international Communism are of a global concern, I have always been of the view that the defeat of the Chinese Communists and the deliverance of our mainland compatriots are a responsibility which we alone should assume.

DOCUMENT 68:   ROC PRESIDENT CHIANG KAI-SHEK'S
ANSWERS TO QUESTIONS SUBMITTED BY THE
HONOLULU ADVERTISER, JULY 9, 1960[4]

3. Q. Will the Republic of China be willing to surrender Kinmen
(Quemoy) and Matsu?   That is, will the Republic of China ever compromise on these offshore islands?

A. Kinmen and Matsu are part of the territory of the Republic
of China and have been consistently administered by the Chinese
government.

From the military point of view, Kinmen and Matsu, because of
their geographical position, are of great strategic importance. On
the one hand, they are outposts indispensable to the defense of Taiwan
and Penghu; they are the free world's lifeline in the Western Pacific;
they are useful observation posts to keep a close watch on Communist
shipping movements in the Foochow and Amoy harbors, thereby
forestalling any possible Communist military build-up for the invasion
of Taiwan. On the other hand, our garrison forces on these islands
are tying up 500,000 Communist forces along the Fukien and Chekiang
coasts, thus keeping them from launching armed aggression in other
parts of Asia.

From the political point of view and also in relation to people
on the Chinese mainland, the very presence of our armed forces on
Kinmen and Matsu, only a stone's throw from the mainland, makes
our compatriots across the Taiwan Straits feel that help is within
reach. This keeps alive their hope for deliverance from under the
Communist yoke. Encouraged by this knowledge, anti-Communist
revolutionary forces on the mainland are bound to grow rapidly to
shake the very foundation of the Communist regime and to hasten the
recovery of the mainland.

From the international point of view, Kinmen and Matsu today
have become West Berlin in the Far East. They stand as a symbol
of the democratic world's determination to resist aggression and to
defend freedom. If anything should happen to them, it would not only
mean the loss of two bulwarks protecting Taiwan and Penghu, but
also the unleashing of the Chinese Communist forces for aggression
against other areas with impunity. In that event, the security of Asia
and the whole free world would be seriously endangered.

In view of the aforementioned reasons, under no circumstances
will the government of the Republic of China ever consider giving up
Kinmen and Matsu. This stand permits no compromise whatsoever.

DOCUMENT 69: PRC PREMIER CHOU EN-LAI'S
REPLIES TO QUESTIONS SUBMITTED BY
FELIX GREENE, SEPTEMBER 5, 1960[5]

Question: It would seem that no fundamental improvement in the relations between China and the United States is possible as long as the issue of Taiwan (or Formosa as we call it) remains unresolved. Am I right?

Answer: You are right. So long as the United States continues to occupy Taiwan, there can be no basic improvement in the relations between China and the United States. Supposing Long Island in the United States were occupied by another country, could the United States improve its relations with that country? The Chinese Government has always stood for the settlement of international disputes through negotiations, without resorting to the use or threat of force. It is even willing to sit down and talk with the U.S. Government, which has invaded and occupied China's territory Taiwan. The Chinese-United States ambassadorial talks were started on China's initiative. But, as the United States Government persists in occupying Taiwan by force, the talks have dragged out for five years, through a hundred sessions without results so far.

Question: Are there any conceivable arrangements regarding Taiwan under which China would be prepared to consider a compromise?

Answer: Taiwan is an inalienable part of China's territory. This is a historical fact. The Cairo and the Potsdam Declarations, both signed by the U.S. Government, confirm that Taiwan is Chinese territory. After the Japanese surrender, Taiwan was formally restored to China on October 25, 1945, and was taken over and administered by the then Chinese Government. Liberation of Taiwan by the Chinese people, like the liberation of the mainland of China, is purely China's internal affair in which no foreign country can interfere. The question now is that the U.S. Government is occupying China's territory Taiwan with its armed forces and blocking the Chinese Government from exercising its sovereignty in Taiwan. There is only one way to settle this question. The U.S. Government must agree to withdraw all its armed forces from Taiwan and the Taiwan Straits.

For quite some time now, the U.S. Government has been scheming to create "two Chinas." In this regard, both the Republican and the Democratic Parties in the United States have the same policy. The United States seeks to set up what they call an "independent state" of Taiwan, or a "Sino-Formosan nation," or to conduct what they call a "plebiscite" in Taiwan, or even to place Taiwan "under trusteeship," and so on. All this is aimed at dismembering Chinese territory,

violating China's sovereign rights and legalizing the seizure of
Taiwan by the United States. All the Chinese people, including those
on Taiwan, are firmly opposed to these schemes; even those members
of the Chiang Kai-shek clique who have the slightest concern for the
national interest don't approve of them.

DOCUMENT 70: "100 MEETINGS OF SINO-U.S. TALKS,"
PEOPLE'S DAILY, SEPTEMBER 8, 1960[6]

Five years have elapsed and one hundred meetings have been held
since the Sino-U.S. ambassadorial talks opened on August 1, 1955. . . .

. . .

        The root cause of the failure of the Sino-U.S. talks to achieve
any positive results thus far lies in the fact that U.S. imperialism
stubbornly persists in its aggressive policy of hostility toward China.
This was demonstrated most clearly in the discussion of the main
subject of the Sino-U.S. talks—the question of easing and eliminating
tension in the Taiwan area. The U.S. occupation of Taiwan is an act
of naked aggression against China. The Chinese people have every
right to take any measure to oppose aggression and safeguard their
sovereignty and territorial integrity. Since the tension was created
by U.S. persistence in its aggression, the responsibility for it
naturally does not lie with China—the victim of aggression—but with
the aggressor, U.S. imperialism. Even so, in order to safeguard
Asian and world peace, the Chinese side is still prepared to sit down
and negotiate with the United States. This alone is adequate proof
that we are for the settlement of international disputes by means of
negotiation and without resort to force.
        During the talks, our country has time and again proposed that
China and the United States issue a joint statement to the effect that
they would settle disputes between the two countries by peaceful means
and without resort to force or threat of force and also suggested ways
of negotiating toward this end. However, the United States deliberately
confuses the international dispute between China and the United States
with the internal affairs of China. It not only continues to forcibly
occupy our territory of Taiwan, but also demands that China renounce
the use of force to liberate its own territory of Taiwan. Taiwan is
Chinese territory. Whether the Chinese people use force or peaceful
means to liberate Taiwan is China's internal affair and the Chinese
people's own business. The United States has no right whatever to
interfere. What should be settled at the Sino-U.S. talks is the international dispute between the two countries resulting from U.S. armed

occupation of China's territory of Taiwan. This dispute can be settled only by the United States agreeing to renounce the use of force and withdrawing all its armed forces from Taiwan Straits area. But the United States insists that it has the so-called "right of self-defense" in Taiwan. This is carrying absurdity to an extreme. On Chinese territory the United States can have no so-called "right of self-defense"—only the obligation to withdraw from China's territory.

The United States demand that China should not use force under any circumstances in the Taiwan area is, in fact, a demand that China recognize that the United States has the right to permanently occupy China's territory while the Chinese people are to be deprived of their right to liberate their own territory. U.S. designs to permanently occupy our territory of Taiwan and turn it into a U.S. colony are unmistakably clear. But the Chinese people will never allow this U.S. imperialist scheme to be realized. Is it for the purpose of legalizing the U.S. occupation of Taiwan that we have held talks with the United States? Is it to beg peace from U.S. imperialism at the expense of our own territory of Taiwan that we have held talks with the United States?

What have been the policies and actions of China and the United States in international affairs during the Sino-U.S. talks? The Chinese Government has in the past five years given active support to all proposals favorable to the relaxation of international tension put forward by the Soviet Union and other socialist countries regarding disarmament, abolition of military bases on foreign soil and the banning of nuclear weapons. The Chinese Government has also repeatedly put forward proposals aimed at easing tension, not only in the Taiwan area but also in Asia and the Pacific region. Recently, our Premier Chou En-lai once more proposed that all countries of Asia and the Pacific region conclude a peace pact of mutual non-aggression and turn this area into one free of nuclear weapons. This peace proposal has evoked a warm response from the people throughout the world. Yet it was openly opposed by the U.S. Government, which is unwilling to see the easing of tension in Taiwan and the Far Eastern area. Not only do the U.S. armed forces hang on to Taiwan and the Taiwan Straits, they carry out incessant military provocations and armed threats and repeatedly intrude into China's air space and territorial waters. The United States continues to expand its network of military bases in Asia and the Pacific region and reinforce its aggressive military blocs; it has signed a new treaty of military alliance with Japan, dispatched to the Far Eastern area cruisers, submarines and aircraft loaded with or capable of carrying nuclear weapons and openly clamors and prepares for a nuclear war.

At the same time, the United States, vainly attempting to turn Taiwan into an "unsinkable aircraft-carrier" for aggression against

China and the Far Eastern area, stops at nothing in carrying out its plots to create "two Chinas." It even advanced such absurd proposals as the setting up of a so-called "Sino-Formosan nation" and placing Taiwan under "trusteeship," all for the purpose of permanently occupying China's territory of Taiwan.

All this is in no way different from what Japanese militarism did in the past—first occupying the Chinese territory of Taiwan and creating the so-called "Manchukuo" after invading China's northeast, then launching an all-out war of aggression against China and the Far East as well as the Pacific region. All this reveals most clearly that what U.S. imperialism seeks is to continue its aggression against China, plot to expand this aggression, maintain and aggravate tension in the Taiwan Straits area and the Far East and create "two Chinas." It is therefore not at all surprising that the Sino-U.S. talks have lasted more than five years without making the least progress.

DOCUMENT 71: U.S. SECRETARY OF STATE RUSK'S REPLY TO A QUESTION ASKED BY A REPRESENTATIVE OF THE BRITISH BROADCASTING CORPORATION, MARCH 3, 1961[7]

. . . The United States has very specific commitments to the [Chinese Nationalist] Government on Formosa and to the security of that island. . . . Those commitments stand, and there is no question about them.

. . .

The [Chinese Nationalist] leadership from the mainland, not just Government officials but their professors, their scholars, their scientists, their artists that came over there [to Taiwan], were to us and are a much more genuine representation of the China that we have known. . . . I'm talking in this context about the great cultural heritage of China. I think you would find a more direct expression of that in Formosa than you would in another regime.

DOCUMENT 72: ROC PRESIDENT CHIANG KAI-SHEK'S ANSWERS TO QUESTIONS SUBMITTED BY MARVIN LIEBMAN, JUNE 11, 1961[8]

[4.] (d) What would be the effect of U.S. recognition of Red China on such Chinese?

A. In such an eventuality, all Chinese in this area would
lose faith in the United States and the free world as a whole. More
important, the governments and peoples of all countries in this part
of the world would conclude that the leading force of the free world
has already decided to hand the entire continent of Asia to the International Communists on a silver platter. Under such circumstances,
they would be compelled to turn from the free world to the Communist
orbit. The consequences would be unthinkable. I do not believe that
the United States, for the sake of her own interest and the interest of
the entire free world, would take such a rash step.

5. Q. Both the Republic of China and the Peiping regime have
expressed opposition to a "two Chinas" policy. Do you believe there
is any chance that the Peiping regime will change its tactics in view
of the possible benefits which might result, and agree to a "two
Chinas" policy? If such an eventuality takes place and the United
States recognizes Peiping and also continues its recognition and
alliance with the Republic of China, what would be the attitude of your
Government?

A. In the first place, I do not think it is advisable for the
United States to permit her policy to be determined by manipulations
of the Chinese Communists. Such a purely passive line of thinking
would get the United States into trouble in whatever move she may
make. Whether the United States should recognize the Chinese
Communists must be considered as a matter of basic policy, as it
has been in the past. Should undue emphasis be laid upon tactics,
basic policy considerations would inevitably suffer and the initiative
would be lost to the Communists.

Second, the so-called "two Chinas" concept is, to put it bluntly,
only wishful thinking entertained by neutralists who hope to achieve
peace without paying any price for it. Our friends in the United States
and other free countries must realize that the existence of free China
is based upon the conviction that free society must in the end triumph
over the Communist system of slavery. The "two Chinas" theory
totally negates this conviction and would, therefore, deprive free
China of the only basis on which its sacred mission could be carried
out. Here it should be very clear that the "two Chinas" theory,
whether or not accepted by the Peiping regime, would in effect
facilitate the Chinese Communists in their attempt to destroy free
China. Any arrangement derived from this line of thinking, therefore,
not only will be totally unacceptable to the Government of the Republic
of China, but should not receive the consideration of any responsible
quarters in the free world.

DOCUMENT 73: PRC VICE-PREMIER CHEN YI'S
TELEVISION INTERVIEW WITH RUSSEL
SPURR AND ALEXANDRE DES
FONTAINES, JUNE 29, 1961[9]

Question three: Do you see any hope of a settlement of the long-standing disputes between China and the United States?

Answer: The United States has occupied China's territory Taiwan by force. And the Chinese people are resolutely opposed to this aggressive and interventionist policy of the United States. Such is the essence of the Sino-American dispute. If the United States withdraws all its armed forces from Taiwan and the Taiwan Straits and stops interfering in China's internal affairs, it will be entirely possible to settle the dispute peacefully. We hope that the dispute will be settled peacefully and we have worked for this. Indeed, we have been doing so for eleven years. But whether there will be a settlement depends entirely on the United States. Taiwan was already an inalienable part of China's territory long before Columbus discovered the new continent of America. We are deeply convinced that, no matter how long Taiwan may continue to be seized by the United States, it will in the end return to the motherland. The more the United States puts off a settlement of this question, the more disadvantageous will be the position of the United States.

DOCUMENT 74: "THERE IS ONLY ONE CHINA,
NOT TWO," PEOPLE'S DAILY,
JULY 14, 1961[10]

The Kennedy Administration of the United States, in pursuance of its "two Chinas" policy, is now playing a new trick—the . . . "successor state" formula.

According to the reports of U.S. papers and news agencies, the U.S. State Department, basing itself on the so-called "successor state" theory, holds that both the new China and the Kuomintang clique entrenched in Taiwan are "successor states" to the China which joined the United Nations when that organization was founded. It therefore advocates that China's seat in the United Nations be divided into two: the Kuomintang clique is to continue to usurp China's lawful seat and the People's Republic of China is to "apply" for admission to the U.N. In other words, it flagrantly attempts to create a situation in which "two Chinas" will exist side by side in the United Nations.

As everyone knows, since its inauguration, the Kennedy Administration has continued the Eisenhower Administration's policy of hostility toward the Chinese people. The heart of this policy is to continue the occupation of China's territory of Taiwan. To achieve this end the Eisenhower Administration conceived the idea of legalizing the U.S. occupation of Taiwan by creating "two Chinas." What the Kennedy Administration is now after is to speed up the process of creating "two Chinas." Kennedy said before assuming office that "Formosa would be recognized as an independent country." Chester Bowles, now Under-Secretary of State of the Kennedy Administration, declared even more bluntly on November 11, 1960: "In the long run we can only solve this situation in China through some kind of two Chinas policy—that is, an independent Formosa and an independent China." Since its inauguration, the Kennedy Administration's activities in creating "two Chinas" have become still more open. The application of the so-called "successor state" formula, the proposition of arranging two seats for China in the United Nations, is a concrete step taken by the United States in its attempt to create "two Chinas" more directly and undisguisedly.

The reason for the haste with which the United States is trying to create "two Chinas" is because its China policy is in a hopeless mess: up a blind alley that offers no way out. The U.S. Government's policy of "non-recognition" of New China, far from preventing New China from growing strong or damaging its international prestige, has had the opposite results. Instead of isolating New China it has isolated the United States itself. The U.S. Government's setting up a handful of Kuomintang elements as the representatives of China has become a laughing-stock of public opinion in and outside the United States. The United States is having an increasingly difficult time in the United Nations. The number of countries voting against the U.S. obstruction to the discussion of China's representation has been increasing every year. The U.S. voting machine is getting more and more run down. Even Adlai Stevenson, U.S. representative in the United Nations, has lamented that "apparent support for our position has been declining in recent years," and that "it will become more difficult to keep Red China out of the organization." U.S. Secretary of State Dean Rusk, replying to correspondents on June 27, also admitted that "there is an increasing feeling in the United Nations . . . that this moratorium formula will no longer suffice to deal with the question." But, in spite of all this, the Kennedy Administration still refused to give up its policy of deep-rooted hostility toward the Chinese people, its occupation of China's territory of Taiwan and its basic policy of aggression and threats against China. As the U.S. ruling circles see it, it won't do to recognize China and it won't do not to recognize it. They have got themselves into a fix. They look on the creation of "two Chinas" as a way of extricating themselves from the ever worsening predicament.

But in trying to find a way out through the policy of creating "two Chinas" the U.S. ruling circles will only be walking from one blind alley into another.

There is only one China in the world and that is the People's Republic of China. Taiwan is an inseparable part of China's territory and is not a state. The Chinese people have, through revolutionary struggles, overthrown the Kuomintang's reactionary rule and established a new China. There has only been a revolution in China and there has been no splitting into two states. How then can the question of two "successor states" to China arise? The Kennedy Administration is only racking its brains to fabricate a theoretical justification for its "two Chinas" policy, but is unaware that it has landed itself in self-contradiction. So confused is Kennedy's logic that he is incapable of answering the question: Has or has not the Kuomintang regime of the old China been overthrown? If not, how does the question of "successor states" crop up? If it has been overthrown, how then can the Kuomintang clique, which represents nobody, become a "successor state" to China?

Still fresh in everybody's memory is the fact that Eisenhower and Dulles, in the earlier days of their office, utterly refused to recognize the existence of the People's Republic of China. Later, they regarded the Kuomintang clique in Taiwan as an "independent political entity"; in other words, they wanted to name it a small China so as to create a situation of a big China and a small China existing side by side. Kennedy is now attempting to name the Kuomintang clique a "successor state" to China in the United Nations so as to create a situation of "two Chinas" existing side by side and on a par with each other. Like its predecessor, the Kennedy Administration, while continuing to "recognize" on the one hand the Kuomintang clique discarded by the Chinese people, tries on the other to create "two Chinas." The only difference is that Kennedy's predecessor used the "half-and-half" division method to break China up into two, while Kennedy is using the "two-times-one-is-two" multiplication method to transform one China into "two Chinas." Kennedy may think he is smarter than his predecessor, but his proposition, in fact, is more absurd. After all, when was this other China suddenly dropped from the heavens, adding 9.6 million square kilometers of land and 650 million people to the earth? What else can this be if not daydreaming?

No question whatsoever should have arisen concerning China's legitimate rights and place in the United Nations. China and the Soviet Union, the United States, Britain and France are all sponsors of the United Nations and permanent members of its Security Council. This question has arisen solely because the United States has shielded the

Kuomintang clique, which has been repudiated by the Chinese people, and has made it usurp China's seat in the United Nations, thus depriving the People's Republic of China—the representative of 650 million people—of its legitimate rights. There can be no question of China "applying" for admission to the United Nations; the only question is for the United Nations to expel the Kuomintang clique and restore to China its legitimate rights and place. This just stand of the Chinese people is firm and unshakable and has won the sympathy and support of ever more countries.

The Kennedy Administration is well aware that the Chinese people are resolutely opposed to any plot of creating "two Chinas." The idea of the so-called two "successor states" to China now publicized by the United States is obviously a sly trick. Should China agree to this idea, it would fall victim to the United States' "two Chinas" plot—this is exactly what the United States wants; and should this idea be resolutely rejected by China, the United States could say with some show of plausibility: Look, it is not that the United States is blocking China's "admission" to the United Nations but that China itself does not want to enter the U.N. The U.S. magazine Newsweek, in its July 10 issue, has explained the U.S. plan clearly: "Bowles' proposal is to offer Peking a seat in the General Assembly, on a par with Chiang Kai-shek's Nationalists. If Peking refused, this would at least remove from the U.S. the onus of blocking its admission." But how can such a clumsy U.S. trick deceive anybody? The absence of lawful representative of China in the United Nations is, of course, a disgrace to the United Nations Organization. It merely shows that the United Nations is still under the control of a U.S.-dominated majority. As long as this absurd situation remains unchanged, the United States cannot absolve itself from the criminal responsibility for violating the U.N. Charter and depriving China of its legitimate rights in the United Nations.

The U.S. plot to create "two Chinas" has not only met with the firm opposition of all the Chinese people, including the people in Taiwan, but has also aroused strong reactions among the authorities in Taiwan. The authorities in Taiwan have of late openly declared that they would resist the United States' "two Chinas" policy. The press of the authorities in Taiwan has said: "If we yield on every point and dare not make even a slight resistance, [it is likely that] we shall become a dependency of others." In fact, the present danger is far more serious than the question of "becoming a dependency." The U.S. plot to create "two Chinas" is, in fact, an important step to put Taiwan into its pocket completely. As is generally known, the United States has long planned to turn Taiwan into a so-called "independent country" or place it under international trusteeship.

The recent big U.S. efforts to win over Liao Wen-yi,* diehard traitor, to engineer a "Taiwan independence movement" are made with an eye to this end.

If the authorities in Taiwan continue to live under the thumb and the dictates of others, they will eventually be thrown overboard by them. Patriotic compatriots in Taiwan, like all patriotic Chinese, are resolutely opposed to any plot of creating "two Chinas." As for the authorities in Taiwan, so long as they consider their own future and weigh the pros and cons, they will not fail to see that to follow the "two Chinas" policy of U.S. imperialism is tantamount to digging their own graves. It is true, of course, that there is a handful of extremely pro-U.S. traitors in Taiwan who overtly or covertly follow the U.S. policy of creating "two Chinas" in a vain attempt to sever Taiwan from the motherland. All those who participate in these conspiratorial activities and favor "two Chinas" will be condemned by posterity as archcriminals betraying their motherland. They can never escape the severe punishment that will be meted out to them by the Chinese people.

The "two Chinas" policy of the United States is a continuation of the U.S. policy of aggression and hostility toward China. It is essentially an attempt to occupy China's territory of Taiwan permanently and a threat to the security of China and the peace in Asia. Therefore, anyone who has a sense of national self-respect and cares for peace in Asia will firmly oppose, as the Chinese people do, this criminal policy of the United States. There is only one China. Taiwan is China's territory. The Chinese people are determined to liberate Taiwan. They will never tolerate any interference in China's internal affairs, any encroachment on China's sovereignty or the splitting of China's territory. The attempt of any state or person to create "two Chinas" in whatever way and under whatever circumstances will only be an illusion that can never be realized.

DOCUMENT 75: ROC-U.S. JOINT COMMUNIQUÉ, AUGUST 2, 1961[11]

President Kennedy and Vice-President Chen have concluded a series of cordial and constructive talks on a broad range of

---

*In April, 1965, Mr. Liao dissolved his Provisional Government of the Taiwan Republic in Tokyo and returned to Taiwan. He is currently a member of the Mainland Recovery Commission of the Nationalist government and Vice-Chairman of the Tseng-wen Dam Construction Committee of the Taiwan Provincial Government.

international problems and matters of common interest to the Governments and peoples of the United States and the Republic of China.
Foreign Minister Shen [Chang-huan], Secretary Rusk, Ambassador
Yeh, Ambassador Drumright, and other Chinese and U.S. officials
participated in the conversations, which were characterized by a
spirit of understanding and mutual interest consonant with the deep
and lasting friendship between the two countries.

The President, who at his personal initiative had invited the
Vice-President to the United States for these discussions, welcomed
this opportunity to reaffirm the close ties between the Governments
and peoples of the United States and the Republic of China.

. . .

In their discussion of Chinese representation in the United
Nations there was a candid and comprehensive exchange of views on
all relevant issues, including the pending applications for United
Nations membership of Outer Mongolia and Mauritania. The President
reiterated firm United States support for continued representation of
the Republic of China in the United Nations, of which she is a founding
member. He also reaffirmed the U.S. determination to continue to
oppose admission of the Chinese Communist regime to the United
Nations.

. . .

The President and the Vice-President reviewed conditions on
the China mainland. In the economic field, they noted that Communist
mismanagement, unworkable agricultural policies, and the commune
system have brought serious food shortages and grave hardships to the
Chinese people. They noted that reports from refugees and visitors
indicate the magnitude of the apathy, discontent, and disillusionment
on the mainland of China. They agreed that these developments provide vivid proof that the Communist regime cannot meet the genuine
needs and desires of the Chinese people for economic and social
progress.

The President and the Vice-President discussed United States
assistance for the continued economic growth of free China. The
President noted the remarkable achievements of the past ten years
in Taiwan, which have brought unprecedented improvements in the
standard of living, in public health and education, and in industrial
and agricultural output. He noted that, in contrast with the disregard
for human rights manifested by the Chinese Communist regime, this
record was accomplished without violence to the great traditions and
human values which have been cherished throughout history by the

Chinese people. The President confirmed the intention of the United States Government to continue its military aid program in the Republic of China and to provide substantial assistance to the Republic of China in support of its economic development program designed to achieve accelerated social and economic progress for the welfare of the people of free China.

In conclusion, the President and the Vice-President recognized the importance of further strengthening the close cooperation and coordination of both countries in matters affecting their common security interests.

DOCUMENT 76: "A BRIEF ACCOUNT OF THE U.S. TWO CHINAS PLOT," PEOPLE'S DAILY, AUGUST 7, 1961 [12]

It has been a long time since the United States began to plot the creation of "two Chinas." Since its inauguration in January, 1961, the Kennedy Administration has acted more impetuously than its predecessor—the Eisenhower Administration—in pushing forward this plot of hostility to the Chinese people in order to achieve its purpose of permanently occupying Taiwan—an inalienable part of China—and to end its utter isolation which its policy of hostility to China had brought about.

Soon after the founding of New China, some U.S. bourgeois newspapers and political commentators started talking about the creation of "two Chinas," though the U.S. official quarters then had not yet taken this as an established policy. However, after the United States suffered a disastrous defeat in its war of aggression against Korea, the U.S. ruling circles, in the face of the growing strength and consolidation of New China, began their plot to create "two Chinas." The late Secretary of State John Foster Dulles said in November, 1953, that on the question of Chinese representation in the United Nations, there was "the possibility that Communist China might be represented in the U.N. General Assembly while Nationalist China was represented in the Security Council." Eisenhower admitted in early 1955 that the "two Chinas" issue was "one of the possibilities constantly being studied" by the United States. Later in 1955, when the Chinese People's Liberation Army liberated Tachen Island, the United States refused to undertake, in explicit terms, obligations to "help defend" Quemoy and Matsu and other offshore islands of China and attempted to force the Chiang Kai-shek clique to withdraw from Quemoy and Matsu Islands so as to create "two Chinas" by making the Taiwan Straits a democration line. In certain international conferences and organizations the U.S. Government also made active

efforts to push ahead its "two Chinas" plot. For instance, at the 16th
Olympic Games in . . . 1956, at the meeting of the Special International
Geophysical Year Committee in June 1957 and at the 19th International
Red Cross Conference held in New Delhi in October 1957, the United
States did everything possible to thrust the Kuomintang clique as
"another China" into these organizations; it attempted to create a
situation in which representatives of "two Chinas" would sit side by
side in these international organizations.

During the latter years of the Eisenhower Administration, the
U.S. Government's efforts to push ahead its plot of creating "two
Chinas" became more and more blatant. In 1958, after suffering an
ignominious defeat in its policy of military provocations and war
threats against China in the Taiwan Straits, the U.S. Government
came out with more noisy talks about the creation of "two Chinas."
High-ranking officials of the United States, including John Foster
Dulles, continuously revealed the intention of the United States to
create "two Chinas." Some bourgeois politicians in the United States
frequently gave advice to the U.S. ruling circles on this question.
In an interview with a correspondent of the British Independent
Television on October 16, 1958, Dulles said that "there is no doubt
we [the U.S.] recognize Communist China as a fact, as we deal with
Communist China." At the same time, Dulles openly called the
Chiang Kai-shek clique the "Republic of China in Formosa" and said
that he wanted the Chiang Kai-shek clique "not to use force to go
back to the mainland or against the mainland."

Later, in his talks with Chiang Kai-shek, Dulles called the Chiang
Kai-shek clique "spokesman" for . . . "free China." In commenting
on the communiqué on the talks between Dulles and Chiang Kai-shek,
the New York Post correspondent Joseph P. Lash said that "this last
[the designation of Chiang Kai-shek as the "spokesman" for "free
China"] is significantly different from regarding Chiang as the spokesman for all China, as we have done up to now. It would seem to free
Dulles to negotiate with Red China on the basis of a 'two Chinas'
approach." The Washington Post . . . said that the U.S. Government
"has taken steps toward a disengagement in Formosa Strait and in
actuality is supporting the concept of two Chinas, or an independent
Formosa."

Later, on October 8, 1959, the U.S. State Department reiterated
its stock argument that the "status of Taiwan" was "unsettled." At
his press conference held on October 22, Eisenhower tried his utmost
to describe the Chinese people's determination to liberate their own
territory of Taiwan as an "international question" and not an "internal
one" of China. He also alleged that "a great number of nations
recognize the independence of Formosa." Certain idea men in the
United States also energetically advocated a "two Chinas" policy.

In November, 1959, the U.S. Senate released a study prepared by . . .
Conlon Associates, Ltd. which put forward such absurd proposals as
the "admission of Communist China to the United Nations," "recog-
nition of the Republic of Taiwan" to be "protected" by the United
States, "the seating of the Republic [of Taiwan] in the [U.N. General]
Assembly, and the "enlargement of the Security Council to include
India and Japan as permanent members as well as China."

After the inauguration of the Kennedy Administration in January,
1961, U.S. conspiratorial activities to create "two Chinas" became
more intensified. This was because, as the U.S. press pointed out,
the question of China policy was "one of Mr. Kennedy's toughest"
(Washington Evening Star), and "one of the thickest items" (Christian
Science Monitor). "The most distasteful inheritance which our
President receives from the Eisenhower Administration," says The
Nation "is the quagmire which currently goes under the misnomer of
the China policy of the United States." By creating "two Chinas" the
Kennedy Administration attempted to find new tactics for its China
policy "to take some of the heat off Washington," but it "contemplates
no change in basic policy" (UPI).

Before he was elected president, Kennedy himself and other
Democratic politicians who are now high-ranking officials in the . . .
Democratic administration actively advocated the creation of "two
Chinas." In an interview with a correspondent of the British Sunday
Times on July 3, 1960, Kennedy said that "it might be possible that
Formosa would be recognized as an independent country."

U.S. ruling circles and their idea men, both before and after
the inauguration of the Kennedy Administration, have been cooking up
various formulas for the creation of "two Chinas." This includes old
stuff inherited from the Republican administration and new tricks
devised by the Democratic administration. These formulas can be
summarized as follows:

No. 1. "An independent state of Taiwan." According to this
formula, the United States will make the Chiang Kai-shek clique
withdraw its troops from Quemoy and Matsu Islands, and then Taiwan
will be declared "independent" and made a new member of the United
Nations, while China will be "admitted" into the United Nations and
the Security Council on condition of undertaking "not to liberate
Taiwan by force."

In an article in the April, 1960, issue of the American quarterly
Foreign Affairs, the present U.S. Under-Secretary of State Bowles
urged the formation of "an independent Sino-Formosan nation . . .
predominantly Chinese by culture but Formosan in outlook." He
stressed that only by beginning with imaginative policies based on
"two Chinas" could the United States start to exert a "constructive
influence" on Asia. On November 11 of the same year he told a

correspondent of the British Associated Rediffusion Company, "In the long run we can only solve this situation in China through some kind of 'two Chinas' policy—that is, an independent Formosa and an independent China."

John Kenneth Galbraith, President Kennedy's nominee for U.S. Ambassador to India, testifying before the U.S. Congress on March 24, 1961, said: "When mainland China agrees to the independence of Formosa and accepts the principles of the United Nations Charter, it seems it might be possible to negotiate with them [on the question of "admittance" to the United Nations] . . . . United States' commitments to defend Formosa and see that it remains an independent nation must be recognized by the Chinese Communists before they could gain admittance to the United Nations." He also said: "I should hope that the time will come when it will be possible to see the existence of two Chinas."

In an article in the November 15, 1960, issue of the Foreign Policy Bulletin, Professor Robert A. Scalapino of the University of California, who prepared for the Foreign Relations Committee of the U.S. Senate a study of the United States' policy toward Asia (i.e., the study by . . . Conlon Associates, Ltd.), demanded that the United States carry out the policy of "one China and one Taiwan (Formosa)."

No. 2. Placing Taiwan under U.N. "trusteeship" or "protection." According to this formula, the United States will leave the Kuomintang clique in the lurch. The status of Taiwan will remain "unsettled for the time being," and it will be placed under U.N. "trusteeship" or "protection" for a number of years, at the expiration of which time a "plebiscite" will be held to decide its future.

In the January, 1960, issue of Foreign Affairs, Adlai Stevenson, now permanent representative of the Kennedy Administration to the United Nations, advocated "acceptance of the right of the inhabitants of Formosa to determine their own destiny by plebiscite supervised by the United Nations." Testifying before the U.S. Senate on January 18, 1961, Stevenson stressed that "the security, independence and self-determination of Formosa is vital" and reiterated his demand for China's "acceptance of the right of the inhabitants of Formosa to determine their own destiny by plebiscite supervised by the United Nations."

In a statement made on April 29 last year James Warburg, banker and a member of the late President Roosevelt's "brain trust," advocated placing Taiwan under . . . United Nations "guardianship" for at least five years, at the end of which time a plebiscite would be held to let the "Formosan people" decide if Taiwan should belong to China or should be an independent state.

In collusion with the reactionary circles in Japan which have been attempting to lay their fingers once again on Taiwan, the United

States has for years been fostering the Chinese traitor Liao Wen-yi as a ready tool for pushing ahead this plan. The <u>Taiwan Kung Ping Pao</u>, published in Japan, said that there already existed openly in Japan a . . . "Provisional Government of the Taiwan Republic" and a "Taiwan Independence and Freedom Party." The movement for the "independence of Taiwan" "is closely related, both in personnel and material resources, with the U.S. government organizations in Japan, financial and industrial circles of Japan, the Liberal-Democratic Party, the Ministry of Foreign Affairs, and the National Defense Agency"; "it is supplied with huge sums of funds from all sides." According to reports circulated in the United States recently, Liao Wen-yi is planning to visit the United States. This throws fresh light on this U.S. plot.

No. 3. "One and a half Chinas." The main idea of this formula is, in the name of recognizing so-called Chinese "suzerainty" over Taiwan, to turn Taiwan into an "autonomous" area which would retain the right of handling its foreign affairs independently; and to restore to China its seat in the United Nations while giving Taiwan a separate seat in the U.N. General Assembly.

This formula was proposed by John Fairbank, former director of the U.S.I.S. in China, on January 20, 1961. Fairbank admitted that the "two Chinas" concept was unpopular, so he proposed that "instead of imposing the obnoxious term 'two Chinas' from the outside, we might better describe the situation realistically in Chinese terms as one of Peking's 'suzerainty' and Taipei's 'autonomy.'"

No. 4. The "two successor states" formula. This is the latest U.S. formula for creating "two Chinas." In the latter part of June, 1961, just around the time when Japanese Prime Minister Hayato Ikeda was visiting the United States, the new . . . "successor states" formula was reported in the U.S. press. The substance of this formula is to regard both the People's Republic of China and the Kuomintang clique in Taiwan, which has been repudiated by the Chinese people, "as 'successors' to the China that entered the United Nations at its founding"; and to allow the Kuomintang clique to continue to usurp the position of permanent member of the U.N. Security Council and the seat in the U.N. General Assembly, while the People's Republic of China will "apply to the Credentials Committee of the General Assembly for approval to occupy an assembly seat."

As the American journal <u>Newsweek</u> (July 10) disclosed, the author of this formula was Chester Bowles, U.S. Under-Secretary of State. The journal admitted that "there is not the slightest chance" that China "would accept" this formula. It revealed that this U.S. plot was but a crafty tactic aimed entirely to escape condemnation of world opinion. It said: "If Peking refused, this would at least remove from the United States the onus of blocking its admission," and would enable the United States "not to lose its allies and neutrals which no longer supported Washington's non-recognition policy."

No matter how they may vary in form, these U.S. formulas for the solution of its "China policy" question have only one aim, i.e., to persist in the forcible occupation of the Chinese territory of Taiwan.

There is, however, only one China in the world, i.e., the People's Republic of China. Taiwan is an inalienable part of China's territory and the Chinese people are determined to liberate it. The Chinese people resolutely oppose the plot of the United States or of any other country to create "two Chinas" in any form. All U.S. imperialist armed forces must get out of Taiwan and the Taiwan Straits. The legitimate rights and seat of the Chinese People's Republic in the United Nations must be fully restored. The "representatives" of the Kuomintang clique in Taiwan must be expelled from the United Nations. Opposed by the people of all China (including those now in Taiwan who do not want to be traitors to the nation by completely selling Taiwan to the United States) and the just public opinion of the whole world, the U.S. plot to create "two Chinas" by all conceivable means will never succeed.

DOCUMENT 77: NCNA CORRESPONDENT, "CHIANG KAI-SHEK GANG PREPARES FOR MILITARY ADVENTURE," JUNE 23, 1962[13]

A Hsinhua correspondent has learned from authoritative sources that the Chiang Kai-shek gang entrenched in Taiwan, with the support and encouragement of U.S. imperialism, is preparing for a large-scale military adventure, an invasion of the coastal areas of the mainland.

. . .

Why does the Kennedy Administration instigate and support the Chiang Kai-shek gang for an invasion of the mainland coastal areas? Any thoughtful person can see that U.S. imperialism wishes to kill two birds with one stone. It calculates that if by luck the military adventure of the Chiang Kai-shek gang should succeed, U.S. imperialism would be able to set up a bridgehead on China's mainland and deal a blow to the prestige of the People's Republic of China, and also spread the armed forces of the Chiang Kai-shek gang thin and aggravate its financial difficulties so that it would have to be even more obedient to U.S. imperialism. Conversely, if the adventure should fail, then with the strength of the Chiang Kai-shek gang greatly weakened, U.S. imperialism would be able more easily to attain the aim it has been pursuing for many years, namely, the realization of its "two Chinas" plot by kicking out Chiang Kai-shek and using a new puppet to take over Taiwan. Recent talk in the New York Herald Tribune about the need for "a man even wiser" than Chiang Kai-shek to rule Taiwan is obviously not accidental.

DOCUMENT 78: PRC GOVERNMENT SPOKESMAN'S COMMENT ON THE U.S.S.R. GOVERNMENT's STATEMENT OF AUGUST 21, 1963, SEPTEMBER 1, 1963[14]

We have not forgotten and will not forget the support the Soviet people have long given China on the question of Taiwan.

Likewise, however, we have not forgotten and will not forget what the Soviet leader, Khruschev, said about the question of Taiwan after his visit to the United States in October, 1959.

He said that the question of Taiwan was an incendiary factor in the international situation and that because the United States supported Chiang Kai-shek and the Soviet Union supported China, the atmosphere was like that on the eve of a great war; but the Soviet Union stood for the creation of all conditions to ease international tension and eliminate war.

He said further that there was more than one way to solve every complicated question, depending on what basis you took. For example, after the October Revolution, the Far Eastern Republic was established in the Soviet Far East, and Lenin recognized it at the time; this was a temporary concession and sacrifice, since later on it was united with Russia.

The meaning of this statement by the Soviet leader was quite clear. To put it bluntly, it was asking China to agree to the U.S. scheme of creating "two Chinas."

This absurd view was of course rebutted and rejected by China, whereupon the Soviet leader made several speeches hinting that China was "craving for war like a cock for a fight," and, like Trotsky, wanted "neither peace nor war," etc.

In accordance with the procedure mutually agreed upon by the Soviet Union and the United States, the Chiang Kai-shek clique, swaggering like a sovereign state, has now signed the tripartite treaty. Not only has the Soviet leader asked the Chinese Government to sign the same tripartite treaty along with the Chiang Kai-shek clique spurned by the Chinese people, and thus to create a "two Chinas" situation, he has also threatened that, if the Chinese Government opposed this treaty and refused to be bound by it, the United States would help the Chiang Kai-shek clique to manufacture nuclear weapons.

It turns out that in order to "save millions of Chinese from nuclear death," one China has to become two Chinas! It is evident that the Soviet leaders will stop at nothing in order to curry favor with the U.S. imperialists. The international position of the German Democratic Republic is beneath their notice and so is China's sovereignty and territorial integrity.

Although the truth has been so fully exposed, they still assert that the nuclear strength of the Soviet Union guarantees China's independence and sovereignty. What effrontery!

DOCUMENT 79: PRC PREMIER CHOU EN-LAI'S PRESS CONFERENCE IN DACCA, FEBRUARY 25, 1964[15]

Premier Chou En-lai in his press conference strongly denounced the U.S. Government for persisting in a policy of hostility toward China. He declared that U.S. imperialism would never succeed in its scheme to create "two Chinas."

A U.S. correspondent asked whether the principle of self-determination was applicable to Taiwan. In a stern reply the Premier pointed out that the question itself clearly reflected the U.S. Government's attempt to create "two Chinas." He said that "two Chinas" meant severing Taiwan from the territory of the People's Republic of China and creating another country. The Government of the People's Republic of China and the entire Chinese people resolutely opposed "two Chinas." Even the Chiang Kai-shek group opposed "two Chinas." All those countries that had formally established diplomatic relations with the People's Republic of China opposed "two Chinas." The majority of the people throughout the world opposed "two Chinas." The scheme of U.S. imperialism to create "two Chinas" could never succeed. This U.S. State Department scheme hostile to the Chinese people will rot in its own archives, he declared.

Premier Chou En-lai said: Taiwan is a province of China; the inhabitants there are all Chinese, the majority being Hans. In the Sino-Japanese War of 1894 the corrupt Chinese dynasty was defeated and Taiwan was annexed by Japan. During World War II, China, Britain and the United States in the Cairo Declaration affirmed that Taiwan should be returned to China after the war. When Japan was defeated in 1945, the then Chinese government sent representatives to Taiwan to accept the surrender of Japan and formally took it over from the hands of the Japanese rulers. Since then Taiwan has returned to the fold of the motherland and become a province of China enjoying the same status as the other provinces. Even the Chiang Kai-shek group recognizes this fact. The question now is that since the Chiang

Kai-shek group was driven off the Chinese mainland by the Chinese people, it has entrenched itself in Taiwan under the protection of U.S. troops and has continued the civil war with the Chinese People. The liberation of Taiwan is entirely an internal affair of China which brooks no foreign interference. Therefore, with regard to this inalienable Chinese territory of Taiwan, there can simply be no such questions as whether it is of indeterminate status, whether there should be a plebiscite, and so on; they are questions of a different nature.

Vice-Premier Chen Yi added: Isn't it ridiculous that Chinese should hold a plebiscite to decide whether they are Chinese?

DOCUMENT 80: ROC FOREIGN MINISTRY SPOKESMAN'S REPLY TO A QUESTION ASKED BY A REPORTER, MARCH 3, 1964[16]

Question: Recently, the question of the legal status of Taiwan was mentioned in the parliament of a friendly state. What's your comment?

Answer: So far as the Republic of China is concerned, the question of the legal status has not arisen since the return of Taiwan to the Republic of China in 1945.

In order to clarify this matter, I wish to state briefly as follows:

When China declared war against Japan on December 9, 1941, all treaties between China and Japan, including the Treaty of Shimonoseki ceding Taiwan and concluded after the first Sino-Japanese War, were abrogated.

Article 4 of the Sino-Japanese Peace Treaty of April 28, 1952, provides: "It is recognized that all treaties, conventions and agreements concluded before December 9, 1941, between China and Japan have become null and void as a consequence of the war."

The return of Taiwan to China was explicitly provided in the Cairo Declaration of December 1, 1943. The Potsdam Proclamation of July 25, 1945, reaffirmed this stipulation. When Japan surrendered on September 2, 1945, she recognized and accepted the Potsdam Proclamation.

According to Article 2 of the Sino-Japanese Treaty, "Japan has renounced all right, title and claim to Taiwan and Penghu. . . ."

China recovered Taiwan on October 25, 1945, and reestablished it as a province.

DOCUMENT 81: ROC PRESIDENT CHIANG KAI-SHEK'S
ANSWERS TO QUESTIONS SUBMITTED BY
ARMANDO RIVAS TORRES,
MARCH 26, 1964[17]

1. Q. What is the attitude of your government toward the
establishment of diplomatic relations between Paris and Peiping?
What is the stand of your government toward this matter?
    A. After the French recognition of the Chinese Communists,
the government of the Republic of China formally severed diplomatic
relations with the government of France. This was done on the basis
of the traditional Chinese principle that a legitimate government and
a regime of traitors do not exist side by side, just as there is no
room for coexistence between justice and evil.
    2. Q. What does Your Excellency think of the impact of
diplomatic measures underlining the "two Chinas" concept on the
world?
    A. I myself and the Chinese people are resolutely opposed
to the "two Chinas" concept. The Republic of China will never consent
to any "two Chinas" arrangement. Meanwhile, I believe that the
conspiracy for "two Chinas" can produce only a negligible effect on
the free world as a whole. It can in no way affect the international
position of the Republic of China.
    3. Q. Is a local war, as waged by your country for many years
against the Chinese Communists, the only way to avoid a worldwide
conflagration?
    A. Yes, you are right. A local anti-Communist war mainly
for the purpose of recovering the Chinese mainland, can help stop
further foreign aggression by the Chinese Communists on the one
hand and is the the only way to avoid a world war on the other. I
have explained this in great detail in my book "Soviet Russia in China,"
which is available for your reference.

· · ·

    6. Q. If the Chinese Communists should attack Taiwan with all
their might, has free China adequate military strength to expel them?
    A. The Republic of China has the necessary military strength
to defeat any Communist attack. In the past, though the Reds had
every intention to attack Taiwan, they just didn't dare to try because
of our military might and strong defenses. Meanwhile, they have been
plagued by internal instability, economic difficulties, and low morale.
In recent years, they have ceased to entertain any illusion of their
ability to attack Taiwan. On the contrary, the Communists now are

afraid of our counterattack because once our armed forces attack, the Red regime will crumble from within and that would be the end of the puppet regime.

DOCUMENT 82: "CHINA'S SOVEREIGNTY OVER
TAIWAN BROOKS NO INTERVENTION,"
PEOPLE'S DAILY, MAY 12, 1964[18]

U.S. imperialism and its followers now are asserting that in 1945 [sic] Japan only "renounced" its "claim" to Taiwan, but that "no government or regime has since been named as recipient of this territory." This not only is inconsistent with the Cairo and the Potsdam Declarations and the fact that the Chinese Government recovered its sovereignty over Taiwan; it is an absurdity fabricated by imperialism's bandit logic. Because it is Chinese territory the Chinese people have an absolute right to recover Taiwan whether Japanese militarism occupied it for 50 or 100 years. After the robber has been captured everything he has seized should be returned to the original owner. The Japanese militarists have been driven out and Taiwan therefore should be returned to China, just as Alsace-Lorraine was returned to France after World War I and the southern part of the island of Sakhalin was returned to the Soviet Union after World War II. The Cairo and Potsdam Declarations merely confirmed that the Chinese people have the inalienable right to recover their territory of Taiwan from Japanese militarism. With or without the Cairo and Potsdam Declarations the Chinese people want Taiwan restored to China. If Taiwan ceased to be China's territory because it was occupied by Japanese militarism for 50 years, then should the territories of Asian, African and Latin American countries, which have been occupied for scores of years and centuries by imperialism— for instance the Suez Canal area of the United Arab Republic, India's Goa, Panama's Canal Zone and Cuba's Guantanamo—eternally be imperialist colonies and not be allowed to return to their motherland? If such imperialist logic is allowed to be enforced, then "might makes right" will become the sole guiding principle in international law. Of course, imperialism welcomes such logic, but the Chinese people and the oppressed nations of the world firmly oppose it. Certainly it is not accidental that advocates of "Taiwan's undetermined status" are all imperialists who have committed or are committing colonialist aggression around the world.

As a legal basis for its spurious "undetermined status of Taiwan," U.S. imperialism and its partners use the allegation that the San Francisco treaty did not decide the future of Taiwan. But the Chinese people are the main force in the defeat of Japanese militarism, and the Government of the People's Republic of China, the only legal government which represents them, was excluded from the preparation, drawing up and conclusion of the peace treaty with Japan. As far back as December 4, 1950, the Chinese Government declared that this so-called peace treaty with Japan is illegal and null and void. Although U.S. imperialism can make demagogical use of the San Francisco peace treaty with Japan, it is completely impossible for it to impose its aggression on the great 650 million Chinese people by means of this so-called treaty which has no binding force whatsoever for the Chinese Government. The dark years when the imperialists could manufacture a treaty at will to decide the fate of the Asian, African and Latin American peoples have gone for ever. U.S. imperialism and its followers should clearly bear this in mind.

U.S. imperialism and its follower, Britain, are doing everything they can to propagandize the idea that Taiwan is an international question, and are advocating its solution by an international meeting. This is utter balderdash. For the Chinese people to liberate their own territory of Taiwan is China's internal affair in which nobody can interfere. True, there is an international aspect to the Taiwan question—the question of U.S. armed occupation of Chinese territory, the province of Taiwan. The only solution is the withdrawal of U.S. forces from Taiwan. Whoever tries to confuse the two entirely different aspects of the Taiwan question and to interfere with Chinese sovereignty over Taiwan in the guise of an "international problem" is doomed to failure.

In order to sell its scheme of "one China and one Taiwan" U.S. imperialism asserts that the "realistic" path to improve Sino-U.S. relations is for China to give up its sovereignty over Taiwan. This is a barefaced fraud. The Chinese and American peoples have always been friendly. The present state of relations between the two countries is entirely the result of U.S. Government policy of hostility to China and occupation of the Chinese territory of Taiwan. As Premier Chou En-lai repeatedly pointed out in his recent tour of Asian-African countries, the only way to improve Sino-U.S. relations is for the U.S. Government to show by deed its readiness to change its policy of hostility to China; there can be no other way. It is pure daydreaming to expect the Chinese people to barter away principle and sovereignty.

Some people, unfamiliar with the actual situation, may be confused for a time by the false arguments of U.S. imperialism on the question of Taiwan but in the end they will see the truth. However, this is entirely not so for the British Government. Willing to act as a cat's-paw, it is actively supporting the U.S. imperialist scheme for infringing on Chinese sovereignty. In return for its support the British Government hopes to obtain U.S. assistance in maintaining its colonial rule in Asia and other parts of the world. This is clear

miscalculation. It can be said with certainty that no matter how
actively the British Government supports U.S. imperialism's scheme,
it can expect no mercy from U.S. imperialism. An important and
component part of U.S. imperialism's global strategy for world
domination is discrimination against, breaking up and taking over
Britain's large empire. This is a decided policy of the United States.
No amount of flattery and service by the British Government can
change it. Frankly speaking, the action of the British Government
will not benefit it but can harm others. Britain has established
partial diplomatic relations with China. To what point does the British
Government want to push Sino-British relations now that it is giving
support in such a flagrant way to the U.S. scheme to invade and occupy
China's territory of Taiwan?

The province of Taiwan is an integral part of the sacred territory
of the People's Republic of China. China's sovereignty over Taiwan
needs no approval by others, nor will any interference be permitted.
The Chinese people's determination to liberate their own territory
of Taiwan is unshakable. Taiwan will be returned to the embrace of
the motherland. Anyone trying to play the trick of severing Taiwan
from the People's Republic of China is doomed to utter bankruptcy.

DOCUMENT 83: HSU MENG-SHAN, "RESOLUTELY
OPPOSE THE 'ONE CHINA AND ONE TAIWAN'
SCHEME," PEOPLE'S DAILY, MAY 24, 1964[19]

On May 24, 1957, the people of Taiwan province held an anti-
U.S. patriotic demonstration. Several tens of thousands of people
surrounded the American "Embassy," loudly shouting "Yankees, get
out of Taiwan!" Ten years before this incident, i.e., in January,
1947, more than 5,000 youths and students and people from various
circles in Taiwan Province held a demonstration and surrounded the
American Consulate in Taipei, in response to the nationwide popular
anti-U.S. hightide, which was caused by an American soldier raping
a Chinese girl student in Peking (the Shen Ch'ung Incident). After
U.S. imperialism occupied Taiwan province in 1950 by force of arms,
our compatriots in Taiwan province have always struggled against
the U.S. aggression. During these years, our compatriots in Taiwan
province have constantly longed for their own liberation. Their wish
to return to the bosom of the motherland cannot be repressed by anybody.

U.S. imperialism has always been preventing the people of China
from liberating Taiwan, and vainly attempts to cut Taiwan province
from China. In the past decade and more, in order to achieve this
end, the U.S. has hatched many schemes to create on the international
scene "two Chinas." However, as a result, the China policy of

U.S. imperialism has gone into a blind alley, and the "two Chinas"
scheme is becoming more and more impracticable. Under this
situation, officials of the U.S. government recently spread the absurd
"one China, one Taiwan" theory. About the time when Fulbright,
Chairman of the Senate Foreign Relations Committee, shouted "Let
Taiwan become independent," the American press and Great Britain
and other followers of U.S. imperialism vigorously maintained that
"one capital of China is in Peking, and another is in Taiwan," said
that "the status of Taiwan is not yet determined," saying that the
problem of the future of Taiwan should be "solved in accordance with
the wishes of the people of Taiwan," and suggested to "enforce the
principle of self-determination" and build a so-called "independent
republic" in Taiwan.

Obviously the . . . "one China, one Taiwan" scheme is simply
a variant of the "two Chinas" trick. Nothing can alienate it from its
origin, whatever change it may undergo. The scheme of U.S.
imperialism is to legalize its permanent occupation in Taiwan and
turn Taiwan into its colony. But, it is making efforts in vain. As
Premier Chou en-lai once said: "Now, more and more facts have
proved that any scheme to create 'two Chinas' or any variant of this
scheme can under no circumstances be realized. Taiwan is an
inalienable part of China, and has been returned to China by Japan
in 1945, i.e., after the Second World War. China's sovereignty over
Taiwan needs no approval by anybody and brooks no intervention."

. . .

It is absolutely futile for the U.S. government to turn China's
Taiwan province into another China or an independent political unit.
Taiwan has belonged to China since ancient times. Though the
Japanese militarists occupied Taiwan by force for 50 years, yet, as
a result of the victory won by the people of China in the War of
Resistance against Japan, the Japanese bandits capitulated and Taiwan
was restored to China. The example of the end of Japanese militarism
is still fresh. If the U.S. government wants to follow the example of
Japanese militarism and occupies Taiwan by force, can it get anything
good? The world today is no longer in a period in which imperialism
can do whatever it wants, and seize colonies at will. Today China
cannot be split by anybody as it was in the past. If U.S. imperialism
attempts to legalize its aggressive position of occupying Taiwan, the
people all over China, including the people of Taiwan, will never
allow it.

U.S. imperialism hatches a scheme of creating "an independent
Taiwan" and even spreads the rumor that "the people of Taiwan are
not Chinese" and "the people of Taiwan oppose the Chinese." This is

absolutely absurd! The people of Taiwan are Chinese. Has this to be ratified by anybody? Over 98 percent of the residents in Taiwan province are Hans; the overwhelming majority of them have come from Fukien and Kwangtung provinces, and the other 2 percent are people of Kaoshan nationality, which is one of the minority nationalities of China. This is a fact which nobody can alter. During the period of the Japanese military occupation of Taiwan, our compatriots in Taiwan still adopted the surnames of the Chinese, spoke the Chinese language, wore Chinese clothes, offered sacrifices to their ancestors on the mainland, longed for return to the motherland, and opposed the Japanese imperialists' rule unremittingly. In the 50 years under the Japanese occupation, over 500,000 people of Taiwan sacrificed themselves and consistently preserved the Chinese people's anti-imperialist and patriotic character.

As people in other provinces on the China mainland do, the people in Taiwan province oppose their reactionary ruler, that is, the Chiang Kai-shek clique which fawns on the U.S. and betrays China. They do not oppose the "people of other provinces," nor the "people of China." Similarly, the people of Taiwan also oppose those natives of Taiwan who are jackals of U.S. imperialism or the Chiang Kai-shek clique. On the contrary, those compatriots who have come from the China mainland to Taiwan and who have served the interest of the people and opposed the U.S.-Chiang reactionaries, win the love and support of the compatriots who are natives of Taiwan. In the history of revolution in China, our compatriots in Taiwan always linked their fate with that of the people of the motherland. Leaving the ancient times aside, during the periods of the Great Revolution and the Second Revolutionary Civil War, many compatriots in Taiwan rushed to take part in the revolution on the mainland. During the period of the War of Resistance against Japan, many of them rushed to the resist-Japan democratic base. During the period of the War of Liberation, large numbers of compatriots rushed from Taiwan to take part in the war. After the establishment of the People's Republic of China, several thousand compatriots who were natives of Taiwan returned from Taiwan, Japan and other countries to the bosom of the motherland. These facts show that our compatriots in Taiwan have entrusted their future with the liberation of the motherland and with the socialist motherland.

For the sake of realizing its ambition of permanently occupying Taiwan, the U.S. bribed a handful of turncoats in the motherland and instigated them to clamor for "a Taiwan for the Taiwanese" or "Taiwan wants independence." This is a scheme, the Taiwan compatriots understand clearly. The so-called "Taiwan people's Taiwan," to speak frankly, is "America's Taiwan." Our compatriots in Taiwan know clearly that, to win emancipation and to make the people master of the house, it is definitely necessary to drive U.S. imperialism out of Taiwan and to enforce a system free from the oppression and exploitation by feudalism and bureaucratic capitalism. To achieve this end, obviously, there is only one way, which is to support the struggle for liberating Taiwan being undertaken by the people on the mainland, to restore Taiwan to the motherland, and to build a new China together. Our compatriots in Taiwan resolutely spurn the turncoats, such as Liao Wen-yi, who betray Taiwan to their American master for a bit of leftover food.

Today, the struggle of the people in the whole world against U.S. imperialism is rising in storms, and U.S. imperialism is encircled by the people of the whole world. By occupying Taiwan, which is part of our territory, and pursuing a policy of antagonizing, threatening and encircling China, U.S. imperialism has eventually dragged itself into a dead alley. The prestige of the People's Republic of China is rising unceasingly, our country's influence over international affairs is increasing continuously, and more and more countries have established relations with China. The strength of the people of China today is unprecedented in history. The people of China have full confidence in restoring Taiwan province to their motherland. The attempt of U.S. imperialism to cut Taiwan province from the territory of the People's Republic of China will be futile forever. Any "two Chinas" or "one China and one Taiwan" scheme, or any variant of this scheme will end in total bankruptcy.

DOCUMENT 84: ROC PRESIDENT CHIANG KAI-SHEK'S NEW YEAR MESSAGE, JANUARY 1, 1965[20]

Fellow countrymen! No matter what changes will take place in the world situation or how confused the people in the world may become, we believe implicitly that as long as we are fortified with the strength due to our national sense of justice, and as long as we persist in our determination to win the struggle against the Communists, eventually right will prevail over wrong, freedom will overcome slavery, the Three Principles of the People will vanquish Communism, and the righteous army of the National Revolution will win the Armageddon over the Communist forces of violence.

Consequently, the people of this island bastion of national recovery, military and civilian alike, are not frightened by the Chinese Communist atomic explosion, but regard it as the siren ahead of a fire engine, or the beacon that calls by its illuminating shaft of light, summoning us to the rescue of our compatriots on the mainland and to speed there as if we were speeding to save someone from death by burning or drowning.

In the international scene, we are not perturbed by threats to our representation in the United Nations. Our feelings are related to the fact that the letter and spirit of the U.N. Charter that we helped propose and sponsor have not been upheld and that the world organization, instead of having attained its intended purpose of maintaining world peace, is faced with a crucial test involving the choice between good and evil, between right and wrong, and between international justice and injustice. But we are worried lest the United Nations should repeat the League of Nations' history of more than twenty years ago. We are concerned, too, about the widespread popular fear of the Communists, fear of aggressive might. This has opened a door to evil in the hearts of some people and increased the danger of nuclear calamity.

However, our actions of national recovery and reconstruction which concern our domestic affairs are not to be linked to the fate of the United Nations, which deals with international politics. To crush the Communist rebellion is our own undertaking. No one can deny or ignore the fact that the territory, sovereignty, and people of the mainland are Chinese and belong to the Republic of China. The Republic of China has contributed so much and so loyally to the United Nations and her title and status in that organization are so transparent that no one can with legal or moral justification usurp her rights or take her seat. There will always be a place for the Republic of China in the history of the United Nations, and it can never be obliterated.

DOCUMENT 85: "THE CHINESE PEOPLE ARE DETERMINED TO LIBERATE TAIWAN," PEOPLE'S DAILY, JUNE 27, 1965[21]

To perpetuate its occupation of Taiwan, U.S. imperialism has for many years been tirelessly engaged in underhanded activities to create "two Chinas." Besides egging on its followers to advance different kinds of preposterous proposals, such as an "independent state of Taiwan," "internationalization of Taiwan," "U.N. trusteeship," "one China and one Taiwan," it has used every opportunity to try and bring about a "two Chinas" situation. The tricks vary but the aim is the same: to sever Taiwan from China and legalize the U.S. occupation of the island.

Taking advantage of the Japanese militarists who eagerly covet Taiwan, U.S. imperialism has recently enlisted the services of the Sato government in the "two Chinas" plot. Sato has openly proclaimed that "Taiwan's status is unsettled," and that the Taiwan question "is not a question of China's internal affairs." The American press disclosed that the question of "independence" for the Chiang Kai-shek gang on Taiwan was discussed last January at the Johnson-Sato talks in Washington. The forces of Japanese militarism, revived under U.S. patronage, are now dreaming of making a comeback, of occupying Taiwan and invading other parts of China. Designating China as the imagined enemy, the Japanese Government has flagrantly drawn up its "Three Arrows Plan." All this cannot but provoke the Chinese people to great indignation and arouse their sharp vigilance.

The Chinese people have not for a moment forgotten that their territory Taiwan remains to be liberated, and their 11 million compatriots there are still groaning under the reactionary U.S.-Chiang Kai-shek rule. Nor can they forget that their ferocious enemy, U.S. imperialism, is just around the corner, posing a threat to them day and night. They must take it seriously. They must redouble their efforts to increase their country's strength. The Chinese people are determined to liberate Taiwan and accomplish the great cause of unifying their motherland. All U.S. armed forces must quit Taiwan and the Taiwan Straits area. Together with the people of Asia and the whole world, the Chinese people are also determined to throw U.S. imperialism out of Asia and out of all places that are victims of its aggression.

DOCUMENT 86: VICE-PREMIER AND FOREIGN MINISTER CHEN YI'S PRESS CONFERENCE, PEKING, SEPTEMBER 29, 1965[22]

The Japanese correspondents asked about the possibility of cooperation between the Kuomintang and the Chinese Communist Party. Vice-Premier Chen Yi said: At present there are Revolutionary Committees of the Kuomintang in the provinces and municipalities as well as in Peking, which are co-operating very well with the Communist Party. New China is a country in which eight democratic parties co-operate with the Communist Party and are led by it. We welcome Mr. Li Tsung-jen's participation in this cooperation. Chiang Kai-shek and Chiang Ching-kuo are also welcome to join in this cooperation as Mr. Li Tsung-jen has done. Taiwan Province and any individual or group in Taiwan are welcome to come back to the embrace of the motherland and join in this cooperation. Only one condition is required: To break away from U.S. imperialist control and be loyal to the motherland. There are no other conditions. In my view, the possibility of Kuomintang-Communist co-operation is great and is, moreover, increasing.

DOCUMENT 87: "THE FIVE-STAR RED FLAG MUST BE
PLANTED ON TAIWAN PROVINCE," PEOPLE'S
DAILY, JUNE 27, 1966[23]

China's territory of Taiwan Province was occupied by force of
arms on June 27, 1950, by U.S. imperialism, which is extremely
hostile to the people of China and all Asia, when it launched its war
of aggression against Korea. Since then, step by step, U.S. imperialism
has transformed Taiwan into its colony and military base from which
to menace the Chinese mainland and to commit aggression in Asia.

U.S. imperialism is the sworn enemy of the people of China and
the people of Asia.

Chairman Mao Tse-tung has pointed out that the Chinese
territory of Taiwan Province, which U.S. imperialism has occupied,
and the other military bases it has set up outside its own territory
are all nooses which U.S. imperialism itself prepared and put around
its own neck. Chairman Mao said: "The longer the U.S. aggressors
remain in these places, the tighter the nooses round their necks will
become." And the facts fully corroborate this wise thesis of Chairman Mao's. In the past 16 years, U.S. imperialism has occupied the
Chinese province of Taiwan, and conducted vicious aggression everywhere in Asia. It has thus added noose after noose around its neck.
The more frantically it strives in a vain attempt to suppress the
revolutionary struggles of the people of Asia, the tighter become the
nooses.

. . .

The Soviet revisionist leading clique is playing the shameful
role of accomplice in the U.S. imperialist schemes to commit
aggression in Asia, to threaten China. The Soviet leaders are doing
their best to serve the U.S. imperialist "peace talks" schemes by
sham support and actual betrayal of the Vietnamese people's struggle
against U.S. aggression and for national salvation. They advocate
the establishment of a "European security system," which helps U.S.
imperialism shift the focus of its counter-revolutionary strategy of
global war to Asia, and thus cater to the requirements of U.S.
imperialism in its encirclement and "containment" of China and its
aggression against Vietnam. They even send their representatives
to sit at the same conference table at international meetings with
delegates of the Chiang Kai-shek gang, south Vietnamese and south
Korean puppet cliques, thus flagrantly serving the U.S. imperialist
schemes for splitting China, Vietnam and Korea. These acts of
treachery by the Soviet leaders are enough to show that they are the

enemy of the revolutionary people of Asia and the world. They will
come to no better end than the U.S. imperialists.

Taiwan Province is an inalienable part of China's territory.
It is the sacred task of the Chinese people to liberate it, to drive out
the U.S. imperialists, to enable our compatriots in Taiwan who are
living a miserable life under the U.S.-Chiang Kai-shek reactionary
rule, to return to the embrace of their motherland, and to fulfill the
great cause of unifying the motherland. The Chinese people certainly
will liberate Taiwan Province, certainly will plant the five-star red
flag on Taiwan Province and certainly will drive out the U.S. aggressors.
Unswervingly, the Chinese people support the revolutionary struggles
of the people of all countries in the world and, along with the people
of Asia and the rest of the world, they are determined to drive U.S.
imperialism out of Asia and of all the places it occupies!

DOCUMENT 88: PRC FOREIGN MINISTRY'S NOTE TO THE SOVIET EMBASSY IN CHINA, MARCH 21, 1968[24]

The note declared: The 700 million Chinese people, who are
armed with the all-conquering thought of Mao Tse-tung, are not to be
trifled with. By collaborating with U.S. imperialism in the "two
Chinas" plot, the Soviet revisionist ruling clique will only further
expose its shameful features as U.S. imperialism's accomplice before
the people of the whole world.

The note said: The so-called "national emblem" of the Chiang
Kai-shek bandit gang has appeared in an inside cover picture publicizing
the Olympic Games in New Books, U.S.S.R. No. 6, a bulletin published
this year by the Soviet revisionists' International Publishers. Even
more, the Soviet side provocatively sent this bulletin to the Chinese
side. This is a new, grave crime committed by the Soviet Government
in actively collaborating with U.S. imperialism for the creation of
"two Chinas," a flagrant political provocation against the 700 million
Chinese people, and new iron-clad proof of the Soviet Government's
collusion with the Chiang Kai-shek bandit gang to oppose the great
People's Republic of China. The Chinese Government hereby lodges
a strong protest against this with the Soviet Government.

It continued: The Soviet revisionist ruling clique has long been
actively collaborating with U.S. imperialism in its criminal plot to
create "two Chinas." Soviet representatives have long since been
accustomed to sitting at the same table with "representatives" of the
Chiang Kai-shek bandit gang at so-called international conferences.
The Soviet press has openly described China's Taiwan as a "state"
and preached that "both Taiwan and Peking should be members of the

United Nations." The Chinese Government has more than once lodged protests with the Soviet Government against participation by the Soviet authorities in U.S. imperialism's maneuvers to create "two Chinas." But the Soviet Government, time and again ignoring the Chinese Government's just and firm stand, has collaborated with U.S. imperialism in an even more shameless and active way in this plot.

The note said in conclusion: We should like to tell the Soviet Government in all seriousness: Taiwan is an inalienable part of the sacred territory of the People's Republic of China. All plots to create "two Chinas" by anybody and in any form will never succeed and will meet with the Chinese people's resolute opposition.

DOCUMENT 89: ROC AMBASSADOR TO THE UNITED STATES CHOW SHU-KAI'S LETTER ON THE "STATUS OF TAIWAN"[25]

I am amazed to read the editorial in the April 4 [1968] issue of your paper under the caption "A Two-Montana Policy," making certain references to matters concerning Taiwan which are contrary to the facts.

The legal status of Taiwan and Penghu (the Pescadores) is beyond the shadow of a doubt. Our title to them is firmly based on the historical connections between China proper and these insular territories from time immemorial, the formal declaration of war on Japan (Dec. 9, 1941) nullifying the treaties, conventions, agreements and contracts concerning the relations between China and Japan; the Cairo Declaration (Dec. 1, 1943); the Potsdam Declaration (July 26, 1945); the Instrument of Surrender by Japan (Sept. 2, 1945); the Declaration of Sovereignty over Taiwan and the Pescadores by my Government (Aug. 30, 1945); the taking over of the territories (Oct. 15, 1945); and the formal retrocession, which was held in Taipei on Oct. 25, 1945.

The Instrument of Surrender is an important document, for it was signed by the representatives of Japan, the Supreme Commander of the Allied Powers, and the representatives of the Republic of China, the United States and seven other countries. It imposes on Japan an obligation which states that "we hereby undertake for the Emperor, the Japanese government and their successors to carry out the provisions of the Potsdam Declaration in good faith." I am not unaware of the fact that my government was prevented from the exercise of its legal right to sign with the other Allied powers the peace treaty with Japan on account of diplomatic intrigue, but this unwarranted action should not affect our legal title.

Regarding Taiwan's status, it is pertinent to quote two official statements of the United States. On Jan. 5, 1950, President Truman declared:

"In the joint declaration at Cairo on Dec. 1, 1943, the President of the United States, the British Prime Minister and the President of China stated that it was their purpose that territories that Japan had stolen from China, such as Formosa, should be restored to the Republic of China.

"The United States was a signatory to the Potsdam Declaration on July 26, 1945, which declared that the terms of the Cairo Declaration should be carried out. . . .

"In keeping with these declarations, Formosa was surrendered to Generalissimo Chiang Kai-shek and for the past four years the United States and other Allied Powers have accepted the exercise of Chinese authority over the islands."

On the same day, Mr. Dean Acheson, then Secretary of State, said:

"The Chinese have administered Formosa for four years. Neither the United States nor any other ally ever questioned that authority in that occupation. When Formosa was made a province of China raised any lawyers' doubts about that. That was regarded as in accordance with the commitments."

The inhabitants in Taiwan are also part of the Chinese people, whose forebears came mainly from Fukien and Kwangtung Provinces. In spite of their separation from the mother country for 50 years, they share and continuously retain the Chinese heritage and traditions.

I am constrained to take strong exception to your statement that our rule on Taiwan was "forcibly and violently imposed." When Taiwan was restored to our sovereignty, my government governed it as other provinces were governed and there was no discrimination whatsoever. There has been continuous freedom of action and expression and private initiative for all the people there regardless of their provinces of origin. It is natural, however, that we have to maintain order and internal security against Communist infiltration, subversion and other harmful activities. But our vigilance is always exercised in accordance with law and justice.

DOCUMENT 90: PRC FOREIGN MINISTRY'S STATEMENT
ON SINO-AMERICAN NEGOTIATIONS,
NOVEMBER 26, 1968[26]

Over the past 13 years, the Chinese Government has consistently adhered to the following two principles in the Sino-U.S. ambassadorial talks: First, the U.S. Government undertakes to immediately withdraw all its armed forces from China's territory Taiwan Province and the Taiwan Straits area and dismantle all its military installations in Taiwan Province; second, the U.S. Government agrees that China and the United States conclude an agreement on the Five Principles of Peaceful Coexistence. But in the past 13 years, while refusing all along to reach an agreement with the Chinese Government on these two principles, the U.S. Government, putting the cart before the horse, has kept on haggling over side issues. The Chinese Government has repeatedly told the U.S. side in explicit terms that the Chinese Government will never barter away principles. If the U.S. side continues its current practice, no result whatsoever will come of the Sino-U.S. ambassadorial talks no matter which administration assumes office in the United States.

DOCUMENT 91: COMMUNIQUÉ ON TALKS BETWEEN
CHINESE AND JAPANESE REPRESENTATIVES OF
MEMORANDUM TRADE OFFICES,
APRIL 4, 1969[27]

The Chinese representatives of the China-Japan Memorandum Trade Office and the Japanese representatives of the Japan-China Memorandum Trade Office held talks in Peking between February 22 and April 4, 1969. Both sides exchanged frank views on the present relations between China and Japan and other questions of common interest.

. . .

Both sides reaffirm that the three political principles confirmed by both sides in 1968 (One, not to pursue a policy of hostility toward China; two, not to participate in any conspiracy to create "two Chinas"; and three, not to obstruct the restoration of normal relations between China and Japan) and the principle that politics and economics are inseparable must be abided by in the relations between China and Japan, and are also the political basis for our relations.

. . .

The Chinese side strongly denounces the Sato government for stepping up its efforts to follow U.S. imperialism, for participating in the conspiracy to create "two Chinas." . . .
The Chinese side reiterates that to liberate Taiwan is China's internal affair and that the Chinese will definitely liberate Taiwan. The so-called "peace treaty" concluded by the Japanese Government

with the Chiang Kai-shek gang . . . is hostile to the Chinese people and is illegal and is resolutely opposed by the Chinese people.

The Japanese side agrees with the just stand of the Chinese side. It explicitly states that the Government of the People's Republic of China is the only legitimate government representing the Chinese people, that Taiwan Province is an inseparable part of China's territory, that this must be the basis for . . . the promotion of the normalization of diplomatic relations between Japan and China, and that it opposes the conspiracy of creating "two Chinas" in any form.

DOCUMENT 92: "U.S.-JAPANESE REACTIONARIES STEP UP 'TAIWAN INDEPENDENCE MOVEMENT' PLOT," PEOPLE'S DAILY, FEBRUARY 24, 1970[28]

Today, U.S. imperialism and the reactionary Sato government of Japan are ganging up to push their scheme for a . . . "Taiwan independence movement" in a vain effort to permanently occupy and annex China's sacred territory Taiwan.

Merely a variation of the "two Chinas" plot long carried out by the U.S. and Japanese reactionaries, the . . . "Taiwan independence movement" is nothing new. Its aim is to sever China's sacred territory Taiwan from the great People's Republic of China and turn it into a colony of the U.S. and Japanese reactionaries. Always dreaming of getting their hands again on China's sacred territory Taiwan, the Japanese reactionaries are conspiring and collaborating with U.S. imperialism in this scheme and acting as its front man.

The criminal activities of the U.S. and Japanese reactionaries in plotting the "Taiwan independence movement" have become even more rampant since the November talks of last year between the U.S. imperialist chieftain Nixon and the head of the reactionary Japanese Government Eisaku Sato. It was disclosed early this year that the U.S. and Japanese reactionaries smuggled their running dog, Peng Ming-min, one of the . . . "Taiwan independence movement" chieftains, out of Taiwan and let him engage in extensive activities. American reporters lost no time in arranging an "interview" with him. The American magazine Newsweek disclosed that the "Taiwan independence movement" was being pushed by Peng Ming-min* at

---

*Peng Ming-min was arrested by the Nationalist authorities in September, 1964, on a charge of advocating Taiwan independence. He later repented his act and publicly announced his support of the Nationalist cause of recovering the mainland. He was released from prison in November, 1965.

the instigation of U.S. imperialism. A henchman of the U.S. and Japanese reactionaries declared in Tokyo on January 15 that they have rigged up a so-called world-wide organization, the "Taiwan independence league," with "headquarters" in New York. On January 22, an organization under the signboard of the . . . "United Formosans in America for Independence" publicly distributed reactionary leaflets in New York, raising a clamor that Taiwan should be made what it called a "nation." U.S. imperialism's propaganda organs also made lots of noise at the same time in peddling . . . "Taiwan autonomy." Former U.S. Ambassador to Japan Edwin O. Reischauer, who had been trumpeting "Taiwan independence," also cried out for "a change of Taiwan's status" with the United States pulling the strings and Japan playing an on-stage role. Following the instructions of U.S. imperialism and harboring their own ulterior motives, the Japanese reactionaries have retained a number of . . . "Taiwan independents" since the war, allowing them to use Japan as a stamping ground for their activities and giving them big support in the way of manpower and facilities. It has been reported that the Japanese reactionaries are the string-pullers and the backstage managers of the recently concocted "Taiwan independence league." Not very long ago, they instigated and encouraged the so-called "Taiwan independents" to publish reactionary books and journals in Japan in a frantic bid for . . . "Taiwan independence." The Japanese bourgeois newspapers have also stirred up an evil gust "supporting the independence of Taiwan." A number of scheming Japanese politicians posing as religionists have traveled between Tokyo and Hong Kong and flagrantly conducted sinister activities on behalf of "Taiwan independence." One report said the reactionary Japanese authorities' request to their U.S. masters to let Japan play its role in "changing the status of Taiwan" had received wide circulation in Washington recently.

Put together long ago by U.S. imperialism, the "Taiwan independence movement" is inseparable from its consistent plot of creating "two Chinas." From Truman, Eisenhower, Kennedy and Johnson to Nixon, every master of the White House has persisted in being hostile to the Chinese people, occupying Taiwan and pushing the "two Chinas" plot. At a time when U.S. imperialism is riddled with worsening crises at home and abroad and is at the end of its tether, the Nixon government is using counter-revolutionary dual tactics more cunningly and resorting to various sinister tricks on the creation of "two Chinas." To carry out his . . . "new Asian policy" after taking office, an anxious Nixon wanted the Japanese reactionaries to share important "responsibility" and play "a key role" in U.S. aggression in Asia. To encourage the Japanese reactionaries to serve its policy of aggression in Asia, U.S. imperialism has allowed the Japanese reactionaries to get a foothold in Taiwan and other places under U.S. occupation in return for their service.

The Japanese reactionaries have a tacit understanding with U.S. imperialism on this scheme. Consistently following U.S. imperialism in creating "two Chinas," they have long cherished the ambition to grab China's sacred territory Taiwan once again. The Japanese militarist forces have never been reconciled to their expulsion from Taiwan and its return to China. From Yoshida and Kishi to Sato, there has been incessant clamoring that the . . . "territorial right over Taiwan is unsettled." Sato went to Taiwan himself on a sinister mission in 1967. On many occasions he has sent Japanese militarist elements and "survey missions" of all descriptions to get into Taiwan for unbridled counter-revolutionary activities and for collusion with the Chiang Kai-shek bandit gang to antagonize the Chinese people. The counter-revolutionary arrogance of the Japanese reactionaries has become even more rabid recently as a result of the instigation of their U.S. masters. In Washington, Sato shouted himself hoarse asserting that China's territory Taiwan is a "most important factor for the security of Japan." Not long ago, Japanese Foreign Minister Aichi also openly declared that the Japanese Government "must always bear in mind the Taiwan question." Having ulterior motives, he even described China's territory Taiwan as a "unique nation." It is as clear as daylight that the Japanese reactionaries are again dreaming their fond dream of seizing China's territory Taiwan.

Soviet revisionist social-imperialism has played an extremely despicable role in connection with the criminal activities of the U.S. and Japanese reactionaries in engineering "two Chinas" and cooking up the "Taiwan independence movement." A short time ago, TASS, mouthpiece of the Soviet revisionists, took U.S. Vice-President Agnew's visit to Asia as an opportunity to label China's sacred territory Taiwan as a "country," so as to act in coordination once again with the U.S.-Japanese scheme to create "two Chinas." The Soviet revisionists last year "invited" a U.S.-Chiang special agent Liu Chieh (who used the name Sydney Liu) to the Soviet Union for two weeks of sinister activities on the suggestion of bandit Chiang Ching-kuo. Earlier, the Soviet revisionists had sent a Soviet citizen under the pseudonym of Victor Louis to Taiwan to carry out clandestine activities as a "journalist." From these facts alone, it can be clearly seen that Soviet revisionist social-imperialism has been collaborating more and more closely with the Chiang Kai-shek bandit gang, the political mummy discarded long ago by the Chinese people!

Taiwan has been China's sacred territory ever since ancient times. The Chinese people will definitely never allow U.S. imperialism to perpetuate its occupation of Taiwan or Japanese militarism to lay hands on Taiwan again. No matter how the Chiang Kai-shek bandit gang looks upon the enemy as its father, no matter what intrigues or tricks the U.S. and Japanese reactionaries and Soviet revisionist social-imperialists cook up, all their attempts to sever Taiwan from China only amount to wishful thinking. The Chinese people's iron will to liberate Taiwan will never waver! We will definitely liberate Taiwan!

DOCUMENT 93: ROC PRESIDENT CHIANG KAI-SHEK'S INTERVIEW, MAY 23, 1970[29]

President Chiang told the IPI [International Press Institute] members that the prosperity and progress in the island province of Taiwan are in sharp contrast to the terrorism and disorder on the Communist-held mainland.

. . .

He said the Communists alleged that Taiwan is a police state and its people are under control of the armed forces.

"Have you seen here anything to justify their allegation?" the President asked his audience.

He also pointed out that the . . . "Formosan Independence Movement" is also a false propaganda campaign of the Maoists aimed at driving a wedge between the Chinese people so as to fulfill Mao Tse-tung's dream of "liberating Taiwan."

"In fact, the . . . 'Formosan Independence Movement' has no followers in Taiwan. They are only a handful of professional students abroad lured by others to work hand in glove with the Communists and become 'Communist Formosan Independents.' They are actually secretly financed by the Maoists while overtly being attacked by them."

He told the IPI members to go to the villages in Taiwan and ask the villagers about their ancestry. "Whether they are mainlanders who came to Taiwan 20 years ago or they are natives of the island, they will tell you they are of the same race and have the same blood and history. The only difference is in the time of their arrivals in Taiwan."

The President also reiterated that the Republic of China will recover the mainland with democratic politics, national spirit, . . . and culture instead of military force alone.

President Chiang said the government and people of the Republic of China are confident of achieving their mission of mainland recovery and of delivering their compatriots.

The President pointed out the political, economic and social contrasts and the difference in living conditions under the rule of the Maoists and that of the Republic of China.

He said the mainland has totalitarian tyranny while the Republic of China has a government of benevolence.

"History has told us that tyrannical rule will collapse in the long run," he said.

. . .

He said progress of the Republic of China may serve as a blueprint for construction of a new China after the recovery of the mainland. It is for this purpose that the government is endeavoring to build the island into a model province of the Three Principles of the People, he added.

"The Principle of Social Well-Being of Dr. Sun Yat-sen is the deadliest weapon against Communism. The Maoists sugarcoat their evil doings as socialism. In fact what they want is to control society and deprive the people of their freedoms to live and to work. You members of IPI, having compared what you have seen in Taiwan with the situation on the Communist-controlled mainland, will be able to distinguish between a government which is for the welfare of the people and a regime bent on persecuting them."

DOCUMENT 94: ROC FOREIGN MINISTER WEI TAO-MING'S STATEMENT ON THE REPRESENTATION OF CHINA IN THE UNITED NATIONS[30]

The Government of the Republic of China, which I have the honor to represent, is the legally constituted government of China. And as such, it commands the allegiance of all Chinese people, including those on the mainland and elsewhere. This is the only Government that can give expression to the authentic aspirations of the Chinese people, speak in their name as well as in their interest, and bring to bear their peace-loving traditions on world affairs.

It is true that the mainland of China has for two decades been under Communist occupation. But this does not give the Communists any right to represent the Chinese people at international forums. This simply means that the civil war in China has not yet come to an end.

The Government of the Republic of China is not an exile government. It is, as my delegation has time and again reminded the Assembly, a Chinese Government on Chinese soil. Its struggle with the Communist regime is purely an internal matter which can be resolved only by the Chinese people.

The Republic of China is a founding Member of the United Nations and is specified by the Charter as a Permanent Member of the Security Council. The Government of the Republic of China that participated in the San Francisco Conference in 1945 is the same Government of China on whose behalf I am speaking today. Indeed, I was myself privileged to serve as a delegate to that historic conference. There has been no break in the continuity of leadership, institutions and policy. Its legal status has not changed. The fact that Communist rebels are in occupation of the mainland does not affect this legal status. The Republic of China continues to exist and functions as a sovereign State.

DOCUMENT 95: U.S. DEPARTMENT OF STATE'S STATEMENT ON THE STATUS OF TAIWAN, APRIL 28, 1971[31]

. . . Press Officer Charles Bray . . . gave the following description of the U.S. attitude toward mainland China.

"We must deal with the practical situation as we find it. We recognize the Republic of China and have diplomatic relations with it. We have a treaty commitment to the defense of Taiwan and the Pescadores Islands on one hand. On the other hand, mainland China has been controlled and administered by the People's Republic of China for 21 years and for some time we have been dealing with that government on matters affecting our mutual interest."

. . .

Bray, in a prepared statement on the question about who exercises sovereignty over Taiwan, said:

"In our view sovereignty over Taiwan and the Pescadores is an unsettled question subject to future international resolution. Both the Republic of China and the People's Republic of China disagree with this conclusion. Both consider Taiwan and the Pescadores Islands are part of the sovereign state of China."

"Obviously we cannot hope to resolve the dispute between these two rival governments," Bray added.

"Our position has been and remains very firmly that whatever the ultimate resolution of the dispute between the Republic of China on Taiwan and the PRC on the mainland, it should be accomplished by peaceful means."

[He] said there were two ways this could be worked out—internationally, or directly by the two governments.

. . .

He said that the statement on Taiwan was a considered statement. He explained that the U.S. regards the status of the island as
unsettled, because in the Cairo and Potsdam declarations of World
War II, the allied powers "stated as their purpose that Taiwan should
be part of China."

"This statement of purpose was never formally implemented or
executed," he said.

There was an opportunity at the time of the San Francisco 1951
treaty of peace with Japan to settle the question of Taiwan, but the
subject was not dealt with.

"We regard the Republic of China as exercising legitimate
authority over Taiwan and the Pescadores by virtue of the fact that
Japanese forces occupying Taiwan were directed to surrender to the
force of the Republic of China," he said.

Bray also recalled President Truman's June 27, 1950, statement,
when he announced that the U.S. Seventh Fleet was being interposed
between Taiwan and the mainland of China, that the determination of
the future status of Taiwan "must await the restoration of security in
the Pacific, a peace settlement with Japan or consideration of the
United Nations."

The Nixon administration also follows this policy, Bray said.

DOCUMENT 96: ROC FOREIGN MINISTRY STATEMENT, APRIL 30, 1971[32]

The government of the Republic of China is astounded by Mr.
Bray's remarks on the so-called status of Taiwan and the Pescadores
and by his proposal for a direct negotiation between the government
of the Republic of China and the Peiping regime. Soon after the Chinese
government learned of the aforementioned statements, a ranking official
of the Ministry of Foreign Affairs made enquiry at the embassy of
the United States on April 29th.

Subsequently, Foreign Minister Chow Shu-kai asked American
Ambassador Walter P. McConaughy for a conference at 11 a.m. on
April 30. The Minister expressed the Chinese Government's extreme
concern with and took strong exception to the contents of the State
Department press officer's remarks.

Mr. Chow pointed out that both the Cairo Declaration and the
Potsdam Declaration clearly provided that Taiwan and the Pescadores
should be returned to the Republic of China. Moreover, the Sino-
Japanese Peace Treaty signed in 1952 and the Sino-American Mutual
Defense Treaty signed in 1954 have definitely recognized Taiwan and
the Pescadores as part of the territories of the Republic of China.

It is, therefore, beyond comprehension that the State Department press officer should have made at this time a statement touching upon the legal status of Taiwan and the Pescadores.

Minister Chow stressed the necessity for the U.S. government to make a clarification of this matter as soon as possible.

In reply, the American Ambassador told the Foreign Minister that he had made a telegraphic enquiry about this incident to the State Department and was instructed to assure the Chinese government that Mr. Bray's statement does not represent any change in the U.S. policy concerning the status of Taiwan and the Pescadores and the Republic of China's legitimate jurisdiction over Taiwan and the Pescadores.

The Ambassador added that it is the consistent policy of the United States that issues relating to this area should be settled by peaceful means, but this should not be construed as the United States advocating a direct negotiation between the Chinese Government and the Peiping regime.

Minister Chow made particular mention to the American Ambassador of the statement made by President Richard M. Nixon on the evening of April 29th (Washington time) at a press conference that any such suggestion for a direct negotiation is completely unrealistic. As far as the Chinese government is concerned, it is simply inconceivable.

Minister Chow emphatically asked the American Ambassador to convey the Chinese Government's firm and just stand to the State Department, to which the American ambassador agreed.

The Ministry of Foreign Affairs has also instructed today the Chinese embassy in Washington to make a strong representation to the State Department to the same effect.

DOCUMENT 97: COMMENTATOR, "FRESH EVIDENCE
OF THE U.S. GOVERNMENT'S HOSTILITY
TOWARD THE CHINESE PEOPLE,"
PEOPLE'S DAILY, MAY 4, 1971[33]

U. S. State Department spokesman Charles Bray made statements twice on April 28, openly claiming that the sovereignty over China's territory Taiwan and the Penghu Islands "is an unsettled question subject to future international resolution"; he also clamored that this is a question of agreements which ought to be reached between the . . . "two Chinese governments." . . . What self-contradictory and nonsensical remarks! The two statements by Bray are new evidence of the U.S. Government's crime in flagrantly interfering in China's internal affairs, persisting in the forcible occupation of China's territory Taiwan, and taking a hostile attitude toward the Chinese people.

Taiwan is part of Chinese territory from time immemorial. At the end of the 19th century, Japanese militarism forcibly occupied China's territory Taiwan by launching a war of aggression. But no country in the world has ever acknowledged that Japan's occupation of Taiwan was justified. The "Cairo Declaration" and the "Potsdam Declaration," to both of which the United States was a signatory, clearly proclaimed the restoration of Taiwan to China. Upon its surrender, Japan also accepted this stipulation. This is well known, universally acknowledged and irrefutable. How can it be said that sovereignty over Taiwan is an "unsettled" question? In a statement issued on January 5, 1950, former U.S. President Truman also openly admitted that Taiwan is China's territory and acknowledged "the exercise of Chinese authority over the island." He also declared that "the United States has no predatory designs on Formosa [Taiwan] or on any other Chinese territory." Later, Truman perfidiously sent armed forces to occupy China's territory Taiwan and the Penghu Islands. But this cannot change the fact that Taiwan is China's territory. Now the hue and cry made by the U.S. State Department spokesman Bray about the so-called "unsettled" sovereignty over Taiwan can in no way negate China's sacred sovereignty over Taiwan and the Penghu Islands. . . .

In order to patch up the tattered fallacy of . . . "unsettled" sovereignty over Taiwan, Bray arbitrarily said that although the Cairo and Potsdam Declarations stipulated that Taiwan should be returned to China, "this statement of purpose was never formally implemented." This is all the more a barefaced lie. In fact, Taiwan and the Penghu Islands were taken over by the then Chinese Government as early as October 25, 1945. From then on, China has resumed the sovereignty over Taiwan. In a comment on February 9, 1950, the U.S. State Department also admitted: "Formosa [Taiwan] has been administered by China since 1945. . . . It was incorporated into China as a province." Today, 26 years after Taiwan's return to China, the U.S. State Department has gone so far as to claim that there has been no such thing at all! This clumsy act of slapping oneself in the face indicates nothing but the stubbornness of U.S. imperialism in carrying on its aggressive ambitions toward China's territory Taiwan Province.

Bray's claim that the soverignty over Taiwan and the Penghu Islands is a question subject to "international resolution" or to be resolved on the basis of . . . "agreements arrived at between the two governments" of China is not only preposterous, but a flagrant interference in China's internal affairs. It is crystal clear that Taiwan and the Penghu Islands are an integral part of China's

territory and the question of "international resolution" does not exist
at all. The Chinese people will never permit the U.S. Government to
play with the plots of "two Chinas" or "one China, one Taiwan."
When and how the Chinese people liberate Taiwan is entirely China's
internal affair, and no foreign country has any right to interfere.

Our great leader Chairman Mao has pointed out: The Chinese
people "are determined to liberate Taiwan, to safeguard the national
sovereignty and territorial integrity of China." The U.S. armed forces
must pull out of Taiwan and the Taiwan Straits. The U.S. aggressors
have to pull out in any case and are not allowed to behave otherwise.
China's sacred territory Taiwan and the Penghu Islands must be
returned to the embrace of the motherland.

DOCUMENT 98: ROC PRESIDENT CHIANG KAI-SHEK'S STATEMENT ON THE WITHDRAWAL OF THE ROC FROM THE UNITED NATIONS, OCTOBER 26, 1971[34]

The twenty-sixth session of the United Nations General Assembly
has elected to violate the provisions of the Charter of the United
Nations and adopted a resolution proposed by Albania and other nations
which are currying favor with the Chinese Communists. As a result,
the Mao Tse-tung bandit regime has usurped the Republic of China's
rightful position in the United Nations and the Security Council.
Before this infamous resolution could be put to a vote, this country
announced its withdrawal from the United Nations, an organization
which it took part in establishing. We declared that neither the
Government of the Republic of China nor the Chinese people will ever
recognize the validity of an illegal resolution adopted by the current
United Nations session in flagrant violation of the provisions of its
own Charter.

The Mao Tse-tung bandit regime is a group rebelling against
the Republic of China. Internally, it has committed enormous crimes
against the people of China. It is the common enemy of all the
Chinese people and especially of our seven hundred million compatriots on the mainland. Externally, the Mao regime stops at
nothing in promoting subversion and committing aggression, and still
stands officially condemned by the United Nations as an aggressor.
The Chinese Communists may occupy the mainland for the present.
But the Government of the Republic of China, with its base in Taiwan,
Penghu, Kinmen [Quemoy] and Matsu, is the true representative of
the seven hundred million Chinese on the mainland, expressing their
common will, heeding their anguished outcries and inculcating within
them a maximum of courage and hope with which to struggle against

the violence of the Mao regime and win back their human rights and freedom. It is clear, therefore, that the Chinese Communists should never be permitted illegally to occupy the General Assembly and Security Council seats held by the Republic of China, whether this be judged by the principles of the United Nations Charter or on a basis of humanitarianism, the law of nature or, in particular, the common will of all the Chinese people.

In 1942, China signed the United Nations Declaration and subsequently took part in the Dumbarton Oaks Conference. This country then participated in the United Nations Conference on International Organization held at San Francisco and helped write the Charter. These efforts were dedicated to saving "succeeding generations from the scourge of war, which twice in our lifetime has brought untold sorrow to mankind." To achieve this goal, the purposes and principles of the United Nations were set forth for the faithful adherence of all the participants. But the current session of the United Nations General Assembly has decided to destroy these very purposes and principles of the Charter, thereby ignoring and completely disregarding law and justice, shamelessly bowing to the forces of evil and timorously yielding to violence. Thus the United Nations, which this country helped to establish after so many trials, has finally degraded itself and become a den of iniquity. History will surely show that our announcement of withdrawal from the United Nations actually presaged the demise of the United Nations itself.

The Chinese cultural tradition is to uphold justice and love peace. Although we have withdrawn from the United Nations, which we helped establish, we shall continue to be guided by the purposes and principles of the United Nations Charter in the international community and shall continue to fight courageously for international truth and justice and for world peace and security.

I hereby solemnly declare:

—That the restoration of human rights and freedom to our 700 million compatriots on the mainland is the common will of the whole Chinese race and is our unalterable national purpose and the holy task which we must accomplish.

—That the Republic of China, an independent sovereign state, will tolerate no external interference.

—That regardless of the changing international situation, we shall unhesitatingly make whatever sacrifices may be required and persevere in our struggle. We shall never waver. We shall never compromise.

DOCUMENT 99: NIXON-CHOU COMMUNIQUÉ,
FEBRUARY 28, 1972[35]

President Richard Nixon of the United States of America visited
the People's Republic of China at the invitation of Premier Chou En-
lai of the People's Republic of China from February 21 to February
28, 1972.

. . .

The two sides reviewed the long-standing serious disputes
between China and the United States. The Chinese side reaffirmed
its position: the Taiwan question is the crucial question obstructing
the normalization of relations between China and the United States;
the Government of the People's Republic of China is the sole legal
Government of China; Taiwan is a province of China, which has long
been returned to the motherland; the liberation of Taiwan is China's
internal affair, in which no other country has the right to interfere;
and all U.S. forces and military installations must be withdrawn from
Taiwan. The Chinese Government firmly opposes any activities which
aim at the creation of "one China, one Taiwan," "one China, two
governments," "two Chinas," and "independent Taiwan" or advocate
that "the status of Taiwan remains to be determined."
    The U.S. side declared: The United States acknowledges that
Chinese on either side of the Taiwan Straits maintain there is but one
China and that Taiwan is a part of China.
    The United States Government does not challenge that position.
It reaffirms its interest in a peaceful settlement of the Taiwan
question by the Chinese themselves. With this prospect in mind, it
affirms the ultimate objective of the withdrawal of all U.S. forces and
military installations from Taiwan.
    In the meantime, it will progressively reduce its forces and
military installations on Taiwan as the tension in the area diminishes.

DOCUMENT 100: ROC FOREIGN MINISTRY'S
STATEMENT ON NIXON-CHOU
COMMUNIQUE, FEBRUARY 28,
1972[36]

Concerning the so-called "Joint Communiqué" issued by
President Nixon and Chou En-lai, the Government of the Republic of
China hereby reiterates its solemn declaration made on February 17,
1972, that it will consider null and void any agreement, which has been

and which may not have been published, involving the rights and
interests of the Government and people of the Republic of China,
reached between the United States and the Chinese Communist regime
as a result of the visit, because the regime now occupying the Chinese
mainland is a rebel group which has no right whatsoever to represent
the Chinese people.

. . .

The "Joint Communiqué" touched upon the . . . "question of
Taiwan." The Government of the Republic of China wishes to declare
solemnly that the Chinese Communist regime is the public enemy of
all the people of China and that it is also the source of troubles of
Asia and the entire world. The effort exerted by the Government of
the Republic of China and the Chinese people both at home and abroad
in overthrowing the brutal rule of the said regime has as its objectives
not only the salvation of China but also that of Asia and the world.
The destruction of the tyranny of the Chinese Communist regime is a
sacred responsibility of the Government and people of the Republic of
China which will never waver or change under any circumstances.
Our question can be solved only when the Government of the Republic
of China, the sole legitimate Government elected by all people of
China, has succeeded in its tasks of the recovery of the mainland,
the unification of China and the deliverance of our compatriots. There
is definitely no other alternative.

. . .

According to President Nixon, he made the trip to the Chinese
mainland with the hope that it might bring a "generation of peace" and
relax tensions in Asian and the Pacific region. Actually, the effects
caused by the visit of President Nixon are diametrically opposite to
what he expected, and the countries in Asia and the Pacific area will
be among the first ones to suffer from its aftermath. It is the considered opinion of the Government of the Republic of China that countries
in this area either have already tasted the bitter cup of political subversion and armed aggression by the Chinese Communists or are now
confronting . . . such menace. In order to assure their freedom and
security, countries in this area must rely upon their own determination
and strength and spare no efforts in consolidating the unity and
cooperation among themselves. They should not entertain the slightest
illusion of coexisting peacefully with the Chinese Communists.

On its part, the Republic of China has the utmost confidence in
overcoming all dangers and difficulties. Henceforth, we shall continue
to strengthen ourselves through calmness and dignity as well as to

keep the destiny in our own hands. We shall redouble our efforts in striving for the sacred tasks of the early restoration of freedom to our compatriots on the Chinese mainland.

NOTES

1. Excerpt from American Foreign Policy, 1959, Current Documents (Washington, D.C.: U.S. Government Printing Office, 1963), p. 1188.

2. Current Digest of the Soviet Press, XVI, 25 (July 15, 1964), 5-6. The article is reprinted from the magazine Problemy mira i sotsializma [Problems of peace and socialism], No. 6, in somewhat condensed form.

3. Excerpt from President Chiang Kai-shek's Selected Speeches and Messages in 1960 (Taipei: Government Information Office, 1960), pp. 22-24.

4. Excerpt from ibid., pp. 95-96.

5. Excerpt from Oppose the New U.S. Plots to Create "Two Chinas" (Peking: Foreign Languages Press, 1962), pp. 3-6.

6. Excerpt from (Peking Review, III, 37 (September 14, 1960), 26-29.

7. Excerpt from American Foreign Policy, 1961, Current Documents (Washington, D.C.: U.S. Government Printing Office, 1965), p. 946.

8. Excerpt from President Chiang Kai-shek's Selected Speeches and Messages in 1961 (Taipei: Government Information Office, 1961), pp. 47-49.

9. Excerpt from Peking Review, IV, 28 (July 14, 1961), 8-9.

10. Oppose the New U.S. Plots to Create "Two Chinas," pp. 17-23.

11. Excerpt from American Foreign Policy, 1961, Current Documents, pp. 949-51.

12. Oppose the New U.S. Plots to Create "Two Chinas," pp. 100-08.

13. Excerpt from Peking Review, V, 26 (June 29, 1962), 5-6.

14. Excerpt from ibid., VI, 36 (September 6, 1963), 13-14.

15. Excerpt from ibid., VII, 10 (March 6, 1964), 18-19.

16. Translated from the Chinese text supplied by the ROC Ministry of Foreign Affairs.

17. Excerpt from President Chiang Kai-shek's Selected Speeches and Messages in 1964 (Taipei: Government Information Office), pp. 37-38, 39.

18. Excerpt from Peking Review, VII, 20 (May 15, 1964), 7-8.

19. Survey of China Mainland Press, No. 3235 (June 10, 1964), pp. 28-30. Hsu Meng-shan is the secretary-general of the Taiwan Democratic Self-Government League.

20. Excerpt from President Chiang Kai-shek's Selected Speeches and Messages in 1965 (Taipei: Government Information Office), pp. 7-8.

21. Excerpt from Peking Review, VIII, 27 (July 2, 1965), 9-10.

22. Excerpt from ibid., No. 41 (October 8, 1965), p. 12.

23. Excerpt from ibid., IX, 27 (June 1, 1966), 38-39.

24. Ibid., XI, 13 (March 29, 1968), 9.

25. The Washington Post, April 15, 1968, p. A16.

26. Excerpt from Peking Review, XI, 48 (November 29, 1968), 31.

27. Excerpt from ibid., XII, 15 (April 11, 1969), 38.

28. Ibid., XIII, 10 (March 6, 1970), 21-22.

29. Excerpt from Free China Weekly, XI, 22 (May 31, 1970), 1.

30. Delivered at the 1902nd plenary meeting of the General Assembly of the United Nations, November 12, 1970. (Excerpt from text supplied by the ROC delegation to the United Nations.

31. Excerpt from Associated Press, Washington, D.C., April 29, in China Post, Taipei, April 30, 1971, p. 1.

32. News from China (New York: Chinese Information Service, May 1, 1971), pp. 71-352.

33. Peking Review, XIV, 19 (May 7, 1971), 13-14.

34. Excerpt from The China News, Taipei, October 27, 1971, p. 8.

35. Excerpt from Peking Review, XV, 9 (March 3, 1972), 5. Although the communiqué was dated February 28, it was released at Shanghai on February 27.

36. Excerpt from The China News, Taipei, February 29, 1972, p. 8.

8

**UNOFFICIAL MATERIALS
RELATING TO THE QUESTION
OF TAIWAN, 1925-69**

ITEM 1: THE FIRST MANIFESTO OF THE TAIWAN
COMRADES ASSOCIATION AT AMOY,
April 18, 1925 [1]

The day of May 9 is coming. The inhuman and treacherous 21 Demands have not been terminated.* The lease of Port Arthur and Dairen expired two years ago. Compatriots of China! We Taiwanese are also Han Chinese. Our ancestors came from Chang-chou and Ch'uan-chou of Fukien [Province] and Ch'ao-chou of Kwangtung [Province]. They came to Taiwan because they wanted to escape the cruel administration of the Manchus and to develop the Han Chinese. In the twenty-first year of Kuang-hsu Emperor [1895], the Sino-Japanese War ended. The Manchus ceded Taiwan to Japan. They let the most valuable treasured land in the Far East fall into the hands of the Japanese.

Japan is a dictatorial monarchy. It has been thirty years since Japan took Taiwan. The Japanese usurp the land which we cultivated. They occupy the mines and forest which we exploited and confiscate the agricultural outputs which we produced. They have taken away

---

*In 1915 Japan presented a secret ultimatum to Chinese President Yuan Shih-k'ai (1859-1916) that demanded Japanese control over German interests in Shangtung Province, control over Mongolia and Manchuria, exploitation of China's main coal deposits, exclusion of other powers from further territorial concessions, and guidance of China's military and domestic affairs. On May 9, 1915, President Yuan accepted the Japanese demands. From then on, all Chinese regarded May 9 as a day of national shame.

all the people's rights. They adopt an evil economic policy for Taiwan and suppress us with methods only a demon would use. They oppress our spirit as well as our material life. Consider the fact that there are more than 50,000 Japanese officials on Taiwan, who constitute more than 40 percent of the entire Japanese population on the island. These officials carry out a cruel policy. They collect heavy taxes, inflict torture on people, deprive us of the freedom of expression and press. Moreover, the Japanese have the ambition to annex Fukien [Province].

Since they took over Taiwan, the Japanese have prevented Taiwanese from returning to their motherland. Not even communication between people on Taiwan and relatives on the mainland is allowed. They prevent the people from loving and helping each other. They are pursuing a dirty policy of taking over Fukien [Province]. What they do is to use the evil elements among Taiwanese to open prostitution houses, gambling houses, and opium shops in Amoy. All this is designed to cause chaos in the society. They will do every evil thing to achieve their purpose. We are considering ways of curbing this confusion.

Taiwanese in Amoy! We Taiwanese are not Japanese. The Japanese are our enemies. We must reject them and not cooperate with them. We Taiwanese are Han Chinese and are compatriots of China. We must help ourselves and not harm each other.

Taiwanese in Amoy! We must understand our own position. We have no place of our own to live and we all are oppressed people under the Japanese rule. Thus, we have to live a hard life and be prepared to revenge what we have suffered. We in Amoy must engage in decent business and avoid being used by the Japanese.

Chinese compatriots in Amoy! We must keep in our memory the national shame which we have sustained and never forget the day when that national shame was imposed on us. We must consolidate ourselves and pledge to recover the lost territory, to abolish unequal treaties and to get rid of foreign domination. We want to establish an independent and democratic state [in China]!

ITEM 2: "EDITORIAL:
CHINA MUST RECOVER TAIWAN"[2]

Taiwan has been an old enemy-occupied territory of China for a long time. We cannot tolerate its being ruled by a foreign country. After the war, China must recover this land.

First of all, according to the principle of occupation in public international law, Taiwan is unquestionably a territory of China. From the beginning, it was the Chinese who . . . cultivated the

Pescadores. Since the Sui dynasty (A.D. 589-618), when General
Ch'en Lin opened the history of Taiwan, Chinese have occupied Taiwan
and the Pescadores. The Yüan dynasty (A.D. 1280-1368) appointed a
Commissioner to the Pescadores, and the administration continued
without interruption. Although Taiwan, like America during the
colonial period, was subjected to foreign exploitation, the Chinese
finally triumphed over others in the area. The Portuguese admired
the beauty of Taiwan and called it "Formosa," and the Spanish fleets
once occupied Keelung. The Dutch took and ruled Taiwan for thirty-
seven years. But the land finally came to China. During the reign
of T'sung-cheng, Emperor (A.D. 1627-1644) of the Ming dynasty
(A.D. 1368-1644), Cheng Chih-lung led thousands of poor people from
Fukien to cultivate Taiwan. Thereafter, immigrants from Chang-chou
and Ch'uan-chou [of Fukien Province] came to cultivate the land and
resources of Taiwan. It was they who built up towns and villages on
the island, cultivated farms and transformed a wild land into a place
of culture. When Cheng Ch'en-kung led his great fleet to attack the
Dutch on Taiwan, and fought the Dutch in a decisive battle at An-p'ing,
his pledge was "to recover the lost land of our ancestors which, after
recovery, will be subject to you and your offspring to exploit!"

At that time, Cheng Ch'en-kung considered Taiwan a land which
in the past belonged to Chinese ancestors. After he recovered Taiwan,
Cheng's administration established a state on Taiwan. He brought
about a prosperous agriculture, built up a strong military force,
designed and promulgated a legal system, and established schools.
He encouraged migration from Chang-chou and Ch'uan-chou [of Fukien
Province], and Ch'ao-chou and Hui-chou [of Kwangtung Province].
The whole island of Taiwan then became a rich land. After 23 years
of cultivation and development on Taiwan, the Cheng administration
had transformed Taiwan into a place of brilliant civilization. Therefore, we say Taiwan belonged to Chinese through occupation. Moreover, the Ch'ing dynasty (A.D. 1644-1911) ruled this land for more
than two hundred years, subjecting it to the Commissioner at Fukien
and constituting it a part of Fukien Province.

Second, Japan took Taiwan away from China; therefore the island
should be returned to China. According to public international law,
the Chinese loss of Taiwan and the Japanese acquisition of Taiwan
occurred in the form of cession—the Shimonoseki Treaty concluded
on April 17, 1895, which provides, inter alia, that "China cedes to
Japan in perpetuity . . . the Island of Formosa and the Pescadores
Group. . . ." Before this treaty became null and void, we did not talk
much about the restoration of Taiwan. During the period between
[July 7, 1937] and [December 8, 1941], China made no formal comment
on the problem of Taiwan. During this period, China's goal was
merely to restore the situation prior to the Mukden Incident

[September 18, 1931]. It was when China declared war on Japan in 1941 that the Shimonoseki Treaty lost its validity as of midnight on December 9, 1941. From that time, China has pursued the course of liquidating the Sino-Japanese relations begun by the 1895 Sino-Japanese War. That is, when war was formally declared, the sovereignty over Taiwan was no longer bound by any treaty. Taiwan became an old enemy-occupied territory of China, just like the four provinces in Manchuria and other places occupied by the Japanese after July 7, 1937. China resisted Japan for the purpose of protecting the territorial integrity of China. China fought because it wanted to liquidate the Sino-Japanese relations since 1895. We have sacrificed and suffered. We naturally want to recover all our lost territories, including Taiwan.

Third, according to the Atlantic Charter, Taiwan ought to be returned to China. Article 3 of the Atlantic Charter provides that "[the United States and Great Britain] respect the right of all peoples to choose the form of government under which they will live; and they wish to see sovereign rights and self-government restored to those who have been forcibly deprived of them. The change of sovereignty over Taiwan was without "the freely expressed wishes of the peoples concerned" as provided in Article 2 of the Atlantic Charter. When the Japanese occupied Taiwan through imperialist means, the Taiwanese revolted against them with their lives. On May 2, 1895, Taiwanese elected T'ang Ching-sung as their President, and gave birth to the first republic in East Asia. They fought the Japanese for nine years and lost half a million lives. Taiwanese had no freedom, nor had they the right to determine the form of their government. The peace settlement after the present war should inquire: What people are Taiwanese? What kind of government do they want?

We can answer this inquiry in definite terms. The five million-person population of Taiwan, except for the 150,000 aborigines of Malay origin living in the mountains and the 200,000 Japanese living as the ruling and exploiting class on the island, is all Chinese, either from Fukien or from Kwangtung. Its language and customs are all identical to those prevailing in Kwangtung or Fukien. The people's political aspiration is very simple: They want Taiwan to return to their motherland.

The above three points illustrate the fact that China has every reason to recover Taiwan. It simply is not proper to arbitrarily separate Taiwan from China. If any citizen of the allied powers indulges himself in the notion that Taiwan be separated from China, he will be strongly opposed by the Chinese.

From the viewpoint of national defense, Taiwan constitutes a stronghold in the southeast part of China. Taiwan and Hainan Island are a pair of eyes of China. Who wants other people to destroy a stronghold for China's defense? Who wants other people to take its eyes?

We also would like to take this opportunity to express our hope that the Government will design appropriate measures in preparation for recovery of Taiwan. It should treat Taiwan as one of our enemy-occupied provinces. It should frankly announce our reasonable aspiration in order to prevent disputes and different opinions from developing in the future.

ITEM 3: LETTER FROM THE TAIWAN REVOLUTION ALLIANCE ASSOCIATION TO THE NATIONAL GOVERNMENT REQUESTING THE ESTABLISHMENT OF A TAIWAN PROVINCIAL GOVERNMENT, 1943[3]

Taiwan today is a strategic stronghold of our country. We must now be prepared for its recovery. This preparation not only will signify our determination to maintain our territorial integrity, but also will concentrate the revolutionary zeal of people on Taiwan and unify their steps in the anti-Japanese movement. This Association is an organization for the direction of revolution on Taiwan. Because of the demands of the time and the urgency of the current situation, we cannot keep silent but want to express our considered opinion [on China's policy toward Taiwan]. We sincerely request the Government to consider the situation with which we are faced and permit the establishment of a provincial government of Taiwan. This will stir up the spirit of the people there and justify their hope. It will enable and encourage them to subscribe to the Three Principles of the People and facilitate the restoration to the motherland of the territory whose loss China has suffered for fifty years. Whether or not our proposal is feasible is subject to your approval by an official reply.

ITEM 4: SHAO CHIN-FU, "THE ABSURD THEORY OF 'TWO CHINAS' AND PRINCIPLES OF INTERNATIONAL LAW"[4]

In the past years, the conspiratorial activities of American imperialists to create "two Chinas" have become more active and exposed. On the one hand they have used all means, including the threat of war and diplomatic negotiations, to frustrate the people of our country from liberating Taiwan. On the other hand, [American imperialists] have exercised pressure upon the Chiang Kai-shek clique by compelling them "to abandon the use of force" to counterattack the mainland and even to withdraw from Quemoy and Matsu so as to create a factural situation of the concurrent existence of "two Chinas" by limiting [the Chiang Kai-shek clique] to the small areas of Taiwan and Penghu.

The genuine purpose of such activities by American imperialism is to permanently occupy Taiwan, and the creating of "two Chinas" is merely a tactic for achieving this purpose. In order to facilitate the carrying out of this [policy], [American imperialism's] tactics are divided into two steps: Firstly, [American imperialism] appoints the Chiang Kai-shek clique as "small China" and stations the Seventh Fleet in the Taiwan Straits to separate Taiwan from the mainland, so as to create the situation of a confrontation of "two Chinas." In other words, this is a step "to isolate Taiwan." Secondly, [American imperialism] will overthrow the Chiang regime by repeating the Huang-ku-t'un Incident* at the appropriate time and then will use the name of the United Nations "trusteeship" or some other to establish a "trusteeship of Taiwan" so as to transform Taiwan into its permanent colony.

From the very beginning American imperialism's conspiracy of creating "two Chinas" has been firmly opposed . . . by the Chinese government and people and solemnly condemned . . . by the just public opinions of the world. But American imperialists do not retreat when facing such difficulty, nor do they abandon such activities. On the contrary, in order to realize this criminal conspiracy, they have made great effort to spread the absurd theory concerning "two Chinas" and some of their accomplices and running dogs in various states have also come out for such shouting in an attempt to create an atmosphere to confuse the understanding of the world's people. Recently, the internal circle of the American ruling clique has been fomenting new ideas for "two Chinas"; therefore, we still have to be always on the alert, to give violent strikes against these conspiratorial activities of the United States and to solemnly refute the absurd theory of "two Chinas." Specifically, when American imperialists are fabricating this type of absurd theory, they frequently usurp some legal concepts to confuse right with wrong. Therefore, it is necessary to rely on general recognized international law and established historical facts to thoroughly expose the lies of the imperialists and to disclose the criminal essence of their intervention in the internal affairs of China and encroachment upon China's territorial sovereignty.

---

*Marshal Chang Tso-lin was a Chinese warlord in control of Manchuria after the founding of the Republic of China in 1911. In 1926 he went to Peking to assume leadership for resisting the Nationalist North Expedition Force. In early June, 1928, he decided to withdraw to Mukden in defiance of the Japanese advice. On June 4, 1928, a serious explosion occurred when his train was passing under a Japanese bridge at Huang-ku-t'un, just outside Mukden. Marshal Chang was severely injured and died within a few hours of the incident. It is believed that the incident was planned by Japan.

[The following translation is from <u>Oppose the New U.S. Plots to Create</u> <u>"Two Chinas"</u> (Peking: Foreign Languages Press, 1962), pp. 76-99. Footnotes renumbered.]

(1)

In the last few years the U.S. imperialists and their followers have concocted many "theoretical justifications" concerning "two Chinas." Generally they boil down to two sets of logic.

The first set begins with the allegation that the Chiang Kai-shek clique in Taiwan is a "sovereign state" existing side by side with the People's Republic of China. It follows that the relationship between the Chinese people and the Chiang Kai-shek clique is "not a civil war" but an international question. With the United States meddling in as an ally of the Chiang Kai-shek clique, a tripartite relationship between the United States, the Chiang Kai-shek clique and the People's Republic of China is thereby framed. Then certain principles and concepts of international law are cited, and the efforts of the Chinese people to liberate Taiwan will turn out to be "the use of armed force to seize new territory," "eliminating Free China," "crude violation of the principles upon which world order is based," and consequently they "endanger vital free world positions and the security of the United States." Therefore, China must agree to make "a declaration of renunciation of force" and carry out a cease-fire. On the other hand, by its occupation of China's territory and interference in China's internal affairs the United States is "living up to treaty obligations," helping "a loyal ally" and enjoying the "right of self-defense" in the Taiwan area. If China does not accept the U.S. demands, then the United States "reserves the right to bring the matter to the United Nations" or to the International Court of Justice, and so on and so forth.

The second set of logic is for the purpose of refusing to recognize China's sovereignty over Taiwan, alleging that the "legal status of Taiwan is unsettled," that China cannot by a unilateral declaration recover her sovereignty which she had ceded by treaty, that the Cairo Declaration was "merely a declaration of intention" and the question "cannot be solved merely by reference to the Cairo and Potsdam Declarations," and that Taiwan, Penghu, Quemoy and Matsu "have never been under the authority of the Chinese Communists," and should, therefore, be "placed under U.N. trusteeship" or "settled by a plebiscite," and so on and so forth.

Obviously these two sets of logic serve two schemes, two steps, i.e., "isolating Taiwan" and "placing Taiwan under trusteeship." The imperialists use the first set of logic to deny the legality of the right of the Chinese people to liberate Taiwan, claiming that the Chiang

Kai-shek clique is another China so as to legalize U.S. intervention in China's internal affairs and its armed occupation of Taiwan. Then they use the second set of logic to deny the Chinese people's sovereignty over Taiwan altogether; that is, to create a legal basis for kicking out the Chiang Kai-shek regime and placing Taiwan under trusteeship and, as a further step, to seize Taiwan for themselves and use it as a base for extending aggression.

These arguments are gangster logic. . . .

First of all, the premises of the first set of logic used by the U.S. imperialists, that the Chiang Kai-shek clique in Taiwan is a state, are extremely absurd.

According to the principles of international law concerning sovereign equality and national self-determination, the adoption of any form of state is the affair of a nation itself. In other words "the establishment of a state organization—a subject of international law—depends upon the free decision of the nation itself.[1] No foreign country has the right to interfere.

China has always been a unified state. Article 3 of the Constitution of the People's Republic of China has made this provision.[2] As national unity is the highest interest of all nationalities in the country and the safeguarding of national unity is their common will, even the reactionary governments of the past could not but recognize this point in their constitutions. In international relations China has always played its part as a unified sovereign state, a single subject of international law. Furthermore, long diplomatic practice has shown that whether at international conferences or in international treaties, China has always participated or signed in the name of a single state. This basic situation did not change even in the periods of mélées between the warlords or revolutionary civil wars. It is still less likely that the question of "two Chinas" will ever arise since the victory of the people's revolution in 1949, when nationwide unification was achieved as never before.

As to the Chiang Kai-shek clique still entrenched in Taiwan, it is the remnant of old China's reactionary ruling clique. . . . This clique depends for its existence entirely on U.S. support and has no mass basis to speak of. It is out of the question that this clique is a "sovereign state." Furthermore, it does not claim to be a new state; on the contrary, it styles itself the "Republic of China," and emphasizes that "Taiwan and the mainland belong to one entity." Notwithstanding

---

1. G. I. Tunkin, The Bases of Modern International Law (Russian), 1956, p. 17.

2. Article 3: "The People's Republic of China is a unitary multi-national state."

its dream for a comeback which will never come true, one point is quite clear, that is, all Chinese recognize Taiwan as a part of China, but not as a state outside of China.

To bring up the matter in a false light, the U.S. imperialists purposely call the People's Republic of China "Communist China" or "mainland China" to distinguish it from Chiang Kai-shek's "Republic of China," in an attempt to create an impression that the People's Republic of China is a new member in international relations while the Chiang Kai-shek clique is the continuance of old China. However, people with some common sense all know that the overthrowing of an old government and the replacing of it with a new one by the people of a country through revolutionary means is an internal question and does not affect the qualification of that country as a member in international relations. In its class nature the People's Republic of China is a new state entirely different from old China, but it is not a new member in the family of nations. In international law it is not a new subject, but continues to exist as a member in international relations in the place of old China. All rights of old China are the rights of New China; all territories of old China are the territories of New China. Taiwan is a part of China. Naturally it is within the sovereignty of New China. The imperialists' insistent allegations that it is a "state" are nothing but lies with ulterior motives.

The U.S. imperialists' allegation that the local authorities controlled by the Chiang Kai-shek clique in Taiwan are the legitimate government of China is likewise without any foundation.

According to international law, "In such single States there is one central political authority as Government, which represents the State, within its borders as well as without, in its international intercourse with other International Persons."[3] "It [international law] recognizes the government which actually and independently exercises power on the territory of the state as the representative of that state in international relations."[4] To quote the Italian jurist Anzilotti, "He who actually holds the power of command has the quality of organ of international personality in international relations; he who in fact loses this power ceases to represent the state internationally."[5] Whether the government of a state is legal or not, only the people of

---

3. Oppenheim, International Law, H. Lauterpacht, ed. (7th ed.; London, New York, and Toronto: Longmans, Green, 1948), pp. 161-62.

4. Tunkin, The Bases of Modern International Law, p. 23.

5. D. Anzilotti, A Course in International Law, French ed., I, p. 179.

that state can decide; "Nobody has the right to examine . . . the question of the legality of the government chosen by the people themselves."6

The Government of the People's Republic of China has been set up after the Chinese people, under the leadership of the Chinese Communist Party, overthrew the Kuomintang reactionary rule through long years of struggle. It exercises state power within the country. Naturally, therefore, it is this government alone that can represent China in foreign relations as the only legitimate government of China.

The reactionary Kuomintang government has already been overthrown by the Chinese people. As to the regime set up in Taiwan by a remnant part of old China's reactionary ruling clique, it may at best be regarded as a local authority of China and absolutely has not the qualifications of a central government. Undoubtedly it cannot represent China in foreign relations and has no right to deal with foreign countries. Moreover, since October 1, 1949, "The Republic of China" has ceased to exist. This title, like the titles of the different dynasties in China, has become a historical relic. The using of the signboard of the "Republic of China" up to the present by the Chiang Kai-shek clique is an act of usurpation; it is of course illegal.

. . .

The relationship between the People's Republic of China and the Chiang Kai-shek clique is the continuation of the internal struggle in the last thirty years between the Chinese people under the leadership of the Chinese Communist Party and the Kuomintang reactionaries. It is China's internal question, a matter between the Chinese themselves. No foreign country, whether it has recognized the People's Republic of China or not, has the right to intervene.

(2)

In order to prove that there exist "two Chinas" the U.S. imperialists try to draw a parallel between the relationship of the Chinese mainland with Taiwan and that of East Germany with West Germany, North Korea with South Korea and North Viet Nam with South Viet Nam. This is also preposterous.

Let us first take the case of Germany.

With the defeat and unconditional surrender of Nazi Germany, the situation was: "There is no central government or authority in

6. L. A. Modzhoryan, "The Identity, Continuity and Succession of the Subject of International Law," The Soviet State and Law (Russian), No. 9 (1958), p. 63.

Germany capable of accepting responsibility for the maintenance of order, the administration of the country and compliance with the requirements of the victorious Powers."[7] On the basis of the relevant provisions of the Crimea statement of February, 1945, the declaration of the four Powers—the Soviet Union, the United States, Britain and France—on June 5 regarding the defeat of Germany and the assumption of supreme authority in Germany, and the Potsdam Declaration of August 3 of the same year, the four governments "assumed the supreme authority with respect to Germany," which was exercised by the commanders-in-chief of the four Powers in their respective zones of occupation. Later, on account of the obstructions of the Western Powers, a united German government was never set up nor was a peace treaty with Germany concluded. On September 7, 1949, under the manipulation of the United States, the "German Federal Republic" was established in the occupation zones of the three Western Powers. In October of the same year the people in East Germany set up the German Democratic Republic in the Soviet occupation zone. "At first these two states were subject to certain restrictions by the respective occupying Powers in the exercise of their state functions, but gradually these restrictions were removed. Now both are sovereign states though there are essential differences in their conditions."[8]

It can be seen that: First, the Hitler government of Germany was not overthrown by the German people. It was destroyed in its war of aggression, and according to international agreements the supreme authority of Germany was assumed by the four victorious Powers. Secondly, on account of the obstructions of the Western Powers the German people were unable to establish a united government to succeed the old government. Instead they set up two states in the eastern and western occupation zones. From a legal point, "with the appearance of the German Democratic Republic and the German Federal Republic, Germany, formerly a subject of international law, has ceased to exist."[9] Each of the two Germanys becomes at

---

7. Declaration Regarding the Defeat of Germany and the Assumption of Supreme Authority with Respect to Germany by the Governments of the United States of America, the Union of Soviet Socialist Republics, the United Kingdom and the Provisional Government of the French Republic, signed at Berlin, June 5, 1945, Documents on American Foreign Relations, 1944-45, VII, p. 217.

8. Gerhard Raintantz, "The German Democratic Republic— Subject of International Law," The Soviet State and Law (Russian), No. 6 (1958), p. 41.

9. Ibid.

present a subject of international law by itself. Thirdly, the German question is one of the important international questions left over from World War II. The existence of two Germanys is a result of this war.

Similarly, the stationing, by agreement, of the Soviet and U.S. armed forces in Korea in 1945 and the Korean Armistice Agreement in July, 1953, had a bearing on the division of Korea into northern and southern parts. This was also a question left over from World War II. The division of Viet Nam into northern and southern parts was a temporary state of affairs provided by the Geneva Agreements of 1954. Fundamentally speaking, the division of Germany, Korea and Viet Nam was a result of the imperialist policy of aggression, particularly that of the United States. The people of these three countries are striving for the peaceful unification of their motherlands.

What about the Taiwan question?

First, the Chinese people themselves overthrew the old reactionary government by revolutionary means and in its place they set up the People's Government. This does not affect in any degree China's status as a member in the family of nations. Secondly, the question of restoring Taiwan to China was already settled after the Chinese people's victory in the War of Resistance Against Japan; it does not belong to the questions left over from World War II. Thirdly, the Chinese people's liberation of Taiwan is a continuation of the Chinese people's revolution after the war. It is purely an internal question which has nothing to do with international agreements and involves no international question. It can be seen, therefore, that the question of China's liberation of Taiwan is different from the cases of the aforementioned countries. The imperialists try to cite the instances of the temporary division of these countries, of which they themselves are authors, to justify their own infamous doings. They will gain nothing except exposing their own helplessness and stupidity.

(3)

While discussing the Taiwan question, former U.S. Secretary of State Dulles advocated that "no country should use armed force to seize new territory," and that it was a principle "upon which world order is based." He demanded that China agree to "make a declaration of mutual and reciprocal renunciation of force, except in self-defense" and to carry out "cease-fire" and "peaceful solution," and so on.

True, "to refrain from the use of armed force to seize new territory" is a generally recognized "principle upon which world order is based." But this is a principle of international law. International law consists of principles for the settlement of questions concerning the relations between states, but not principles for settling internal questions of a state. An internal question is different in nature from

an international question. Municipal law and international law have
different scopes of application; the two should never be confused.
The well-known German bourgeois jurist Liszt said, "International
law is the body of legal norms which define reciprocal rights and
obligations between states"[10] and "International law concerns only
states as states."[11] The Soviet jurist Tunkin said, "International law
does not apply to the internal relations of a country. As is laid down
by the United Nations Charter, international law cannot be invoked in
internal disputes and conflicts."[12] Even the American scholar Wilson
. . . admitted: "Its scope should not be extended so as to interfere
with domestic affairs or to limit domestic jurisdiction."[13] Since the
Chinese people's liberation of their own territory Taiwan is China's
internal question, naturally it has nothing to do with international law.
It should be settled by the Chinese Government according to its municipal law. Here Dulles purposely evaded the nature of the Taiwan
question and applied, without the least justification, a principle of
international law to China's internal question. What was he after if
he was not deliberately calling black white and confusing truth with
falsehood?

It is the business of the Chinese people themselves as to how
the Chinese Government is to deal with the Chiang Kai-shek clique
and what form is to be adopted to liberate Taiwan. The Chinese
Government has the absolute right "to recover these areas by all
suitable means at a suitable time."[14] To use or not to use force,
"cease-fire" or no "cease-fire," "peaceful solution" or otherwise—
these questions are not within the scope of application of international
law. The United States can in no way meddle.

Since there is no firing between China and the United States in
the Taiwan area, there is no "fire" to "cease." When the United
States brings up this question, it is raising a hue and cry for no reason.

U.S. imperialists' assertion of the "right of self-defense" in
this connection is also out of place. It is true that both international
law and the United Nations Charter recognize that each country enjoys
the "inherent right of individual or collective self-defense" (Article
51 of the U.N. Charter). But such a right can only apply to the

---

10. F. von Liszt, International Law, 4th Russian ed., (1923),
p. 1.

11. Ibid., p. 3.

12. G. I. Tunkin, "Time to Restore China's Representation in
the United Nations," International Affairs, No. 10 (1956), p. 27.

13. G. G. Wilson, International Law, 9th ed. (1935), p. 5.

14. "Declaration on China's Territorial Sea," September 4,
1958, Peking Review, No. 28 (1958), p. 21.

relations between states and only a "state" can enjoy it, because "the purpose of the non-aggression principle is to maintain international peace; it only applies to relations between states,"[15] not to internal conflicts within a country. Therefore, as far as the Chiang Kai-shek clique is concerned, there is no right of self-defense to speak of.

As to the United States, it is the side which first used force toward the Chinese territory (Taiwan), grossly violating the obligation "not to be the first to use force toward another country." Still less is it entitled to the right of self-defense.

Some time ago U.S. imperialists declared that they would bring the question of the situation in the Taiwan Straits before the United Nations for settlement. Dulles openly announced at the 12th session of the U.N. Assembly that "The United States reserves the right to bring the matter to the United Nations." He also said he would submit it to the International Court of Justice for settlement, and so on.

But we would like to ask: What question did he want the United Nations to settle? If he meant settling the question between the Chinese Government and the Chiang Kai-shek clique, obviously it is sheer nonsense. It is expressly stipulated in Article 2, Paragraph 7 of the U.N. Charter that "Nothing contained in the present Charter shall authorize the United Nations to intervene in matters which are essentially within the domestic jurisdiction of any state. . . ." The United Nations, therefore, has no right to discuss this question. Likewise, the International Court of Justice, as the principal judicial organ of the United Nations, has no jurisdiction over China's internal question. If Dulles meant the settlement of disputes between China and the United States over the Taiwan area, then as China's right of representation in the U.N. has been illegally taken away and has not hitherto been restored, the United Nations is morally and legally not qualified to deal with such question. As to the International Court of Justice, since China has never agreed to accept its jurisdiction, it has no right to handle cases concerning China.

(4)

The U.S. ruling circles have time and again displayed the . . . "Mutual Security Treaty" signed between the United States and the Chiang Kai-shek clique in 1954 as a legal basis for their dispatching armed forces to the Taiwan Straits area and interfering in China's internal affairs, and they term the movements of the U.S forces in the Taiwan area as "living up to treaty obligations." But this so-called

---

15. Tunkin, The Bases of Modern International Law, p. 29.

"treaty" is illegal and invalid with regard either to its subjects or to its contents.

First, according to international law, "The subjects of a treaty are states."[16] American jurist Wilson also said, "The parties to the treaty must have the international capacity to contract, i.e. ordinarily they must be states."[17] Since Taiwan is not a state, and the Chiang Kai-shek clique is not the legal representative of China, it has absolutely no right to conclude a treaty and cannot be a subject of a treaty. A treaty concluded by an unqualified subject should of course be regarded as null and void.

Secondly, as to the contents of the treaty, "The treaties must be in conformity to law, as embodied in the generally recognized principles of international law and the established usages of states"[18]; and "obligations which are at variance with universally recognized principles of International Law cannot be the object of a treaty."[19] Article 103 of the U.N. Charter states: "In the event of a conflict between the obligations of the Members of the United Nations under the present Charter and their obligations under any other international agreement, their obligations under the present Charter shall prevail." In other words" . . . to the extent of their [treaties'] inconsistency with the Charter all these agreements are, for all practical purposes, void and unenforceable."[20] The aim of the U.S.-Chiang "treaty" is "to resist armed attack and communist subversive activities directed from without against their territorial integrity and political stability" (Article II). Here, "to resist armed attack" means to resist the Chinese people's liberation of Taiwan, on the pretext of which the United States can provoke war at any time. To resist "communist subversive activities" means that the United States can send troops to suppress the Taiwan people, because the United States and the Chiang Kai-shek clique are always in the habit of calling any revolutionary activity as "directed from without." The contents of the U.S.-Chiang "treaty" are to empower the United States to split China, provoke war and interfere in China's internal affairs. This, of course, contravenes the principles of international law and the U.N. Charter, and what contravenes these principles has, of course, no validity at all.

---

16. International Law, F. I. Kozhevnikov, ed. (Russian) (1957), p. 242.

17. Wilson, International Law, 9th ed., p. 219.

18. Ibid.

19. Oppenheim, International Law, Lauterpacht, ed., 7th ed., p. 808.

20. Ibid., p. 807.

(5)

The imperialists' second set of logic is also baseless.

Since ancient times Taiwan has been a part of China. More than 1,000 years ago China set up government offices in Taiwan and Penghu to administer these places. After the Sino-Japanese War of 1894 the government of the Ching Dynasty, by signing the Treaty of Shimonoseki, ceded Taiwan and Penghu to Japan. With the outbreak of China's War of Resistance Against Japan in 1937, in accordance with international law, the treaties between the two countries became null and void. The Treaty of Shimonoseki was no exception. In 1945, after China's victory in the Anti-Japanese War, China recovered these two places from Japan. No question has ever been raised about the legal status of Taiwan. Since Taiwan has always been Chinese territory, it is a matter of course for China to take it back like a thing restored to its original owner. It is not a case of China taking a new territory from Japan, which must be affirmed by a peace treaty. Particularly since the United States and Britain signed the Cairo Declaration, which clearly recognizes that Taiwan and the Penghu Islands are "territories Japan has stolen from the Chinese," and "shall be restored" to China, they are still less in a position to raise the . . . "question of the legal status of Taiwan." Despite the U.S. and British imperialists' clamors that the Cairo Declaration was "merely a declaration of intention" and was not in the nature of a treaty, anyone with some legal knowledge realizes that the Cairo Declaration, like the Yalta Agreement and Potsdam Declaration, was neither a unilateral expression of the policy of one allied country nor merely a statement of general principles between allies. It was an agreement reached between the heads of government of the Allied Powers on a specific question in the interest of joint military operations during the war, having definitely a legal binding force. Regarding the nature and contents of such documents, even the bourgeois authorities on international law admit their validity. For example, Oppenheim's International Law says: "Official statements in the form of Reports of Conferences signed by the Heads of States or Governments and embodying agreements reached therein may, in proportion as these agreements incorporate definite rules of conduct, be regarded as legally binding upon the States in question."[21]

In fact, in October, 1945, the Chinese government at that time had already recovered Taiwan from the Japanese aggressors and exercised sovereignty there, and made it one of the provinces of China. Such hard facts were known to the whole world and were publicly

---

21. Oppenheim, International Law, p. 788.

recognized even by the Truman Administration. The Chinese people overthrew the reactionary rule and set up the People's Republic of China; the sovereignty of this Republic naturally extends to Taiwan. The Chinese people's liberation of Taiwan, like their liberation of other places in the whole country, is a legal act of exercising their sovereign rights. It can never be called "extending new territories."

Dulles said, "Neither Taiwan [Formosa] nor the islands of Quemoy and Matsu has ever been under the authority of the Chinese Communists." This is true, but who does not know that it is precisely owing to U.S. aggression that Taiwan has up till today been unable to come under the authority of the People's Republic of China? This point brought up by Dulles can on no account deny the Chinese people's sovereign rights over Taiwan. On the contrary, it is a confession on the part of the United States of its occupation of Chinese territory and intervention in China's internal affairs.

As to "plebiscite" and "U.N. trusteeship," which the United States and some of its accomplices clamor for, they are even less grounded.

Of the total population in Taiwan, 98 percent are Hans who are exactly the same as the Hans on the mainland. Only a very small section are Koshans, who have been a member of China's big family for a long time and China is their motherland. Here the question of national self-determination does not exist, nor is there any controversy over the territory. On what grounds do the imperialists want them to vote in a plebiscite? Since they do not want to establish a new state or belong to any foreign country, what is the objective of imposing a plebiscite on them?

The United Nations trusteeship system is the result of mutual compromise between the Allied Powers after World War II on questions dealing with the colonies of the defeated nations and the former League of Nations mandates. The "basic objectives" of the system are to promote the local inhabitants' "progressive development toward self-government or independence " (Article 76 of the U.N. Charter), and according to Article 77, the "Trust Territories" are confined to: (1) territories now held under mandate; (2) territories which may be detached from enemy states as a result of the Second World War; and (3) territories voluntarily placed under the system by states responsible for their administration. China was a victorious Power in World War II and Taiwan, being always China's territory, is entirely different from the three categories of territories mentioned above. Obviously the "trusteeship system" is not applicable.

. . .

(6)

The "two Chinas" scheme is a temporary tactic rather than the aim of the U.S. policy toward China. For, as far as its original intention goes, the United States does not even wish to see a truly independent China. It only wants a China of "open door and equal opportunity," a colonial or semi-colonial China. It helped the Chiang Kai-shek clique fight a civil war with the object of maintaining the continued existence of such a China. At present it adopts the policy of creating "two Chinas," its purpose being precisely to occupy by force a part of Chinese territory, foster a counterrevolutionary clique on it so as to detach it from China and make it a base for extending aggression, and to look for an opportunity to overthrow the people's state power and further its aggression on the whole of China.

Today the U.S. imperialists are just treading the old path of the Japanese bandits in their aggression against China. The aims and even many concrete measures of the two are identical.

In 1931, when Japan launched aggression against China's Northeast, it claimed that it had "vital interests" in Manchuria, and that its purpose was "maintaining peace in the Orient." Today, in occupying Taiwan, the United States claims that Taiwan concerns the "U.S. defense interests" and its purpose is for "the security of the free world." In order to detach the Northeast from China, Japan used the feudal remnants of the Ching Dynasty such as Puyi and Cheng Hsiao-hsu, who had been long ago repudiated by the Chinese people, as figure-heads to set up . . . "Manchukuo." In order to sever Taiwan from China, the United States supports the . . . "Republic of China" —the remnants of the reactionary Kuomintang ruling clique. In order to deny China's sovereign rights over the four northeastern provinces, the Japanese militarists said that these were the "old imperial domain" of the Ching Dynasty and should be "detached from China proper,"[22] in other words, turned over to Japan. In order to deny China's sovereign rights over Taiwan, the United States and its accomplices say that "the legal status of Taiwan is not decided" and it should be placed under "United Nations trusteeship," in other words, turned over to the United States. In order to create a "legal basis" for occupying the Northeast, the Japanese Government signed a "Japan-Manchukuo Protocol" with its collaborator Cheng Hsiao-hsu. For a similar purpose the United States has concluded a "Mutual Security Treaty"

---

22. From the opinion of the Japanese Government on the Lytton Report, November 18, 1932, as reported by Kuzuu Yoshihisa in The Unofficial History of Japan-China Negotiations (in Japanese).

with the Chiang Kai-shek clique. The "Japan-Manchukuo Protocol" states: "Manchukuo and Japan, recognizing that any threat to the territory or to the peace and order of either of the High Contracting Parties constitutes at the same time a threat to the safety and existence of the other, agree to co-operate in the maintenance of their national security; it being understood that such Japanese forces as may be necessary for this purpose shall be stationed in Manchukuo"[23] (Article 2). The U.S.-Chiang "Security Treaty" states: "Each party recognizes that an armed attack in the West Pacific area directed against the territories of either of the parties would be dangerous to its own peace and safety and declares that it would act to meet the common danger in accordance with its constitutional processes" (Article V), and the United States has "the right to dispose such United States land, air and sea forces in and about Taiwan and the Pescadores as may be required for their defense, as determined by mutual agreement" (Article VII). Is there any difference in phraseology between the Japanese and U.S. imperialists? When Japan attacked China's Northeast, it said that it was exercising the "right of self-defense," and that the action of the Japanese army "conforms with Webster's definition of the right of self-defense."[24] Now the United States claims that it enjoys the right of self-defense in the Taiwan area which is Chinese territory and that this is based on the "United Nations Charter." Again how similar are their claims!

The matter is crystal clear. . . . "Manchukuo" was only a signboard; Puyi, Cheng Hsiao-hsu and others were only a group of puppets in the hands of the Japanese invaders who regarded them as negligible elements. The real motive of the Japanese was to turn "Manchuria" into an "imperial domain," in other words, a Japanese colony. Today the . . . "Republic of China" is also a signboard. The Americans, too, regard the Chiang Kai-shek clique as negligible elements. As U.S. Vice-President Nixon said, the Americans never intended "to keep the symbol of Chiang Kai-shek on Taiwan island" but to "look beyond Chiang." In other words, if the Chiang Kai-shek clique refuses to act obediently as puppets, the Americans will kick them out and turn round to "keep the symbol of a free government." In the last

23. The Manchukuo Year Book, 1934 (Tokyo: East-Asia Economic Investigation Bureau, 1934), p. 152.

24. From the opinion of the Japanese Government on the Lytton Report, November 18, 1932. Webster, the American Secretary of State, defined the necessity of self-defense as being "instant, overwhelming, and leaving no choice of means and no moment for deliberation." See Oppenheim, International Law, 7th ed., p. 266, note.

analysis, U.S. imperialists only want to turn Taiwan into an "island of freedom," in other words, seize it as their own, and turn it into a colony of the United States.

ITEM 5: THE CONLON REPORT, NOVEMBER 1, 1959[5]

. . .

The third alternative represents the basic recommendation of this report, and is supported, in our opinion, by its findings.

(3) Exploration and negotiation—a third approach to Communist China.

This policy would be multifaceted and would have three basic objectives:

(a) To test the willingness of Communist China to coexist with us.

(b) To seek an expanded policy that would retain certain firm commitments, but also present a more dynamic, flexible, and positive tone.

(c) Through the actions, to make possible a greater degree of collective agreement on the China issue among the major nations of the free world, and hence provide a firmer basis for collective action if and when necessary. This policy contains the following proposals, based upon a sequence of stages.

1. Stage one:

a. An offer for the mutual exchange of journalists with Communist China; if this program is successfully inaugurated, to be followed by proposals for the exchange of scholars and commercial representatives.

b. Permission for some prominent individual or group not in the national executive branch of the Government to go to Communist China and conduct such informal discussions with the leaders as are possible.

c. The launching of informal, private discussions between the United States and our European allies, Japan, and some of the leading "neutrals," particularly India, Burma, and Indonesia, to solicit ideas and some cooperative thinking about the problem of China.

This first stage would seek to test the position of Communist China and its interest in improving relations with the United States. It would also test the position of our allies and some of the "neutrals," indicating our possible interest in a more positive, flexible policy, and one in which they might assume some joint responsibility. If the results of these actions showed some promise, the next stage should be undertaken.

2. Stage two:

a. Abandonment of CHINCOM restrictions and permission for trade on the same basis as that with the U.S.S.R.

b. Informal discussion with our allies and "neutrals" on the following four-point program: admission of Communist China to the United Nations; recognition of the Republic of Taiwan; the seating of this Republic in the Assembly; the enlargement of the Security Council to include India and Japan as permanent members, as well as China.

c. Simultaneous discussions with our small allies, pledging full and continued support to all of our treaty obligations.

d. Simultaneous special discussions with the National Government on Taiwan, looking toward the following agreement:

1. The United States would continue to honor its existing obligations to Taiwan and the Pescadores. It would underwrite the defense of the Republic of Taiwan, and would support an expanded economic-technical assistance program.

2. The military forces of Taiwan would be withdrawn from the offshore islands, together with those civilians desiring to leave.

3. The United States would endeavor to help in the resettlement of any mainland refugees who wish to leave Taiwan following the establishment of the Republic of Taiwan.

e. If feasible, the United States would negotiate a treaty of commerce with Communist China, and if successful, this would be followed by de facto recognition.

Under any conditions, this would be a complex and difficult stage. It is obviously unrealistic to consider the above proposals as more than general suggestions of the directions in which we should move and the positions that we should hold. Both improvisation and basic changes might be required. Moreover, the precise timing of this policy in each of its phases would have to be determined with respect to the international scene.

The offshore island issue is extremely serious. It might become critical again at any point. Thus it is possible to argue that irrespective of this program, we should extricate the Nationalists and ourselves from this area. These islands bear no relation to the defense of Taiwan, and can only be considered steppingstones to the mainland. They are an integral part of the mainland. Militarily they are very vulnerable. Politically, they are a liability, both in terms of world opinion and in terms of the unhealthy psychology they foster in Taiwan. In the event of full military action over them, the American people themselves would be of divided opinion.

The four-point program raises a number of difficulties which should be admitted. It would be acceptable at present neither to the Communists nor to the Nationalists. Either might refuse to sit in the United Nations if the other were present under any designation.

Communist China is likely to hold to its claim on Taiwan tenaciously.
It might also be impossible to get Taiwan into the United Nations, even
if the government of that time were willing to sit, due to a Russian
veto. Various techniques should be explored, including that of treating
Taiwan membership in the Assembly as a matter of the continuing
membership of a government already recognized, but given a changed
designation.

What are the alternatives? Continued recognition of the Nationalist Government as that of China seems most unpromising unless we
are forced into this by Communist intransigence. The acceptance of
Taiwan as a part of mainland China? This alone would satisfy the
Chinese Communists at present, and therefore remove what is otherwise likely to be a continuing source of trouble. Indeed, it has been
argued that Taiwan is not so important from a military or political
viewpoint as to warrant ipso facto the enormous cost and risk of a
long-term U.S. commitment for its defense. It has been suggested
that a general settlement in Asia might be attempted whereby Taiwan
would be united with the mainland in exchange for a Communist agreement to accept free elections under U.N. auspices throughout Korea,
leading to the unification of that country.

To adopt this policy, however, would be to jeopardize the American position with respect to other small nations dependent upon our
protection and aid. It would seriously affect morale in South Korea,
South Vietnam, the Philippines, and other areas. In addition, if it
were done without the consent of the people of Taiwan, it would represent an immoral action. In the event of a bargain between some
political leaders on Taiwan and the Communists, to be sure, the United
States might be placed in an extremely awkward position whereby it
would have to decide hastily whether it should intervene in an attempt
to protect the Taiwanese right of self-determination. Such a development is possible, but it does not appear likely.

The program suggested above forms the only basis for any possible agreement among major elements within the free world. It also
accords with the existing facts. There is a separation between mainland China and Taiwan at present and two separate governments are
operating. The United States, moreover, takes cognizance of these
facts, having tried to persuade the Nationalists to abandon any idea
of returning to the mainland by force, and having guaranteed the
military defense of Taiwan. There are no legal obstacles; the status
of Taiwan has not been fixed by international pact, although admittedly
we did promise during World War II that it should belong to China.
The Taiwanese people themselves have given considerable indication
of wishing to remain separate from the mainland, and could be tested
by plebiscite if this were agreed.

The broad program suggested above does not contemplate a
world without problems or without fear. It assumes that our military

defenses will have to be strong, and that we will need a bold, dynamic program of international economic cooperation with non-Communist nations, especially in the Asian-African world. And, clearly, this program is not without its risks and difficulties of execution. But among the alternatives that confront us, it deserves serious consideration as the best long-range policy to serve American national interests.

ITEM 6: LIN YUTANG AND CHIN-TUNG LIANG,
"AN ANALYSIS OF THE CONLON REPORT: ITS FALLACIES
AND CONTRADICTIONS AS VIEWED BY ASIANS, 1960*

The main theme of the [Conlon] report's approach to the China problem is its emphasis on being realistic. But our objection to the proposed policy is precisely based on its lack of realism. In the following sections, we shall endeavor to point out that both its findings and recommendations are utterly unrealistic.

1. The lack of realism in the findings:

. . .

5) Between the Taiwanese and the mainland refugees there are no racial or cultural differences. The only difference is that they come from different localities. The Taiwanese view toward the future of Taiwan may be different from that of the mainlanders, but, at most, it is only a difference of opinion between the older emigrants from China and the newcomers, no more than that. In matters relating to taxation, conscription and local elections, the Taiwanese and the mainlanders enjoy the same privileges and are under the same laws.

---

*Lin is a famous Chinese writer whose publications include My Country and My People (New York: John Day, 1939), The Wisdom of China and India (New York: Random House, 1942), and The Importance of Understanding (Cleveland: World Publishing Co., 1960).

The paper was also signed by the following Chinese: Y. Y. Pan, Paul K. T. Sih (professor and director, Center of Asian Studies, St. John's University, New York), H. W. Chan, Paul Chen, William L. Tung (professor of political science, Queens College, New York), Chi-pao Cheng (president, Institute of Chinese Culture, New York), Y. C. Chen (correspondent in U.S., Chung-yang jih-pao [Central daily news], Taipei), H. M. Wang, and S. T. Chen.

The excerpt is presented with editorial changes.

In recent years, many elected public officials, such as city mayors, county magistrates, and council chairmen have been Taiwanese. Hence, the assertions that Taiwanese have to support "unproductive" refugees, that they alone bear the responsibility for Taiwan's defense, and that they have no access to official positions, etc., is a gross exaggeration used to support Mr. Conlon's incorrect reasoning.

2. The lack of realism in the recommendations:

1) The existence of the Republic of China is a fact and the "Republic of Taiwan" exists only in Mr. Conlon's imagination.

2) Communist China's anti-American attitude is a part of her national policy. It would be wishful thinking to expect that Communist China would change her attitude after gaining recognition from the United States.

3) Communist China has insisted on "liberating" Taiwan with force. It would be a conscious self-deception to expect that Communist China would recognize "the Republic of Taiwan," even if it could be established.

4) The Republic of China is physically in occupation of the territory of Taiwan and is its undisputed master. To obliterate the Republic of China from the map without first consulting her, and to solicit opinions of third parties such as India, Japan, Indonesia, and Burma, would be high-handed imperialism in Chinese eyes. We refuse to believe that the United States will or can sell out her friend and ally so easily.

From the above, it is easy to see that these recommendations are far from realistic. There is no possibility that they would constitute a practical solution to the China problem. Aside from this criticism there are other points in the report that deserve our scrutiny.

First, with regard to the statement that "the Kuomintang does not enjoy the genuine support of the Taiwanese," the report provides no concrete illustration or proof. Even if it were true, it could not justify the suggestion for the creation of a "Republic of Taiwan."

Secondly, in the proposed third alternative, a scheme is devised to select four Asian countries—Japan, India, Indonesia and Burma—as the co-conspirators in an attempt to annihilate the Republic of China. At the same time, Japan and India are promised seats in the Security Council of the United Nations. It is evident that these promises are nothing but bribes to induce their participation in an infamous international deal in which an ally would be the innocent victim. As friends of the United States of America, we would hate to see such underhanded dealings tarnish her honor. Mr. Conlon at best seems to be unaware of the possible loss of respect for the United States by the Asiatic peoples that this course would lead to.

Thirdly, the Republic of China has lost the mainland to the Chinese Communists, but it does not follow that it has also lost the support of the people on the mainland. This is revealed by the fact that among the Chinese war prisoners of the Korean War 14,000 of them have chosen freedom and also by the fact that when the Nationalists withdrew from Ta Chen Island, only 19 of its inhabitants chose to remain. The Chinese Communists have physical control over the mainland, but they have no control over people's hearts and longings. The testimony of articulate elements, given during the "Hundred Flowers Blooming" period, and that of escapees from behind the bamboo curtain are eloquent witness. If the question of "who really represents China" were posed today, Communist China would be the first to suffer from its answer. The report suggests that a plebiscite should be held in Taiwan—where no real minority problem exists— and arbitrarily appoints the United States to supervise and to force the inhabitants of Taiwan to participate in the vote. On the other hand there is no suggestion of holding a plebiscite—which now seems to be a popular device for settling political disputes—in Communist China, where an opinion poll is urgently needed. This is what baffles us most.

Fourthly, the Chinese government has withdrawn from Ta Chen Island and has denounced the use of force as a means for the recovery of the mainland on the advice of the United States, but it does not follow that the Chinese government would blindly consent to the arguments for the elimination of the Republic of China, advocated by an ally, however powerful and strong. The "Republic of China" was created through the bloody sacrifice of numerous martyrs under the leadership of Dr. Sun Yat-sen. It cannot be stealthily destroyed by the substitution of the three inconspicuous words "Republic of Taiwan." Over the past decade, the Chinese Communists have noisily protested against the so-called American "occupation" of Taiwan and have instigated the hate-America campaign, but the people on the mainland know that Taiwan remains under the control of the Chinese government and that the United States has not occupied Taiwan. Hence, the hate-America campaign turns out to be a farce. Should the suggestions of the Conlon report be put into effect, it would provide ample reason for the people on the mainland to hate America because it would have been the United States that forced Taiwan to become a non-Chinese state. The United States has no territorial ambitions toward Taiwan. Then why should it assume this unnecessary responsibility and thereby justify the criticism of "territorial aggression" made by the Chinese Communists, thus tarnishing its national reputation and paving the way for international communism to achieve final victory?

Throughout the report, we have found only two sensible and intelligent statements: (1) "do not entertain the idea that the United States can do everything," and (2) "the United States should not impose her ideas on other countries." These timely warnings turn out to be apt criticism of the third alternative policy recommended in the report.

Taiwan is an integral part of the Chinese territory. The national government is the legal representative of the Republic of China. These facts are clearly stated in the pamphlet entitled "The Republic of China," published in October, 1959, by the State Department (pages 4 and 50).

Speaking in practical terms, moreover, in order to protect the ocean communication links between free countries and to fulfill its obligation under the Charter of the United Nations, the United States must give its full and continued support to Taiwan. Consequently, the United States should not abandon Taiwan's legal owner, the Republic of China. However, if the United States is only interested in a piece of real estate and wishes to treat its occupants like dirt, then even with the help of high-sounding words (i.e., promising independence to Taiwanese), skilled maneuvers (i.e., holding discussions with Japan, Burma, and India) and shameful bribes (i.e., offering Security Council seats to Japan and India), she would not be able to escape the stern judgment of history and would stand condemned as having committed the following crimes:

1. Creating puppets,
2. Betraying her ally,
3. Committing aggression in disguise.

All of us are aware of the fact that the China problem is only a phase of the impasse created as the result of the struggle between the Communist bloc and the free world. The impasse can only be solved with a global strategy; local solutions are of no avail. Today, there are two German, two Vietnamese and two Korean states; impasse exists everywhere, not only in the Taiwan Straits. If we compare the situation of China with that of Germany, although the Western countries as yet have not produced a plan for the achievement of German unity, no one has ever suggested the elimination of West Germany as the first step toward the solution of the German problem. May we venture to ask what enables Mr. Conlon and his associates to make such a preposterous suggestion with regard to a similar situation in Asia? Could it be dictated by the traditional Europe first, Asia second attitude or by the indifference of the American people toward the affairs of the mysterious Orient? Yet here lies the key to the problem of security of the U.S. Pacific and Atlantic coastal defense.

Far Eastern experts like to compare the development of India with that of Communist China. They are convinced that if the democratic method practiced in India should prove to be successful, then the totalitarian method of Communist China would fail to impress the newly emerging nations in Asia. This is true to a certain extent, but there are other aspects that need to be explored. Today the real competitor of Communist China in the Far East, so far as socioeconomic development is concerned, is not India but Nationalist China. During the ten years of Nationalist rule on Taiwan, spectacular achievements, both in raising the living standard of the people and in maintaining the stability of the society, have been achieved. This presents a dramatic contrast to what has happened on the mainland, where people are languishing under tyrannical rule. Sooner or later, the situation there will reach an exploding point, and then will sound the death knell of the Communists. On the basis of past records, if the free world feels that it is obligated to help India gain influence with other Asian states, then it should help the Republic of China for the same reasons. This is another Asian suggestion for the solution of the Asian problem.

We earnestly hope that the freedom-loving American people, mindful of the security and honor of the United States and the peace of the world, will consider carefully the views presented by us as Asians and reject the Conlon report, which is more tendentious than objective and therefore cannot solve the China problem but, rather, will only lead to more complicated problems in the future.

ITEM 7: "'ONE CHINA, ONE TAIWAN' PLOT DENOUNCED"[6]

Avery Brundage, President of the International Olympic Committee, in his recent talk in Tokyo with Hideji Kawasaki, President of the Japanese Dietmen's League for the Promotion of Sports, stated that the I.O.C. recognized the existence of "one China and one Taiwan." This preposterous formula shows that Brundage, acting as an agent of U.S. imperialism, is once again trying to saddle international sports with a political scheme that is simply a revamped version of the old U.S. plot to create "two Chinas."

The All-China Athletic Federation issued a statement on June 21 denouncing this attempt. It recalls that Brundage, abusing his authority as President of the I.O.C., has for years carried out in world sports the U.S. imperialist policy of hostility toward New China, and defended and pushed the U.S. imperialist plot to create "two Chinas." "However," the statement points out, "Brundage's disreputable activities to exclude the People's Republic of China and to create 'two Chinas' in world sports have been rejected and censured by all fair-minded sportsmen and peoples of the world."

Taiwan was restored to China after Japan's surrender. Even the United States Government has publicly recognized Taiwan as "part of China." "Brundage's talk about 'one China, one Taiwan' is sheer nonsense and certainly cannot change the facts," declares the statement. "On the contrary, he reveals himself all the more clearly

as an imperialist agent in international sports whose job it is to carry
out the political schemes of the United States."

ITEM 8: "EDITORIAL: NO NEED FOR CONCEAL-
MENT, NO ROOM FOR APPEASEMENT–ON THE
GOVERNMENT'S ATTITUDE TOWARD THE SO-
CALLED 'TAIWAN INDEPENDENCE' CONSPIRACY"[7]

It is well-known that the Chinese Communists have a strategic
tenet, namely, "a fortress is always taken from within." Since our
government's removal to Taiwan, it has constantly dedicated itself to
improving administrative measures. It has made remarkable progress
in various fields. The signing of the Sino-American Mutual Defense
Treaty and the failure of the Chinese Communists' bombardment of
Quemoy have taught them that any military aggression against Taiwan
would surely fail; now they no longer dare to try again. On the other
hand, due to the effective enforcement of the counterespionage work
done by the government and due to the increasing vigilance of all
levels of society against Communist infiltration and activities, the
bandit Mao has been forced to let his spies in Taiwan hide underground
in order to escape exposure. However, the Chinese Communists'
plot to annihilate Free China will never be changed, since our existence
constitutes a standing menace to them, and our ever-growing strength
causes them great anxiety. Based on the tenets of Marxism-Leninism
and their "historical experience" of rebellion, the Chinese Communists
are fully aware of the tactic of using various and sundry means to
achieve a single end. Therefore, on the one hand, they make use of
their international fellow travelers to mislead public opinion by fabricating the . . . "Taiwan Question." In addition, they also instigate a
few ignorant individuals in Taiwan to respond to their appeals for a
. . . "Taiwan Independence Movement." They also urge other dissident
elements to unite with the movement abroad. This is the background
of the emergence of the . . . "Taiwan Independence Movement." Although at the present time this movement is not very influential, it
can by no means be allowed to develop to such an extent as to endanger
our national security and national unity. We definitely should not take
this matter lightly. We should work out positive and effective measures, such as the following:

First, on ideological education, we should clarify some historical
facts. Taiwan was first cultivated by the Chinese in A.D. 610. It was
formally listed as a part of Chinese territory in the Yüan Dynasty
[A.D. 1279-1368?]. The 1943 Cairo Declaration, the 1945 Potsdam
Proclamation and the 1952 Sino-Japanese Peace Treaty all confirmed
that Taiwan is an integral part of Chinese territory. Hence there is

no doubt whatsoever as to its legal status. Furthermore, all the 12 million people on Taiwan today, except for a few aborigines in the mountains, come from the Chinese mainland and are descendants of Huangti [the Yellow Emperor]. They are 100 percent nationals of the Republic of China. They share the same culture, language, history, blood, customs and habits. Their ancestors' tombs are all on the mainland. Their common cause and their future hinge upon returning to the mainland. With only a few exceptions, no patriotic Chinese would ever think about "Taiwan Independence." All these are undeniable and irrefutable facts and truth which could be used to clarify the distorted arguments set forth by a few traitorous people and their fellow travelers. We hold that there is no need to avoid touching on this subject, since any form of debate on this matter would be helpful in promoting the genuine understanding of this problem both at home and abroad. As for the few youth who are bewildered by the absurdity of "Taiwan Independence," we should intensify their education in national spirit.

Secondly, as to those fellow travelers of the Chinese Communists who are striving to destroy our national unity, we should employ diplomatic channels to urge our allies to stop their activities if and when we possess convincing evidence and witnesses. Their activities can no longer be ignored, for they seriously damage our national interest as well as the friendship between our country and others.

Thirdly, as to those who engage in this conspiracy at home, the Government has the responsibility for making intensive and thorough investigations. Once caught, they should be tried in accordance with the relevant laws and regulations for the punishment of treason and espionage. . . . There is no room for tolerance and appeasement of traitors who try to endanger the foundation of our country.

ITEM 9: STATEMENT OF PRESIDENT LIAO WEN-YI
ON THE DISSOLUTION OF THE PROVISIONAL
GOVERNMENT OF THE REPUBLIC OF TAIWAN,
MAY 14, 1965[8]

For the cause of improving the interest and welfare of the Taiwanese people, I have been in exile abroad for nearly twenty years. Since the world situation has recently gone from bad to worse, I have come to realize clearly that the great danger at the present moment is from the Chinese Communists' infiltration and subversion. I have decided, therefore, to give up my activity in organizing for Taiwan independence, to respond to President Chiang's call for an alliance of anti-Communism and national reconstruction, and to return to Taiwan immediately. I shall henceforth contribute all my strength to struggle resolutely for the grand cause of anti-Communism and national reconstruction.

ITEM 10: STATEMENT OF LIAO WEN-YI, MAY 17, 1965[9]

I have been away from the motherland for more than a decade. It is really a great delight for me to come back to my native land.

Since returning from abroad, I have had the honor to receive a hearty welcome and encouragement from governmental officials, from my fellow countrymen on every level, and from my relatives and friends. I am very grateful and I wish to express my appreciation to all of you.

As for my political stand, I have already made a statement in Tokyo; namely, I have decided to dissolve the Taiwan independence activities, and to join the grand cause of anti-Communism and national reconstruction. I have been expressing my sincerity in interviews with people from every level. Here I wish to make a few further simple comments by way of explanation:

Firstly, the natives of Taiwan are an integral part of the Chinese nation. All the natives of Taiwan, be they Hakkas or Southern Fukienese, are descendants of Huangti [the Yellow Emperor]. The ancestors of the Hakkas migrated southward from the central China plains; as for the Southern Fukienese, they are descendants of the big families who crossed the Yangtze River from the North in order to escape from the chaos caused by the invasion of the northern barbarian tribes. Blood is thicker than water. Our Chinese nation possesses a natural cohesive strength. Family records further illustrate this point. Therefore, no one in the world can ever create dissension between us by any means.

Secondly, the anti-aggression movement in Taiwan in earlier years not only is deeply rooted in the National Revolutionary Movement, but also, all along, has been connected closely with that movement. History affords many examples of this relationship. After graduation from a university in Tokyo, I myself served the cause of National Revolution and participated in the anti-Japanese war until Taiwan was recovered. Today, we Taiwanese, under the leadership of President Chiang, contribute all we have in order to win victory in the holy war to counter-attack the Communists and engage in national reconstruction. This is an even better concrete manifestation of our dedication to the National Revolutionary Movement.

Thirdly, the present chaos and crisis in Southeast Asia all comes from the infiltration and subversive activities of the Chinese Communists. I engaged in a fierce face-to-face struggle with the Chinese

Communists—Hsieh Hsüeh-hung and Hsiao Lai-fu—in Hong Kong and Macao during the period from 1947 to 1949. During my years in exile abroad, I acquired deep understanding of the plotting and intrigue carried on by the Chinese Communists. Henceforth, I will contribute the experience I have gained from the revolutionary struggle to my fellow countrymen for the struggle of anti-Communism and national reconstruction.

Fourthly, the marked progress made in the past decade and more in various fields, the prosperity, and the improvement of the living standard in Taiwan have attracted notice the world over. I felt great longing for my native land—Taiwan—during the many years I was in exile abroad. Hereafter, I wish to make trips around the island in order to further appreciate what has been accomplished here in Taiwan. As for my future plans, I wish to say that I will contribute my strength to anything which will be beneficial to the cause of national reconstruction and the welfare of the people of Taiwan.

ITEM 11: STATEMENT OF CHENG WEN-FU, PRESIDENT OF THE TAIWAN DEMOCRATIC-POLITICAL PARTY, MAY 20, 1965[10]

According to the reports of the Asahi Shimbun, Mainichi Shimbun, and other Japanese newspapers, Dr. Liao Wen-yi, "President of the Provisional Government of the Republic of Taiwan," repented and realized that the . . . "Independence Movement" is nothing but an intrigue of the Chinese Communists, and has returned to Taipei from Tokyo. He believes that the correct path for him to follow is to cooperate with the policy of the Government of the Republic of China. His decision has aroused interest and attention in various quarters here.

In light of this new development and the cruel fact of the military aggressions wantonly launched by the Chinese Communists against the various countries of Asia, our Party deems that the action taken by Liao Wen-yi is wise and deserving of our praise. We have concluded that the continuous promotion of the [Taiwan] Independence Movement can only benefit the Chinese Communists and, in addition, would be harmful to the people of Taiwan.

For the foregoing reasons, we unanimously hold that it is most glorious to be a citizen of the Republic of China, which is completely dedicated to building Taiwan and resisting the Chinese Communists. We decide, therefore, to dissolve our Party, ceasing all activities after May 20, 1965, to fully support President Chiang and to respond to the call for organizing a unified alliance of anti-Communism and national reconstruction.

ITEM 12: WANG SHAO-P'ING, "CAN TAIWAN BECOME
INDEPENDENT ?"[11]

If the "Taiwan independence movement" did succeed in driving
out the Chiang Kai-shek group from Taiwan and did establish an
independent state, what would be the situation in Taiwan and Asia?

First, Communist China definitely would not recognize Taiwan
as an independent state. Without Communist China's recognition,
Taiwan's independence would be meaningless, for Taiwan's independence means to be independent of Communist China, and without Communist China's recognition what is the significance of this independence?

Second, once Communist China refused to recognize an independent Taiwan, all the countries in the world which either have diplomatic
relations with Communist China or are neutral certainly would not
recognize Taiwan. This would certainly diminish to a great extent
the significance of Taiwan's independence.

Third, because the Taiwanese are in fact Chinese, once Communist China or any government on the mainland had achieved steady
progress toward prosperity, the people on Taiwan would undoubtedly
desire to return to the motherland and to incorporate Taiwan with
China again. As a result of this inevitable tendency, Taiwan's independence, even if achieved, could not last long.

Finally, the present stalemated confrontation between the mainland and Taiwan will sooner or later be upset for the following reasons:

The reason why Taiwan now can maintain the status quo is
entirely dependent upon the United States Seventh Fleet, and the fact
that the military strength of Communist China has so far been unable
to eliminate the Seventh Fleet. A few years from now, if the Communist regime continues to exist, its military strength will become
much stronger and it will possess atomic bombs and missiles. . . .
By that time, the United States certainly will not risk an atomic attack
at its homeland to protect the independence of Taiwan, and China's
liberation of Taiwan will be carried out easily. On the other hand, if
the Communist Chinese regime undergoes desirable internal changes
and eventually takes the direction of "revisionism," China's progress,
economic growth and improvement of the people's living standard will
certainly enhance her national prestige to an unprecedented degree.
If this should happen, the Sino-American relationship will be greatly
improved. Consequently, the United States will not become involved
in any conflict between China and Taiwan, in order to maintain that
good relationship and preserve world peace. In the meantime, the
people on Taiwan will also come to desire to return to a powerful
and prosperous China.

From this analysis it seems clear that, from whatever standpoint or perspective, even if an independent state should be established on Taiwan after a long and bloody struggle, the independence could not last long. Why, then, should the people do this in the first place?

To speak objectively, the "Taiwan independence movement" is in fact encouraged and supported by the Japanese militarists and some Americans. Its emergence has been due largely to their taking advantage of the dissatisfaction of some Taiwanese. Thus, the movement is neither reasonable nor realistic. It does not have wide popular support. It is doomed to failure. Otherwise, the leaders of the "Taiwan independence movement," such as Liao Wen-yi and Cheng Wang-fu, would not have submitted to Chiang Kai-shek after so many years of struggle.

ITEM 13: CHAO KUANG-YU, "MR. TS'AI PEI-HO TALKS ABOUT HIS TRIP AROUND THE WORLD"[12]

Mr. Ts'ai strongly criticized the people abroad who advocate independence for Taiwan. He said: "Although those who advocate Taiwan's independence use the pretext of anti-Communism, their views coincide with the mainstream of appeasement; in fact, their views often support the policy of appeasement."

. . . This old gentleman, who has always maintained a sense of justice and has not been afraid of undue power, further stated: "It is absolutely impossible to separate Taiwan from mainland China, just as limbs cannot be severed from the body. . . ."

Mr. Ts'ai pointed out emphatically: "The illusion of setting up an independent Taiwan is permeated with the fundamental characteristic of pessimism. It is self-degenerating, retrogressive, confusing, and not clear-minded. It reflects an ignorance of the historical background, blood ties, geographical relationship, and cultural affinity between Taiwan and mainland China. Except for the aborigines in the mountains, all inhabitants on Taiwan are of Chinese origin. Their language and way of life are inherited from China. Moreover, 20 years ago, the Chinese on the mainland contributed immeasurably, sacrificing their lives and blood, to emancipating Taiwan from the oppressive rule of Japan. Today, the mother country is in crisis, and the Chinese on the mainland are suffering under Communist rule. This is an opportunity for the people on Taiwan to offer aid to those on the mainland. All people of other countries who have a sense of justice should also show their spirit of chivalry to save the Chinese from Communist tyranny. It simply cannot be sensibly said at this time . . . that Taiwan has no relationship with China."

He continued: "Anyone who denies Taiwan's ties with China must have forgotten his ancestors, disobeyed tradition, and intended to sever his blood ties with his ancestors. He must have intended to be an 'orphan of the world.'"

Mr. Ts'ai pointed out: "It is not easy to be an 'orphan of the world.' A country like China, which has a long, brilliant cultural history, and a people like the Chinese, who have an enduring character, shall not long tolerate the oppressive rule of Mao Tse-tung and his Party. They will not lie asleep before the eyes of the world. Now, there are a few people who, due to their blindness to and ignorance of reality, advocate independence for Taiwan, attempting, under the pretext of pessimism, to escape their responsibility toward their brothers on the mainland. Even if this independence did come about, the millions of Chinese and their offspring would no doubt dislike and hate the people on Taiwan for generations to come. One day, then, when China becomes strong, her first target would certainly be the recovery of Taiwan. . . . On the other hand, if all the Chinese at home and abroad use Taiwan as a base to wipe out the Chinese Communists and build up a strong and prosperous China, the great contributions that the people on Taiwan would make to China will be recorded in the history of China and remembered forever. Moreover, the 11,000,000 square kilometers of land of China will be open, under the principles of freedom and equality, to be used and exploited by all the people, including those on Taiwan."

Once this point of view is understood, Mr. Ts'ai urged, those living in a foreign country who advocated independence for Taiwan should be careful not to become guilty of betraying their history and ancestors.

ITEM 14: SSU-MA LU, "FOREWORD TO 'A TAIWANESE
SPEAKS ABOUT THE FUTURE OF TAIWAN'"13

The original title of Mr. Wu Yu-lin's article was "The Future of Taiwan." . . . Because he clearly identifies his own standpoint as a Taiwanese, we have changed the title to "A Taiwanese Speaks About the Future of Taiwan."

Since this magazine published articles advocating the independence of Taiwan, it has received about a thousand letters of protest from the readers. We have selected and published some of these letters; the others have not been printed because they are largely repetitious. . . .

. . .

On the problem of the future of Taiwan, we whould listen to what Taiwanese want to say. Each Taiwanese, of course, may have his own view. For example, we have published Mr. Liao Min-hsiung's article, where he opposed the theory of an independent Taiwan and two Chinas.

I have long since expressed my own view opposing the independence of Taiwan in my book entitled Chung-kuo ho-p'ing yen-pien lun (On the peaceful transformation in China). I hope that the Nationalists and Communists might unite China by way of a peaceful and democratic competition for leadership.

ITEM 15: WU YU-LIN, "A TAIWANESE SPEAKS ABOUT THE FUTURE OF TAIWAN"[14]

The only future for Taiwan is independence—an independent Taiwan republic, not the Republic of China nor the People's Republic of China.

The Taiwanese do not deny that they are Han Chinese, but Han Chinese are not necessarily of [Chinese nationality]. The overseas Chinese in southeast Asia are not of Chinese [nationality]. The Han Chinese in Singapore can establish their own country. And the Han Chinese in Hong Kong can use a passport of the British Empire; and in the future they may establish a new country. One hundred and ninety-two years ago, Anglo-Saxons could declare themselves independent of England and establish an independent United States. Are not the Taiwanese today qualified to declare their independence?

Some people might say Taiwan is too small to be an independent state. This is nonesense. Eighty percent of the countries in the United Nations have less population than does Taiwan, and they are independent and members of the United Nations. The small countries in Europe, such as Switzerland, Monaco and Luxembourg, do not possess better conditions and resources than Taiwan. But each of them has a stabilized society and enjoys a high standard of living.

Not only does Taiwan have many conditions for being an independent state, but there are many advantages to be derived from its independence. First, politically, Taiwan would no longer be under the influence of the deteriorating politics of mainland China. Under the experience of the past hundred years, when Taiwan was part of China, the people of Taiwan were at all times fearful due to the fact that warlords or bandits were in control of the island. The Taiwanese were always given an inferior position, and never had the opportunity to manage their own land. After Taiwan becomes independent, it will have nothing to do with China, whether the latter is being ruled by Mao Tse-tung or Chiang Kai-shek. Under these circumstances whatever fruits of their achievements the Taiwanese may have will no longer be denied to them by a regime on mainland China. The lives of the Taiwanese will no longer be subject to the mercy of a Chinese regime. Thus,

such strange phenomena as Cheng Ch'en-kung using Taiwan as a base
to try to destroy the Manchus and restore the Ming, China's cession
of Taiwan to Japan as a condition for peace after the Sino-Japanese
war in 1895, and the Nationalist use of Taiwan as a base to return to
mainland China would not repeat themselves.

Secondly, economically, the national income of Taiwan has been
much higher than that of China, and the Taiwanese live a better life
than do Chinese on the mainland (had it not been for the present regime
in Taiwan, the living standard of the Taiwanese would have been even
higher). If Taiwan should one day be integrated with China, then Mao
Tse-tung's ridiculous programs of manufacturing steel with bare hands
and people's communes would be imposed on the Taiwanese.

Of course, the independence of Taiwan does not mean that it will
sever ties with China, or that all the overseas Chinese on Taiwan (i.e.,
the Chinese refugees who came to Taiwan after 1949) will be slaughtered. Although these refugees have in the past contributed to the
development of Taiwan, most of them have also oppressed the Taiwanese. Only when these people dispense with their attitude as con-
querors and change their bureaucratic manner can they become citizens
of Taiwan, sharing with all Taiwanese the rights and duties of citizen-
ship. With regard to the relationship between Taiwan and China, we
may well follow Western precedents. Once the regime on mainland
China becomes democratized, and stops pursuing programs such as
the Cultural Revolution, Taiwan will become a friendly, fraternal
neighbor of China, working together with it. . . . When this is done,
Asia will no longer remain a region for colonization by Westerners.

Judging on the basis of the current situation, the chances for
an independent Taiwan are abundant. The Mao regime is engaged in
the Cultural Revolution and has no spare power to "liberate" Taiwan.
The refugee regime of Chiang on Taiwan certainly will not be able to
resist the trend toward independence. The slogan of "anti-communism
and resistance to Russia" is no more than a camouflage designed to
oppress the Taiwanese and . . . is becoming a joke in international
affairs. From the standpoint of the United States, an independent
Taiwan is inevitable. The United States policy of opposing the Soviet
Union and Communist China will not change in a short time. And
those overseas Chinese who live in Taiwan are not necessarily anti-
Communist—once they have the opportunity, they will go back to their
homeland on mainland China, whether from Quemoy and Matsu or
during the Olympic Games. The Americans clearly understand this
situation. They know that if the United States desires to stay on Taiwan in order to prevent Communist China from expanding into the
Pacific, they must rely on the Taiwanese, who will devote themselves
to protecting their native island.

Thus, there are two alternatives open for the Nationalist regime in the near future: (1) to continue its deteriorating administration, practiced formerly on the mainland and now on Taiwan; or (2) to open the door for more power to the Taiwanese and gradually give up its policy of "counterattack against the mainland." The first alternative is doomed to failure. Under that circumstance, it is not clear whether in the future a military junta or a Taiwanese regime will assume political power in Taiwan. The second alternative is the only chance of survival for the Chiang regime.

ITEM 16: CH'EN SHAO-SHUN, "ON THE PROBLEM OF TAIWAN'S INDEPENDENCE—A COMMENT ON 'A TAI-WANESE SPEAKS ABOUT THE FUTURE OF TAIWAN'"[15]

What is most ridiculous is that Mr. Wu refers to Cheng Ch'en-kung's use of Taiwan as a base for restoration of the Ming as a "strange phenomenon." By saying this, Mr. Wu himself is strange. Before Cheng administered on Taiwan, the island had been in the hands of the Dutch, not to mention Wu's ignorance of the fact that the whole epoch of Cheng was far earlier than Wu's periodization of "the past hundred years." In fact, the Cheng period began in 1661, which was about three hundred years ago. For the purpose of establishing a base for restoring the Ming and resisting the Manchus, Cheng Ch'en-kung led his troops, most of whom were Fukien Chinese, to attack and drive the Dutch from Taiwan. The purpose of Cheng's taking Taiwan was to restore the Ming and resist the Manchus. On what ground can this be viewed as a "strange phenomenon"?

. . . How have the Han Chinese become the Taiwanese today? It is because most of Cheng's troops and followers were Fukien Chinese, who subsequently resided in Taiwan. Moreover, after Cheng took Taiwan, mass migrations came often, and most of the migrants were from Kwangtung and Fukien. The migrations during the Cheng period, which were subsequently reinforced by migrations during the Ch'ing Dynasty, then formed the population of Taiwan. Their offspring constitute the Taiwanese today. . . .

It is difficult to agree with what Mr. Wu believes to be the future development in Taiwan, that is, that after Taiwan becomes independent, there will be no warlords or bandits, as there were when Taiwan was a part of China. In Wu's contemplation, the Taiwanese are those who came to Taiwan before 1949. None of them has ever had the experience of administering a government. How can it be guaranteed that there will be no warlords or bandits after Taiwan is independent? . . .

The central theme of Mr. Wu's article is, in his words, "after Taiwan becomes independent, it will have nothing to do with China,

whether the latter is being ruled by Mao Tse-tung or Chiang Kai-shek."
But the difficulties lie exactly in this thesis. If Taiwan wants independence, Chiang's consent must first be sought. It may be possible that
the Taiwanese will achieve this purpose by revolt, mutiny, or through
American support. But even if the Nationalist regime under Chiang
were overthrown, Mao Tsetung would still remain in the way. If there
were no American fleet to defend Taiwan, Mao's forces would be able
to cross the Taiwan Straits to take Taiwan notwithstanding Taiwanese
resistance. But do the Americans love the Taiwanese so much that
they would be willing to fight for them on this island far away from
their home? If they were to fight for Taiwan, would it be because they
want to keep this island as a military base for their national defense?
If the Taiwanese gained their "independence," Taiwan would be no
more independent than a military base of the United States. And in
world history, there has never been a country which has depended
totally upon another country for its existence but could still be properly
considered an independent state. Moreover, would it be more glorious
to be a base for the United States than a part of China? And who can
guarantee that the United States would not reach a compromise with
China irrespective of the interests of the Taiwanese? Even if the
Taiwanese desired to transform their island into a military base of
the United States, could peace and order be ensured on a military
base?

Of course, Mr. Wu envisages some economic and political
advantages to be derived from Taiwan's independence. Mr. Wu believes
that the national income on Taiwan is much better than that on mainland China, fearing that once Taiwan is put under Mao's regime, it will
suffer great economic setbacks due to Mao's economic programs.
Independence would, in Wu's opinion, eliminate this possibility. Also,
he alleges that had it not been for the present regime, the living
standard on Taiwan would have been even higher. The first point has
its truth. But if the present political situation is maintained, the
danger of Mao's policy being enforced on Taiwan is also ruled out.
As to the second point, I do not have statistics in hand but, as a
businessman, I would believe that there has been great economic
progress in Taiwan. Also, I would believe, as everybody does, that
since the land reform program was put into force in Taiwan, the net
income of the farmers has rapidly increased. These are facts. In
my view, the natural conditions of Taiwan are no better than those in
most provinces on the mainland. The difference is that in the past
hundred years Taiwan has enjoyed peace and order. Also, the Japanese
contributed to some extent to the development of Taiwan. As a result,
the net income of an individual on Taiwan is at present higher than that
of an individual on mainland China.

There might be some advantages in obtaining independence for
Taiwan, since the new administration would not have to inherit the
heavy burdens from the present system of government. Nonetheless,
there have to be capable politicians, together with a great number of
able officials at the basic levels, to ensure that the administration
would be sufficiently and reasonably carried on so that the economic
growth would continue. Countries like Indonesia and Burma have in
the past been ruthlessly exploited by imperialists, and should have
been able to advance the living standards of their people after they
achieved their independence. But twenty years have passed while,
except for a few politicians and warlords who have been enriched,
there has been little improvement in the life of the people. The
situation in those countries is much worse than that of Taiwan under
the Nationalist administration. Therefore, no one can guarantee that
once Taiwan achieves its independence, there will be many leaps forward, or progress in Taiwan's economic development.

Mr. Wu thinks that there are good chances for realizing the plan
for Taiwan's independence. But what are his reasons? There is only
one reason—the Americans would like it this way. However, the
Americans have never expressed an official view to that effect. Even
if they do desire Taiwan's independence, there is no reason to predict
that whatever they desire will eventually come true. That up to this
moment there is no "Republic of Taiwan" speaks for the fact. . . .

In my opinion, the factors which, when combined . . . , form a
country are blook, language, customs, historical background, geographical conditions, and religious beliefs. Judged on the basis of these
factors, Taiwan is plainly a part of China. It is one thing to say that
it is separated from China by military force; it is quite another to say
that [lack of] cultural affinity and other factors demand its permanent
independence from China. If historical reasons are to be invoked, no
persuasive argument can be made to advocate separation of Taiwan
from China. A country depends upon a permanent organization, and
no short-range interests should dictate the establishment of a state.
Otherwise, any part of a country could declare independence. Even
the people in Taichung or Tainan could argue for independence of their
local regions!

ITEM 17: SUN CH'IH-P'ING, "WHILE WU YU-LIN'S
OPINION MAY SPEAK FOR SOME PEOPLE, ITS
REASONS ARE NOT CONVINCING"16

To consider whether or not Taiwan should gain an independent
status, either from the standpoint of a Taiwanese or from that of a
Chinese, two points must first be carefully examined. First, does the

present environment permit Taiwan's independence? Second, what are the advantages of Taiwan's independence for its inhabitants?

From Wu Yu-lin's standpoint, the answer to the first question is that there are good chances for establishing a Taiwan republic; but his principal reason is that "from the United States' standpoint, an independent Taiwan is inevitable." His next reason is that Taiwan must rely upon "the United States to defend Taiwan so as to prevent Communist China from expanding into the Pacific." Under these circumstances, can it be said that Taiwan would acquire a genuine independence?

With regard to Taiwan's geographical and economic conditions, the island is not qualified to become an independent state. Wu Yu-lin refers to Switzerland, Monaco and Luxembourg as precedents, asserting that the size of a country does not matter. In fact, except for Switzerland, which is surrounded by Germany, France, Italy and Austria and has historically been considered by the European Powers as a buffer zone, small countries like Monaco and Luxembourg have had to be protected by one or more strong countries in order to survive. Are they independent in the true sense of the word? . . .

As to the second question, I think that Taiwan's independence would do harm rather than good to the people there. Why? . . .

If a revolution for independence should take place in Taiwan, neither the Chiang Government nor the Mao Government could possibly tolerate such a development. That the Mao Government has not taken military action to recover Taiwan is due to the fact that it considers Taiwan a part of China which will eventually be unified with China. Once the Communist Chinese leaders find out that Taiwan would become a separate country, who can guarantee that they would not undertake a military adventure? Why can't Mao start a fight with the United States in Taiwan, as he did in Korea? And it should be pointed out that the Communist Chinese intervention in Taiwan [to suppress independence] would be legitimate, for it would be an act of safeguarding China's territory. If there should be a military conflict, the people of Taiwan would be the first to suffer. . . .

ITEM 18: NIXON-CHOU JOINT COMMUNIQUÉ AND THE FUTURE OF TAIWAN[17]

Nixon and Chou En-lai, in the joint communiqué issued in Shanghai recently, openly ignored the will of 15 million Taiwanese people, presuming to resolve the Taiwan problem while they have no right to do so. We, the Taiwanese people, resolutely oppose this.

. . .

The future of Taiwan is by no means pessimistic for the following reasons:

A. Communist China is unable to develop armed forces large enough to invade Taiwan in the near future, and this is the reason why she has adopted political and diplomatic offensive [instead]. Before Communist China possesses the capacity to invade Taiwan, the unstable phenomenon in Communist China or the Chiang regime, arising either from death in the leadership or from transfer of the leadership, the development of the Taiwanese independence movement on the island, etc., are factors capable of changing the direction in the development of the Taiwan situation.

B. In the Nixon-Chou communiqué, the U.S. policy on the future of Taiwan is still flexible. The U.S. Government, except for blaming the Chiang regime for its responsibility of adopting the "one China" policy with a view to alleviating its sense of guilt, indicated two points: First, presently the U.S. Government raised no objection to the claim, taken by both Communist China and the Chiang regime, that Taiwan is a part of China. Therefore, if the Chiang regime or a [new] government representing Taiwanese people claims that Taiwan is not a part of China, the U.S. Government has no obligation to raise objection to the new position. Second, the U.S. Government has conditioned its withdrawal from Taiwan on two elements, i.e., a peaceful settlement [of the Chinese civil war] and the relaxation of tension [in the Taiwan Straits]; this is apparently aimed at reserving a backdoor for a change of policy. . . .

NOTES

1. Translated from Lin Hsiung-hsiang and Huang Wang-cheng, eds., T'ai-wan sheng t'ung-chih kao (Draft history of Taiwan Province), IX, Ke-min chih—K'ang jih pien (History of revolution—resistance against Japan) (Taipei: T'ai-wan sheng wen-hsien wei-yuan hui, 1954), pp. 230-31.

2. Ta-kung pao (Impartial daily), Chungking, January 7, 1943, p. 2.

3. Translated from Huang Shun-ch'ing, Lin Hsiung-hsiang, and Kuo Hai-ming, ed., T'ai-wan sheng t'ung-chih kao (Draft history of Taiwan Province), X, Kuang-fu chih (History of restoration) (Taipei: T'ai-wan sheng wen-hsien wei-yuan hui, 1952), p. 3.

4. Excerpt from Kuo-chi wen-t'i yen-chiu (Studies in international problems), No. 2 (Peking, February 1959), pp. 7-17.

5. Excerpt from Conlon Associates Ltd., United States Foreign Policy, Asia, Studies prepared at the request of the Committee on Foreign Relations, United States Senate (Washington, D.C.: U.S. Government Printing Office, 1959), pp. 153-55.

6. Peking Review, VII, 27 (July 3, 1964), 4.

7. Excerpt from Tzu-li wan-pao (Independent evening news), Taipei, February 28, 1965. p. 2.

8. Translated from Chung-yang jih-pao (Central daily news), Taipei, May 15, 1965. p. 3.

9. Translated from ibid., May 18, 1965, p. 3.

10. Translated from ibid., May 21, 1965, p. 3.

11. Excerpt from Chan-wang (The outlook), No. 103 (Hong Kong, May 16, 1966), p. 14.

12. Excerpt from Tzu-li wan-pao, November 9, 1966, p. 3.

13. Excerpt from Chan-wang, No. 163 (November 16, 1968), p. 2.

14. Ibid.

15. Excerpt from ibid., No. 171 (March 16, 1969), pp. 3-4.

16. Excerpt from ibid., p. 8.

17. Excerpt translated from T'ai-tu [Taiwan Independence], I, 1 (Kearny, N. J., March 28, 1972), p. 4.

SELECTED BIBLIOGRAPHY

Appleton, Sheldon L. "The Political Socialization of Taiwan's College Student," Asian Survey, X, 10 (October 1970), 910-23.

_____. "Taiwanese and Mainlanders on Taiwan: A Survey of Student Attitudes," The China Quarterly, No. 44 (October-December 1970), 38-65.

_____. "Taiwan: Portents of Change," Asian Survey, XI, 1 (January 1971), 68-73.

Barclay, George W. Colonial Development and Population in Taiwan. Princeton: Princeton University Press, 1954.

Brandt, Karl. "Economic Development: Lessons of Statecraft in Taiwan," Orbis, XI, 4 (Winter 1968), 1067-80.

Campell, William. Formosa Under the Dutch. London: Kegan Paul, Trench, Trubner, 1903.

Chang Han-yu and Ramon H. Meyers. "Japanese Colonial Development Policy in Taiwan, 1895-1906: A Case of Bureaucratic Entrepreneurship," The Journal of Asian Studies, XXII, 4 (August 1963), 433-49.

Chen, Lung-chu, and W. M. Reisman. "Who Owns Taiwan: A Search for International Title," The Yale Law Journal, LXXXI, 4 (March 1972), 599-671.

China and U.S. Far East Policy, 1945-1967. Washington, D.C.: Congressional Quarterly Service, 1967.

China Yearbook, 1969-1970. Taipei: China Publishing Co., 1970.

Chinese People's Institute of Foreign Affairs. Oppose U.S. Occupation of Taiwan and "Two China" Plot. Peking: Foreign Languages Press, 1958.

Chung-hua min-kuo wai-chiao wen-t'i yen-chiu hui. Chin-shan ho-yueh yu chung-jih ho-yueh ti kuan-hsi (The relationship between the San Francisco Peace Treaty and the Sino-Japanese Peace Treaty). Taipei: Chung-hua min-kuo wai-chiao wen-t'i yen-chiu hui, 1966.

Clark, Gregory. In Fear of China. Melbourne: Lansdowne Press, 1967.

Davidson, James W. The Island of Formosa. N. p., 1903; reprinted Taipei: Wen hsing shu chu, 1964.

Goddard, W. G. Formosa, A Study in Chinese History. London: Macmillan, 1966.

Gurtov, Melvin. "Recent Development on Formosa," The China Quarterly, No. 31 (July-September 1967), 59-95.

_____. "Taiwan in 1966: Political Rigidity, Economic Growth," Asian Survey, VII, 1 (January 1967), 40-45.

Hsieh Chiao-min. Taiwan-ilha Formosa, A Geography in Perspective. Washington, D.C.: Butterworths, 1964.

Hsieh, S. C., and T. H. Lee. Agricultural Development and Its Contributions to Economic Growth in Taiwan—Input-Output and Productivity Analysis of Taiwan Agricultural Development. Taipei: Joint Commission on Rural Reconstruction, 1966.

Huang Ching-chia. Jih-chü shih-ch'i chih T'ai-wan chih-min-ti fa-chih yü chih-min t'ung-chih (Taiwan colonial legal system and colonial rule under the Japanese occupation). Taipei, 1960.

Important Documents Concerning the Question of Taiwan. Peking: Foreign Languages Press, 1955.

Jacobs, J. Bruce. "Recent Leadership and Political Trends in Taiwan," The China Quarterly, No. 45 (January-March 1971), 129-54.

Jacoby, Neil H. U.S. Aid to Taiwan: A Study of Foreign Aid, Self-Help and Development. New York: Frederick A. Praeger, 1966.

Koo, Anthony Y. C. The Role of Land Reform in Economic Development, A Case Study of Taiwan. New York: Frederick A. Praeger, 1968.

Kuo Ting-yee. T'ai-wan shih-shih kai-shu (General history of Taiwan). Third printing. Taipei: Cheng chung shu chu, 1964.

Lamley, Harry J. "The 1895 Taiwan Republic," Journal of Asian Studies, XXVII, 4 (August 1968), 739-62.

Lien Chen-tung. Chiang tsung-t'ung yü T'ai-wan sheng ti kuang-fu ch'ung-chien (President Chiang and the restoration and reconstruction of the Taiwan Province). Two volumes. Taipei: Chung-yang wen-wu kung-ying she, 1967.

Lien Heng. T'ai-wan t'ung shih (A comprehensive history of Taiwan). Two volumes. Edited from 1921 Taiwan edition. Taipei: Chung hua ts'ung shu wei yuan hui, 1954.

Lin Hsiung-hsiang and Huang Wang-cheng, eds. Tai-wan sheng t'ung-chih kao (Draft history of Taiwan Province), IX, Ke-min chih-k'ang jih pien (History of revolution—resistance against Japan). Taipei: T'ai-wan sheng wen hsien wei yuan hui, 1954.

Lin, Ken C. Y. "Industrial Development and Changes in the Structure of Foreign Trade," International Monetary Fund Staff Papers, XV, 2 (July 1968), 290-318.

MacFarquhar, Roderick. Sino-American Relations, 1949-71. New York: Praeger Publishers, 1972.

Mancall, Mark, ed. Formosa Today. New York: Frederick A. Praeger, 1968.

Moorsteen, Richard, and Morton Abramowitz. Remaking China Policy. Cambridge, Massachusetts: Harvard University Press, 1971.

Morello, Frank P. The International Legal Status of Formosa. The Hague: Martinus Nijhoff, 1966.

Myers, Ramon H., and Adrienne Ching. "Agricultural Development in Taiwan Under Japanese Colonial Rule," The Journal of Asian Studies, XXIII, 4 (August 1964), 555-70.

O'Connell, D. P. "The Status of Formosa and the Chinese Recognition Problem," American Journal of International Law, LII, 2 (April 1956), 405-16.

Oppose the New U.S. Plots to Create "Two Chinas". Peking: Foreign Languages Press, 1962.

Plumber, Mark. "Taiwan: The 'New Look' in Government," Asian Survey, IX, 1 (January 1969), 18-22.

_____. "Taiwan: Toward a Second Generation of Mainland Rule,"
    ibid., X, 1 (January 1970), 18-24.

Pye, Lucian W. The Spirit of Chinese Politics, a Psychological Study
    of the Authority Crisis in Political Development. Cambridge,
    Massachusetts: The M.I.T. Press, 1968.

Tai Hung-chao. "The Kuomintang and Modernization in Taiwan," in
    Samuel P. Huntington and Clement H. Moore, eds. Authoritarian
    Politics in Modern Society. New York: Basic Books, 1970.

United States Security Agreement and Commitments Abroad, Republic
    of China. Hearings before the Subcommittee on United States
    Security Agreements and Commitments Abroad of the Committee
    on Foreign Relations, U.S. Senate, 91st Congress, 2nd Session,
    Part 4, November 24, 25 and 26, 1969, and May 8, 1970. Washing-
    ton, D.C.: U.S. Government Printing Office, 1970.

Wei Yung. "Elite Recruitment and Political Development [on Tai-
    wan]," Chung-yang jih-pao (Central daily news), international
    edition, Taipei, October 18, 1970, p. 2.

Weiss, Thomas. "Taiwan and U.S. Policy," Orbis, XII, 4 (Winter 1969),
    1165-87.

Wilson, Richard W. "A Comparison of Political Attitudes of Tiawanese
    Children and Mainlander Children on Taiwan," Asian Survey,
    VIII, 12 (December 1968), 980-1000.

Yang, Martin M. C. Socio-Economic Results of Land Reform in
    Taiwan. Honolulu: East-West Center Press, 1970.

Yen, Sophia Su-fei. Taiwan in China's Foreign Relations 1836-1874.
    Hamden, Connecticut: The Shoe String Press, 1965.

Young, Kenneth T. Negotiating with the Chinese Communists. New
    York: McGraw-Hill, 1968.

ABOUT THE EDITOR AND THE CONTRIBUTORS

HUNGDAH CHIU, Research Associate in Law at Harvard, is the author of The Capacity of International Organizations to Conclude Treaties (The Hague: Martinus Nijhoff, 1966); Agreements of the People's Republic of China, 1949-1967: A Calendar (Cambridge, Mass.: Harvard University Press, 1968), with Douglas M. Johnston; Law in Chinese Foreign Policy: Communist China and Selected Problems of International Law (Dobbs Ferry, N.Y.: Oceana, 1971), with Shao-chuan Leng; The People's Republic of China and International Law, 2 vols. (accepted for publication by the Harvard University Press), with Jerome A. Cohen.

GEORGE PO-CHUNG CHEN, Assistant Professor of Political Science at Augusta College, Augusta, Georgia, is currently writing a book concerning China's border problem with the Soviet Union.

JOHN CHUNG KUAN, a doctoral candidate at the Fletcher School of Law and Diplomacy, is now writing a dissertation concerning the early history of the Chinese Communist Party.

TING-YEE KUO, formerly Director of the Institute of Modern History of the Academia Sinica in the Republic of China, and currently Senior Research Fellow at Columbia University, is the author of Modern History of China, 2 vols. (Changsha: Commercial Press, 1940-41); Chronology of Modern China, 2 vols. (Taipei: Commercial Press, 1963); Sino-Japanese Relations 1882-1927 (New York: Columbia University East Asian Institute, 1965); and General History of Taiwan (3d. ed.; Taipei: Chung-cheng Press, 1967).

SHAO-CHUAN LENG, Doherty Foundation Professor of Government and Foreign Affairs at the University of Virgina, is the author of Japan and Communist China (New York: IPR, 1958); Sun Yat-sen and Communism (New York: Frederick A. Praeger, 1961), with N. D. Palmer; Justice in Communist China (Dobbs Ferry, N.Y.: Oceana, 1967); and Law in Chinese Foreign Policy: Communist China and Selected Problems of International Law (Dobbs Ferry, N.Y.: Oceana, 1971), with Hungdah Chiu.

RAMON H. MYERS, Professor of Economics at Miami University, is the author of The Chinese Peasant Economy (Cambridge, Mass.: Harvard University Press, 1970) and a forthcoming book on the industrial development in the Republic of China on Taiwan.

LUNG-SHENG TAO, Research Fellow at the Chinese Center of Cornell, is the author of "The Criminal Law of Communist China," Cornell Law Quarterly (Fall 1966); and "Recent Studies on Chinese Law in the United States," Ost-europa Recht (June 1969).